TVA

Bridge Over Troubled Waters

Also by **North Callahan:**

The Army
The Armed Forces as a Career
Smoky Mountain Country
Henry Knox: General Washington's General
Daniel Morgan: Ranger of the Revolution
Royal Raiders: The Tories of the American Revolution
Flight from the Republic: The Tories of the American Revolution,
  Vol. II
Carl Sandburg: Lincoln of our Literature
George Washington: Solider and Man
Revolutionary War Leaders of Connecticut
Leaders of the American Revolution Series (editor)

TVA
Bridge
Over Troubled Waters

North Callahan

SOUTH BRUNSWICK AND NEW YORK:
A. S. BARNES AND COMPANY
LONDON: THOMAS YOSELOFF LTD

A. S. Barnes and Co., Inc.
Cranbury, New Jersey 08512

Thomas Yoseloff Ltd
Magdalen House
136-148 Tooley Street
London SE1 2TT, England

Library of Congress Cataloging in Publication Data

Callahan, North.
  TVA: bridge over troubled waters.

  Bibliography: p.
  Includes index.
  1. Tennessee Valley Authority—History. I. Title.
HD9685.U7T33   353.008′23   79-21586
ISBN 0-498-02490-3

Printed in the United States of America

To Helen

Contents

8 TVA: BRIDGE OVER TROUBLED WATERS

Illustrations

Acknowledgments

Excerpts from *The New Republic,* Aug. 17, 1938 and Nov. 10, 1973. Reprinted with permission.

Excerpt from *Nation's Business,* August 1935. Reprinted with permission.

Excerpts from the Oral History Project of Memphis State University, Dr. Charles W. Crawford, Director. Reprinted with permission.

Excerpt from *American Forests,* July 1934. Reprinted with permission.

Excerpt from *The Economist,* June 10, 1939. Reprinted with permission.

Excerpts from the writings of A. E. Morgan. Reprinted with permission.

Excerpt from *In Brief Authority* by Francis Biddle, published 1962 by Doubleday & Company. Reprinted with permission.

Excerpt from the *Journal of Land and Public Utility Economics,* Nov. 1933, published by the University of Wisconsin Press. Reprinted with permission.

Excerpts from Arthur Robert Burns, *Electric Power and Government Policy* (New York: The Twentieth Century Fund, Inc., 1948)

Excerpt from *The Chattanooga Country: From Tomahawks to TVA* by Gilbert E. Govan and James W. Livingood. Copyright 1963, University of Chattanooga. By permission of The University of North Carolina Press.

Excerpt from *Geothermal Energy,* Paul Kruger and Carel Otte, eds. 1972 published by Stanford University Press. Reprinted with permission.

Excerpt from *American Quarterly,* Winter, 1970, "The TVA" by Edward Shapiro, Copyright 1970 Trustees of the University of Pennsylvania, Philadelphia. Reprinted with permission.

11

Excerpt from *Should We Have More TVA's,* edited by Walter M. Daniels, published by H. W. Wilson Company, 1950, New York.

Excerpt from *The Atlantic Monthly,* October, 1937, "A Consumer's View of the TVA," by George Fort Milton. Reprinted with permission.

Excerpt from *A Study of the TVA Power Business* published by the Edison Electric Institute, New York, 1965. Reprinted with permission.

Excerpt from *TVA: the First Twenty Years* by Roscoe C. Martin, published by the University of Alabama Press, 1956. Reprinted with permission.

Excerpt from *TVA: Adventure in Planning* by Julian Huxley, published by The Architectural Press, Cheam, Surrey, England, 1943. Reprinted with permission.

Excerpt from a study by Dean Russell on "Taxation and the TVA", published by The Foundation for Economic Education, 1949. Reprinted with permission.

Excerpts from an article on the efficiency of our energy system by S. David Freeman in the March-April 1973 issue of *Public Power.* Reprinted with permission.

Excerpt from an article by Shirley Scheibla in *Barron's,* Dec. 16, 1974 on the proposal of the TVA to buy the Peabody Coal Company. Reprinted with permission.

Excerpt from an article about the Clinch River Breeder Project in *Mechanical Engineering,* the November, 1974 issue. Reprinted with permission.

Excerpt from an article regarding the Clinch River Breeder Project appearing in the September, 1972 issue of *Fortune.* Reprinted with permission.

Appreciation is also expressed to the Tennessee Valley Authority Office of Information for the illustrations used in this book.

Introduction

When the initial research was undertaken on this immense project, I had already come to realize that the Tennessee Valley Authority was a significantly important institution with national and international implications. And with the onset of the worldwide energy crises, I came to understand how crucially pivotal this dynamic organization is.

The TVA is the most visibly enduring of the many New Deal creations of the late President Franklin D. Roosevelt, and some regard it as the most important achievement of his memorable administration. It is the largest producer of electric power in the United States, the nation's biggest user of coal, and the leading investor in nuclear power. It is spending some $10 billion on nuclear power plant construction planned for completion by the mid-1980s.

At times the copious criticism of the TVA has been as overflowing as the water gushing from one of its power dams. The range has been as extreme as the statement by the late Congressman James B. Frazier, Jr., who described it as "the greatest good that ever came to the people of the Tennessee Valley," to the evaluation of *Time Magazine* in 1937: "Its chief product has been costly lawsuits with private companies." In later years, the biggest complaints regarding costs centered around power rates. And at the peak of the price-spiraling 1970s, the TVA was described as standing at bay before a public disenchanted with its inflationary aspects. Still, its supporters held on.

Between these polarized opinions, I have tried to steer an academic and objective course. My personal impressions, as set forth in the text, have come largely from firsthand knowledge and a searching examination of a complicated subject. William Blake wrote, "Tell me the Acts, O historian, and leave me to reason upon them as I please." This has been my guiding principle in writing this book.

In a conversation with TVA officials several years ago, I made the suggestion that a full history of the Authority would be desirable. The idea was met with enthusiasm and an offer to cooperate in every way. Such help was given, with the understanding that my work would be a strictly independent, scholarly effort. I obtained mounds and pounds of research material from the TVA as well as many outside sources, but no one tried to impose a single subjective word upon the manuscript.

Having "grown up" with the TVA, my approach was somewhat facilitated. It was decided to structure the history along chronological-topical lines. There followed not only delving into seemingly endless documentary materials but personal interviews with many TVA personnel, from workers in the field to the chairman and other high officials. Retired employees were glad to reminisce about their days with the Authority, and most (but not all) were commendatory. The Technical Library of the organization at Chattanooga was especially helpful.

Without injecting too much of a personal nature into the unfolding story, I decided to include some of my own close contacts with the TVA, especially in its early years to point up the contrast of what it was then and what it seems today. Having written about the organization for newspapers and to a small extent in a previous book, I felt as if I were on familiar ground.

Scholars who are particularly conscious of footnotes are referred to the extensive bibliography in this volume. Also, most of the specific references to sources are set forth in the text itself. An effort has been made to balance as far as practicable the pros and cons which have surrounded the TVA and which have been vividly expressed by the protagonists. There is no doubt of sincerity on either side, with differing views based upon the relationship of those concerned. Most of all, I have attempted to cite only responsible sources and to offer reasoned comment to enable the reader to make an individual conclusion.

Appreciation is expressed to the Arts and Science Research Fund of the Graduate School of New York University for a grant-in-aid which has been helpful in the research on this volume. The University of Tennessee at Chattanooga provided a visiting professorship which enabled me to be in proximity to TVA territory and to have access to informative data. My academic colleagues have shown a warm and wholesome interest in the project and have made many valuable suggestions for the treatment of the subject.

Finally, my wholehearted thanks go to my relatives and friends as well as to numerous others who have lightened and brightened the way to the end of this challenging enterprise.

North Callahan

Prologue

The rays of the setting sun were changing from gold to red that day in 1934 when I made my way in an old Ford roadster along the winding dirt road toward my destination. It was TVA-CCC Camp Number 297 and was located near a tiny place called Loyston, which proved difficult to find.

I finally arrived at the newly built camp, located several feet above and to the left of the rocky road, and was greeted by its commanding officer from the U.S. Army Reserve and the camp superintendent from the U.S. Forest Service. More details could be given about the Civilian Conservation Corps (CCC) enrollees and their officials—a story in our nation's history which has never been fully told—but that is not the object of this account. The CCC was a valuable, colorful, important, and necessary organization which helped to bring human rehabilitation to the economic recovery days of the Great Depression. General George C. Marshall served with the Corps before he became chief of staff of the U.S. Army. He said that his experience with the CCC was "the most instructive service I have ever had and the most interesting."

The function of the 200 men in this camp was to help build Norris Dam and its environs. These men were mainly from the Lower East Side of New York City. They were about as familiar with this rustic, mountainous, East Tennessee countryside as many of the local "hillbillies" were with Manhattan. There were 11 other such camps under my educational supervision, but the Loyston one was my headquarters. From there I could participate in and observe at close hand the growing challenge of the TVA to the low economic conditions of the Tennessee Valley. This region, about the size of England, at that time had about 2 million people in portions of several states covering an area of some 40,000 square miles.

When I arrived at Loyston the TVA was a little over a year old. The organization began by an Act of Congress on May 18, 1933. Besides Tennessee, the other states in TVA territory were Virginia, North Carolina, Georgia, Alabama, Mississippi, and Kentucky. The purpose of the new organization was to embrace many facets of social development, but the one with which we were primarily concerned evolved around a huge dam to be used principally in the production of electric power.

One morning after I had familiarized myself with the camp, its displaced enrollees, and the genial officials, I had an opportunity to view the pristine work of the TVA at first hand. The camp's superintendent took me in his pickup truck to see Norris Dam. This behemoth was being built on the picturesque Clinch River 20 miles northwest of Knoxville, Tennessee. As we approached the uncompleted dam, along a winding gravel road from below, the structure already appeared impressive. The dam was being plugged into a 400-foot gorge of the river and was to be about 2,000 feet in length, 200 feet thick at the base, and 266 feet tall. I was told that it would be one of the six largest dams ever built and would back water up the valleys of the Clinch and Powell rivers above to a distance of 47 miles.

We took a look at the hundreds of workers swarming over the dam, and then, being hungry, we ducked into a nearby improved wooden restaurant where I enjoyed the best chili I had ever eaten. It cost 10 cents, and crackers were included.

Meanwhile, the CCC personnel were busy supplementing the TVA activity in the Norris basin. Mainly they were building check dams to stop erosion. The dams consisted of burlap bags filled with soil and sprinkled with grass seed. Also used for these dams were rocks, logs, brush and, when needed, concrete. One of the most difficult jobs was to slow the runoff of water on the steeper slopes and banks of gullies. Bermuda grass was used and even honeysuckle, which was not popular with Tennesseans generally because it often grew where it was not supposed to.

I found it interesting to watch the workers, who were young men from 18 to 25 years of age, as they struggled with their new environment. Here were Italians, Jews, Irish, and others from the poorer sections of New York City, some of whom apparently had not had a square meal for months before they entered the Civilian Conservation Corps. (Each received $30 a month, $25 of which was usually sent home to an indigent family.) Their pale faces, puny muscles, and cynical attitudes soon changed into weathered faces, stronger bodies, and a calmer acceptance of their new life. This was indeed a vivid example of human rehabilitation. It was amusing, however, to watch a man's first encounter with a cow or a hog or an irate farmer with whose daughter he had flirted.

This was more than a national event to me. I had been born 25 years before in the pleasant little community of Fork Creek, Tennessee, some nine miles from Sweetwater, one of the small indigenous towns which dot the picturesque Tennessee Valley. Education at the universities of Chattanooga and Tennessee and a few years of teaching school had placed me squarely in the midst of the Depression. So I welcomed the TVA and its related opportunities for employment and possible promise.

"A river went out of Eden to water the Garden . . ."
Genesis II, 10

1. The Outlook

The purposes of Norris Dam were representative of the early aims of the TVA:

Benefits of Navigation. From the higher reaches of this river system to the shoals at Florence, Alabama, there were periods of low water on the river. TVA's dams were to provide a minimum depth of water and thus to improve navigation.

Flood Control Benefits. The U.S. Army Corps of Engineers had estimated that the average annual flood damage between Norris Dam and Wilson Dam (named after Woodrow Wilson) at Muscle Shoals was close to a million dollars.

Power Development Benefits. It was planned that Norris Dam would be a storage dam which would be pressed into service during the low-flow periods of the Tennessee River, into which the water from the dam would flow. The water stored would be used to generate power at Norris and in addition increase the available power at each hydroplant down the river. For the most part this system worked out well.

Other TVA activities such as the production of fertilizer, the development of recreational facilities, and urban planning were to come later, although the town of Norris, which was to serve as a model, was already being built near the dam.

For centuries the Tennessee River has been interwoven with the history of America. It was used extensively as a trade route by Spanish, French, and English explorers as well as by the Indians. The first recorded expedition to the river by white men was that of Hernando de Soto and his Spanish soldiers who came upon the Tennessee River near Chattanooga in 1540. They then continued down the river for about 150 miles to the vicinity of what is now Guntersville, Alabama.

Some two centuries later the Cherokee Indians remained in possession of the Tennessee Valley, as indeed they had since the expedition

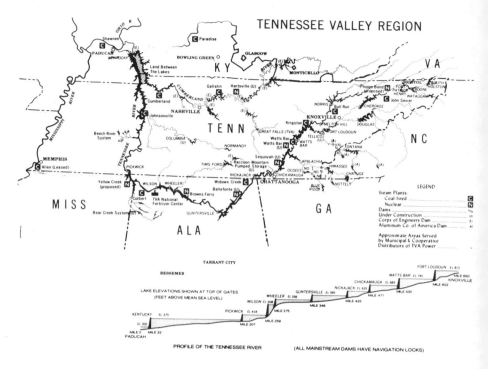

TENNESSEE VALLEY REGION

LEGEND

Steam Plants:
Coal-fired — C
Nuclear — N
Dams:
Under Construction — U
Corps of Engineers Dam — (E)
Aluminum Co. of America Dam — A

Approximate Areas Served
by Municipal & Cooperative
Distributors of TVA Power

PROFILE OF THE TENNESSEE RIVER   (ALL MAINSTREAM DAMS HAVE NAVIGATION LOCKS)

LAKE ELEVATIONS SHOWN AT TOP OF GATES
(FEET ABOVE MEAN SEA LEVEL)

of de Soto. These Indians, among the most civilized tribes in America,
used the river for transportation within their own nation. The large
Cherokee towns were located on the banks of the river and on some
islands in it and its tributaries. This picturesque and meandering
waterway was used by the French traders in the latter part of the
seventeenth century as part of their commercial route between the
Mississippi Valley and South Carolina. They built a number of trading
posts at strategic points along the stream.

The French and Indian War saw both England and France seeking to
acquire trade with the Indians. In furtherance of this goal, the British
built Fort Loudoun in 1756 on the Little Tennessee River not far from
the present city of Maryville, Tennessee. This was in the midst of the
Cherokee country, but the location proved to be unwise because in
1760 the Cherokees turned against the British and captured the fort. Of
course the British won the war. (Fort Loudoun has been restored and is
an historic site for tourists today.)

Professor Howard K. Menhinick of the Georgia Institute of
Technology and TVA official Lawrence L. Durisch made a study of
TVA plans and operations and found that construction of the reservoirs
presented an opportunity for exploring some prehistory. For generations the Tennessee River was a major travel route for the American

Indians. They moved over its waters in their swift canoes, stopping now and then to eat the mussels which flourished there and discarding the shells which they placed in great mounds along with broken utensils, tools, and weapons. The purpose of the TVA was to study these mounds before they were covered with hundreds of feet of water and the records they contained were lost forever.

The first step was to identify and locate on maps the important Indian burial mounds and shell mounds. The most promising of these were then scientifically sampled, a few completely explored. The results were reported in a series of monographs published by the Bureau of Ethnology of the Smithsonian Institution. The findings shed new light on phases of early life in the region and on the migration of these early inhabitants of the American continent. As a result of these archaeologic investigations, the University of Tennessee created a new department of anthropology and archaeology.

According to a sociological study by Professor William E. Cole of this university, the Indians' bones have been better preserved than those of the white settlers because the latter used wooden coffins and, as these decayed, the wood acids disintegrated the bones of the dead. As to the Indians in the region today, it is pointed out that

on the edge of the Valley, in Swain and Jackson Counties, North Carolina, is the Cherokee Indian Reservation where the Federal government has committed "Unto These Hills" the remnants of the Cherokee tribe which fled General Winfield Scott's soldiers in 1838 at the time the Indians were being removed westward over the "Trail of Tears" to beyond the Mississippi. Here on their reservation, mostly mountainous with arable coves, near the beautiful Oconaluftee River, which in the Indian vernacular means "near the river," live 3,500 Indians engaged in marginal agriculture, handicrafts, servicing tourists and acting out each summer for tourists an historic drama depicting the historical removal of the Cherokees and the heroism of their young Chief Tsali who rebelled at removal.

Here Chief Tecumseh came from the North in the War of 1812 to try to get the Cherokees to help the British. They refused. The Indians now live somewhat apart, and some of them have worked on TVA projects. Otherwise the Authority has had little influence on them.

The early white settlers came down the Great Valley of Virginia and entered this mountainous region through various routes. Some followed the Holston River southward; others entered through North Carolina and came down the Watauga and Nolichucky rivers. Kingsport, Tennessee, was established on the Holston River in 1770. Knoxville became the capital of the Territory South of the Ohio in 1791, being named after then Secretary of War Henry Knox. The original site of Chattanooga was an Indian trading post named Ross's Landing, after renowned Indian Chief John Ross. The City of Chattanooga was incorporated after the removal of the Cherokee Indians to Oklahoma in 1838.

Flatboats, rafts, and keel boats were built upriver, loaded with cotton, corn whisky, and other produce and floated down the Tennessee River to the Ohio and then to the Mississippi down to New Orleans where the goods were disposed of. Because of the difficulty of upstream traffic, the boatmen then had to walk back to their homes over a winding and dangerous road, the Natchez Trace. The passage of a steamboat over the Muscle Shoals and up the Tennessee River to Knoxville was first achieved in 1828, the year Tennessee's Andrew Jackson was elected President.

The origin of the name Muscle Shoals is uncertain. There are two versions. One is that it was at first "Mussel Shoals" because the currents there were agreeable to the shellfish; another version is that it was called "Muscle Shoals" because the Indians felt it required "heap big muscle" to get their canoes around the place.

The early settlers of the Tennessee Valley, according to the census of 1790, were English 65 percent, Scotch 12 percent, Ulster Scotch 7 percent, German 12 percent, Irish 5 percent, French 2 percent, and Dutch 0.4 percent.

According to Cole, these people settled on the flatlands, and in the hills and mountains of the South they developed and have preserved a close-to-nature environment. Since that time in general, the Tennessee Valley has proven to be a place not only of heavy rainfall but of high birth rates. In 1947 the average birth rate of the seven valley states, after corrections for underregistration, was 34.3 per 1,000 as contrasted with the national average of 27.8 per 1,000. Between 1940 and 1947, it is estimated that the excess of births over deaths caused a natural increase of over 361,000 in the Tennessee Valley watershed. Between 1940 and 1950 the natural increase of the population of the nation was 18,029,000, of which 7,246,000, or 40.2 percent, was produced by the Southeast, Texas, and Oklahoma; 5,634,000, or 31.2 percent by the Southeast alone; and 3,977,000, or 22.1 percent, by the seven Tennessee Valley states.

The Tennessee River is not unusual in size or length, but it is a picturesque stream that wanders in a curious way. One distinctive thing about it is that the river flows just about as far north as it does south. After rising in the mountains, it flows through hills and valleys, some timbered with hardwood, others open and rolling like the New

England countryside. After passing through narrow and rocky valleys near Chattanooga, the Tennessee flows southward into Alabama through wide fields that once grew more cotton than they do now. After dropping more than 100 feet in 30 miles, the river turns northward and veers across the state of Tennessee again and then into Kentucky to the Ohio River.

With the exception of a few small streams, all of the water courses of East Tennessee flow into the Tennessee River and find their way out of the valley through one common channel near the southern boundary of the state, west of Chattanooga. If one could stand on the northern ledge of the mountain range that lies along the Alabama state line and look northeast, the streams of East Tennessee would be like a figure of a big oak tree, its trunk stretching across the state northward with its head far up in Virginia and its numerous branches stretching on both sides far and wide. East Tennessee lies between parallels 35 degrees and 36 degrees and 4 inches north, and its mean altitude is 1,000 feet above sea level. The prevailing winds are from the southwest and west and bring a constant supply of rain from the Gulf of Mexico. This region has been called the "poor person's rich country" because of the undeveloped resources of the valley.

There was little traffic on the river before 1818 when the House of Representatives passed a bill to appropriate money for roads and canals. Six years later the federal government was authorized to make necessary plans, surveys, and estimates for national roads and canals for transporting the public mail. Secretary of War John C. Calhoun designated Muscle Shoals as one of the most important projects. In 1831 the State of Alabama built a canal around Muscle Shoals, but it was unsuccessful and was abandoned after a year.

In 1852 Congress allotted $50,000 for improvement of navigation on the Tennessee River. Difficulty was encountered in a stretch of the river below Chattanooga because of the dangerous and unpredictable waters there. However, it was not until 1905 that anything permanent was accomplished in this respect on the river. At that time, to promote interest, the government granted a 99-year franchise for the construction of a dam to produce electric power. This dam was to be located 33 miles below Chattanooga, with navigation locks to be provided by the federal government.

At the end of 1908 the National Conservation Commission under the leadership of Gifford Pinchot reported that "it is an irrefutable proof that the conservation of our resources is the fundamental question before this Nation, and that our first and greatest task is to set our house in order and begin to live within our means."

Under the National Defense Act of 1916, President Woodrow Wilson selected Muscle Shoals as a site for the construction of two nitrate plants, a steam-electric generating station and Wilson Dam. The plants were to be used to produce the ingredients of munitions and fertilizer in peacetime. The dam was planned as part of a navigation, flood control, and power development project with other such dams to follow. Wilson Dam was completed in 1925.

But after the end of World War I there was a question of what to do with Muscle Shoals. Since it was not active, there was much pressure for sale of the properties to private interests. (In fact from 1921 to 1933 there were 138 bills introduced in Congress concerning the disposition of Muscle Shoals, some involving proposals of private companies and others advocating public operation.)

The most conspicuous of these proposals was that of Henry Ford, who in July of 1921 offered to pay $5 million for the nitrate plants and all government property connected with it. Objections to the Ford offer, which was withdrawn in October 1924, were outlined in a report of the Senate Committee on Agriculture and Forestry, written by its chairman, Senator George Norris of Nebraska. The report stated that this was a poor financial deal for the government, since Ford was offering to pay only $5 million for facilities and property which had cost $88 million. Also, if the offer were accepted, it would nullify the principles of conservation which had been set forth by the government over many years. In conclusion, the committee stated, "If the Ford offer is accepted then the fight for conservation that has been waged by public-spirited and patriotic men and women all over the country is not only lost and given away but those who are unwillingly compelled to make the gift are to be taxed 100 years to make the gift more profitable. It is the greatest gift ever bestowed upon mortal man since salvation was made free to the human race."

Gilbert Govan, writing in the *Chattanooga Times,* observed that on May 3, 1923, this newspaper carried an interview which was prophetic about the TVA. W. C. Waldo of Washington, D.C., consulting engineer for the Tennessee River Improvement Association, outlined a plan for protecting Chattanooga and other communities in the valley from the "flood menace." Proposed by the U.S. Army Corps of Engineers was a series of dams and storage lakes to form a navigable channel from Paducah to Knoxville as well as to develop electric power. "It is interesting," commented Govan, "to note how simliar this plan of the early 1920s was to that adopted a decade later by the Tennessee Valley Authority."

In 1927 there was a big flood involving the Mississippi River which focused national attention on the responsibility of the federal government in the field of flood control. The next year the Boulder Canyon Act was passed, authorizing construction of a great dam on the Colorado River for the purpose of improving navigation, irrigation, flood control, and power production. Senator Norris introduced five bills in Congress for the purpose of government production of power, the last of which passed in May of 1928, only to be vetoed by President Calvin Coolidge. A subsequent bill was passed in 1931 but was vetoed by President Herbert Hoover.

Said Senator Norris:

> From the beginning to the end, there was that irreconcilable conflict between those who believe the natural wealth of the United States best can be developed by private capital and enterprise, and those who believe that in certain activities related to the natural resources only the great strength of the Federal government itself can perform the most necessary task in the spirit of unselfishness, for the greatest good to the greatest number.
>
> I did not ask for the job of leading in the battle for TVA. I thought, as chairman of the Committee on Agriculture of the Senate, that I should be spared its great burden. I felt deeply I lacked the strength, the time, and the technical background to discharge that task creditably.

The Senator contended that it was by accident, the result of America's participation in World War I, that the Tennessee Valley was selected as a testing ground for the TVA experiment. He had been alarmed over the real estate boom which had resulted from the belief that Henry Ford was going to buy Muscle Shoals. He explained:

> In that boom centering around the Muscle Shoals development, a town had been incorporated and plotted, covering several square miles. It was these town lots which were being sold. Offices of the real estate speculators were established in some of the leading cities of the country, including Washington. Special trains were run from New York City to Muscle Shoals, filled with prospective land purchasers. People were taken up in airplanes to view the wonderful sweep of country where a city, rivaling even New York, was to rise when this great power development had been turned over to Mr. Ford and his genius for ultimate development. In that boom thousands of lots were sold to people living in scattered sections of the United States so that every purchaser of a lot became a committee of one to help Mr. Ford gain possession of Muscle Shoals. I am certain that, had Mr. Ford known of this, he would have frowned upon it and rebuked it with all the power at his command.

Senator Norris on March 1, 1931, ridiculed Herbert Hoover's efforts to shift Muscle Shoals from a political to a technical basis. Said the Nebraska Senator:

> The President, being an engineer, it seemed he would have no difficulty in solving the problem and, therefore, it is rather surprising to learn from his statement that he is referring the matter to the heads of his departments, none of whom is an engineer. The great engineer is asking advice on an "engineering project" from those who are not engineers, and when those who are not engineers tell the engineer what to do with "an engineering project" the engineer will know whether to sign or veto the bill. It reminds me of the New England country justice who, at the close of a lawsuit, said he would take it under advisement for three days, at which time he would render judgment for the plaintiff.

A writer in *The New Republic* stated that the proponents of the Henry Ford offer "use precisely the same arguments which led honest men at one time to accept the Teapot Dome leases as legitimate." Frank Smith, a one-time member of the TVA board of directors, recalled:

> There are still remnants of the Ford mirage at Muscle Shoals. Even though the TVA stimulus increased the population of the Shoals urban area from 23,000 in 1930 to 58,000 in 1960, there are still hundreds of acres of empty lots, some with weed-grown roads and sidewalks, that were sold during the days of real estate speculation. A half dozen brick store and bank-type buildings in the small-town style of fifty years ago can be found at strategic road corners over the still-undeveloped area, vestiges of the evidence built to show the prospective lot-buyers that the boom was already under way.

Smith also recalled that, ironically, Senator Norris worked out with Senator McKellar of Tennessee a change in his bill about Muscle Shoals, obligating the government to produce 40,000 tons of nitrogen fertilizer from the chemical plants within five years after taking it over. "McKellar was to prove a tower of strength to Norris in the critical days of the fight against sale to the power companies." To many, Senator McKellar was an enigma. Evidently he could not brook any lack of adherence to the old practice of political patronage. So he turned from cooperation to bitter opposition to the TVA and its officials.

Senator Norris once wrote:

> From boyhood I have seen first hand the grim drudgery, and grind which had been the common lot of eight generations of American

farm women seeking happiness and contentment on the soil. I had seen the tallow candle in my own home followed by the coal oil lamp. I knew what it was to take care of the farm chores by the flickering, undependable light of the lantern in the mud and cold rains of the fall, and the snow and icy winds of winter.

Fundamentally I felt the farmer would become a better and a more satisfactory consumer of electricity than the individual in the town and city. His needs were greater. Electric power could be used to pump water, to grind feed, to meet all the needs of the dairy, and to perform other useful and beneficial services not within the grasp of a city home. I knew the heat of those summer days in a farm kitchen. I had seen the drudgery of washing and ironing and sewing without any of the labor-saving electrical devices. I could close my eyes and recall the innumerable scenes of the harvest and the unending, punishing tasks of hundreds of thousands of women.

Between 1800 and 1930 there occurred in the United States a change in the distribution of population which received comparatively little notice. The proportion of people living on farms decreased from 85 to 23 percent. From 1920 to 1930 alone almost 6 million migrated from farms to cities. So great became the concentration of population in the cities that it was said, "The social distance between human beings increases so that the art of living and the business of making a living have come into intense conflict."

This drain upon the rural population in the valley was noted early by the TVA. A survey of agricultural Grainger County in Tennessee showed that federal and state tax payments going into it were $91,000 in excess of tax revenue produced there. County buildings had depreciated $80,000 during 1932. Depletion of soil and forests amounted to about $55,000. The estimated deficit between cash coming in and cash going out was $212,000. It was apparent that something was needed to be done here.

Without a doubt, 1933 was not a good year in the Tennessee Valley. The per capita income was $163, or 44 percent of the national average. Twenty years later such income was still only $1,005, or 61 percent of the national average. The land of the region was in poor condition with 150 billion tons of rainfall annually pounding the land, much of it laid bare by reliance on row crops and destruction of forest cover, resulting in thousands of tons of topsoil being carried down the streams into the Tennessee River and below. Private power companies served fewer than 300,000 customers. Twenty years later over four times as many were served by the municipally owned and rural electric cooperative systems which distributed TVA power in the same area. Part of this increase was due to a 19 percent increase in the population during this time and the growth of the cities, but most of the increase was the result of extension of electric power service to rural areas.

Historian Broadus Mitchell, himself a native Southerner, exclaimed in deprecating the local lethargy in the South:

> We had the rock and the rivers, the labor and the lumber, the iron and steel, but never exploited them until a man of superior intelligence, George Norris, prompted FDR to undertake the greatest of public works. Norris was a latter-day Henry W. Grady. Remember Grady's tale of going to a funeral in Tennessee or Georgia? The grave was dug through marble, but the headstone came from Vermont; the body was shrouded in cloth woven in Massachusetts, though cotton grew in sight of the mourners; the coffin came from elsewhere, though hardwood abounded in the locality. In short, all that Georgia contributed was the corpse and the hole in the ground!

Private power interests had come into low standing. The record of the public utility and its pyramiding holding companies had reached a low status. So it was not illogical that in May of 1933, only a little more than two months after the advent of the New Deal, the Tennessee Valley Authority Act was passed. President Roosevelt in his bell-toned, resonant voice said to Congress:

> The continued idleness of a great national investment in the Tennessee Valley leads me to ask the Congress for legislation necessary to enlist this project in the service of the people. It is clear that the Muscle Shoals development is but a small part of the potential public usefulness of the entire Tennessee River. Such use, if envisioned in its entirety, transcends mere power development: it enters the wide field of flood control, soil erosion, afforestation, elimination from agricultural use of marginal lands, and distribution and diversification of industry. . . . I, therefore, suggest to the Congress legislation to create a Tennessee Valley Authority—a corporation clothed with the power of government but possessed of the flexibility and initiative of a private enterprise. It should be charged with the broadest duty of planning for the proper use, conservation, and development of the natural resources of the Tennessee River drainage basin and its adjoining territory for the general, social, and economic welfare of the nation.

From the national public works fund there was set aside for TVA use $50 million, a like amount being authorized in U.S. bonds. Time was to prove this to be only a financial drop in the bucket for this huge new enterprise. The TVA was to be administered by a board of directors consisting of three members and appointed directly by the President. The personalities of these officials were to form a dynamic if conflicting image of the organization.

It was to be located in the Tennessee Valley itself and an independent agency which reported directly to the President and Congress and was solely responsible for its success or failure.

Paeans of praise reverberated in the valley. Many of the local people, especially the poorer ones, saw in the coming of the TVA a providential panacea for their social and economic ills. Regional members of Congress hailed the advent in glowing terms, and the Democrats especially hugged the TVA to their political breasts. However, all was not affirmative in Congress. Representative Joseph Martin, a Massachusetts Republican who later became Speaker of the House, said, ''Painting rainbows is always a delightful and inspirational pastime. . . . We are painting a beautiful picture for the good people of the Tennessee Valley and the United States, a fine dream that will eventually end in disappointment.''

Proclaimed Representative John Taber, New York Republican: ''This bill is going to turn out bad.''

Representative Everett Dirksen, the Illinois Republican who later became a Senator and the father-in-law of U.S. Senator Howard Baker of Tennessee, had this to say: ''In the days to come some of you gentlemen who are giving birth to this beautiful child, I am afraid, will not be as proud of it after it grows up.''

But another noted Republican, Representative J. Will Taylor of Tennessee, was more sanguine: ''I look forward with keen anticipation to fishing and duck hunting on the placid surface of that great lake that will result from the construction of Norris Dam.''

The day the bill was signed was a proud one for George Norris. ''It is emblematic,'' he said, ''of the dawning of that day when every rippling stream that flows down the mountain side and winds its way through the meadow to the sea shall be harnessed and made to work for the welfare and comfort of man.''

Press reaction to the passage of the TVA Act varied with different parts of the nation. Here are only a few typical quotes:

> The conservatives see in the Roosevelt Tennessee Valley proposal a great stride toward national ownership of public utilities. They believe it will involve the expenditure of untold millions of government money, the creation of many more Federal jobs, and the embarkation on a dangerous economic path, which ultimately means a control over business almost fantastic in its scope and a centralization of power in the Federal government abhorrent to the believers in private initiative, and particularly in conflict with Democratic principles. [*Baltimore Sun*]

> The Tennessee Valley is not an Eden waiting, uninhabited, for

development. On the contrary, it has a settled population, established industries, entrenched customs, which necessarily must be readjusted unless the scheme is to become merely a horn of plenty instead of an instrument of planned economy. [*Hartford Courant*]

The time is long since passed when the country could be roused to fever heat or divided against itself by wordy war in the national capitol over Muscle Shoals. We think that Congress senses the popular feeling and will break the deadlock which has virtually paralyzed this national enterprise through three administrations. [*New Orleans Times-Picayune*]

With the passage of the act, there was rejoicing in the valley. Chattanooga, Tennessee, was one of the fervent examples. Leaders of the city were watching Congress, and when word came that the Senate and House had approved the TVA bill, excitement broke loose. It had been arranged beforehand, and it happened. As soon as the local announcement was made, a whistle blew at the O. B. Andrews Company, a box factory. Immediately a large number of other factory whistles throughout this industrial city were in full cry. Mayor Edward Bass exultingly pronounced the news. The president of the chamber of commerce received a wire from U.S. Senator Nathan Bachman which said: "By this act the Tennessee Valley is started on its way to a full development as a great industrial and agricultural empire."

All sentiment was not unanimous, however. Mercer Reynolds, prominent chamber of commerce official, resigned when President Roosevelt signed the act. He gave as his reason: "I am opposed to the government going into the power business, just as I would oppose the government starting up flour mills all over the country to grind up wheat or going into the cotton mill business. . . . I cannot feel that Chattanooga will receive the benefits from the bill that most citizens are expecting." This remark was typical of a conservative element which still exists in this city.

A Town Called Norris

The towering Norris Dam was not the only happening there. The town of Norris itself was a new entity. A total of $3.5 million was spent on land, buildings, streets, water supplies, sewage disposal, and electric service. It was laid out a few miles from the dam and planned to accommodate eventually 10,000 people. Norris was designed like an English garden city, concentrically within a swath of woods. Gardens ranging in size from one-half acre to four acres per family were a part of the pattern. The houses were divided into three types: most of them brick and frame ones but many simply built of cinder blocks which were found to be cheap, insulative, termiteproof, and yet not unpleasant to the eye. Some of the larger buildings had fireplaces and baths. For many families who had been living in wooden shacks and even log cabins, the town of Norris was a real innovation.

The land was acquired in an unusual way. Two TVA appraisers visited each tract and prepared independent estimates to be approved by a TVA board. The landowner received an offer in the mail, and two weeks later the buyer showed up. Since there was little recourse, there was little bargaining, although these farmers were largely of Scotch-Irish descent and were ordinarily shrewd traders.

In many cases the history of night life in construction camps was a story of gambling, drinking, and prostitution. Not so at Norris. Recreation was an important part of the scheme. For leisure activity there were games in the community building which had been built for this and other purposes. Ping-Pong, shuffleboard, and movies were available at night, as well as boxing which proved to be extremely popular especially with the young men. Outside there were baseball, tennis, horseback riding, and horseshoe pitching.

One of the survey parties working in the Norris basin came across a farmer who started complaining about his loss of acreage. One of the survey crew told him that he should be glad that the dam was being built, that the whole region would be benefited, and that all the farms would have electricity. "Now listen," said the farmer, "you can't tell me that. You know dang well that all the dams you have built upstream from here will sift all the electricity out of the water before it gets down here."

Another incident occurred in the same Norris area when a woman called "Old Aunt Rachel" wanted to know if the water was going to cover her house. The surveyor said it probably would but that she would get an even better place. Nevertheless, she insisted that she was not going to move. "I ain't goin' to sell," she said, "but I ain't goin' to give you no trouble. I am just goin' to set here in my rocking chair and let the waters come up around me and drown me."

A TVA buyer pled with her in desperation. "This project will be a great thing for this valley and the people," he cried. "It seems that the least you could do is cooperate."

"Cooperate!" shot back Aunt Rachel, "I'm goin' to die for the government. What more do you want?"

For the Norris library, it was recommended to TVA officials that they limit their selection of reading materials largely to comics, Western stories, and other such literature. It was said that these were the only things the men from the mountains and rural areas would read. Instead the shelves were stocked with publications such as *Time Magazine, National Geographic, Scientific American,* and *Colliers,* and a reasonably good range of fiction, science, and biography. The Norris residents and their families devoured this reading.

To manage the cafeteria, a woman trained in dietetics and well acquainted with the region and its appetites was brought in. Some had said the local people would eat only such things as cornbread, pork, and turnip greens. Instead they enjoyed salads, vegetables, milk, and other foods. "Scotty" Forbes, who was director of recreation at Norris, worked out a plan of booking motion pictures only of good quality, without accepting a block of weak film. He also developed a series of dramatic productions using local talent. At night the workers were very interested in learning machine tooling, welding, and electrical and carpentry work. Master craftspersons were brought in, one from a Highpoint, North Carolina, furniture factory and a couple from the Berea, Kentucky, craft shops. In an effort to localize their endeavors they made models of typical early American furniture used in the valley.

But all was not play. The adults of Norris also went to school. Holders of college degrees volunteered to teach night classes, and the courses ranged from the "three R's" through literature, current events, and American history. University professors and Tennessee officials also lectured at Norris. There were woodworking, metal, automotive, and electrical courses.

After having observed these interesting and valuable night courses, I dropped into the Knoxville office of Chairman A. E. Morgan one day and told his secretary that I had an idea in which he might be interested. To my surprise, she asked me to wait, and within a few minutes I was in Morgan's office talking with him. My idea was that the CCC workers of the surrounding camps be allowed to attend the night classes in the town of Norris. He approved the idea almost instantly, and soon on the winding roads into town the roar of Army trucks could be heard hauling scores of interested enrollees toward courses.

It was not the policy of TVA to force God on anyone, so He at first was left out of the program. This showed that the TVA did not understand the people of the valley. They wanted God and murmured about the lack of Him at Norris. TVA called a vote among the townspeople, and almost unanimously they asked for a preacher. On Thursday nights several hundred of them gathered in the auditorium to hear a sermon and sing for half an hour.

With little fanfare the TVA in line with its policy initially began hiring blacks until their employment percentage tallied with the population percentage of the communities. (A fairly recent book, *The Glory and the Dream* by William Manchester, erroneously states that no blacks were hired for the first TVA construction.) This amounted to about 20 percent. They were paid the same wages and were given equal housing.

Architect Roland Wank had a theory that government architecture would be good "if given the right encouragement at the beginning." He went to the TVA board of directors and said that this was the time for new things because, as a result of the Depression, there had not been much original architectural work going on for several years. Now the TVA was here as a new organization with a great deal of opportunity to do something better and different. Wank also pointed out that in the past very few visitors were permitted or encouraged to visit hydro-electric projects. In his opinion the TVA was a government corporation and the money for it was coming from the taxpayers of the United States; therefore the taxpayers were the actual stockholders in this corporation and should be invited to visit the TVA projects to see what their money was buying. The board of directors felt this was an excellent idea. Another attractive feature was the fact that most of the dams were located in scenic areas in the woods and near the hills where the lakes themselves make pleasant places to visit, especially for picnickers.

A related idea which Wank introduced was the inclusion of reception facilities inside the powerhouses. This can be seen today. Visitors can sit in comfortable chairs, have a soft drink and, if they desire, listen to a talk by a trained guide. The design of the power buildings took on a special character. It was realized that a dam represents a massive and heavy restraint on water and therefore its holdings should look powerful.

"A new architecture, bold as the engineering from which it springs, is rising in the Valley. Look at it and be proud that you are an American." Thus spoke Stuart Chase at the exhibition of TVA architecture at the Museum of Modern Art in New York in June 1941. Often-glum Lewis Mumford this time was cheerful. Writing about the exhibit in the *New Yorker* of June 7, 1941, he commented, "Thanks to these dams, the colossal forces of the Tennessee River are held back or released almost as easily as one turns the water on and off at one's private faucet, and instead of wasted water, there is an abundance of electricity. Aren't we entitled to a little collective strutting and crowing?"

There were 312 houses built in the town of Norris. Considerable pioneering was done in electric heating of houses. Some of the designers thought these houses should be quite modern in design, "but the wiser heads prevailed on the TVA directors to stick with house designs that were more indigenous to that particular area. They were more in keeping with the mountain cabins and the other types of housing that existed before TVA came into being in that area—that remote area of Anderson County. So these houses actually reflected in their design and the choice of materials a certain amount of character that was prevalent in that area in the housing prior to TVA."

When Norris Dam was finished, the construction personnel for the most part moved away, many of them being transferred to other TVA projects such as Pickwick, Chickamauga, and Guntersville Dams. Those who remained in Norris were the personnel who operated the powerhouse and employees of the forestry department, of the ceramic laboratories, the drugstore, and other facilities that were operated by the TVA for the benefit of Norris residents.

A town council came into being which worked with the town manager who was a representative of the Authority. "I happened to be elected the mayor of the first council," recalled Harry Tour:

> Looking back over my files I found we covered a great deal of territory. We enacted a dog ordinance, which the TVA enforced. We enacted a milk ordinance, which caused TVA to put caps on the milk bottles so that they wouldn't be contaminated. We had quite a hassle over a beer situation. TVA operated a restaurant and after the construction of the dam was over it occurred to some people that TVA ought to sell beer at the restaurant. It would be nice for the residents to be able to buy beer at the restaurant. We found that it was not illegal for TVA to do that, hence it was brought up at the council for the council to decide whether the residents would want beer or not. There was a very strong feeling among some of the people—among some of the women in Norris at least—that they shouldn't sell beer there. Yet there was a strong movement on foot to sell beer and the discussion became a hassle when the wife of Dr. Morgan, the Chairman of the Board, who was very much opposed to the selling of beer, went around circulating a petition calling for the council to disapprove it. And the situation got to be rather difficult because just her presence made it more or less obligatory on TVA employees' wives to sign the petition. In spite of that, the council voted in favor of selling beer.

After the construction personnel left the town of Norris, a number of other TVA people who worked in Knoxville moved to Norris because they thought it was a more pleasant place to live. In the words of Tour:

It was picturesque. The houses were nicely designed. They were nicely sited. We were living among talented people from all over the country, in fact all over the world. It was quite an interesting and pleasant experience for all of us who lived there. We had study groups, book review clubs, music clubs and such things. When the Atomic Energy Commission constructed Oak Ridge, there were quite a few people from there who came over to Norris to live.

The school in the town of Norris was distinctive. The school building was located in the town center and reflected Early American architecture. Simple in structure, it fitted in with the low-mountain landscape. Constructed on a terraced slope, its walls consisted of bricks within and without and paint was applied directly to the interior.

The lighting for the building was of the soft, indirect type, yet sufficiently strong for schoolwork, as tested by a sight meter. The athletic coach served both as an instructor and "engineer" who turned switches on and off to regulate the supply of fresh air in the classrooms. The Norris school attracted wide attention and was visited frequently by outside teachers who sought to learn the effectiveness of this new educational setting.

The schedule of the Norris school was a very definite one not only in the daytime but also in the evening classes. Monday evening was reserved for a general public program of lectures, concerts, or plays. Entertainment films were shown every Tuesday. Wednesday evening saw an educational film dealing with the natural or social sciences. Often a group met at the request of the workers to discuss economic questions. The community forum met every Thursday for general discussion. Friday evening was reserved for intermural sports. Dancing and motion pictures were provided on Saturday nights.

The shorter work days of the TVA were one reason why the employees could take advantage of evening courses. They worked five and one half hours a day for six days a week, and their schedule was so arranged that those working on any shift could have training opportunities.

A distinctive phase of the Norris educational schedule was an arrangement whereby groups of selected members of the construction crew were allowed to rotate every five weeks for experience and training in about ten different types of work. These included electricity, carpentry, pipe fitting, rigging, machine shop, crusher plant, mixing plant, quarry work, and concrete carrying. Often those who successfully completed these courses became job foremen.

Much credit for this early educational expansion was given not only to the TVA but to the educational program of the Civilian Conservation Corps, by which "thousands of young men were being given an opportunity to find themselves socially and vocationally." Perhaps not enough recognition has been given to the fact that the employees of the TVA, except for the professional and technical classes, were generally residents of the valley. Almost 150,000 applications for positions were received. Of these, 40,000 men were given examinations to determine their occupational proficiency, mechanical aptitude, and intelligence. Upon the basis of these tests, along with the judgment of personal interviews, a few thousand men received employment.

A cooperative arrangement was worked out with Anderson County, in which the TVA conclave was located, so that Norris High School was available to county students outside of the town. Similar contractural arrangements were made between the Authority and Hardin County, where the Pickwick Landing Dam is located. In this same area an agricultural program got under way, conducted with the cooperation of the extension services of the three states involved here, Alabama, Mississippi, and Tennessee.

In the last weeks of 1935, a report showed that almost 400 employees in the central TVA offices at Knoxville were enrolled in training activities. These included courses in personnel administration, public ownership and operation of utility services and discussion groups on TVA aims and purposes, philosophy and social trends, hydro-mechanics, mathematics, and stenographic and clerical services. The program at Norris was administered by the superintendent of education, said to be the only instance in the United States of a superintendent of education administering a community educational program which reached from the nursery school through adult education.

At Wilson and Wheeler dams a large part of the instruction was carried on by volunteers who did this in their extra time without pay. One of their major functions was to train leaders to carry on educational programs with their respective groups, such as those in the fertilizer plant. This activity also included the training of leaders among members of the labor unions.

A divergent outgrowth was the Norris School Cooperative. It was organized soon after the advent of the main school. To correlate science with agriculture, a small produce company was organized to sell products from the garden to the residents of Norris. The social science classes studied different kinds of business organizations before the cooperative was started. A board of three directors with a chairperson was elected by the students.

The TVA sponsored a kind of traveling classroom. It was mostly in the form of Bill Baird, a young man with a background in science and education. In the summer of 1971 he set out with a small van to visit junior and senior high schools in the Tennessee Valley. His mission was to help students better understand the basic principles and peaceful uses of atomic energy. He traveled almost 20,000 miles and spoke to approximately 100,000 students, visiting four or five different schools each week. He began by presenting an hour program for the entire student body. Then he called students from the audience to help him move through a number of experiments and demonstrations designed to show the highlights of basic nuclear science, chain reactions, reactor, and the application of nuclear energy for the generation of electricity, for medicine, for agriculture, and for research.

Baird spent the remainder of the session in science classrooms at the same school, where he lectured, answered questions, and discussed with the students in more detail the material they had seen in the assembly. As a part of both sessions, he explained TVA's nuclear power generation facilities, how they work, and how they would contribute to supplying the electric needs of the region. During the latter part of the year, the breeder reactor came in for discussion.

"I think we were able to dispel a large number of misconceptions about radiation," the lecturer said. "I was amazed at the lack of understanding. Almost every school, for example, had students who thought a person exposed to radiation would become radioactive himself."

As for myself, when I walked through the town of Norris, I was impressed with the beauty of its picturesque simplicity. Not only the inviting-looking houses stood out, but also the community building, restaurant, drugstore, barber shop, beauty parlor, general store, and post office. Naturally I was especially interested in the educational facilities. They, too, were an innovation, certainly different from the proverbial one-room school, not many miles away, which I had once attended. The Norris High School students were studying government weather station recordings and, on the basis of these, making weather forecasts and thus learning about physical geography, astronomy, barometric pressure, rainfall, and temperatures. Lower grades were studying, among other things, modern homes and contrasting country and city life. Agriculture courses included landscaping, gardening, poultry raising, dairying, cooking, sewing, and child care. Athletic activities at Norris were strictly intramural. No games were played with other schools, and every pupil had a chance to take part.

In the electrically heated modern classrooms, the idea of failure was not even considered by the alert and well-trained teachers. If the required amount of work was not finished by the end of the term, the next term the pupil would begin where he left off, thus not repeating the entire year.

According to Harry Tour, former TVA official, the school facilities operated by the local Anderson County

were pretty minimal. They may have had school that went to the eighth grade. A lot of the kids would drop off in about the seventh grade. A lot of them were old for their school grade and were dropping out. When the school was opened in Norris, an effort was made to get a lot of these children to come to Norris to go to school and complete their education. And the way it worked out was that people like us and others would take some of these county pupils, usually girls, in our own homes and give them a room, and give them their board, their lodging, buy their clothes, and permit them to go to school during the school hours. Then they would help around the house with the cooking, and the dishes, and the house cleaning, and baby sitting, and that sort of thing in the evening. And we did that for several years with these county girls and it worked out very well. They went on through. It was quite hard to persuade them to go to school because they were large for their school grade. They were older, considerably older than the Norris youngsters in the same grade, so it was a little embarrassing for them. But after you talked them into it and they go in there for about a year or so, then they liked it. And they went on to school and made good grades and turned out very well—most of them did.

We used to see these girls who had worked for us, after they had left Norris and were married and had children. They would come back and bring their children to show them off to us. But they were dressed up well—dressed nicely. Hair was done in a beauty parlor. Their nails were manicured. They were then very refined, which was a far cry from what they were. When they first came over there to work for us a lot of them had never seen running water. You had to teach them how to turn on the water in the sink and teach them how to turn on a light switch. They had never seen electricity. And to show them how to use the telephone. But they were honest. They were hard working. They were conscientious. Trustworthy. They had the very highest kind of personal attitudes on things which just hadn't been exposed to these areas of modern civilization. They didn't understand some of our words. You talk about putting something on the buffet—they didn't know what a buffet was. But after a few years in Norris they turned out very, very well.

On June 15, 1948, the town was sold by the TVA to Henry David Epstein, a Philadelphia, Pennsylvania, real estate dealer. He was high bidder for the 1,284-acre model townsite of 341 dwellings having a population of 1,250. The buyer represented a group of Philadelphia business men and bought the town for $2,107,500.

"We intend," said Epstein, "to give the present residents an opportunity to purchase their homes. Our plan is to continue the pleasant residential character of Norris. The town will continue as a home for people who work for TVA."

As he spoke, nearly every resident of Norris—men, women, and children—were on the school lawn for the auction sale. Others, hundreds of them, had driven in from elsewhere. There was emotion in the voice of George M. Baker, the TVA land branch chief, as he described the little city: "Norris is known throughout the world as the perfectly planned community of the green-belt type," he said. "Its fame has been carried around the world by its visitors."

After the town of Norris was purchased by Epstein, according to ex-mayor Harry Tour:

> The former came down and worked with the corporation and gave us his ideas of what he was planning on doing. And he was going to do a lot of things that we didn't think were particularly good in the way of chopping up some of the undeveloped areas for commercial development. By selling those he was going to make a lot of his money first by charging higher prices for the houses than we had appraised them and second by selling a lot of vacant land for commercial development and for real estate development. We pointed out to him the fact that we had a planning commission, which had authority by state law to control the zoning, and to control the major thoroughfares, and set up standards for subdivision regulations and enforce them. Mr. Epstein didn't like that very well. He thought, of course, if he owned the town why it was his to do anything that he wanted to do. But our foresight in creating a planning commission with that kind of authority and having developed a zoning ordinance and subdivision regulations in advance, before the town was sold, stood us in good stead because that did prevent him from doing a lot of the things that he had planned on doing before hand. Because we could prevent him from doing it by authority we had under the state law. It worked out pretty well that way and as a result the town has grown under private ownership in a rather attractive way.

Board of Directors

The TVA Act itself stated that it planned "the economic and social well-being of the people living in said river basin." President Roosevelt himself had observed that "many hard lessons have taught us the human waste that results from the lack of planning. . . . We are fully persuaded that the full success of the Tennessee Valley development project will depend more upon the ability, vision and executive capacity of the members of the board than upon legislative provisions."

Who were these first members of the TVA board of directors? One was Arthur E. Morgan. Although not a graduate of any college himself, had been president of Antioch College in Ohio, a liberal institution tending toward benevolent, socialistic ideas for its students. He also had been a successful water conservation engineer in the Midwest. He and his wife had very definite concepts of a society that should rest upon broad, humanitarian ideals. Some thought the Morgans were admirable and altruistic; others, more conservative, regarded them as impractical, intellectual crackpots.

Another director was Harcourt A. Morgan, president of the University of Tennessee from 1919 to 1933 and a noted agricultural expert, who had brought this state institution into national eminence particularly in his special field. His confirmation in Congress, however, was opposed by a former member of his faculty, John R. Neal, a would-be political figure who in this effort as well as many others was highly unsuccessful.

In the early 1900s there spread through the United States an expanding agricultural and extension program designed by universities to meet the needs of more and more people. H. A. Morgan was a foremost leader in this movement and was said to have "brought the college to the farm and made Tennessee the campus of the university." To people who could not attend the university in person, it undertook through its extension program the task of disseminating knowledge of agriculture, education, engineering, and home economics. In 1913 Morgan was offered but declined the presidency of the University of Virginia and also the Maryland College of Agriculture. But he remained at Tennessee and was termed by a successor "a remarkable salesman who proved a genius at making friends with the farmers and helping them solve their problems."

The third director was David E. Lilienthal of Wisconsin. John P. Ferris, a former TVA official, said:

Lilienthal was imaginative and daring. But he always persuaded people to recognize realities. One of the realities that he tied back to was that electric power in the modern age was a key tool and that TVA's having control of a big block of it enabled us to undertake a tremendous task—to find out what electric power was good for in the Valley. And then he had of course, this great talent of saying things understandably; of interpreting what TVA was doing in speeches and in writings that would seem plausible to politicians and others who had the "yes and no" power over it all.

The first meeting of the board of directors was held in Washington, D.C., in the historic old Willard Hotel (a mellowed hostelry where

Presidents had stayed) on the dark and rainy afternoon of June 16, 1933. According to the minutes, it was formally announced that Chairman Arthur Morgan had been appointed by the President of the United States, confirmed by the Senate, "and who had previously subscribed to support the Constitution of the United States." Each board member was to receive a salary of $10,000, together with the occupancy of a dwelling house furnished by the government.

Although the first meeting of the board was of a preliminary and procedural nature, there was one event of significant interest. The board was in receipt of a letter from Wendell Willkie, president of the Commonwealth and Southern Corporation, a holding company which controlled most of the large utility operations in the Southeast. Willkie asked to meet with the chairman of the board to discuss problems of mutual interest to the TVA and his corporation. This brought about a discussion as to what attitude the board should take toward private utilities. Lilienthal received the impression that there was some difference of opinion regarding tactics and strategy between him and Arthur Morgan. On the other hand, Harcourt Morgan seemed to be in the middle of the road as far as the proper approach to dealing with private industry. This was to be a harbinger of opposing forces to come. How prophetic this was, Lilienthal could not know!

Here at this very first board meeting appeared the embryo of a great controversy which was eventually to split the board and almost the Tennessee Valley Authority, because the differences between Lilienthal and A. E. Morgan were really never worked out.

Chairman Morgan was to be responsible for integration of the whole program, including Norris Dam, the educational program except agricultural engineering, regional planning, social and economic organization and planning, forestry, soil erosion, and the conservation corps.

H. A. Morgan was to handle all matters relating to agriculture, phosphorus, potash and nitrate plants, research in fertilizer, rural life planning, public relations, and matters pertaining to localized industry and its relation to agriculture.

Lilienthal was to be in charge of power distribution and relations with its purchasers. This supervision included the operation of the electric plant at Muscle Shoals, construction and operation of transmission lines, accounting methods; legal matters, acquisition of land, and transportation.

A. E. Morgan lost no time in stating what he thought the TVA program ought to be. In his opinion it should be based entirely upon the inhabitants of the valley. He knew that thousands of local people had left their native homes to work in mill towns. When the Depression threw them out of jobs, they drifted back to practicing subsistence farming on the hillsides of Tennessee and Virginia. What Morgan probably did not realize was that these people were still proud and individualistic. So when he suggested the setting up of small, highly specialized cooperative industries in each locality—he suggested those making fine textiles, furniture, and scientific instruments—he was surprised at some local reaction.

One feather in Morgan's cap, on the other hand, was his honest approach when he assumed his TVA position. He filed with Secretary of State Cordell Hull an inventory of all property possessed by himself and his family and announced that he intended to submit a similar statement upon the termination of his job. How many such public officials do we presently have?

This early effort of Arthur Morgan was to establish in connection with the TVA certain cooperatives which would, in his words, "help remove people from public relief or keep from public relief people whose resources are nearly exhausted." Accordingly there was organized early in 1934 the Tennessee Valley Associated Cooperatives, Inc., the principal office of which was to be located in Knoxville.

The specific purposes of this subsidiary organization were to promote, organize, establish, manage, finance, coordinate, and assist in developing cooperative enterprises in the Tennessee Valley; to produce and sell farm products, livestock, and merchandise, to extend financial assistance to cooperative firms; to borrow money and issue bonds for the purpose; to improve and manage property of the corporation; to handle such things as licenses and trademark or patents which might be involved; and "to do all and everything necessary, suitable and proper for the accomplishment of any of the purposes or the attainment of any of the objects" of the corporation.

By now it was obvious that much of the future of the TVA would hinge upon its relationship with other social and industrial institutions of the Tennessee Valley. And the valley was far from devoid of natural resources. Nationally known writers who visited the development in its early stages often were asked to view the poverty and the poorest people and then rush back to their northern editorial offices and write vivid stories about the squalid hillbillies who lived in rickety shacks. Actually a good proportion of the people of the valley resided in comfortable homes, were fairly well educated, and compared well with the top people in other parts of the nation.

As for material resources there were lumber mills in several towns not far from Norris. Chattanooga, Knoxville, Kingsport, Johnson City,

Elizabethton, and Cleveland had knitting and spinning mills as well as foundries. Kingsport produced wood alcohol, acetone, and charcoal. There was a large paper mill at Canton, North Carolina, and copper smelters at Ducktown and Copper Hill, Tennessee. The Alcoa plant at Maryville, Tennessee, is one of the largest aluminum manufactories in America. Interestingly enough, while there is bauxite in the valley, it is not rich enough to be mined in competition with ores elsewhere. The aluminum smelted here has come largely from South American ores, first carried to St. Louis for reduction to aluminum oxide. Zinc, lead, and marble are obtained from sources in the valley but are not always available in the huge quantities necessary for large-scale production. In addition to these products, the Tennessee valley affords asbestos, asphalt rock, barytes, limestone, iron ore, coal, manganese, mica, phosphate rock, and shales, as well as other products.

Chairman Morgan in an early meeting reported that he had received a letter from the U.S. Army authorizing Major Robert Neyland, who was stationed at Nashville, to cooperate fully with the TVA. This was the same "Bob" Neyland who was to become a famous football coach at the University of Tennessee and who, if he did not work directly with the TVA, certainly bolstered the morale of local football fans by his many winning teams.

Another interesting development in these early meetings was the report of Lilienthal which stated that he was trying to work out a comprehensive plan in cooperation with the Commonwealth and Southern Corporation. This plan would enable the TVA to set up an area for its power operations in which its relations with the private utilities would be comparable to the relations which might exist between two privately owned utilities operating in the same area. He stated that he would like to integrate the existing facilities but not in any way relinquish any of the rights that the Authority was trying to establish in connection with its experimental power project.

This early attitude of Lilienthal seems rather odd because later he not only lessened his cooperation with the private power companies but fought them relentlessly and effectively.

In 1935, The Southern Highlanders, Incorporated, was formed by 25 members of the Southern Highland Handicraft Guild. In order to extend the marketing of the handicraft products of the region into other parts of the nation, Chairman Morgan was quick to see the possibility here of an affiliation. Consequently, a rather extensive contract was drawn up between the Authority and The Southern Highlanders. The document pointed out that large numbers of people were living in the

Tennessee River basin and adjoining areas and were engaged in producing handicraft products as a means of earning money as a chief or supplemental source of family cash income. By 1938 the Southern Highlanders had 54 stockholders, including organizations and individuals, representing 2,500 craftspersons. Their products have been sold in every state and several foreign countries, and stores have been established in Chicago and New York City.

Good Workers

Since this was during the Depression, much good talent was readily available—in fact out of work and anxious. One veteran TVA official has stated that in its early days the Authority had more personnel of a high caliber than any other organization in the country.

Another special aspect of the TVA personnel was that the act creating the Authority made a definite stipulation that in no instance were political tests or qualifications to be considered in making appointments. Writing in the *Commonweal* of August 31, 1934, E. Francis Brown stated:

> This stand, though it has caused untold anguish in many a politician's heart and may in the end prove to be a boomerang against the TVA, has been upheld in the face of the greatest pressure. As a result, the TVA personnel has been spared the hampering if not paralyzing effects that would have arisen from the presence of a hoard of office-seekers. . . . As a result of this policy the workers are obviously of a high type—bright-eyed, clean-cut, vigorous and intelligent. Already they have proved themselves hard-working and efficient.

TVA wages were considered liberal for those days, approximating the prevailing rate in the region which ranged from 45 cents an hour for unskilled workers to $1 an hour for skilled. Work was scheduled on the basis of four 5½-hour shifts each day, six days a week.

The availability of labor turned up some unusual results. For example, the janitor in the TVA school at Norris had a college degree—and in those days made as much money as some school principals. At first he worked on the Norris Dam, but when the school was established, he asked for a place on the faculty. The only job open was that of janitor. He took it so that he might eventually take charge of the recreational work. In his spare time he organized athletic clubs and Boy Scout groups and helped the children find play activities during their lunch hour. A thermostat regulated the electric heating as well as a humidifier which provided the proper amount of moisture. There was also an air circulating system in the comfortable building.

Relief for unemployment was not a major purpose of the TVA, but it was a problem which the Authority inevitably had to deal with. In some communities in the valley, the unemployment situation was not extreme. In others it was different. For instance, in early November of 1933, C. C. Killen, TVA director of labor relations, came upon conditions which were startling. His primary purpose was to help select some 50 single young men for reforestation work in the CCC camps. He went to the Wilder coal mining district near Cookeville, in the rugged Cumberland Mountain region of East Tennessee, to interview the applicants. There he found awful starvation among adults and malnutrition in hundreds of children.

He reported that the help offered by the Red Cross was "wholly inadequate and for a time was unfairly dispensed." He found that many of the children had not tasted fresh milk for 18 months, a few of them getting canned milk:

> A diet of flour and water, or corn meal and water, is all they get for days at a time. Their pinched faces and thin bodies show signs of actual starvation. Boiled greens from weed tops often are eaten. The only medical aid available in the community is the Company doctor. The families of the miners get little of this aid. . . . Pellagra, rickets and bloody flux (bowel infection) are prevalent and increasing.

The TVA representative learned that foraging parties had ranged through the adjoining territory at night, killing cattle and hogs and taking them back to their families. He recommended immediate relief in the form of food and clothing for these suffering people and employment for as many of their men as possible. Out of the anguish of his own heart, he spent about $15 personally for sandwiches and coffee to give them. As a result of this investigation, the TVA was able to hire a number of the men for work at Norris Dam as well as to help place them in local CCC camps for similar work.

Relocation

The plan of the Authority was to relocate families displaced by Norris Dam in other places as suitable as possible. But all did not work smoothly. The James Randolph family waited so long to move that they were evicted because the waters of the dam reservoir would soon cover them. Having no place to go to immediately, they lived in a tent on the

Campbell County poor farm while they looked for a farm to buy. The tent was provided by the TVA, had a floor and side walls, and was not too bad. The family cows were housed in a second tent. University of Tennessee extension workers helped the Randolphs find a new farm which was paid for by the money which the TVA gave the family for its previous property.

Ras Lindamood lived in a picturesque place known as Big Valley. He was a happy man and knew his neighbors and everything about his farm. It seemed he never threw anything away. So when it came time for him to move out of the Norris Dam reservoir basin, he was sad, but he did not sit around moping about it. He found a place near the Clinch River in Anderson County and borrowed $14,000 from his friend Walter Lynch, a storekeeper and squire.

Lindamood bought the farm, but it took him several weeks to move from Big Valley in Union County to the new place. He insisted on taking everything with him, his smokehouse board by board, the front yard stepping stones, hundreds of locust fence posts, chestnut rails, saddles, wagons, buggies, scrap iron, and even a worn-out bellows from his old farm blacksmith shop.

The thing that attracted most attention, however, was the publicized fire in his fireplace. He said it had been burning there for a hundred years and had been brought down, still burning, from Virginia by one of his ancestors. Lindamood told the TVA that he had never let his fire go out and did not intend to do it now. Here was a stickler. There was some head scratching in the headquarters of the Authority. What could be done? Somebody had a bright idea. The TVA agreed to move the fireplace intact to the new Lindamood farm and left the fire burning, which it did until the death of the owner in 1940.

Not only the living cried out for adjustment. The dead did also. In the Norris Dam area there were 92 graveyards which would be flooded by Norris Dam. In these cemeteries were 4,200 graves. It was no little matter for the relatives and friends of those deceased to think of a hundred feet of water covering the hallowed resting places of their loved ones. The TVA handled this touchy matter in a low-key way. It did not make noisy speeches about the problem of the graves, although there was wide publicity on the poignant matter, some of it played up to a maudlin extent by feature writers. The TVA knew better than to offer money for these acres. It quietly offered to move the cemetery to suitable places elsewhere, working through the preachers of the region as well as civic and veterans organizations. Where tombstones and monuments were needed, the Authority furnished them. One thing that helped in the smooth accomplishment of this delicate operation was that not a grave was touched without religious services.

It was definite TVA policy that every effort be made to keep grave removal activities from becoming a gruesome ordeal. The operation was looked upon by the TVA as a "regrettable necessity," and special efforts were extended to make the removals as easy as possible upon the nearest relatives. In and around Norris, several generations of old first-settler families were buried in a single small ancestral cemetery. Some of the local families were so resentful of the intrusion that they would not sign a permit for the graves to be moved. In such cases the TVA simply left the graves intact unless they interfered with construction. In Norris alone 5,226 graves were relocated, the largest number the TVA has had to relocate in any one reservoir.

Where possible, monuments and markers were transferred to the new locations. The largest monument weighed 14 tons. Jewelry, Bibles, ornaments, buttons, and sometimes coins were found in the graves. Some bodies were found to be petrified. This was probably due to the limestone water which often flowed into the graves of the region.

Early in 1934, about 200 TVA-CWA workers began investigating the Norris Reservoir basin to see what was present in the way of historic remains. On the Powell River in Campbell County several open caves were discovered. In one of these were found eight skeletons in sitting positions. Officials believed that these had been prehistoric Algonquin Indians. Some 40 Indian mounds also were discovered in the basin as well as primitive village sites, and these were excavated. Shells and bones indicated that these early inhabitants lived largely on fish from the rivers. In the center of each village was a "temple" ranging from 40 to 60 feet long by 30 to 35 feet wide. In the center was a raised baked clay alter with a fire pit in the center. American Indian pottery was found nearby. According to the scientific authorities, none of the artifacts found indicated contact with white persons.

One burial mound was found to contain 49 skeletons, believed to have been those of early Cherokee Indians. These and their ancestors, the Iroquois, have been described by archaeologists as "the Romans of the American Indians." Two oddly shaped copper ceremonial objects were found in a depression beneath one grave. This was believed to have been made from copper mined nearby. Remains of weapons found suggested that these Indians lived before the bow and arrow was in use.

In Pleasant View Cemetery near Maynardville, Tennessee, there is a tombstone inscription that is revealing:

Major Allen Hurst
son of
John and Elizabeth Thompson Hurst
March 4, 1810, Tazewell Co. Virginia
May 26, 1873
First Circuit Court Clerk of Union County

During Reconstruction Days Robbed by
the Carpet Baggers of 4,000 acres.
60-odd years later the TVA
Confiscated Several Thousand acres
of Mineral Land left
to his Grandchildren
GONE WITH THE WIND

But TVA was not heartless; an example of its consideration occurred at Dandridge. There elderly Anna Hynds had a spring of water which flowed through the yard of her home. For centuries, she told the TVA men, this spring had been in her family, secure in its cool little cove from which issued crystal clear water. Now the efficient thing for the TVA to have done would have been to plug up the spring so as not to interfere with the nearby lake, which was filling from a dam. Instead, out of consideration for the feelings of Hynds, the men installed a pump to lift the spring water over the wall and into the lake.

Slightly different is the story of a bootlegger who was living contentedly in the Smoky Mountains, operating his still beside a roaring creek, when the National Park Service bought up all the land around for the new national park. The bootlegger had to move and went to Union County, where he resumed his occupation of making moonshine. After being here a few years, the TVA moved in and took his land for the Norris Dam basin. He next moved down on the Clinch River, and there was again engaged in his favorite vocation when the Oak Ridge project came along. This was the last straw. "Used to be, the only Federal men I dealt with was the revenooers," he snorted, "and we understood each other. Now it seems that every time I come home from a run, theys a guvermint man a-settin' on my doorstep with papers orderin' me to move. Ef I knowed of a place where there weren't no guvermint men but revenooers, I'd shore go there."

As for the Norris families, 62 percent relocated in one of the five reservoir counties in East Tennessee: Anderson, Campbell, Claiborne, Grainger, and Union counties. About 10 percent went to other counties nearby and the rest elsewhere, but only 7 percent moved outside the state, most to Kentucky. More than 85 percent purchased farms for less than $1,000 in the reservoir counties. One study showed that both owner and tenant families who resettled within the reservoir counties had smaller farms than they had prior to removal. Nearly all the families who were farmowners before the coming of the TVA remained owners of farms in their new locations.

One TVA contact man who went out to see the local residents was forced to proceed on foot when the road became too rough for his car. Suddenly he came upon a local resident who looked at him suspiciously. Not thinking of anything else to say, the TVA man asked, "What time is it?"

The local man replied, "Nigh on to three o'clock."

The former then asked, "Is that sun time or railroad time?"

This drew the laconic answer, "Can't see what difference it makes. You are as far from one as you are from the other."

Through the basin, contours were marked at elevation 1020 to indicate the location of the normal pool and to show the upper limit of reservoir-clearing-operations. This numeral 1020 was painted in white on fences, buildings, and surfaces of state highways. One day a Hancock County visitor stopped at a drugstore in the nearby town of Tazewell and asked for "a bottle of that 1020 medicine which is advertised all over the country."

The TVA adopted the policy of giving the landowners permission to remove the improvements on their property, provided the removal was made by the surrender-of-possession date. Such a date was established when possible at the end of the calendar year between crop seasons preceding the date set for the completion of construction. One helpful factor was that the TVA appraisers had been realtors or they had represented banks or insurance companies in the appraisal and management of real estate.

If a dispute over land could not be otherwise settled, the courts were available. But in the decade following its creation, during which time most of its land was acquired, the Authority had to litigate in less than 5 percent of the property it sought. These contested condemnation proceedings involved 801 tracts of land consisting of 46,891 acres and resulted in price increases amounting to $456,008 over the $2,716,801 offered for the property, or an increase of 16.8 percent.

The magazine *Nation's Business* for August, 1935, took a rather sanguine view of the TVA's progress. In it Herbert Corey wrote, "So far as I was able to discover the dwellers in the Valley accept with gratitude the material benefits showered on them by the TVA. Money has poured on them in a flood.'' Corey took a dim view of the writers from New York who poked fun at the local mountain people: ''If I were a mountain man I would cock the spring gun and turn loose the dog whenever I saw a writer approaching.''

''You are on the right road,'' one man said when I feared I was lost on a distressing detour. It did not seem possible that wheeled vehicles could be taken over it except as a stunt. The man explained, ''There ain't no other road.''

The article showed that not only did the TVA officials in general understand the people and characteristics of the surrounding countryside, but some of them grew up there. One TVA department head emphasized this by explaining, ''My father and mother would not have understood what you were talking about if you had said that I was hungry. We always had enough to eat by our way of thinking. We always had enough clothes to wear. We lived in a 'storm-house,' but it was a good enough storm-house. I did not want to get away because I felt myself deprived of any of the essentials of life. I wanted to do something else. My folks aided me to go.'' Apparently there were enough such people in the region to fill the requirements of the Authority.

Two of the writers which Corey may have referred to were Drew and Leon Pearson, who went down to the Valley and wrote about it somewhat with columnist tongue-in-cheek. They first visited Norris Dam and viewed its spectacular construction with surprised appreciation. (Incidentally, the dam was scarcely completed when an exceptionally heavy rain fell over the watershed. The gates were closed, and the entire flow above the dam was stored. The flood stage at Chattanooga was reduced about 4 feet, and an estimated $750,000 damage was prevented.)

The Pearsons found some colorful opposition to the TVA. They ferreted out a Squire John Keck, who claimed that the intrusion of the government behemoth was against what he had learned in his Bible. ''This TVA is like the seven-headed monster that rose up out of the sea and had dominion over man and beast,'' stated Keck, claiming to be quoting Genesis. ''The Lord made a covenant with Noah never again to destroy the earth with water. . . . They'll be punished! It's profanation to dig from the Lord's holy ground the bodies that have been given to His care. There is not a man among us would do so much as tread upon a human grave, and here's the TVA with picks and shovels turnin' up the bones of the dead and leavin' graves yawnin' like the Judgment Day.''

Near the village of Loyston, it was found that a merchant sold his store when he learned that his land was to be flooded. Evidently, he could not endure the drastic change. Depressed and inactive, he went inside his barn one night and hanged himself.

Isabel Brantley lived on Cedar Creek in the house where she was born and her father before her. The TVA offered her $1,200 for her log cabin and a few eroded acres of land. At first she stoutly refused, but when the TVA laborers offered to move the house in their spare time without cost to her to a site below Norris Dam, she softened. "But you have got to find me a place with a spring or a well," she interjected. "I don't want none of this new-fangled pipe water runnin' into my house."

Ezra Hill squinted over the plans for the new home which was to replace his old one in the flood area. He pointed to the place on the blueprint which showed the circles and oval of the bathroom fixtures. "What's all this?" he cried. "I won't have it! I guess a privy is still good enough for me."

The opposition press charged that the TVA was an enemy of religion. It is already stated that the Authority had reduced electric costs so low that private stockholders interests were threatened; now the TVA was held out as an atheistic outfit which denied free Americans the right to worship God. *The Christian Century* magazine of September 14, 1934, reported inaccurately that "the region near Norris happens to be a hotbed of holy rollerism and a similar form of religious obscurantism. Should the permanent population of Norris be drawn from this region, it is conceivable that a majority vote would favor a Holly Roller church. Or if the majority in the community should vote for some other form of church, it is still possible that the Holy Rollers, disdaining comity agreements, might try to storm the place anyway."

Copper Hill

The copper basin of Ducktown in Southeast Tennessee looked like a wasteland. When I first viewed this burned-out basin from a road which ran around its rim, I was depressed by the sight. It was a man-made desert of 23,000 acres. Not a single tree, bird, or blade of grass were in sight. Instead a dead, reddish, dreary badland cut by deep gullies leading into lower, larger ones greeted the eye. Nearby on a rise the huge buildings and tall smokestacks of a copper smelter loomed grimly over the prostrate land. This devastation was caused by the ax, poisonous sulphur fumes from the smelter, forest fires, and cloud-burst rains on unprotected slopes. So millions of tons of silt were washed into nearby creeks and on into the Ocoee River. "Besides the wasted land, the only reminder of mining in the early days was a small brick chimney on one of the hills near Ducktown. This lone sentry stands as a reminder that once a great forest covered the region,'' I wrote in my book *Smoky Mountain Country*.

This naked scar in the once-fertile earth was a challenge to the TVA. So it was not many years before its personnel and the boys of the Civilian Conservation Corps attacked the problem and brought good results. Trees were planted, grass was made to grow on part of the surface, and check dams were placed across the gully scars. Residents of Ducktown nearby Copperhill and Isabella also helped in planting and replanting trees, grass, shrubs, and flowers, until eventually this devastated section began to resemble to a brighter extent its former natural appearance.

Cartter Patten, prominent Chattanoogan and local historian, was not altogether sanguine in his analysis of the TVA, however:

> For a time, TVA was prone to picture the Tennessee Valley as an eroded, poverty-stricken, ignorant and backward land prior to its arrival. A few years later, presumably due to its good works, all appeared to be green, happy, and electrically equipped. This was particularly displeasing to the Valley residents, who had seen their fine and fertile river bottom farms covered by TVA waters. At present, even this is largely forgiven, if not forgotten, because the TVA continues to preach, and usually prove, that it benefits far outweigh its transgressions.

2. Power and Controversy

The early story of the Norris Dam and its related facets is in many ways that of the Tennessee Valley Authority in microcosm. Although this was the beginning, related activities were burgeoning as other dams and plants were coming. The Wilson Dam and power plant were the first links in the chain of the new Tennessee River system. The TVA had taken them over in the summer of 1933. Wilson was one of the largest dams in the world, and Norris was the second of the forthcoming units.

In October of 1933 President Roosevelt requested that the TVA begin construction of another dam to be located 15 miles up the river above Muscle Shoals. It was to be named the General Joe Wheeler Dam and was to be 50 feet high and about 6,000 feet in length, some 1,000 feet longer than the Wilson Dam at Muscle Shoals. Its reservoir was to cover 100 square miles and extend up the river about 80 miles to Buck Island, 5 miles above Guntersville, Alabama. While Norris Dam was primarily a storage dam, Wilson and Wheeler dams are what are called run-of-the-river plants. This means that when the river is high, much power can be produced. On the other hand, when the river is low, little power is available. Norris Dam, with its big reservoir, can store a year's rainfall from several thousand miles.

During the wet season when Wilson and Wheeler dams had an abundance of power, Norris was to be shut down and the water stored. The TVA estimated that such an integrated power system, which embraced the entire watershed, would produce power at half the usual cost. The Wheeler Dam also would provide navigable waters to Guntersville, Alabama, and also would serve to mitigate big floods.

Construction of the Wheeler Dam also provided some insights into the employment conditions of that period. George F. Hull, who eventually became an official in the TVA power system operations, genially recalled his early days in helping to build the dam. "Working was a highly competitive thing in those days," he reminisced:

Men with patches on their pants sat around on the grass outside the

2182-11-16-34.

On 16 November 1934, President Franklin D. Roosevelt, who sponsored formation of the TVA, visited Norris Dam. With him are Mrs. Roosevelt and Chairman Arthur Morgan in the rear seat. Later, the First Lady rode across the dam in a concrete-pouring bucket hundreds of feet high in the air. The author of this book was present and witnessed the visit of the President.

employment office just waiting for some employee to complain about his job. That's about all it took to lose it in those days. I recall seeing a "pink slip" brought to our payroll office by a discharged workman. In the space for "reason for termination" the foreman had written "not worth a damn." Probably the best reason for firing a man that I ever saw. Those men on the grass were not just local sharecroppers, either. Some were unemployed construction superintendents, engineers, and accountants. They came in by freight train, hitchhiking, or walking. Some later became officials in TVA. Probably one of the most over-qualified work forces ever put together—as was all of TVA for that matter. This was a strong factor in the early successes of TVA. We didn't necessarily go home when the whistle blew—we quit when the boss said so. That, incidentally, might be midnight or whenever the work was done. No overtime either. As I said, work was a highly competitive thing.

Since Wheeler Dam was farther south than Tennessee, blacks comprised more of the local population. In line with its policy, the TVA therefore employed a proportionate number of black people on the Wheeler project, this being 20 percent of the work force. A protective belt of land, approximately one-eighth of a mile wide, was acquired around the reservoir above the flood contour line. Average price paid per acre for land and improvements was $42.63.

The third major dam construction undertaken by the Authority was the Pickwick Landing Dam, located on the Tennessee River in West Tennessee about eight miles from the Mississippi state line. This was begun in late 1934 and was the first dam to be designed by the TVA, the others having been designed by the U.S. Bureau of Reclamation. Its length was about 1½ miles, and much of it was enclosed by earth embankments.

Neither the preamble or the caption on the TVA Act mentions production of power by the Authority; yet beginning with the second section of the Act and in half of the section thereafter, the subject of power is a major element. Naturally the private power interests and those who desired to keep the government out of business have been and still are instrumental in blocking public power production. These interests have contended that a government bureau cannot operate as efficiently as private business, which has the incentive of individual profits. They also have contended that government in business is unfair competition and that the government should confine its activity to controlling business practices.

It is true that the TVA was authorized to use as much electricity as it needed in the development of its own projects. Surplus power was to be sold. The TVA was to provide electricity to states, cities, and cooperative associations which would distribute power to towns or farmers. Usually the TVA was to generate the electricity and then transmit it over its lines to a town using it, which had set up its own distribution system. It buys electricity wholesale from the TVA at a fixed price and then sells it to its own citizens. The TVA prescribes the retail rates which the municipalities make to private users. In this way there appeared to be assurance that the cheap electric power benefits would be passed on to consumers. Any surplus power could be sold by the TVA to private companies.

Cities in the valley were not long in answering the invitation. Tupelo, Mississippi, a town of about 6,000 people, was the first to begin use of TVA power. The little city already owned its own distribution system but bought its power from a private company. Service began on February 7, 1934, when the city's franchise with the Mississippi Power

Company expired. Mayor J. P. Manney announced that his city had been paying 1.7 cents per kilowatt-hour but now was paying only 7 mills per kilowatt hour. The retail rates began at 10 cents per kilowatt-hour for the first 50 and stepped down to 7.5 cents per kilowatt-hour for consumption of 300 to 500 kilowatt-hours. Reductions in domestic rates were estimated at a minimum of 67.7 percent, while commercial rates were 50 percent lower.

The TVA announced that the 20-year agreement between it and Tupelo was expected to set a standard for contracts with other cities. The arrangement was to operate strictly as a business enterprise, and books were to be kept separate from other city accounts and carefully audited. Taxes, interest, and depreciation were to be counted as part of the costs, and consumers were to be charged enough to pay all these expenses of distribution and to pay off the indebtedness.

In the first six months that Tupelo was receiving its power from the TVA, there was an increase of 83 percent in the amount of electricity used in the city's homes. Families not previously able to afford electricity were now electrifying their homes. During the first two months of this period, $6,000 worth of electrical equipment was sold in Tupelo, or an average of $1.00 per inhabitant.

Printers' Ink Monthly for April 1935 pointed out "No amount of money could buy the volume of sales promotion that has pushed sales ahead so fast in the Tennessee Valley. The active support of the President has been the spearhead of a campaign of intensive selling, making use of all forms of advertising, including appliance display rooms, the radio, motion pictures, demonstrations, traveling displays and dealer helps. It has been a big push rivaled only by the Liberty Bond campaigns."

Such new measures may have pleased the people of Alabama, but they did not convince many conservative leaders of business. For instance, there appeared an editorial blast from the magazine *Electrical World* for September 16, 1933, as follows: "Water-power projects of the type outlined are not worthy. They should not receive taxpayers' money because they are economically obsolete before they are constructed. To stop these senseless programs, engineers who know the facts should speak out. They will not be consulted by those who sponsor the projects, but they would be heard by the taxpaying public if they would cite facts. Why not seize this public service opportunity?"

Controller General of the United States J. R. McCarl struck at the TVA's authority regarding the letting of contracts, such as those to Tupelo. He advocated an amendment to the TVA Act to compel the agency to use competitive bids. He also questioned the authority of the TVA to purchase a herd of 25 dairy cows and a bull. The controller explained that "they had produced milk of a butter fat content of 6 percent, some of this being exchanged with commercial dairies for milk of a 4 percent butter fat content. Just why an expensive dairy herd was developed to produce a high grade of milk when such milk is to be exchanged for an equal quantity of inferior milk is not apparent," he concluded.

That the TVA was not perfect, even Chairman Arthur Morgan conceded. In a Chicago address on September 30, 1933, he stated: "There is no assurance from on high that public ownership will bring honest and economical administration. Before national Prohibition, when I questioned its advisability, I was told that 'public opinion will grow up behind the law.' The reverse is what actually occurred. I meet enthusiastic public ownership advocates who thrill with the conviction that the achievement of public ownership will perforce reduce public incompetence and corruption. They should take a lesson from Prohibition."

Though he became a controversial figure, Arthur Morgan certainly spearheaded the main efforts of the Tennessee Valley Authority in its formative years. Herbert Corey termed him "schoolmaster idealist, and engineer, a combination of fine, almost saintly enthusiasm, with a hard-headed understanding of ways and means." Morgan himself was a dreamer and expressed his mission this way: "If we keep constantly in view our purposes—the greatest welfare of the whole people, both now and in the future—we shall realize that we must develop a certain spiritual quality of good will—social mindedness, the presence of which can give life to any program and the absence of which can kill any program."

There was another voice, however, raised against such ideas. It was that of Wendell Willkie. He became the spokesman for the holding companies and predicted that the TVA would bring "ruin" to the power industry. At the time, Samuel Insull was establishing his first holding company and Franklin D. Roosevelt was striving to save the St. Lawrence River for the state of New York, Willkie was working his way through Indiana University, laboring in a steel mill. He grew up on an Indiana farm and developed an appearance of boyish simplicity which often misled those who chose to oppose him. After practicing law for several years in the Midwest, Willkie became general counsel for the Commonwealth and Southern Corporation. He became its president in 1933 at the age of 40, with a salary of $75,000 a year, just in time to take on the TVA.

The private power companies making up Commonwealth and Southern were mainly in Georgia, Alabama, and Tennessee. In the first years of TVA, their record could hardly be called that of "ruin." For instance, in December 1936 the electrical output of Willkie's companies was running about 20 percent ahead of the year before. The 1936 net income of the company was nearly $4 million higher than in 1935.

Although Wendell Willkie became known as the spokesman for private power, his son Philip, at one time governor of Indiana, told me just before he died that his father was "liberal but not communistic." The son felt that his father had been misjudged, that he really favored the principles of the TVA, but differed mainly regarding the true cost of power production and its subsequent selling price. The TVA officials felt that if Wendell Willkie was a liberal, then they would have to redefine the word.

The reply of the Authority to the private power spokesman's charge that the TVA was underwritten by the government was answered by A. E. Morgan. He stated that TVA needed no such subsidy. He admitted that opponents asserted that the TVA had lower freight rates, free postage, lower interest rates on bonds, no interest on money appropriated by the government, and unfair allocations and paid no income taxes. Morgan mainly denied these accusations. He contended that freight rates had already been low in the valley, that other government agencies paid most of the TVA postage, that the TVA disposed of its bonds through the Treasury Department and paid the interest charged, and that the rate of interest on TVA bonds and private utility bonds was small.

The verbal tilts between Morgan and Willkie became well publicized, especially in the *Atlantic Monthly*, which termed them "two able protagonists" who practiced fairmindedness. Willkie argued vividly:

> Like England's once famous military formation, the British Square, the TVA has had four fronts to present to the public, and it uses the front most suitable to the group which it is addressing. Before the courts it claims that it is not really a power enterprise, but primarily a conservation activity; it is a project to prevent floods, promote navigation on the Tennessee River, and check soil erosion in the great Tennessee Valley. Only before a more sympathetic audience is it frankly an instrument for the electrification of America.

As for the "yardstick" which the TVA declared it was setting up as a proper rate charge for electric power, Willkie called it

rubber to the last inch by reason of the privileges, benefits and favors which it enjoys at the taxpayers expense as a governmental agency. . . . The private industry in America has been more progressive and effective than that in England, where public ownership has been much more dominant. The larger part of the investment in American utilities is prudent, necessary investment, honestly made and quite generally by people of moderate means.

Using his own yardstick, Willkie estimated that in the year 1935 the TVA paid only $16,900 on property and funds totaling $384 million. He added that if it were a privately owned and operated corporation, it would be paying on the same property and funds from $9 to $10 million in taxes:

Like the cuckoo bird, it has not built a nest of its own but has seized the nest of another bird. If the Federal Government were to give the private utilities of the Tennessee Valley as well as those elsewhere in the United States the subsidies and grants and special advantages, relief from taxes and low cost of money made available to the TVA and the municipalities it serves, the privately owned utilities could and would put in force rates for electricity materially lower than those now charged by the TVA and the municipalities to which it furnishes electricity wholesale.

Since he was probably the strongest voice against the TVA, Wendell Willkie should be considered at further length here. His words were electrifying in more ways than one. He wisecracked:

It has been truly said *the Tennessee River waters four states and drains the nation.* . . . Who is paying the bill? I will tell you who is paying the bill. Whenever a householder in Tupelo, Mississippi, switches on a light, everybody in the United States helps to pay for it. . . . It is tax moneys that are being used to give Tupelo its well publicized "yardstock rate."

He struck hard at what he regarded an invasion of the investment of private stockholders. "But what the TVA can really claim responsibility for," he said, "is the progressive destruction of the savings of some 300,000 stockholders who have invested $650,000,000 in the power properties in that area."

Willkie was reinforced in his charges by Jo Conn Guild, president of the Tennessee Electric Power Company, who stated on July 2, 1936: "Securities of this company are selling as much as 42 percent below par, while the securities of other operating companies in the same group outside of the Tennessee Valley are currently selling above par. . . . The TVA for three long years has carried on uninterruptedly a systematic and all inclusive program of propaganda designed to engender in the minds of the people of the Valley and in the minds of the utilities' own customers, employees, and stockholders, a spirit of distrust, dissatisfaction, and hatred for private enterprise in the power business.''

A TVA report was quoted as saying that the growth earnings of Alabama, Georgia, and Tennessee electric power companies had increased 10 percent. According to Commonwealth and Southern, this statement was incorrect; ''for in this same period the net earnings after preferred dividends of these same companies declined 20 percent . . . even more forcefully brought out in the losses being sustained by these companies through their present inability to refinance their securities. . . . The private utilities in the TVA area are anxious to extend their rural lines to every customer who can possibly use the service and pay the reasonable cost of service.''

Why, asked customers in the area, had this not been done before? The Commonwealth and Southern analysis concluded that the TVA had no right to imply that decline in retail power rates had been due primarily to its activities: ''Retail prices for electricity in this area have been declining continuously for the past twenty-five years, ever since the first holding company began consolidating electric operations in this territory. . . . The power companies could have supplied all of the demands of their customers by generation at their own plants, without purchasing any TVA power.''

In a ringing peroration, the Willkie analysis concluded: ''a total of about 758,000 acres of land, much of which is fertile farm land, will be removed from the tax rolls of the states, counties and cities involved. This is more land than has ever been inundated by any Tennessee River flood. It even exceeds the estimate of the Army Engineers of land which would be flooded by floods so large that it is expected to occur once every five hundred years.''

The voice of the TVA was not stilled. ''It won't be capitalism,'' said Arthur Morgan. ''It won't be socialism; it won't be communism; it won't be individualism; it won't be any of these *isms* that have become little more than labels or battle slogans. It will be none of those things, yet some of all of them. It will be a new Americanism.''

Even President Roosevelt had said in his Portland, Oregon speech: ''I might call the right of the people to own and operate their own utility a 'birch rod in the cupboard, to be taken out and used only when the child gets beyond the point where mere scolding does any good.' The right of the federal government and state governments to go further and to transmit and distribute where reasonable and good service is refused by private capital gives government, viz., the people, that same very essential 'birch rod' in the cupboard.''

A. E. Morgan echoed the man who had appointed him, calling for a ''new deal'' for inhabitants of the Tennessee River basin. In his regional planning he called not only for power production and distribution but for improvement of agriculture, development of domestic industries, production of cheap fertilizer and navigation, flood control, and reforestation along the Tennessee River. He felt that many people of the valley had been forgotten: ''Descendants of the pioneer stock our country has produced, the people of this area have always been hardy, patriotic, honest hospitable and independent. They have never asked for help, and do not ask it now. But it is in the interests of the country as a whole, as well as their own interests, that Uncle Sam now offers them assistance in making the most of this zone of super-power potentialities and one unusually rich in natural resources.''

Taking issue with Wendell Willkie about the Valley, he added, ''for that reason it has immense power, illumination and transportation possibilities.'' He noted that the TVA projects required most of their materials from other parts of the country and therefore believed the enterprise to be a national asset. From Pittsburgh came steel rails, from Detroit autos and trucks, from St. Louis road-building equipment. The things that the workers used included shoes from New England, textiles from the Deep South, furniture from Michigan. Food came from California and Florida, meat from Chicago, and grain and dairy products from the Midwest and Northwest.

R. G. Tugwell of the Department of Agriculture agreed with Morgan about the importance of the TVA in the mind of Roosevelt ''This work of his carries more significance for the future than any other single attempt of the Administration to make life better for all of us,'' said Tugwell. He believed that the TVA was not an emergency measure and did not have to be done, despite the reports of many indigent people living in the area. He felt that the Authority was ''a deliberate turning toward the future, a commitment toward an ideal.''

A. E. Morgan was farsighted. As early as 1933 he had envisioned a shortcut from the Tennessee River in Alabama to the Gulf of Mexico by way of the Tombigbee River with a ship canal and a series of locks and dams. Some day, he believed, this would make Cincinnati an ocean port and shorten the distance from the Ohio River points to the Gulf of Mexico by 500 miles. Such a project was begun only recently.

An Example

As to what is excellent or not, this is an academic account, and the facts must be presented as impartially as possible. But to deny that there was a great change in the Tennessee Valley as a result of the TVA would be much in error. I recall the example of an uncle who lived on an East Tennessee farm as comfortably as the old manner would allow. His acres were on rolling hills, and the crops of corn, tobacco, wheat, and vegetables were necessarily limited by the terrain. He lived in an unpainted wooden house which, though adequate by the current standards, was rather primitive by those of today. The front porch accommodated several rickety chairs, and the front room was a musty parlor containing an old-fashioned soft feather bed covered by a quilt made by women at a quilting party interspersed by the use of snuff.

In the living room was the customary fireplace which burned wood for heat as well as for cooking. The latter was a carry-over from older days when iron "bakers" were used on the hearth, these being round, kettle-like containers with live coals placed underneath and on top to produce what seemed to be the best corn bread in the world.

The dining room jutted out rearward and had a long wooden table which held the crude but wondrous viands of this country life. A breakfast was something at which to marvel. Great steaming platters of succulent country ham, swimming in red-eye gravy, fried eggs by the half dozen, heaping platters of incomparable hot biscuits, country sausage, and sometimes bacon were supplemented with jam, jellies, and marmalade under an enveloping aroma of strong hot coffee. All this was regularly prepared by the women of the household who literally "sweated over a hot stove" fired by hand-split hickory wood.

The kitchen was crude if productive. The range on which such meals as the foregoing were cooked was efficient but back-breaking and blistering for the women. Simple utensils surrounded it, and while it was cozy in the winter, it was the equivalent of a steam bath in hot weather. On the back porch was a wash basin, a bar of Lenox soap, and a towel which was used by everybody. Here took place the family ablutions whenever the weather permitted. In the wintertime, little worry was given to face washing. In the backyard was the black, iron wash kettle which on Monday mornings, with a fire built under it, served as an almost ritualistic center of the laundry activities. Milk and butter were kept in the springhouse, some 50 yards away, and home-canned fruits and vegetables were stored in a musty-smelling cellar beneath the house—accentuated by the odor of a barrel of homemade sauerkraut.

The household as well as the barn were lighted by mellow but dim kerosene lamps and lanterns. Baths were taken infrequently in the recesses of the kitchen in round, galvanized washtubs. At a questionable distance away from the house stood the old-fashioned privy, an institution which has been given much attention in our folk literature. Many anecdotes have appeared about these little outhouses, but it was no joke to use these insect-ridden, oversized wooden boxes in the chill of winter or the steaming heat of summer. Much of this way of life was to change.

Julian Huxley, the English writer, after visiting the Tennessee Valley, swallowed with profound ignorance some well-worn clichés about the region. For his British readers he produced the following: "The Tennessee River is a tributary of the Ohio, which, again is a tributary of the Mississippi. Yet the area of its basin is four-fifths that of England. It is a poverty-stricken region. In the north it is inhabited mainly by backward white mountaineers, the so-called hillbillies, who live in miserable little farms among the wooded mountains. In the south there is an abundance both of Negroes and of race-feeling. Dayton, scene of the notorious Evolution Trial, is in the north; Scottsboro, with its equally notorious trial of four young Negroes, in the south of the area."

The question has been raised many times as to why the Tennessee Valley did not have more rural electrification before the coming of the TVA. Numerous answers have been given, depending usually upon the situations of those who responded. The most general answer has been that regardless of what the reason was, electricity did *not* previously come to the farms.

Ben H. Nichols of Oregon State College made a study which appeared in the conservative magazine *Electrical World* on March 18, 1933. In this rather distinctive article it is pointed out that financing the large original investment per customer was one of the major problems of rural electrification. It was learned that state commissions generally leaned toward the procedure of requiring the utility to pay all the costs of rural electric facility construction, with the customer guaranteeing as a monthly return a certain percentage of that cost.

Out of 35 companies reporting, only 13 paid all the costs, most of them requiring a guarantee of a minimum monthly revenue calculated to return the construction cost within a certain period, the shortest time being three years. Significantly, two companies in the South included an item in the rates separate from the usual charges, levying 25 cents per month per pole beyond existing lines. One Great Lakes utility company required a deposit of $1,000 per mile before construction could be started, refunding $100 per customer after rendering the first bill. A utility required a five-year contract with the consumer in addition to demanding that the consumer pay all the excess costs over $400 per mile.

Public authorities who were questioned about the advisability of requiring customers to pay excess costs unanimously agreed that this practice was detrimental to increased use. The principal reason given was that it left the farmer with no funds with which to purchase equipment. Some officials questioned the justice of customers being required to build a line and then to give it to the utility company.

Both Lilienthal and A. E. Morgan had indicated a need for a large town to become a TVA market. So it was a considerable setback when Birmingham, Alabama, on October 9, 1933, voted down a proposal for municipal ownership and operation of electric utilities. The vote was 10,034 to 7,004 in this city of more than 250,000 with 50,000 electric meters. Ten smaller towns had already decided to go into the power business with TVA. Cheaper electric rates from Muscle Shoals were offered the people of Birmingham, but opponents of the proposal held out the bugaboo of higher taxes, inefficient management, and political control.

Electrical World on October 21, 1933, jubilantly editorialized: "The first error in the Tennessee Valley plan was the endeavor to sustain it upon the basis of electric power. The second was the announcement of retail rates and the endeavor to sell municipalities the idea of going into the power business at these rates. And now the results of the Birmingham election promises to show the fallacy of these conceptions. . . . Birmingham was a fair test sample."

Lilienthal thought that the simple hillside farm with its primitive facilities harked back all too much to the days when the first white settlers came to this territory. People should have in their homes and on their farms the appliances for which electricity was used, he contended.

Those in charge of the TVA were heartened when on November 25, 1933, at a special election, the voters of Knoxville, Tennessee, approved by a two-to-one vote a bond issue for municipal electric lighting and a TVA power distribution system. Knoxville thus became the first large city in the Tennessee Valley to enter the TVA power system. This municipality of over 100,000 population was and is a vital focal point for the Tennessee Valley Authority. The TVA soon constructed a 226-mile transmission line from Muscle Shoals to Norris Dam, and it was not long before Knoxville was receiving the new TVA power.

Rather belatedly it was announced that the Tennessee Public Service

Company, a subsidiary of the Electric Bond and Share Company which had previously served the city, had under consideration drastic rate reductions. However, an engineering firm employed by the City of Knoxville recommended that the TVA system be adopted, reporting that the rates of the Authority were one-half those of the Tennessee Public Service Company.

3. Light in the Valley

Years after I had first seen the TVA blossom, it was elating to view the Tennessee countryside, which I still felt was my valley. A visit to the uncle's farm, which was described in the previous chapter, was revealing. Although it still had that quaint and homey quality and the hospitality held the same welcome flavor, a transformation had come about. Now there was light in the valley—and more.

Something I had written about the TVA 20 years before came to mind: "More than a depression had struck the region in and around the Smoky Mountains. There was a change of life. The old order, held onto so closely and fondly by the settlers for so many years, was at last slipping away."

The uncle still had his rolling hills—he was not one of those who had to move because of flooded land—but the sloping acres now were marked by horizontal terracing for his crops. This had been done by the CCC boys under the guidance of the National Park Service and the TVA. In his barn was a hay dryer which had been built inexpensively on the farm. In a new barn for curing tobacco, electric fans were being used to help in controlling temperature, humidity, and carbon dioxide accumulation. Even in the tomato patch which grew the best ones I ever tasted, there was an electric insect trap which had completely eliminated the once-pesky bollworms.

His one-time unpainted house was now a gleaming white, and the chairs on the front porch were modern and comfortable. The parlor still had its old-fashioned bed, but the mellow, kerosene lamp which had glowed beside it had now been relegated to a back closet. In its place was a handsome electric bedside table lamp with three-way lighting. The living room still had its picturesque fireplace, but it was now more for atmosphere than necessary use. The iron "baker" was gone from the hearth. For heating purposes there now was an electric baseboard which ran around most of the room. One noticed, however, that the fragrant smell of the old-time cooking still breathed faintly from the fireplace.

In the dining room the long table was now covered by a white cloth, and above it was a handsome chandelier, the lights from which reflected in the china and silverware. I was glad to find that those good old country breakfasts were still being served, but somehow the faces of the women did not seem so tired when they came from the kitchen. And no wonder: gone was the big wood-burning stove with all its merits and in its place was a handsome electric range which furnished instant heat for cooking with the turn of dials. Overhead electric

TVA officials with members of the New York Power Commission at Norris Dam in 1934. At extreme **left** *is Chairman Arthur Morgan, typically standing aside from the rest. On his* **left** *is David Lilienthal, a member of the TVA Board of Directors.*

lighting also made it easier to see what was happening on and in the stove. On one side of the kitchen stood a sturdy electric refrigerator, replete with a freezing compartment, ice trays, and shelves for its varied contents—no more trips to the springhouse.

In a small room off the kitchen was a color television set that vied with small electric radios here and there for entertainment and information. Adjoining this was a colorful bathroom containing not only the usual facilities but a combination tub and shower, the water for which was heated by electricity. A small electric heater cut off the chill here in wintertime, a far cry from the lengthy trips to the crude and uncomfortable outdoor privy. On the back porch reposed a large electric freezer into which the family had placed a hoard of foodstuffs which appeared to be enough to last for months. Herein were numerous glass jars filled with green beans, peas, tomatoes, and other such home-grown vegetables. Cuts of beef and pork as well as canned sausage also graced the food supply. The freezing was electrical and automatic.

Food for the Land

Things may have been favorable for many, but for the average farmer in the mountainous areas, conditions were not so good. It would require considerable time even to bring him out of his traditional rut. As has been mentioned, much of the surface soil had been washed from the slopes. In order to eke out a bare living, these hill farmers had planted land which should never have been cultivated. As a result the loose soil had washed away, leaving an unfertile subsoil on the surface. In the low-lying country, farms had been planted in corn, cotton, or tobacco so many years in succession that much of the substance had been worn out of the soil from lack of crop rotation and proper fertilizer.

According to agricultural authorities, four fertilizer elements are needed for proper support of vegetation. These are nitrogen, phosporus, potash, and lime. In the Tennessee Valley, lime is in plentiful quantity and presents no problem. Nitrogen is always needed but was expensive until it was found that it is present in the air everywhere and can be obtained by planting legumes such as clover and alfalfa. Potash which was formerly obtained from abroad was found to be available from livestock manure, particularly when the stock were pastured on legumes.

Phosphorus was found to be the biggest problem, and the TVA went to work on it. This element helped greatly in the growing of the legumes. Since the great nitrate plants at Muscle Shoals were no longer needed, one of them costing originally $75 million and covering 2,300 acres with 14 factory buildings was converted into a station for producing cheap phosphates from which phosphorus-fertilizer is made. The TVA cooperated with agricultural stations in each of the seven states within the valley area.

Harcourt A. Morgan headed the TVA fertilizer program. He was a comparatively quiet man, and not much material can be found on him in researching the TVA.

"There can never be a substitute for phosphorus in the human body," Morgan believed: "Plants that are starved for phosphorus cannot grow a strong root system; they fail to hold the soil. The soil washing away carries with it the prosperity of the farmer and of the farming region in which he lives. Cattle that are fed on plants deficient in phosphate grow listless and torpid; they are easy victims of disease; their milk and meat lack nourishing qualities. Here and there in the world are human populations that already show signs of phosphorus deficiency."

An experiment with a pasture on a worn-out cotton farm showed that with 300 pounds of TVA superphosphate and 1,000 pounds of lime, the yield increased 65 percent. The final verdict on this experiment was given by the cattle which grazed on the new pasture and refused "to waste time on the other." Such experiments were widely noticed, and neighboring farmers kept a close watch on the results. They saw the improvements which took place, and many of them took up similar methods on their own farms. As will be noted, the TVA was only partly instrumental in such activities; it cooperated with county agents, state universities, and other federal departments.

In conversations with various employees of the TVA, this writer frequently heard mentioned the name of C. Neil Bass, who was with the Authority for a number of years. His statement in an interview with Dr. Charles W. Crawford, director of the Oral History Research Office of Memphis State University, helps to explain his position:

> While serving as city manager, the depression hit our city of Knoxville, and we really had a difficult time. All of the banks in the city failed. Earnings were low by the people in the city. They were unable to pay taxes. One of the little devices that we used was to print city warrants, which turned out to be very successful. The warrants, in turn, were used to pay city taxes. So we were very receptive to the approach that the President of the United States, Mr. Roosevelt, made at the time that he proposed the Tennessee Valley Authority."

H. A. Morgan, according to Bass, vetoed any idea that TVA would set up an agricultural program of its own to be carried out by TVA as a federal agency operating in the area:

> He chose, rather, to call together the agricultural colleges of the seven Valley states—their deans of Agriculture, the heads of their experiment stations, and the heads of their extension services—and pose to them the problem and opportunity that was afforded by having these wonderful facilities at Muscle Shoals with which we could carry out a research program to improve and develop fertilizers that could be used in an agricultural readjustment program in the

watershed. As the college scientists pointed out quickly, with the proper applications of phosphate, along with lime which was abundantly available in the region, you could grow pastures and legumes through this natural process and provide the nitrogen needed for the soil through the growth of legumes.

So the major conclusion was reached in this collaboration between the TVA and the land-grant colleges that the research at Muscle Shoals would be pointed, not to the development of nitrogen as a fertilizer, but to the development of phosphorus—phosphate. Bass said:

> One of the earlier problems of the TVA was that the fertilizer industry was very critical of TVA's role in carrying out this fertilizer development. There was quite a public controversy engaged in about the TVA's role. It was interesting to recall the first meeting that we arranged at Muscle Shoals with the leading manufacturers in the fertilizer industry. We sat around the table to describe what we had done, and then showed them through the laboratories how the work was carried out and what had been accomplished and the test results of fertilizer used by these farmers. The TVA demonstrations set a pattern of use and thus created a market which has been very profitable to the private fertilizer industry, as it should be. But the earlier meetings were somewhat of a controversial nature, and the fertilizer industry was skeptical of what TVA intended to do. That is, they would pose the question, "Well, are you proposing to monopolize the nitrogen industry and the phosphate industry?" We made it clear that our role was research and the bringing about of the testing of these products and to have the more efficient fertilizer products generally adopted for use in the industry and by farmers in general. Now, one of the channels that TVA used in marketing its product which it had to produce on a large enough scale to get accepted use, was farmer cooperatives all over the country. The TVA set up a marketing arrangement with the farmer cooperatives and through some 9,000 outlets made the fertilizer available to farmers. Once they had begun to buy it and use it, the market was created in a wide-spread fashion.

A native of Canada, H. A. Morgan, was sold on the TVA region. Said he:

> No other comparable area in the United States offers the diversity of climate, of soil, of vegetation and of resources which we find in the Tennessee Valley. It is the perfect laboratory for an attempt which is of vital concern to the future of every one of us . . . millions upon millions of tons of that all-important topsoil disappear every year. Most of it is washed away by the rains, but wind can be just as destructive. . . . All of our food and more than one-third of the raw products used in industry come off the farms. Our land is our

capital—and we are wasting it! . . . for once we dissipate the growing power of our soil every other advance in our civilization becomes futile . . . with patience, knowledge can be brought to the corners where it has not yet penetrated . . . less than 12 percent of our farms have ever experienced the benefits of electric power . . . we must have electric power to make our phosphates and to promote the economic rehabilitation of the farm, and electric power means dams, and dams mean reservoirs, and reservoirs to remain effective, must be protected from the deposit of silt due to soil erosion. We checked soil erosion through phosphate and our circle is complete.

The CCC boys eventually made themselves quite welcome to local farmers, but as has been observed, at first some of them appeared to be intruding strangers called "Furriners." In the July 1934 issue of *American Forests,* tribute was paid to them: "The CCC boys have pitched in wholeheartedly, have learned how to handle a pick and shovel; they can now swing an ax and pull a cross-cut saw, and at check dam building they have shown wonderful results in helping to make the water "walk off." The "Furriners" may not have been quite as adept at handling tools as the local farm boys, but all work on an equal basis when it comes to building check dams. The record for one week's work for a camp runs well above 200 rock dams or at the rate of better than one dam a week for each man, and these dams average four feet to the wire notch with widths up to eight and ten feet."

About his work, the *Knoxville News-Sentinel* commented: "Under Dr. Morgan's leadership, TVA has made the nation's farmers fertilizer-conscious. It has taught them how to buy and use intelligently and productively the necessary plant foods. It has broken down the wall of secrecy and mystery built over a long period of years by the commercial fertilizer monopoly. As a result, more and much better plant foods are now available on the commercial market, and the fertilizer industry itself is doing more business than ever before in history."

The Maps and Survey Division, organized on July 4, 1933, was the earliest TVA staff organization. At first it was assigned a curious assortment of jobs, from procuring office furniture to moving graves. There seemed to be something individual about the division, a kind of brighter morale, an esprit among the personnel, which has lasted. Ten years later, Ned H. Sayford, its head, recalled: "In the first group no need became so imperative—aside from the need to staff with quality folks—as the need to develop techniques of accuracy. Accuracy of deed, of thought, of utterances. Be it holding a rod, typing a report, drawing a map, solving an intricate complicated situation, contributing to a discussion, preparing an official statement, or making a speech, no amount of other kinds of competence nor heights of brilliance could then or ever substitute successfully for getting the dope and checking it. In offices, in computing and drafting rooms, in laboratories, on inspections, in conferences, out in the field, the watch word of the division became 'Check it.' "

Another function of the division was land acquisition. By tact and persistence, it achieved a smooth record, with few exceptions, in obtaining thousands of acres. One exception was that of a black woman who owned a small tract of land in the area required. After numerous calls on the woman and lengthy explanations to her, the TVA land buyer reported to his superior that he felt he should admit his defeat. The chief buyer accordingly went out himself to see the owner. After briefly explaining that the government would need her property, he stated that the price fixed had been carefully appraised at a fair market price, and that this had all been carefully explained by the land buyer. Then he asked her a direct question. "Now Lucy, won't you agree to sell us the property?"

Lucy looked up at him with a grin and said, "Lawd, Mistah! Sure I'll sell the land. I wants to sell. This other gentleman, he come out here every day and talked and talked; but he nevah ask me if I'd *sell* the land."

Reforestation

In 1935 Bernard Frank of the TVA's Division of Forestry found that in many wooded sections of the Tennessee Valley practically the only cash income received by farmers came from the cutting and sale of farm forest products. Such income often spelled the difference between bare existence and adequate satisfaction of basic needs.

Louis Bromfield, the well-known liberal farmer-writer, did not pull any punches in his expressed opinion of the TVA: "In my travels over the world I have seen many people who are interested in flood control or in nutrition or in forestry; in navigation, in agriculture, and so on. But nowhere, until I visited the Tennessee Valley, had I found all the specialists working together, unifying their efforts and their objectives and making remarkable progress for the overall, long-time good of the land and the people."

Bromfield came across a county school supervisor who described the problem of teaching farming in the elementary grades.

Kenneth Wann, the supervisor said: "For years, the schools of our county taught reading, 'riting and 'rithmetic to boys and girls because these were the things we supposed would fit them for life in the future. Today we realize that the best preparation for life is living and dealing with real problems now as youth grows and matures, because most of the boys and girls who mastered the textbook type of learning returned to live in the same unscreened, unpainted, bare farm houses. They raised the same crops, cotton and corn by the same methods their grandfathers used. They allowed their land to be gullied by water erosion and their children were as poorly nourished as they had been.''

But good teachers of their children or not, many of the people in the valley had to move when the TVA lakes came. Bromfield sensitively recorded the words of one old farmer who had to move but did not know where to go. Said he solemnly, "My wife can't move fast or far but I'll take her by the hand and start down the road."

Reforestation was closely related to the TVA role regarding farming in the valley. Forests help to hold the soil and to store water. Dead leaves of the forest floor protect the ground which is usually filled with worm holes and other small crevices. Where the soil is deep enough to serve as an underground reservoir, a well-protected forest serves as a sifter for conveying the water gently under the ground, where it will not wash away the surface but will feed the springs and valley streams in dry weather. A TVA report capriciously states: "The underground reservoir is the biggest one in the Valley."

On the land that was badly gullied or too poor for pasture grasses and cover crops, forest cover was found to be the best answer. Some 2 million acres in the valley did contain gullies, and about half this number were approaching the same stage. County agents aided the Authority in supplying trees. The idea was to develop trees that would show quick return. One such was the "shipmast" locust which grows fast and straight and resists borers. This tree is one of the best and cheapest means for stopping gullies. Others were found to be native persimmons, walnuts, hickories, and oaks.

In an average year of such activity, the TVA nurseries produced nearly 20 million young trees at an average cost of one-quarter of a cent apiece. Mostly locust and pine, this work was done in cooperation with the U.S. Department of Agriculture. Ten thousand bushels of pine cones and other seeds were harvested by the members of the Civilian Conservation Corps at the direction of its able chief, Robert Fechner. The seeds were gathered largely in Virginia, West Virginia, North Carolina, and Arkansas. Four national forests in these states furnished the seeds, which included 600 bushels of yellow poplar seed pods—and 4,000 bushels of black locust pods. It was estimated that this amount of seedlings would produce 2 million yellow poplar, 10 million short-leaf,

8 million Virginia pine, and 6 million black locust trees. As soon as the ripe cones were picked they were shipped to southern nurseries of the U.S. Forest Service for drying and seed extraction. The prepared seeds were then forwarded to the TVA. Though easier to pick cones from trees felled in lumbering operations, most of this batch had to be picked from standing timber. Where it was necessary for the CCC boys to climb high trees, safety belts were supplied.

The TVA participated in what was then a new quick freezing of small fruits. Strawberries were frozen by dipping in a heavy cold syrup. This freezing required only six minutes, whereas formerly several hours by other methods were necessary. Cleveland, Tennessee, was the scene of most such early fruit freezing. This improved freezing process helped to relieve the excessive supply of fruits in season and spread them over the year at various receiving points. Strawberries had been grown for many years along the river in Meigs County, Tennessee. Such crops were of particular interest to the TVA because it was found that the high profits and intensive work per acre in strawberry culture enabled the farmer to concentrate his cultivation on a small part of his land, thus using the rest for pasture and soil-conserving crops.

Farmers' cooperatives were already in existence in the valley when the TVA came in. These societies were used for buying needed materials and for collecting, grading, and marketing their produce. Now with rural electrification spreading, a new kind of cooperative resulted. There were small cooperative canneries in western North Carolina, some to handle the abundant wild berries of the region, others operating seed mills and creameries. Cooperatives for small handicraft products of the mountain country also were stimulated by the growth of others.

Legal Battles

The beginning of the legal department of the Authority shaped up as both deliberate and accidental, said Charles McCarthy, a former member, in an interview with Dr. Charles Crawford of Memphis State University. Young lawyers at that time, McCarthy recalled, could hardly get a job. The top law students received salaries in New York City of about $2,400 a year. Those who went to Chicago got less. When McCarthy joined the TVA legal staff in 1934, he was paid a beginning salary of $5,200 annually:

> I would say that there were basically three factors attracting people to the TVA: the Depression, the high salaries, and the challenge which was presented by something new and exciting. You would

have to live in the TVA and in that era to realize the grip that this got on people. Some of them were screwballs. Some of them were pretty solid, hard-headed individuals, but they all felt that they were engaged in starting something that was important and was going to do a lot of good for a lot of people.

McCarthy pointed out that the TVA handles practically all of its own legal work, unlike most government agencies for which the Department of Justice does this:

We had some questions involving freight rates before the Interstate Commerce Commission. And that seemed like sort of a vague field that we didn't know anything about. We talked about getting a Washington attorney, and then we decided that it just can't be that mysterious. After all, one lawsuit is pretty much like another. So we decided to handle them ourselves. From that we just expanded in commerce work, and I would say that after a few years TVA had as competent staff of commerce attorneys as any law firm in Washington. I'm not sure we weren't the best in the country. . . .

I can give you another example or two. We went into the bond financing field. Ordinarily you hire a bond counsel. Everybody does. Well, we hired bond counsel, and they prepared some drafts for us. We decided that really they didn't know our business as well as we did, and we ended up drafting all of the bond documents ourselves. We got into the nuclear energy field. We had a question of getting licenses from the Atomic Energy Commission. We didn't go to one of the firms that specializes in that. We learned how to do it, and we did it.

McCarthy made a statement appropriate for the present-day situation involving the financial nature of the TVA. About this experience, he explained:

When we operated under an appropriations process we had to go to Congress to get the money to build a steam plant. There was a big political fight every time about whether TVA ought to be building steam plants; whether they ought to be building it in this location, whether it needed the power. The Edison Electric Institute was in there fighting tooth and nail to keep us from getting the appropriations. We got them sometimes, I guess, by one, two, or three vote margins. The attractiveness of bond financing to TVA was that it would eliminate that. After all, whether you are going to build a steam plant is an economic question. It isn't a political question. Where you put it is an economic question. You put it where it can produce power at the cheapest price where the power is needed.

Interestingly, William C. Fitts, who succeeded Lawrence Fly as general counsel of the TVA in 1939, also considered that the organization had two problematical aspects. One was the beginning of litigation challenging the constitutionality of the TVA Act. Second, Fitts believed, was the necessity for obtaining state legislation in Mississippi, Alabama, Tennessee, Georgia, North Carolina, and Kentucky to permit the municipalities and rural cooperatives to build their own electric power distribution systems and to purchase the power from the transmission lines of the TVA. Fitts related:

> Without that state legislation, the basic power program, which was built upon the distribution systems of the municipalities and rural cooperatives, would never have been able to have gotten off the ground, because enabling legislation was needed in each of these states. So there was a two-fold job here. Part of it was the preparation and drafting of the legislation. But another part of it was the actual job of convincing the political powers in the states—the legislative bodies and the executive—of the necessity of desirability of such legislation. A good deal of this work was done during these early years. The third problem involved federal legislation, because throughout the early period of TVA there was a constant struggle to prevent legislation from being passed that would limit, cripple, and in many cases, make absolutely impossible further development. There was a constant flow of proposed legislation in the Congress that was hostile. There were a great many occasions where appearances had to be made before the legislative committee in Congress, making the arguments and advancing all of the reasons why such legislation should not be adopted. In addition, there were several periods where affirmative legislation was needed. The Act required amendments that would enable us to do better what we were trying to do, and here, also, was a big part of the work that we found in these early years.

As has been shown, the TVA has had to deal with not only conflicting interests outside of but also inside of the government. Fitts remembered a problem with the General Accounting Office (GAO). From the beginning the Authority took the position that it was not subject to all the rules and regulations of the GAO. The settlement of a lawsuit was given as an example of the conflict. The TVA held that since it was a corporation, it was subject to suit and could be sued for anything such as automobile accidents or transmission line electrocution, just like a private corporation. The Authority believed it had the right to settle its own law suits, while the GAO took the position that they had to be settled through it. As a result, many hearings were held on this question because the GAO was trying to get legislation passed which would make the TVA accountable to it. "We got it settled our way," said Fitts.

The constitutionality of the Tennessee Valley Authority Act and the validity of the generation and sale of electric power by the Authority thereunder were challenged in a series of cases beginning in the summer of 1934 and ending with the decision of the Supreme Court of the United States in the case of *Tennessee Electric Power Company et al. vs. Tennessee Valley Authority et al.* on January 30, 1939. Two of these cases finally reached the Supreme Court, and the decisions of that court, when considered together, establish the constitutionality of the provisions of the TVA Act which authorizes the generation of electricity at TVA's multipurpose dams and the transmission and distribution of such electricity.

George Ashwander et al. vs. Tennessee Valley Authority et al. was a suit in equity instituted by a group of preferred stockholders of the Alabama Power Company for the purpose of enjoining the company and TVA from consummating a contract for the sale by the company to TVA of certain transmission lines owned by the company in the northern Alabama area and serving the territory within transmission distance of Wilson Dam. The contract was attacked by the stockholders upon the ground that, insofar as the Tennessee Valley Authority Act purported to authorize TVA to own and operate transmission lines, it was unconstitutional and that, therefore, the contract in question had not been authorized by any valid statute and should be enjoined. The issue presented thus turned on the basic question of the constitutional power of the federal government to authorize its agent to market electric power produced by Wilson Dam by means of transmission lines serving the market in the surrounding area. The Supreme Court, in a decision reported in 297 U.S. 288 (1936), held that the Government did have such constitutional authority, based upon the following reasoning: the federal government was acting within its constitutional powers in constructing Wilson Dam for the purpose of improving navigation on the Tennessee River and promoting the national defense. In constructing the dam, the government was within its rights in providing for the generation of electric energy from the water power created by construction. The electric energy so generated became the property of the United States, and the government had power to dispose of that property in the manner that it believed to be in the public interest. The construction or purchase of transmission lines necessary to the marketing of such energy was merely a means of disposing of the government's property and was accordingly within its constitutional power.

While the decision of the Supreme Court, strictly construed, related only to Wilson Dam and the marketing of power there generated, the rationale of the decision applies equally to every dam which bears a substantial relation to the improvement of navigation, the control of floods, or the national defense and, therefore, applies to all of TVA's multipurpose projects.

The utility companies operating in the area did not accept this decision as conclusive of the controversy and determined to seek a review of the validity of the entire program. Accordingly, 18 of the companies operating in the Tennessee Valley and surrounding territory joined as plaintiffs in the suit of *Tennessee Electric Power Company et al. vs. Tennessee Valley Authority et al.* In this case the bill of complaint challenged the constitutionality of all of the dams constructed or under construction by TVA, except Wilson Dam, upon the ground that they were in reality being constructed for the express purpose of generating power and that their relationship to navigation or any other federal power was too remote to sustain their constitutionality. It was also asserted that even if the dams were being legally constructed, the program for the marketing of the power exceeded the bounds of federal power. The case was heard by a statutory three-judge court, which (following the theory of the *Ashwander* decision) sustained the constitutionality of the Act, the legality of the dams, and the power marketing program. This was appealed to the Supreme Court of the United States. The high court found it unnecessary to decide the constitutional questions involved because it held that the utility companies had no legal right to claim freedom from competition, which was the sole basis relied upon to sustain the suit, 306 U.S. 118 (1939).

If there were any remaining doubts as to the constitutionality of the TVA's program for the generation of electric power at multipurpose dams and the marketing of the power so generated, those doubts were finally put to rest by the Supreme Court's decision in *Oklahoma vs. Atchinson* Co., 313 U.S. 508 (1940), in which the court passed on the issues it had not decided in the *Tennessee Electric Power Company* case. The court held that the federal government, under Article 1, Section 8, of the Constitution could construct dual-purpose projects for flood control and power development and that this power could be sold to help defray the cost of flood control.

People had to move of course as the reservoirs came on. An instance was that of the little town of Newburg, Kentucky. Its mayor, chief of police, alderman, and former postmaster, J. Bodine Henslee, put it this way in August 1938: "Folks in Newburg are not feeling so spry right now. We've all got to move out, lock, stock and barrel, to make room for the great lake TVA will create on land that's been in some of the families' names for a hundred years. Yes, sir; we are going to move, and with us will go Newburg. There was a time when Newburg was a big shipping point on the Tennessee. It doesn't seem very long ago when some of the biggest and finest steamboats on the Tennessee never passed our little town without landing. We lived happily then. All of us boasted of homes in that stretch of valley where the soil is as rich as along the Nile.''

Another disappearing community was that of the village of Harrison, Tennessee, which was covered by the waters of Chickamauga Dam. "From Indian trading posts, to county seat of Hamilton County, to village hamlet, to habitat of fishes''—that is the way John Chadwick described it in the *Chattanooga News* of June 20, 1936. An historic house to go was called the Joe Vann House, after the Cherokee Indian chief who once lived there.

One modern resident of the village did not seem so sorry about its forthcoming demise. He was elderly and talkative J. T. Cooper, who said from under his broad-brimmed black felt hat, "When the flood comes, it will be the best thing for Harrison. It will float all the trash out!''

In March 1956 the *Knoxville Journal* asked what happened to the affected people when the TVA built Norris Dam. An estimated 17,765 persons were obliged to leave 146,347 acres of land in five East Tennessee counties, an area one-fifth as large as Rhode Island. Many of course were unhappy about this exodus. According to the *Journal*, "One such family was that of D.C. (Dap) McCarty, moved from the Mossy Spring community in Union County. His brother-in-law hanged himself rather than be moved and he said there were "several other suicides." A neighbor, Mattie Randolph, remained to the bitter end and finally was moved out in a boat. . . . Mrs. McCarty put down a firm foot. She had no intention of moving below where the dam was built, she said, as 'the thing might give away at any time.' ''

A survey of the reaction of the displaced Norris basin families showed that roughly half of them were pleased with their move to new homes, one-fourth said it made no particular difference, one-fifth were dissatisfied, and the rest had indefinite opinions.

When the TVA reservoirs were being finished, some people believed that they would soon become what was called "biological deserts.'' This meant that the aquatic life in them would die. This had happened in other parts of the country where reservoirs were built and neglected because the people and agencies responsible for their operations did not understand the problems of maintaining aquatic life. The TVA conducted a study of the reservoir conditions and gave the information to the state agencies that had charge of wildlife resources.

At first it was strongly recommended by the U.S. Fish and Wildlife Service that the TVA establish fish hatcheries to replenish such resources. It was soon discovered that hatcheries were unnecessary; with proper water control and correct fluctuation of water levels and silt, the reservoirs reproduce fish far more effectively than can be done by restocking.

It was found that the average life of most game fish was about four years and that most of them died a natural death. At the time fishermen were catching just about 20 percent of the available fish. When these facts became known, the valley states liberalized their fishing laws. Commercial fishing occurred on many of the lakes. Catfish, suckers, and carp competed with the game fish for food and in many instances won out. Commercial fishing helped to thin out the nongame fish and to keep the two kinds in balance.

Flood Control

The Act creating the Tennessee Valley Authority had as one of its principal purposes the control of floods in the valley. More dramatic at times than the need for electricity or navigation was that of flood control. This is a region of heavy rainfall, and in the wettest seasons the water often cascades down the mountains, hills, and valleys. It not only carries the topsoil into the rivers but, if not properly controlled, also floods the farms, highways, and streets. The TVA lost no time in coming to grips with the problem. At the center of the plans was the development of flood storage space in tributary reservoirs and behind high dams along the winding Tennessee River.

The reservoir created by Norris Dam on the Clinch River provided a flood storage capacity of over 2 million acre-feet. (An acre-foot is the amount of water required to cover one acre one foot deep.) The dam was hardly finished when the heavy rains came. Then on March 30, 1936, the Tennessee reached a 37.1 foot stage at Chattanooga. The TVA estimated that enough water was withheld in the dam reservoir to prevent the water reaching a stage of 41 feet, resulting in the flooding of 1,000 acres of city property. Almost an estimated million dollars was saved. I well remember the flooded streets of Chattanooga during and after previous heavy rains. The long length of Rossville Boulevard, for example, resembled a lake, and small boats were actually used on it.

George Hull recalled Chattanooga being so flooded that steamboats came up Market Street, its main thoroughfare. The river was ten miles wide in places and washed bumper crops away. Chicken coops and corn stalks among other items floated upon its wide surface. In contrast, a flood in 1957 caused very little damage there.

Chattanooga seems to have been on the receiving end of much of the flood water. A number of times in 1937 Norris Dam was able to reduce the flood heights there several feet. So it has been since that time, but the area still lacks full protection at this writing. The river itself has been pretty much under control, but tributary streams are not. Like the creek in the town of Sweetwater, which periodically has overflowed its verdant banks and covered the main street with a lake, the Chickamauga Creek at Chattanooga performs in a like manner and causes considerable damage. The TVA is aware of such situations and has recommended additional steps to cope with them. But until local governments take a greater part in financing and controlling these smaller streams, some risk will remain. TVA is finishing a new levee system to lessen the flood damage risk in the Brainard section of Chattanooga.

An interesting sidelight of dam-building along the Tennessee River was its relation to aquatic life, wildlife, and game. The Authority conducted studies and experiments, and in 1938 a large fish hatchery was built on the Elk River in Limestone County, Alabama. It was to serve river reservoirs and covered 111 acres of water. When finished it was taken over by the United States Bureau of Fisheries. Hatching and rearing fish ponds also were completed at Norris Lake and in the Chickamauga area. As examples of resupply, 400,000 bass were dropped in Norris Reservoir and 25,000 rainbow trout were released in one year into the cold water below the dam which comes directly from the bottom of the lake. In order to provide for protection for migratory waterfowl which use the impounded TVA water as resting grounds, a 40,000-acre migratory waterfowl refuge was built on Wheeler Lake to be managed by the U.S. Biological Survey. Similar work was done on the smaller Cove Lake refuge adjoining Norris Reservoir. At the time, these were said to be the only sheltered areas for duck and geese in the interior South. Thousands of game food trees were planted on the Wheeler and Cove Lake refuges.

Flood control may appear as merely physical impediments to the excessive flow of water but actually, as the TVA demonstrated, it goes back to the source of the streams. Tree planting is important as a measure of water control on the land, especially in halting gullying and other such erosion preventives. The landowners in cooperation with county agents used their teams and supplied brush, logs, and other materials to help in this watershed protection. In addition to such work on private land, much reforestation was carried out on TVA property surrounding the reservoirs. In the first few years more than 20 million trees had been planted on TVA land, with 80 million more needed for their proper protection.

Malaria Control

The control of malaria received special attention in the areas of the Wilson and Wheeler reservoirs. Here the artificial lakes made ideal breeding places for the Anopheline mosquito. An example of the need to control this pest was found in the early 1930s in Decatur, Alabama. Typical of such cities in the Depression, Decatur had one small textile mill, representing the only sizable payroll there. It was noted that absenteeism was high in this mill compared to other mills owned by the same company. The management tried to find out why so many employees were absent because of illness. They were asked to submit to a malaria test. The result revealed that nearly one-third of the workers had malaria. George F. Hull recalled:

> Those good men and women, try as they may, could not possibly produce the amount of fabric needed to keep the mill on a paying basis. In self-defense, the management modified its employment requirements to include a malaria smear. Now, this condition was not limited to this one mill. Other industrial plants that were operating, or had operated within the Tennessee Valley, had the same experience with low production. These conditions had helped the people of the region to achieve the title "Lazy Southerners." The states, counties, and cities were not unaware of the fact that malaria incidence was about 16 percent and often ran as high as 30 percent. They knew also that industry was difficult to attract into a labor market with a reputation for low productivity. Now, what could the people of the valley do about malaria? They nursed the sick and fed them quinine. But where was the answer? In destroying the source—the malaria-carrying mosquito. TVA, having an interest in helping to create a balance between industry and agriculture, took an interest in this mosquito. So they built traps, caught him, colored him with dye, released him and caught him again. They learned his life span, his breeding habits, how far the wind would take him, and everything else about him. Then they set out to destroy him. He was sprayed with insecticide, his breeding places were destroyed, the larvae are left to die in the sun when lake levels are fluctuated. The result? The only cases of malaria found in the Valley in ten years have been a very few and all of them of Korean origin. Not one single case of locally transmitted malaria. How much this has had to do with the industrial growth of the Tennessee Valley is a matter of speculation. The fact that industry now considers this area as a good

labor market indicates that the valley's people no longer wear the label "Lazy Southerners."

The TVA has emphasized permanent rather than temporary malaria-control measures. The principal ones are arrangements for periodic fluctuations of the water level and proper cleaning and preparation of the basin prior to impoundage. Adequate drainage was another important measure for the control of malaria, particularly in Alabama where there are many sloughs, limesinks, and other places suitable for mosquito breeding. As a consequence of such measures, malaria has been virtually eliminated in the Tennessee Valley.

The acres of water had increased, and flowing streams had been changed into a system of slack-water lakes. This situation necessitated continuation and expansion of the TVA malaria-control program. After ten years of its operation, the program seemed to have brought results, for out of 11,816 blood samples, only 79 indicated a presence of malaria germs. During World War II the U.S. Army Medical Corps and Sanitary Corps sent 67 officers from lieutenants to lieutenant colonels to the Tennessee Valley for training in methods of malaria control. Data on this work were sent by the surgeon general of the U.S. Army to India, Trinidad, and Puerto Rico. The TVA generally has been imitated, especially in India and South America.

At the large Kentucky Dam Reservoir, malaria control was undertaken on an even bigger scale. Constructed were dikes, drainage ditches, pumping stations, channels, and docks for malaria control boats; some marginal lake areas were deepened or filled in to reduce the extent of mosquito breeding. Experiments were conducted in grazing cattle along the lake shores, and this was found effective in killing the mosquito larvae.

Navigation

In order to consider the navigation phase of the TVA, it is well to keep in mind that the Tennessee River originates on the western slope of the Appalachian Mountains and then flows west, making a long arc southward and then northwestward into the Ohio River at Paducah, Kentucky, which is not far from its confluence with the Mississippi River. The Tennessee is about 650 miles long, and between Knoxville and Paducah drops about 500 feet. Customarily, in the United States, navigable inland waters have been looked upon as a concern of the federal government. Flood control has been divided among local, state, and federal jurisdictions; the development of electric energy has been regarded as a domain of corporate enterprise; and erosion has been considered as the problem of the individual farmer.

When the TVA was created, it was realized that the average rainfall of the headwaters of the Tennessee River was more than 50 inches. Congress directed the TVA "to control the Tennessee River to provide for navigation, flood control and the production of power incidental to such development." In the June 10, 1939, issue of the *Economist,* the New York correspondent of the publication, after discussing the navigation possibilities and merits of the TVA, summed up the objections raised against it: "It is costly; it does benefit a fraction of the country at the expense of the Federal Treasury; it does introduce Government competition with private enterprise in the utilities and potentially with the hard-pressed railroads; it is questionable if a single program can serve with optimum effect three such diverse objectives as navigation, flood control and "incidental" power production: and serving these three objectives, it is a more than dubious "yardstick" of fair costs for privately generated and distributed power. But, on the other side, it is a boldly-conceived, schematic plan of regional development, centered on the conversion of a more or less destructive river into a positive natural resource. As an experiment it is large enough to test its merits and its defects; yet the area and its population are small enough, compared to the whole nation, to be in the nature of a social and geophysical laboratory. That it is raising, and promises to raise further, the standard of living of the area is almost certain; whether this praiseworthy objective might have been realized by other means of lower direct and indirect costs of our political economy is debatable."

It should be pointed out that the Tennessee River is an ice-free, all-weather channel which links the Tennessee Valley region with the 8,000-mile inland waterway system of the United States. In the beginning of the TVA, most of the cargo hauled on the river consisted of sand and gravel. Within 20 years this tonnage included oil, gasoline, automobiles, coal, fertilizer, corn, and wheat, and the river has been connected with such inland water ports as Pittsburgh, Minneapolis, St. Paul, Chicago, St. Louis, and Gulf Coast ports. The first shipment of automobiles ever carried on the Tennessee River passed through the Muscle Shoals area in December of 1941 enroute to Guntersville, Alabama. There were 130 cars in the shipment, which came from the Detroit area to Evansville, Indiana, on the Ohio River, where they were loaded on to a barge especially made for such transportation. At Guntersville, the most southern point on the Tennessee River just as it bends to turn northward, the cars were unloaded by means of derricks for distribution to points in Alabama and Georgia.

There were problems in connection with the opening of the river to commercial navigation. Engineers were concerned about the possible loss of reservoir water through the accumulation of sediment. Opponents of the TVA predicted that the Norris Reservoir would be "silted up within 50 years." As a matter of fact, the deposit of sediment has been at the rate of about half the amount these pessimists predicted. Late in 1934 the TVA undertook to measure the amount of sediment carried in suspension by major streams in the valley. Soundings and probings also were made in the reservoirs. The resulting estimate was that the reservoir would lose less than 4 percent of the acre-feet of its storage in the subsequent 100 years.

A TVA publication harked back into history to contrast the early and later navigation of the river: "For 250 years the fractious Tennessee River resisted the efforts of man to tame her and put her to work. Today she has settled into harness for a long, steady pull. The Cherokee Indians understood in their primitive way the importance of Tennessee River transportation when they felled great pines and poplars, burned out their centers, and created the pirogues which would carry twenty men. Fur traders knew the dollar-and-cents value of a loaded canoe, which would carry bundles of pelts that no man could shoulder over land. Pioneers built covered flat boats and moved their families, livestock, and household goods along the Tennessee to new westward frontiers. Civil War armadas used the river to bring fighting men to battle. Steamboats in their "golden era" struggled against alternate floods and low water. Swift currents and rocky shoals stubbornly opposed their efforts to bring commerce to a vast region between the mountains and the Mississippi. Always the success was only partial—the Tennessee ran recklessly on its way almost unused."

It may accurately be said that the advantage of water transportation which was realized by the Indians and the fur traders has not changed with the years, even though the river has. When the TVA was established in 1933, as has been seen, the Wilson Dam and the locks at Muscle Shoals were already in place. They had been built by the Army Engineers during and after World War I—which shows that something good can come out of a war. Before this time Hales Bar, a private power dam with a navigation lock, had been built just below Chattanooga. The Wheeler Dam was started by the TVA in 1933, was completed in 1936, and was followed successively by six other big dams which created a "water stairway" between Paducah and Knoxville. In this process cargoes are raised and lowered 515 feet. The last of these dams was near the mouth of the Tennessee River with a reservoir extending to the south 184 miles. The new waterway has an

11-foot depth for vessels of 9-foot draft. Channel markings allowed tow boats to move along the river night and day.

There was a difference however, in this water route and others which adjoined. Two-thirds of its length was through an agricultural region. Unlike the Ohio River, the Mississippi, and the lower Missouri, it had no great manufacturing and commercial centers to generate river traffic along its banks. Only Chattanooga and Knoxville came anywhere near industrial bigness, and these two cities were concerned more with local than national needs.

It was a heartening result when producers, consumers, and shippers could rely upon an all-year minimum 9-foot channel for the entire distance from Knoxville to Paducah, a distance of about 648 miles. It meant that large vessels could carry more cheaply the products of the farms, mines, and factories between the Southeast and major inland ports.

First to participate on a large scale in the new waterway were the oil companies. Along the banks they built terminals, and soon a familiar sight was that of their tow boats pushing oil barges from Texas ports up the Mississippi River to customers in the Tennessee Valley. Grain companies began to build mills along the river and brought in large quantities of corn, soybeans, and alfalfa. Coal, chemicals, metals, and lumber also were being shipped commercially up and down the stream. This activity not only increased private investment in plants beside the river but also stimulated the growth of rail and truck transportation. An engineer's profile of the Tennessee River depicts vividly the drop in the water elevation. This illustration begins with the Fort Loudoun Dam in East Tennessee followed by those at Knoxville, Watts Bar, Chickamauga, Nickajack (formerly Hales Bar), Guntersville, Wheeler, Wilson, Pickwick, and the Kentucky Dam near Paducah. All these dams have navigation locks.

In an article in the *Southern Economic Journal* for April 1938, Lilienthal advocated expansion of navigation opportunities. He contended that wherever good navigable channels have been provided, commerce has increased on the waterways of the country. He gave as an example the traffic on the Illinois waterway which also had been improved with federal funds and had increased ten times within ten years.

It was not a new factor, but the high cost of transportation in producing and marketing commodities in the United States was realized and called attention to. According to the federal coordinator of transportation, goods in this country are hauled farther on the average, between their points of production and their points of ultimate use, than in any other country in the world except Canada. Since transportation costs represent a large percent of the total cost of the things consumers buy, it is obvious that a substantial reduction in transportation costs will reduce costs generally and lead to lower prices. The navigation system on the Tennessee River has undoubtedly been a good example of such and also has led to greater production. Unfortunately this trend was not to continue and, at this writing, transportation costs have soared again to contribute to inflation.

The TVA has regarded water transportation as not only the cheapest form of transporting heavy goods over substantial distances but "remarkably cheaper." It was felt that the river really would become "a trunk highway and will be fed not merely from the river's bank but by the other transportation arteries which lead to the river—highways and railroads." It is true that in the 1930s particularly the South had the disadvantage of higher freight rates than some other parts of the country. Economy in shipping aids the prosperity of that region and, as TVA officials believe, has a stimulating effect upon the general economic life of the South. How low the average income of many inhabitants of the valley had become is exemplified in the fact that many of the small farmers received an average cash income of around $100 a year.

Business interests apparently realized the advantage of cheaper transportation by Southern waters. Harvey S. Firestone, chairman of the board of the Firestone Tire and Rubber Company, stated at this time in connection with the location of a plant of his company in Memphis: "We can make quite a saving in transportation costs by shipping rubber right to our plant in Memphis by an all-water route to New Orleans and up the Mississippi, both from our plantations in Liberia and from the Far East."

Henry G. Johnson, president of the National Piano Manufacturing Company, made a similar statement about shipping opportunities on the Southern waterways: "It will allow us to ship pianos to the leading cities along the River."

Certainly Herbert Hoover was no friend of the TVA idea. Yet when he was secretary of commerce he urged the benefits of the development of the Tennessee River as part of an internal waterway system throughout the Mississippi Valley. This is his statement to the Committee on Rivers and Harbors of the House of Representatives on January 30, 1926: "Now, there is a fundamental economic fact that improved transportation facilities cheapens the cost of goods, and thereby increases the volume of consumption, and thus the old saying that new transportation creates business is absolutely true. Every time we can cheapen the cost of producing goods, we increase the volume of production and thereby we increase the volume of traffic.''

Pointing out that wealth, industry, and population flourish along developed waterways, Lilienthal concluded that of the 39 leading counties of the United States which produce 50 percent of our manufactured products, they use 40 percent of our purchasing power, and contain 27 percent of our total population, that only four are without some type of water transportation. He added significantly that only three of these counties were in the Southeast.

At about this time an incident occurred which was recounted in more than the Southeast. Senator Styles Bridges of New Hampshire rose in the Senate and solemnly charged that the TVA paid $2,500 for a jackass and later sold it for $300. This caused a humorous uproar of disbelief, and the story was circulated by news services around the country. The account grew until it was rumored that the TVA lost more than $4,000 on the animal.

This came at a time when the TVA was under attack in the Senate, and Senator George Norris indignantly denounced the story as a deliberate attempt to discredit his favorite agency. This was actually what happened, he said: A jackass was bought on April 2, 1934 from R. E. Snell of Murfreesboro, Tennessee, for $290. The Authority kept the beast for almost a year, used him as a breeding animal, and sold him to J. B. Waters of Sevierville, Tennessee, for $350. Thus instead of losing $2,500, it made $60.

How Senator Bridges got his fictitious story happened this way: One day when the animal was about to be purchased, a newspaper man came into the office of Charles H. Garity, the Purchasing Director of TVA, and said, ''What about the jack?''

Garity thought the reporter was referring to a bid in answer to a TVA advertisement for a giant mechanical jack, and he referred the newsman to a bulletin board on which the purchase was announced. The price paid for the huge implement was $2,500. But the reporter, apparently thinking only of a long-eared donkey, went away and wrote a story that the TVA paid $2,500 for a jackass.

Five years after the advent of the TVA, Jonathan Daniels seemed enraptured by it. He wrote in the *New Republic* for August 17, 1938: ''Come Sunday, any Sunday, through the pretty town of Norris down the green freeway where, in the throat of the Valley of the Clinch, Norris Dam sits, smooth and white and high. There every such day the cars are parked side by side in every permitted space from the fish pools below the powerhouse to the high overlook where one American can look down upon his fellows stirring like proud ants over every part of this high monument to order and conservation and power which his TVA has made for him. Almost as thick as the cars are the pleasure boats on Norris Lake behind the long floating boom which keeps them from going down with the waters by Chattanooga and Florence and Paducah to the Mississippi and the sea . . . like a set for a great drama, loveliness and power and people all are at their best here together.''

4. Morgan versus Lilienthal

The Tennessee Valley Authority has always had many enemies. Naturally, the opposition has come mainly from outside interests. But the dissension within was so great at one time that it threatened the structure and even the existence of the organization.

This was the celebrated controversy between Chairman Arthur E. Morgan and Directors David E. Lilienthal and H. A. Morgan which culminated in the removal of A. E. Morgan by President Franklin D. Roosevelt, who had appointed him. The feud, in one form or another, lasted from the beginning of the TVA until Morgan's ouster in March 1938. At the very first board meeting of the Authority in Washington in 1933, Morgan and Lilienthal struck discordant notes when they first discussed power politics. How ominous this was for their future relationship could hardly be imagined at the time. Even so, they were able to work together, if sometimes divergently, for the first five years of the TVA.

In order to understand the background of this notorious controversy which rocked the TVA and reverberated through the halls of Congress and nation, it seems well to look in some detail at the lives of the two main contestants. Arthur Morgan was born in Cincinnati, Ohio, on June 20, 1878, the son of a surveyor of land who not long afterwards moved with his family to the little town of St. Cloud, Minnesota. Rutherford B. Hayes was President, and the country was just moving from the trauma of the Civil War into a new period which itself was involved in personal and political controversy. Morgan was a year old when he suffered an attack of cerebral meningitis which endangered his life and left physical damage that remained with him. His father was not especially concerned with religion, but his mother was a pious Quaker, a trait that was sharply felt by their son. Sickness, sleeplessness, and weariness were magnified by Morgan in order to avoid attending school or to make excuses for not meeting his mother's standards of perfection. Almost daily he recorded in his diary ailments such as boils, headaches, and colds.

Arthur Morgan thus found his younger days a hard struggle to be a normal boy. But he kept busy. He read children's stories, books on botany, and Edward Bellamy's *Looking Backward*. As to Bellamy, there is no doubt that this famous book deeply influenced Morgan. He simply turned the idea around to "looking forward" and became one of the most conspicuous of modern Utopians. The time would come when Morgan himself would write a good biography of Bellamy.

A young associate in later years who made a study of Morgan's life concluded about his early one: "His dissatisfaction with the present led him to develop a sense of mission and a deep commitment to change for himself and for the world. From his early teens he dedicated himself to self-improvement, especially from a physical and moral standpoint. His strenuous self-discipline made him at times a harsh judge of others—even when committed to free inquiry and open to new ideas."

In the fall of 1899 Morgan entered the University of Colorado. For six weeks he attended classes but soon found that his eyes were failing him. He had purchased a pair of glasses the year before, but these did not seem to solve the problem, so he dropped out of school. With this withdrawal, the formal education of Arthur Morgan came to an end. The doctorates he was to receive in later life were all honorary.

So Arthur Morgan became a self-educated man. He read avidly the works of Charles Darwin, Herbert Spencer, and Thomas Huxley. Morgan embraced the theories of evolution and Social Darwinism and believed strongly in the survival of the fittest. His impression of the Anglo-Saxon "race" was that it was the leader of civilization. Mental and physical exertion would lead to social reform as well as ethical and moral improvement. He was an ardent temperance man and opposed the use of tobacco and liquor. Specifically, he noted that it would be impossible for him to work in a newspaper office and set up type for a tobacco advertisement or work in a store and sell tobacco products. He wrote his mother, "No job is important enough to hold at the cost of any sacrifice of Christian principle.' " (Morgan is said to have once quit a job in a sawmill because the lumber was to be used for a gambling house.)

In a formal way Morgan had not succeeded in Colorado, but he did feel that he had formed some principles by which he could lead his life. He had spent three months meditating in the mountains. Just before leaving the state, he wrote in his diary: "I thank Thee, Lord, for having made me a failure at teaching, at farming, at printing, at carpentry, at mining. Help me to be a failure at all the things till I find my place. There help me to succeed."

His father, John D. Morgan, needed help in his work. The son became a rod and chain man and soon entered into partnership with his father as a surveyor and engineer. Young Morgan began a study of the drainage of wetlands. It happened that this field was booming because of the emphasis at the time on conservation and land reclamation, an ardently followed policy of the Progressive Era.

In 1904 Arthur Morgan married a young osteopath, but his wife died the following year after bearing him a son. Saddened but determined, by the next year he was in full partnership with his father and the firm was called Morgan & Morgan, Civil Engineers. After his father retired, Morgan ran the office by himself and became known throughout the state as a drainage engineer. However, he did not feel that this job had scope enough for his ambitions, so he placed an advertisement in the *Engineering News,* seeking a bigger job. He had an inquiry and answered it with a lengthy letter which concluded with the following: "I use no intoxicants whatever. Am in the habit of keeping my temper and of keeping on good terms with contractors and property owners. Am also in the habit of working 'on the square' with all parties concerned, and would not be interested in any proposition where false reports are expected to be made to public officials, property owners, or anyone else. I can come early in December." He did.

The reputation of Morgan in Minnesota engineering circles caught the attention of the U.S. Department of Agriculture, and in 1907 he was offered a job by Charles G. Elliott, acting chief of the Drainage Investigations Section. Morgan took the Civil Service examination and accepted the job of supervising engineer of the section. In this capacity he traveled over the United States, visiting different areas which had drainage problems, and drew up plans for remedying them. In 1908, however, he left the federal government and with two associates founded the Morgan Engineering Company of Tennessee. For six years his firm worked on flood control projects in the greater Memphis area, constructing more than 2,000 miles of canals and levees.

While going about the countryside around Memphis, Morgan noticed the lack of concern on the part of the farmers for taking care of the ground they owned and cultivated. He directed the reclamation of hundreds of thousands of fertile acres, but the owners seemed most interested in simply getting it back into shape to make the most money out of it quickly. The engineer was depressed by the fact that share-cropper tenants there lived in poverty and bitterness. Morgan also observed that the formal education of his engineers often was not sufficiently practical. Some of them could do a thorough and efficient job but appeared completely unable to write a good report about it. Morgan became convinced that something was lacking in an education which did not enable these engineers to perform their duties through to the end.

Meantime, Arthur Morgan had met a young lady named Lucy Griscom who had graduated from the University of Pennsylvania and was teaching chemistry and home economics at Wellesley College. After Morgan accepted her invitation to visit her on the family farm near Philadelphia, a romance grew, and on July 6, 1911, he and Lucy were married. She was to have a great influence on his life. As for Lucy's impression, she later recalled, "He impressed me as a man who, in spite of his most unusual ability, sadly needed to be taken care of."

On the morning of March 23, 1913, the flooding waters of the Miami, Stillwater, and Mad rivers overflowed their banks and poured through Dayton, Ohio, and surrounding communities. There was 10 feet of water in the main section of the city and to this was added the problems of a heavy snow and a big fire. The flood claimed 400 lives and destroyed over $100 million in property. Arthur Morgan was called in to supervise remedial measures. He set up his headquarters in Dayton and proceeded to supervise the construction of five dams on the Miami River. At each of the dams he constructed villages, and in place of the usual tents and shacks he had small cottages built replete with running water, electricity, and sanitation facilities. There was even a community hall, clubroom, library, and a school combining learning and doing. As a result, the turnover of workers was well below normal. This was to be largely repeated in the TVA two decades later.

At first his ideas were along conventional lines for a flood control system by improvement of the river channel, but his fertile mind, after examination of the situation, decided upon something new. Five dry earth dams and retarding basins would provide the greatest protection, he believed. Looking at these big dams, which resemble huge Indian mounds in steep valleys, one senses that they are there waiting to catch the flood waters. At each of the dams is a block of granite upon which is inscribed: "The dams of the Miami Conservancy District are for flood prevention purposes. Their use for power development or for storage would be a menace to the cities below."

Arthur Morgan was the first man in the United States to utilize the principle of building dry dams to create storage reservoirs. Still another idea developed by him was what he called "dynamic design." This meant that instead of having his office prepare plans to be followed exactly by the engineers, the plans were kept fluid. Each construction engineer took part in the preparation of plans for his dam and thus understood the reasons for the particular design. When unexpected factors cropped up while the construction was going on, the engineer in charge could change the design to fit the new circumstances. Such a practice was used later by Morgan in constructing dams for the TVA.

The next major step in the life of Morgan came when he assumed the presidency of Antioch College in the little town of Yellow Springs, Ohio. The school was as unusual and unorthodox as its new head. It was founded in 1853 by Horace Mann, the famous Massachusetts educator, who hoped that the school would become "the little Harvard of the West."

As president of the college, Morgan had a somewhat novel idea that students should have the ability "to gather together the various tangled threads of forces, conditions, and affairs, which make up the elements of any potential human accomplishment, and to weave them into a perfect fabric, showing the texture and design of a preconceived plan." Morgan believed that too often the student's home had protected him so much that he was unable to adjust to outside life on his own. The college, the new president believed, had an obligation to assist the student in making this transition. The idea of combining academic procedures with practical work attracted wide attention and became known as the Antioch Plan.

Not surprisingly, H. L. Mencken wrote to his friend, H. W. Van Loon: "Whenever a school announces a new scheme it is immediately deluged by all the half-wits who have failed under other schemes. I doubt that Morgan's staff could have the resolution to turn these vermin away. The careful selection of pupils is a fine ideal, but it is hard to execute it. . . . This is the danger that menaces Morgan. He will get plenty of applicants, but most of them will be . . . simply boneheads unable to pass the entrance examination at Yale, Amherst and the Ohio Baptist University."

On the race question, Morgan was definite. In 1910 he had written in his diary: "The extreme and universal immorality of the Negro is a bigger blight on the country than people realize." Morgan apparently did not believe that the blacks, Mexicans, and Asians were sufficiently intelligent and moral enough in many cases to measure up to his own standards.

Some of this philosophy was incorporated in "The Antioch Notes." These had come to the attention of President Roosevelt and helped to familiarize him with Morgan as a likely candidate for the chairmanship of the TVA. James M. Cox, Roosevelt's running mate in 1920, recommended Morgan for the TVA. During the Miami project, Cox had been governor of Ohio and remembered Morgan's notable work there as an engineer. Both the President and his wife Eleanor were familiar with

"The Antioch Notes" and liked the ideas of social reform contained in them. Roosevelt also consulted Louis Brandeis, who considered the "Notes" an American version of *The Spectator Papers*. Morgan said, "The TVA is the kind of thing I have been wanting to do all my life."

Morgan was described at this time as "Tall and stern, indefatigable and abstemious, tinged with mysticism. A compulsive writer, he was given to flights of philosophical speculation, and utopianism was never far from the surface of his thought."

At Madison, Wisconsin, Morgan stated in a speech:

The mountains of Virginia, North Carolina and Tennessee are settled by white people who mostly live on small farms. . . . In this region there are grown men and women who have never seen a Negro. As the Tennessee River sweeps off to the Southwest, making a great loop through northern Alabama, it drains a region of great plantations largely given to raising cotton. Here about a quarter of the population is colored and most of the farmers, both white and colored, are tenants. . . . We are trying to work out possibilities of creativeness in these people.

As an extension of his philosophy, Arthur Morgan said:

I do not have a vision of Utopia. I see problems beyond problems, issues beyond issues, as far as present vision runs. If my outlook is one of aggressive hope, rather than of resignation or of disillusionment, it is because, while I have tried to overlook no doubts, difficulties, or reasons for lack of hope, what I have found gives me an increased sense of value and increased feeling of favorable possibility. . . . The Tennessee Valley is the first place in America where we can sit down and design a civilization.

In what is perhaps his clearest philosophical summation, Arthur Morgan stated admirably:

The greatest of all social aims is that of developing the qualities of character and intelligence that will lead each person of his own volition to try to play that part which is best for society as a whole. Such an attitude would vastly simplify the processes of social adjustment. Enlightened character is a universal solvent of social evils.

It was in early April of 1933 when President Roosevelt first spoke to Morgan about the TVA. This was more than a month before the TVA Act became a law and more than two months prior to the first meeting of the board of directors. The other two board members had not been selected by Roosevelt at this time. He had decided only that one should be an agriculturist, if possible from the South, and the other with special knowledge of electric power. At this time he mentioned the names of several prospects to Morgan and asked him to help in making the final choices. Morgan recalled in an interview with this writer that the President would make diagrams on paper and then wave his arm toward the window, as if the Tennessee Valley were just outside. Morgan remembered that Eleanor Roosevelt a few weeks earlier had made an oddly appropriate statement about the whole New Deal: "One has a feeling of going in blindly, because we are in a tremendous stream and none of us knows where we are going to land."

Arthur Morgan was markedly impressed by his visit with the President. Later he remarked, "I was just a backwoodsman, and he was President of the United States."

Morgan made several suggestions which were incorporated in the TVA bill. But some Congressmen and public utilities executives attacked the bill as being Communistic. However, this was in the famous first One Hundred Days of the New Deal and the recommendations by FDR were magic. He put pressure on Congress, and on May 18, 1933, the TVA Bill as originally submitted by Senator Norris and Morgan was signed into law. On that day Arthur Morgan exultantly wrote, "A new order is opening up in America."

Chairman Morgan immediately went into action. He sent staff members of Antioch College around the country to interview candidates while he himself went to several places for the same purpose. After talking to some public and private power executives, Morgan consulted Supreme Court Justice Louis D. Brandeis who gave him the name of David E. Lilienthal, a member of the Wisconsin Public Service Commission. The chairman interviewed the 33-year old Lilienthal in Chicago, and although some of Morgan's friends had described Lilienthal as a "publicity seeker," Morgan was much impressed by him. He jotted down on the back of an old dog-eared envelope, "Brilliant, square, public minded!" He wired President Roosevelt: "Lilienthal is fine. I heartily recommend his appointment on Tennessee board."

David E. Lilienthal was born in Morton, Illinois, where his father, who was a Jewish immigrant from Austria-Hungary, operated a retail store. The son entered DePauw University and became a prominent student, boxing, playing football, excelling in public speaking as well as scholarship, and becoming president of the study body. He graduated in 1920 and, after thinking of becoming a journalist, he instead entered Harvard Law School.

He did not fool around. In his first year at Harvard, he introduced himself to Professor Felix Frankfurter, who was to have great influence on his career. Then young Lilienthal began a series of letters to such labor leaders as William Green, William W. Johnston, and Frank P. Walsh. The result was that Frankfurter and Walsh helped to land Lilienthal a job with the small Chicago law firm of Donald Richberg. Richberg did not need anyone at the time but was so impressed with Lilienthal that he accepted him.

Lilienthal at once began work on labor cases. So rapid was his progress that he contributed to the legislation which became the Railway Labor Act of 1926. Meantime Lilienthal had met Helen Lamb at DePauw. (She earned her M.A. at Radcliffe while he was at Harvard.) They were married after graduation.

At the age of 31, Lilienthal became the youngest member in the history of the Wisconsin Railroad Commission. Donald Richberg had first been asked to accept this appointment by Governor Philip La Follette. He declined and suggested Lilienthal, who surprisingly accepted, because the change involved considerable financial sacrifice. It was in the midst of the Depression. One of Lilienthal's first duties was to draft a bill increasing the power of the commission and changing its name to the Wisconsin Public Service Commission.

Arthur Morgan was appointed chairman of the TVA nearly three months before the other two directors were selected. When Harcourt Morgan and David Lilienthal joined the board, they discovered that the chairman already had several of his plans in operation. This was a mistake, perhaps unwittingly, of President Roosevelt. The chairman had already hired personnel for some key positions, and they were active in several parts of the organization, under his orders and as if he alone were running the show. Twenty years later John Oliver, general manager of the TVA, stated in a lecture at Florida State University that under this arrangement deficiencies were evident from the start: "A major shortcoming arose from the fact that the Act gave no special authority to anyone of three board members. The relatively independent exercise of authority by any one member without the full knowledge and concurrence of the others would not be conducive to efficiency; and early experience emphasized the need for a strong over-all plan together with a clear-cut system of control."

Lilienthal's outlook was to give the people ways to produce. If the individual did not have such means, the government should assist him. On the other hand, Arthur Morgan felt that the TVA should create a new way of life, not simply improve on an existing one. Harcourt Morgan came into the TVA not siding with either of the other two directors, but because he felt that the chairman was domineering, he came to take more and more the side of Lilienthal. Two of the chairman's most controversial ideas were his suggestion that the states should pass laws to take land away from owners who failed to maintain the fertility of the soil and a suggestion for creating a regional currency for the Tennessee Valley. He believed that the northern financial centers were taking away the wealth of the Tennessee Valley by artificial freight rates, high interest on loans, and wage differentials. So a special currency could be established and maintained within the region. Neither of the ideas was accepted. The *Chattanooga News* derisively suggested "coon skins" as the new currency.

On July 30, 1933, Arthur Morgan presented an outline of what he thought should be the TVA's program. While containing worthwhile elements and new ideas, to the other two directors many of the proposals appeared to be "impractical and highly visionary." In particular the two directors had serious doubts about the plans of the chairman for the total integration and development of all the power sites in the Tennessee River system; his recommendation for manufacturing Portland cement and dry ice at the phosphorus plant at Muscle Shoals; his wide-ranging forestry program, which went beyond that of other government agencies; his proposal for the quick formulation of social and economic plans for the TVA; and the cooperative distribution of local products.

As a result of their surprise and concern, the two directors decided to take action to curb what they felt was becoming the increasing power of the chairman. Lilienthal was more concerned than Harcourt Morgan, especially about the execution of the power policy. As Roy Talbert has aptly noted, "Lilienthal worried that unless restrained, the visionary Morgan would drown the TVA, and his crusade for public power, in a sea of platitudes."

So the two lower ranking directors prepared a "Memorandum on Organization" which allocated various activities of the Authority among the three members of the board. Arthur Morgan was to have charge of constructing Norris Dam, preparing educational programs about the Authority, establishing a policy of employee relationships, planning for the improved navigation of the Tennessee River, and unifying various parts of the work of the TVA. H. A. Morgan was to supervise the Authority's agricultural program. Lilienthal was to have control of the power program and legal department.

The Battle Is Joined

On August 5 the board met in the Andrew Johnson Hotel in Knoxville. The chairman was angry. He later recalled: "The atmosphere was a very hostile one. It was aggressively resentful and dictatorial. I was being told this is what is going to be done. I was not asked shall we do this, but I was explicitly told, as explicitly as I would tell a servant to do anything, except there was discussion, and I secured modifications, but some of these were nullified. It was a case of being told and not discussing, primarily." The other two directors insisted, and the chairman was compelled to go along with their general plans.

Forty years later the aged Arthur Morgan, sitting behind his little desk in his cluttered old home in Yellow Springs, Ohio, told this writer that his agreement with this division of authority was the worst mistake he made in all of his years with the TVA. He said bitterly that this plan opened the door through which Lilienthal and the other Morgan ran roughshod over him.

Not anticipating such internal controversy, Roosevelt had said in his message requesting TVA legislation, "If we are successful here, we can march on, step by step, in a like development of other great natural territorial units within our borders." Why this has never happened, why there are no more TVAs in the United States, is a question which has not been clearly answered. The most cogent reason seems to be that the substantial effects of TVA power production appear to have aroused the strong opposition of private interests in other areas. They have fought expansion of the TVA idea, charging that it is subsidized by the government, socialistic, and unnecessary. Another factor is that of opposition within the government by cabinet departments and such influential groups as the U.S. Army Corps of Engineers, which were directly affected by the operations of the TVA, as well as many conservative politicians.

For his part, Lilienthal sought the support of such old friends as Robert La Follette, Felix Frankfurter, and other "time-tested public men." These were opposed to the chairman's power proposal, Frankfurter particularly, who held it to be fraught with every kind of danger." Morgan's aim was to make the TVA power program an experiment in purely impartial research. Thus his moderate position left him open to charges that he was soft toward the power trust. This made it easy for Lilienthal to convince his friends that Morgan was visionary and a danger to the TVA itself.

In regard to the confrontation among the board of directors, Neil Bass, former Knoxville City Manager at the advent of TVA, recalled:

> Mr. Lilienthal being a man of very sharp mental abilities and characteristically a lawyer with very strong ambition, strong controversies developed in board meetings that sometimes hampered the work of TVA. In fact, some of the board meetings were almost

shouting sessions, and I use that word guardedly. Sometimes the conclusion of the board meetings would not satisfy anyone, because of the atmosphere in which decisions were carried out. Sometimes the board members would have second thoughts after getting out of the board meetings. On more than one occasion, the chairman, Mr. Arthur Morgan, would not carry out things that the board had decided on.

William C. Fitts, Jr., former general counsel of the TVA, stated in a recent interview his interesting, conceptual opinion as follows:

In Arthur Morgan you had a man who was unquestionably a brilliant hydraulic engineer, who had the concept—a broad concept—for the development of the reservoir project; who understood the flood control problem; who had had a great deal of experience in flood control engineering. He also was an idealist. He had a quite broad concept of overall economic development and improvement in the Valley.

In David Lilienthal you had a very fine administrator who was good at building a management; who helped unquestionably in building an excellent personnel department and what I thought was a great legal department, and in general, was what we call now a manager. In my opinion, his greatest contribution was in the field of management. I think that he was far and away the best administrator—the best manager of the three.

In Harcourt A. Morgan you had a man who I think has been greatly underrated. First, he was a great human being. He had a warm personality and was a fine person. But in addition, he knew the Valley, he knew the area, he knew the people. He knew how to approach them. The thing that might have killed TVA, and at one point came close to hurting it, was a feeling in the Valley itself that we ran into—that here was something being superimposed on them. Now, H. A. Morgan insisted from the beginning, strongly supported by Lilienthal (and this was one of the beginnings of the division) that this project had to be coordinated with the local people. You had to have the cooperation of local government, local legislation, and local officials. The grass-roots concept, that this was being done not by superimposition but cooperation and coordinated efforts, was strongly helpful. I think this had a great deal to do with the success, because, as I stated earlier, without the cooperation of the local authorities, we would never have been able to have obtained authorization for the distribution systems, without which the entire power program would have failed, and we would never have been able to get the agricultural program in anything near the shape it reached without the cooperation of the Extension Service and the state universities. In all of this H. A. Morgan was invaluable.

On August 17, 1933, still smarting from the "Memorandum on Organization," Arthur Morgan met privately with President Roosevelt to express his disagreement with the board's decision to divide responsibilities. He also showed FDR some newspaper clippings which he felt were examples of a campaign secretly conducted against him by Lilienthal. The President showed sympathy but said little. The next day Morgan had lunch with Lilienthal and confronted him with reports of what the chairman regarded as intrigue against himself. The suave Lilienthal assured Morgan that his feelings toward him were those of confidence and goodwill.

In spite of such overtures, the position of the chairman did not improve. He seemed to mistrust others, and they mistrusted him. He was more inclined to give directions than to offer his views first to his colleagues, so the friction continued. The accomplished memorandum of Harcourt Morgan and Lilienthal had this effect: In future board meetings these two directors would stand together and support each other's proposals. From now on the chairman was a one-man minority. As Thomas K. McCraw has pointed out: "The Board now lost all resemblance to a private corporate board of directors. In addition to affairs of policy, its members now became actively involved in administering the business of the Authority, business which would normally be entrusted to a general manager. The temporary designation of Arthur Morgan as general manager was ended."

On Sundays, instead of playing golf as the other two directors did together, Arthur Morgan walked through the picturesque countryside along the bend of the Tennessee River. He felt that he needed this calming diversion. The harassed chairman believed as James D. Lorenz, Jr., states: "People had to be provided with an example of the good life. They had to come in contact with a person or institution which they respected, and which could serve as a basis for a newer, improved way of life. Only then Morgan concluded, could the amelioration of many individuals be achieved. . . . Although Morgan was often Lincolnesque in tolerance and kindness, he was also stubborn in his moralism."

In June of 1933 Arthur Morgan had met Jim Farley, chairman of the Democratic National Committee, who pressured the TVA official to appoint a large number of Democrats. Morgan was unmoved. He recalls with some asperity that Farley and his assistants vigorously insisted that the victorious political party which had put Roosevelt in the White House be shown such appreciation. Farley found he was talking to no politician. Morgan told Farley, "If there were two men available but the better man had no political influence, I should appoint him." Morgan added that he had not sought the appointment as chairman and had accepted it only on the condition that no political patronage would be involved. Farley suggested that Morgan see the President, which he did next day at the White House. FDR was eating from a tray on his desk and agreed with Morgan that no political patronage would be foisted on the TVA.

If the politicians could not go through Morgan, they could go around him. Congressmen who had been turned down by the chairman began to deal with David Lilienthal, who was more friendly. So it was that in the fall of 1933 relatives and acquaintances of prominent Democrats were found working for the TVA. One was James Eldredge, a nephew of the Speaker of the House of Representatives, Sam Rayburn, who became an assistant law clerk. Beth Carmichael, who was the daughter-in-law of a Congressman, became a member of the TVA office staff, as did J. B. Knight, formerly a secretary to the Congressional Committee on Military Affairs. A victim of polio, Harold Denton, whom Eleanor Roosevelt had known at Warm Springs, Georgia, obtained a job as research assistant. Edith Jacobs, who had worked for but did not please the Democratic National Committee, came in to supervise the display of scale models of TVA projects, while Claude McReynolds, nephew of the popular and influential Congressman Sam D. McReynolds of Chattanooga, was appointed a land surveyor.

Although some of these appointments seemed to have been made also on the basis of merit, they appear to have had considerable political help as they passed through the Lilienthal office. Even Gordon R. Clapp, veteran TVA official and later chairman of its board of directors, stated that it appeared that Claude McReynolds could not have been appointed to his TVA job had it not been for his political connections.

Arthur Morgan felt that not only was Lilienthal too much in contact with politicians but that he was quite a maneuvering politician within the TVA. One manifestation of this, the chairman believed, was the attitude of Lilienthal and H. A. Morgan in opposition to the chairman's social planning.

In a recent book, *The Making of the TVA*, Arthur Morgan stated:

> Harcourt Morgan was nearly twice the age of Lilienthal and it seemed natural for the younger man to act like a son to the elder. Lilienthal brought Dr. Morgan to the office in the morning, took him out to lunch and home in the evening. He arranged for his office to adjoin Dr. Morgan's, with a connecting door between, and for Dr. Morgan's office to be the farthest distance from mine. I seldom had conversations with Dr. Morgan. While the other two directors were extremely intimate, their relations seemed to be mostly for practical purposes. The arrangement of their offices constituted a somewhat exclusive board headquarters for the two of them, and they soon became the working majority of the board, almost invariably voting

together. . . . With the active campaign against me carried on by Mr. Lilienthal, who dominated the functions of the TVA Washington staff, I did not see how I could bring about a workable administration. On the other hand, it would not be easy to undo my mistake of asking Mr. Lilienthal to select the head of the office. . . . President Roosevelt came to me similarly convinced of my total dishonesty, depravity and disloyalty to the New Deal in favor of the private utilities.

Both sides in the growing controversy appealed to Senator Norris. He had an abiding interest in the ideas and ideals of both sides but of course was not in a position to judge the true nature of the in-fighting. Norris was to come to lean toward Lilienthal in regard to the question of public versus private power interests, but as late as October 1935, he still greatly admired the chairman. Writing to George Fort Milton, editor and publisher of the *Chattanooga News,* Norris said: "Morgan's ideals are high and noble, his ability in this line of work is unquestioned; his honesty is beyond dispute; his heart goes out to the underdog, to the sufferer, to the man who toils and labors, and who does not get sufficient recompense for his toil. . . . I think that when you get on the inside of the man, you find one who is, for our viewpoint, perhaps as near perfect as a human being can become. From this standpoint, he is in my opinion a true man. He is enthusiastic about the TVA; he wants to make it a success in every way; I think it is the ambition of the man's life."

As one can well imagine, the mood of the board of directors during these trying times was not one of great personal happiness. Yet Arthur Morgan still dreamed as he walked along the river which the Indians had named Tennessee ("River of the Big Bend"). Sometimes he was even happy. Sometimes he even got a laugh, as he did when he received the following letter from J. F. Morgan of Athens, Alabama:

I am a righting you a few lines to see what your grat-granfather name is. My grat-granfather was name Markes Morgan and he com from Irlent and settle in Vegenia and was the first settler ther and cauled it Morgantown. He browt 9 suns and 2 doughters. Mr Morgan I have a big roun bottle that holes 3 quarts that has bin handown from ginerashun. My granfather got it and then my father got it and he left it to me and I am in my 87th years. The bottle I won is 200 years ole. I just want to know if your grat-granfather is my grat-granfather.

Morgan replied in kind:

I am very glad to have your recent letter, but greatly fear that your great-grandfather was not my great-grandfather. My great-great-grandfather came from just across the channel in Wales and settled in Montgomery County just North of Philadelphia. I should like to see the big round bottle. I have not a single heir-loom from across the water. Perhaps I can stop to see you sometime when I go through Athens, as I do occasionally.

The Morgan-Lilienthal feud came to a sort of climax in 1936. The latter had been appointed for three years, and his term was to expire in June of that year. Here Morgan saw his chance. So he went to the top and journeyed to Warm Springs, Georgia, to talk with President Roosevelt who was there on one of his customary visits for relaxing treatment of his polio affliction. Morgan felt confident as he approached the chief executive, who at first seemed inclined to agree with the chairman. However, Morgan was in for a disappointment.

Roosevelt was soon to face another election, and he did not wish to rock the boat of his Administration with a radical removal at this time. Morgan did not insist that Lilienthal be left completely out of the government. He would have been glad to see the power director shifted to some other position within the New Deal. The President did go so far as to ask Morgan to name a few people who might take the place of Lilienthal. The latter replied that Neil Bass, assistant to H. A. Morgan, would be satisfactory. The President told Morgan he would consider his suggestions carefully.

The next time Morgan saw Roosevelt was in May 1936 at a meeting in Washington of the heads of federal agencies. On this occasion, Morgan received a setback when the President leaned close to him and asked in a low voice if it was all right "to reappoint Dave." But in a few days FDR again seemed sympathetic with Morgan and commented that both of them were almost entirely in agreement. The chairman then wrote a letter to his wife saying that he was encouraged by the attitude of the President and felt that the chief objectives of the TVA would be fulfilled.

Soon afterward the directors and Morgan got into a dispute about personnel matters, the result of which was that H. A. Morgan went to Roosevelt and urged the reappointment of Lilienthal. Arthur Morgan now felt that his dreams were crashing about him. He recorded in his notes that "the internal organization is suffering disastrously . . . what should be technical decisions are plays for power. The fence sitters in the organization are calculating which way to jump. Intrigue and suspicion of intrigue are becoming the prevailing temper."

It seems that when one of the directors felt himself in trouble, he hied himself off in rabbit-like fashion to Washington, D.C. In this case

Arthur Morgan was no exception. He boarded a train for the nation's capitol and went straight to see Senator Norris. Again Morgan was rebuffed. The Senator from Nebraska was weary and told Morgan that to oppose Lilienthal was futile. "As much as I am opposed to Lilienthal's ethics," said Norris, "I am convinced that the hopes for public power lie with him." According to the Senator, such strong liberals as Frankfurter, La Follette, and Brandeis were behind Lilienthal, and Morgan would have to fall in line.

Back home in Tennessee, Arthur Morgan felt disconsolate. However, as is obvious by now, the chairman did not give up easily. He sat down and wrote the President a final entreaty. He informed the chief executive that Lilienthal had taken part in political patronage with the purpose of making his own position more secure. The power director had not fit in with the crusading character of the TVA. Lilienthal had assumed an attitude "which was belligerent toward the private utilities." In regard to the yardstick, Lilienthal had mismanaged. It was a strong letter; but for some reason Morgan did not mail it.

Instead, within a few days, Morgan saw the President again. He was not surprised when FDR told him that Lilienthal would be appointed to another term. The President had considered shifting Lilienthal to the Securities and Exchange Commission, but he did not want that job. FDR also pointed out that if Lilienthal was removed from the TVA, some members of Congress would feel that the Administration was in cahoots with private utilities. The President appealed to Morgan not to let him down, stating that something could be worked out after the election. Roosevelt then appealed to the board of directors to bring their major disputes to him before acting upon them.

It was a day of train travel, and that evening Morgan sadly boarded one for the South. Melancholy and nervous, he sat up most of the night staring out of his compartment window. What should he do? It was almost morning, and brightness was along the mountain horizon when he made his decision. He would resign. He wrote a letter to this effect but did not mail it.

At his home Morgan continued to suffer the pangs of indecision. He was unable to decide what to do. His wife Lucy pressed upon him to resign. She said she had never trusted Roosevelt anyway and believed he reappointed Lilienthal in order to undermine her husband. At his office in the TVA, Morgan found some support, especially among his chief engineers, who urged him not to resign. They said he was essential to the program of the Authority in the Tennessee Valley. But Morgan was doubtful. He was afraid that suspicion and intrigue and rivalry in an organization were sure to "destroy all possibility for the mutual respect and confidence on which the most effective work is based."

Morgan wrote Senator Norris that he regretted the reappointment of Lilienthal and that his opposition to him was not so much in regard to power policy but "a lack of personal confidence." The chairman added that he could not respect Lilienthal personally and accused him of carrying on a campaign of harmful publicity against him. Newspapers in Knoxville and Chattanooga carried adverse articles about Morgan and hinted that he would resign if Lilienthal were reappointed. The other two directors added insult to injury for Arthur Morgan when they appointed John C. Blandford as "temporary manager." Blandford was known to be opposed to the chairman, so this seemed to be the last straw. Still undecided as to his future, Morgan left Knoxville on June 14, 1936, for his home in Yellow Springs, Ohio.

The old home did not seem so pleasant to him now. It was just before graduation at Antioch College, but there was little of such joy in the heart of Arthur Morgan. He had few outside interests, and so there was no diversion to take his mind off his troubles. For the previous three years he had been away, living, working, and completely absorbed in the TVA. He was unable to sleep, and his wife sat by his bedside at night reading to him from Tennyson. He was still unable to make up his mind about what to do and received differing kinds of advice. One friend, Morris Leeds of Philadelphia, wrote him saying, "You have been placed in a position where you cannot go on with the enterprise without doing violation to your philosophy of life."

There was some consolation in a friendly letter from President Roosevelt, but by this time Morgan's opinion of him had naturally changed. He still thought the President had a "creative personality, active imagination and great readiness to break with social and political precedent." However, Morgan viewed the chief executive as feeling too much the power of his office. He wrote the President a letter in which he suggested changes in the structure of the TVA. These included a requirement for unanimous votes in the board of directors, a bona fide general manager, and the creation of an outside board of consultants to develop new TVA policies. Not illogically, these recommendations were not adopted.

Perhaps Arthur Morgan should have resigned at this time, but he did not. At any rate his loss of the fight against Lilienthal, his threat to resign, and his failure to do so placed him in an untenable position both within and without the organization. He was still chairman of the board but continually voted as a minority against the other two directors.

Most Congressmen now did not favor him, and in the public eye he did not seem beneficial to the TVA, especially to those who felt he was too friendly with private power interests.

In this connection A. E. Morgan commented in a statement to this writer: "the favorable attitude of Mr. Lilienthal, during the period when the Aluminum Company of America greatly needed and desired more power from the TVA, and Mr. Lilienthal's intense opposition to me at that same period involving the relations of the Aluminum Company of America toward power supply from TVA sources convinced me that Mr. Lilienthal's opposition to me was not separate from his support of power needs of the Aluminum Company and their desire to have a share in the power production at the dams of the Tennessee River."

Like the smoldering drama of a Shakespearean play, events came to a climax in late 1937. The issue was the right of TVA to condemn and acquire land. George L. Berry, a labor leader, had been appointed a Democratic U.S. Senator from Tennessee. He owned the mineral rights to some land in middle Tennessee which was to be purchased and flooded by the TVA. Berry filed a claim which stated that his land held valuable deposits of marble and asked that the TVA pay him the sum of $5 million.

In the opinion of Arthur Morgan, this was a preposterous claim and Berry's lands were worth no more than ordinary soil. The other two directors were immediately inclined to make some settlement with Senator Berry and thus avoid unfavorable publicity both in regard to the public and to Congress. Instead of conferring with his associates, Arthur Morgan made an unexpected appearance on the last day of the hearings on condemnation and publicly denounced his fellow directors, accusing them of favoritism toward Berry. Chairman Morgan was right. New evidence showed that the Berry marble was of very poor quality, and even Lilienthal and Harcourt Morgan agreed that the Senator should not receive any compensation. The court ruling was against Berry.

This situation did nothing to alleviate the directors' controversy. Lilienthal wrote to Senator Norris that this was all just part of the same controversy over power policy. It now appeared that the fight was out in the open and no holds were barred. Lilienthal and Morgan made public statements about each other, descending to unbecoming personal invective. The other two directors accused Arthur Morgan of conducting a deliberate campaign to discredit the TVA.

The embroilment in and around the Tennessee Valley Authority had now reached such a disorderly stage that something had to be done.

The other two directors in November of 1937 informed President Roosevelt in substance that they could no longer work with Chairman Arthur Morgan. He was, they said, trying to sabotage the TVA by attempting to outlaw that part of the power program with which he did not agree. By January of 1938 they told the President that they felt Morgan should retire.

The chairman was not one to take this sitting down. In a letter to Congressman Maury Maverick of Texas, released to the press by Morgan on March 7, he cut loose at Lilienthal as "a menace to good government." Morgan said that Lilienthal and his staff were purposely keeping important information from the chairman; that the other two directors met and made their decisions in private; that he was not permitted to learn in advance the subjects which would be presented to the board; and that his views, even though they were in the minority, were not even recorded in the minutes of the board meetings.

In this long letter Morgan singled out Lilienthal as follows: "There is a practice of evasion, intrigue and sharp strategy, with remarkable skill in alibi and the habit of avoiding direct responsibility, which makes Machiavelli seem open and candid. It took me a year or more of close association to be convinced that the attitude of boyish open candor and man-to-man directness was a mask for hard-boiled selfish intrigue; so I am not surprised that Congressmen do not quickly see the situation from a distance."

In this connection Arthur Morgan told this writer in an interview that Lilienthal was "a clever, deceitful and misleading man who would sit in board meetings and take down the proceedings in his own shorthand and then later write them up with his own biased interpretation." Lilienthal, to me, denied strongly all such allegations.

Morgan by now had his verbal gun blazing. He let Harcourt Morgan have the other barrel. He charged that the Tennessee Morgan had become, through his control of TVA grants to land grant colleges and county farm agents, "one of the most powerful figures of the South, though he nearly always chooses to be behind the scenes." Arthur Morgan asked for a Congressional investigation which, he declared, would disclose "disorder, waste, confusion and lack of planning to a startling degree." He added that he had increasingly put up with in the TVA "an attitude of conspiracy, secretiveness and bureaucratic manipulation."

Of course Lilienthal and Harcourt Morgan had to make a public reply to these public charges. In a joint statement they accused Arthur Morgan of obstruction and refusal to cooperate with them. He allegedly had attacked them malevolently and without reason, and they countercharged that he refused to carry out decisions of the board and had collaborated with the private power companies in their actions against the Tennessee Valley Authority.

The gauntlet was now flung down. Arthur Morgan had to prove the serious charges that he had made. But he could not do this. He did not even produce what little evidence he had, such as the charge of Lilienthal's slight involvement with political patronage or statements from staff members showing that Lilienthal had waged verbal war against him.

At last the word came down from on high: Roosevelt's hand was forced. The President preferred to stay out of fights among his subordinates, but he could no longer allow the TVA chairman's claims and charges to go unsettled. So Roosevelt called a meeting at the White House on March 7, 1938, for the purpose of having a showdown. Arthur Morgan was given a chance to substantiate or withdraw his charges against the other two TVA directors. But Morgan had long been sold on the idea of a Congressional investigation. So at the White House meeting he adamantly refused to take part in the hearing. The President patiently gave him a week to reconsider his plan, but at the next meeting Morgan still refused to answer questions. Still another meeting on March 21 brought the same futile results, and the President now felt that he must give Morgan an ultimatum: he must respond within 24 hours.

Arthur Morgan departed from Washington on that same day. Whether he realized the seriousness of his public defiance of the President of the United States is not known. What *is* clear is that Roosevelt dismissed him from office for "contumacious behavior."

In his last years Arthur Morgan looked far back and stated:

As I listened to President Roosevelt's comments, it dawned on me that he had come to believe that I had repeatedly betrayed him, as Mr. Lilienthal had charged. With the benefit of hindsight, I can see that I made a serious error in refusing to defend myself, but at that time, perhaps because of my illness, I did not fully realize the extent of the impact my refusal would have. I tended to further Mr. Lilienthal's efforts to bring to an end my official connection with the TVA. Because the circumstances of these presidential hearings of March 7, 14 and 21, 1938, seemed to be unsuitable for a true review of the facts and because in the absence of an objective hearing before the President, the Congress had responsibility as representative of the people, I asked for a Congressional hearing on the issue. At the hearings, which began May 25 and proceeded through the summer, I was given an opportunity to state my case, but politically and judicially the door was closed. I was barred from obtaining evidence from the TVA files.

Most people would think that being fired by the President himself would be as final as it is possible to be, but not Arthur Morgan. He wrote Roosevelt on March 24, 1938, as follows:

At the meeting in your office on March 21, I challenged the suggestion of my removal and denied your right and power as President to remove me. Now that you have acted, I believe it my duty most respectfully to say to you that I do not recognize your order for my removal as within the power of the President. I am, therefore, notifying you that I am still a member and chairman of the board of directors of Tennessee Valley Authority.

Morgan did get his Congressional investigation. Politicians on both sides had a field day. The hearings lasted from May to December, 1938, and produced 15,000 pages of testimony and technical exhibits, some relating to complicated accounting and engineering. The Republican minority on the joint committee supported Morgan, apparently hoping that his frustrated ideas would discredit the TVA, whose entire program they condemned. The Democratic majority clung to New Deal policy and praised the work of the TVA, at the same time accusing Arthur Morgan of failure to cooperate.

Like Richard Nixon, Morgan was not up to his best intellectual and emotional self during his last years with the TVA. Nonetheless, during his five years as chairman of the Authority, he had made valuable and lasting contributions which shine through to this day.

Almost a quarter of a century later, Francis Biddle, who had been Attorney General of the United States and who headed the investigation, recorded his impressions of the TVA triumvirate. In his book, *In Brief Authority,* Biddle states:

Lilienthal was precise and realistic in his outlook, where Arthur Morgan was loose-minded and touched with mysticism. Once Lilienthal came to see me to ask my opinion as to whether it would be a mistake for him to sue Arthur Morgan for libel—his charges had been grossly libelous—and Lilienthal felt them deeply under his cool and disciplined behavior. I advised him against bringing any action, at least until the investigation had been completed. I hardly knew him then, but much later, when I was vice chairman of the Twentieth Century Fund and he was a director, we grew to be friends. He had a genuinely Christian outlook—perhaps a curious word to apply to a Jew, but one that fits exactly his compassionate sensitiveness.

This was not the only time in which Lilienthal contemplated suing Morgan.

Congressman Thomas A. Jenkins of Ironton, Ohio, a Republican member of the investigating committee, also came under the fire of Francis Biddle. He recalls that when Jenkins did not get the answer he wanted from a witness, he began to shout:

He had once been a football player. He was 'tough,' but not very bright. Every now and then he would run into a witness who was skillful in rejoinder and unafraid, as when George Fort Milton, president of the *Chattanooga News,* was on the stand. . . . Milton's appearance was misleadingly mild. He was not impressive. A short fat man with wide-open, watery blue eyes, he constantly fidgeted in the witness chair. He was gently ironic—which confused the Ohio Congressman—and venomously polite. Jenkins, as one reporter described it, launched his attack with the swift directness of a falling stepladder. Milton, a distinguished historian, had for a year been a special assistant to Secretary of State Cordell Hull. Jenkins kept calling him "Mr. Special Assistant"; and finally said sententiously: "I am just a common congressman," upon which Milton, to the delight of the spectators, addressed him as Mr. Common Congressman.

In regard to the outcome of the Congressional inquiry, *The Nation* editorialized:

The results of the investigation must be set down as one of the most dismal defeats in the whole history of the anti-New Deal campaign. Dr. Morgan has had to back water on his charges of dishonesty made against the other TVA commissioners. What was originally played up as the Teapot Dome scandal of the New Deal has simmered down to the personal differences as to the wisdom of certain administrative decisions on which it is now clear that reasonable men might easily have differed.

The man in the middle, so to speak, was Senator George Norris. It must have been rather painful for him to reach a conclusion which could disrupt the TVA. However, he did come to a decision which can be summed up in his own words:

Dr. Arthur E. Morgan was an eminent engineer, conscientious and honest in all that he did, although in the later phases of the bitter controversy that developed it was difficult to harmonize his attitude then with the history of developments that took place in TVA itself. It has seemed to me that, although magnificently qualified as an engineer, and perfectly conscientious, he did not give his associates on the TVA board proper consideration. Unconsciously he was unfair to them; disregarded their advice and counsel and seemed at times desirous of establishing himself as a dictator in control of every activity of the board. . . . I investigated every charge he made. I conferred with him upon my conclusions, and still never on a single occasion did he produce a thread of evidence that Mr. Lilienthal had been untrue to his trust.

"Reluctantly I came to the conclusion there could be no improvement without the removal of Dr. Morgan. About that time Mr. Roosevelt arrived at the same decision when he issued the order directing the removal of Dr. Morgan from the TVA board.

Senator Norris had reached virtually the end of his fine career. "My years are measured," he said. "If in the peaceful years ahead new vigor comes to old and wooded hills not only in the basin of the Tennessee but throughout America, and in other regions of the world . . . that is well."

5. TVA at War

In a survey of the factors influencing people's attitude toward the TVA, Verner Martin Sims of the University of Alabama in 1938 found the following: southern adults were more favorable toward the TVA than were northern adults; in general business and industry were less favorable than were laborers, farmers, and the professions; teachers were most favorable and engineers least in the professions; and in business and industry salespersons and merchants were most favorable and lumbermen and manufacturers least.

In general, attitudes toward the TVA seemed to be determined by very immediate factors in the environment. Northern adults reacted to it as a political issue, but students coming south very readily took on the attitude of the southern majority; farmers, laborers, merchants, and builders saw improved economic conditions and good business, and therefore reacted very favorably; lumbermen saw the possibility of government control of the lumber supply and were not so favorable; owners of power stock thought it would ruin the country along with their stock; and applicants for jobs or government employees were conveniently favorable.

Julius Krug, who later was to serve as chairman of the War Production Board and Secretary of the Interior under President Roosevelt, worked with the TVA for three years beginning in 1938. He went down from Kentucky, where he was with the state utility commission, to Knoxville. "When I arrived I was given the title of Chief Power Planning Engineer," said Krug.

This is interesting in this respect if I can divert for a moment. I arrived after agreeing to consider this job on a Monday morning on the railroad from Lexington.

This Monday morning it was drizzling half soot and half rain. I got off the train. It was still dark about 5:30 in the morning. I couldn't get a cab or anything. I finally walked from the station over to the Farragut Hotel. I thought, "Oh, my God, how can anybody live and work in this town?" I found that they didn't have room for me until later when someone checked out. My date with Mr. Lilienthal was for nine o'clock. So they gave me a place to clean up and shave, and

113

Badly eroded land in the Tennessee Valley 45 years ago.

A pastoral scene in East Tennessee once eroded by rains and lack of crop rotation. Most such farms now use TVA electricity.

A house in the model town of Norris.

An "all-electric" home in the Tennessee Valley.

The many lakes of TVA receive an average of 45 million recreation visits a year, a good proportion of them made by fishermen and women.

Typical sailboat scene on a TVA lake.

Water skiing has proved popular on TVA lakes.

New "Twin Towers" headquarters of the Tennessee Valley Authority in Knoxville.

I went out. It was still this miserable drizzle. I went down to a drugstore on the corner there and got some breakfast.

All during this time I was building up a definite opinion that I would *not* work with TVA. Any outfit that would pick a place like this for headquarters was just out. So I finally got to the meeting at nine o'clock, and I told Lilienthal that I was sorry that I had caused TVA this expense and him the inconvenience, but the job was out. If you'll let him, he can be a pretty persuasive guy. He said, "Oh, now, wait a minute. Before you do that, why don't you consider taking a look around at what we are doing down here?" I said, "What, in this rain?" "Maybe it will clear up by noon," he said, "and we have an airplane out at the airport and I will have a couple of our men show you around and what TVA is doing. Not just in the power, but in other things. If you can spend a week here and let us take you around and show you, then you can decide how to accept your judgment.' "

So, he was right. It cleared up about eleven o'clock and we took off in this old, single-engine Bilanca that TVA owned in those days. We flew down over Chickamauga Dam, which was under construction then, and down to Muscle Shoals and stopped and saw the fertilizer works, and then on over to Memphis to see the prospects of that tremendous metropolis that was not served by TVA, but one that TVA contracted, then back through Nashville and over the countryside. I was impressed by a number of things; I think first by the people that I met working with TVA. They were guys that were certain. They were doing a real job. They were not just working for a salary, but were accomplishing something.

Krug took the job. On April 25, 1939, President Roosevelt wrote to H. A. Morgan: "Here is one of the rare instances in which I assume the powers of a dictator. Whether you like it or not, I am sending your name to the Senate for appointment for a new term, which will include of course the Chairmanship of the Tennessee Valley Authority."

Morgan accepted. Understandably, the first TVA annual report to be issued after he became chairman contained much more about fertilizer than its predecessors.

H. A. Morgan spoke before the American Society of Agricultural Engineers in Knoxville on June 23, 1941. In his comparatively new position as chairman of the TVA he expressed himself along general as well as agricultural lines. Said he:

Power is no longer the exclusive luxury of urban America. You can see for yourselves—transmission lines riding on thousands of sturdy towers into 100,000 rural homes throughout this Valley. In the homes, on the farms, here and elsewhere in the United States, diffused power is rounding out a cycle of history that began with the perfection of the steam engine more than a century ago.

Louis Bromfield admired the agricultural director. Perhaps it was farming the two had in common or prophecy or both. "Dr. Morgan admonishes us," observed Bromfield in regard to the conserving of energy,

> to use these exhaustibles carefully, to make them last longer, with waterpower and with energy from plants, but to remember that today's plants cannot supply the quantities of energy consumed in coal and oil. We burn these fuels far too fast. It took plants millions of years to create them; millions of years will be necessary for their recreation. I said Dr. Morgan is a teacher. He teaches these things to his Sunday school class; he lectures visiting industrial, agricultural, and political leaders; and they listen to him as to a prophet—which I think he is—an earthy prophet. It is his interpretation of the highest stewardship. His viewpoint represents long-time, worldwide fundamentals in conservation. His key to conservation admonishes that we see to it that nature has the 5 percent of minerals she needs to get the 95 percent of energy. "Of the 92 known chemical elements, only some 15 to 20 go into life," he pointed out. "These are nitrogen and carbon of the air; hydrogen and oxygen of water; and phosphorus, calcium, potassium, magnesium, sulfur, iron and a number of other minerals of the soil."

In a letter of May 4, 1948, to H. A. Morgan, President Harry Truman stated:

> The regret with which all thoughtful men approach retirement should be tempered in your case by the consideration that you have richly earned the right to a little leisure. . . . Your contributions as a farseeing pioneer in a great public enterprise and as a capable administrator will be long remembered in the annals of TVA. For all this you have earned the thanks of the American people whose interest and welfare you have always safeguarded.

Lilienthal, who became chairman of the TVA board in 1941, soon afterward had a little war of his own. U.S. Senator Kenneth D. McKellar of Tennessee was a powerful member of Congress and highly influential in getting appropriations bills through or blocking them. He had been disappointed and rebuffed a number of times when he had tried to obtain TVA employment for his political friends. Now he wanted a dam built by the Authority in upper East Tennessee. Lilienthal and the board did not agree with him. Whereupon the Senator attacked the TVA officials, and in the Senate he tried hard to thwart their progress. "He has taken this as a direct assault upon his Senatorial prerogative and has replied in the way that so often occurs in Congress, namely, a violent unmitigated attack on the administrator who offends," the Board noted. "He happens to be one of the most violent and unrestrained of any, and also because of seniority, a man of great power and influence. He has declared that there will be no appropriations for TVA and no more dams unless we accede."

Lilienthal and his colleagues felt that this was an attack upon the independence and integrity of the TVA itself. They continued to resist McKellar and, somewhat to their pleasant surprise, they won out.

The conflict between the TVA and Senator McKellar was one of the most bitter in the history of the Authority. Here was the senior Senator from Tennessee and ranking Democratic member of the Senate Appropriations Committee, one of the most powerful men in Washington; and ironically, he was fighting the biggest federal organization that had ever been located, with his help, too, in his home state. He was determined that Douglas Dam should not be built. The TVA was equally determined to defend its "adherence to the inflexible standard of nonpolitical engineering."

The TVA said that the dam was necessary if the power was to be produced which other agencies said was required to meet war production schedules. Four other dams as substitutes were proposed by Senator McKellar: two Army Corps of Engineers dams on the Cumberland River and one each on the South Holston and Watauga rivers to be built by the TVA. Its engineers replied that the others would take too long to build and produce too little power. Only the Douglas Dam, they said, could be built in time to meet the schedule. President Roosevelt intervened on the side of the TVA, and Senator McKellar lost.

But this was a loss which the venerable Senator never forgot in the six years in which he remained in the Senate. From then on he fought the Authority tooth and nail. He tried to get legislation passed to force the TVA to return all its power earnings to the national Treasury, funds which TVA had used to defray the costs of operation and maintenance. Another proposed McKellar amendment to the TVA Act would have required Senate confirmation of every TVA employee making more than $4,500 a year.

In a book, *The Tennessee Valley Authority* by Marguerite Owen (for 33 years TVA's Washington representative), a moderate view is taken of the situation. She did believe that the Senator wanted to exercise more control over the Authority, but "there is no reason to believe that Senator McKellar wanted to destroy the TVA power system or to injure the agency as a whole, although that would have been the effect of his amendments," Miss Owen said. "As ranking member and later chairman of the Senate Appropriations Committee, he was doubtless certain that he could make sure that adequate funds would always be provided, and apparently he expected to hold his seat forever.''

Larger battles were looming for this historic region. Here the Indians had lived and fought among themselves. Here were fought some significant battles of the American Revolution. The greatest military conflicts took place here in the ''Civil War Between the States.'' From Virginia to Mississippi major battles raged which were to influence greatly the outcome of the conflict. East Tennessee was an anomoly in this war. From this section of mountains and valleys, members of the same family often took different sides of the conflict, there being few slaves here. Brother fought against brother, and East Tennessee furnished more soldiers for the Union than for the Confederate army. Tennessee became known as ''The Volunteer State.'' Its McMinn County claimed that in World War I it furnished more volunteers per capita for the American Army than any other county in the United States.

It has already been pointed out that the chemical plant at Muscle Shoals was constructed during World War I and was later taken over by the TVA. The chemical plant became a large-scale laboratory and center for the development of fertilizer. With the advent of World War II, it was necessary for this center, so to speak, to beat its plowshares into swords. The TVA facilities manufactured chemicals and munitions for the armed forces.

In fact, the Tennessee Valley seemed singularly quiet on the eve of the great war. R. L. Duffus recalled it well: He wrote: ''One observer who visited the site more than a decade ago remembers the peaceful charm of the scene: the quiet cabin up the draw on the right bank, the unmarred wooded slopes, the green meadows, the cove and beach, and the dirt road that came out to them. Now, after the fury of construction, everything is peaceful again, with the peace of quiet machinery, of controlled power, of the pure green water below the dam, always passing and always there. The maze of wires in the yard beside the powerhouse hums gently, like an aeolian harp in the wind.''

Although the valley was perhaps better prepared for the war than most places, like other places, it did not have the exuberance that was shown in 1917. For here, as over the world, had come a repugnance for war. Men already had been leaving for military service since the Selective Service Act of 1940. Soldiers in uniform from training camps were seen on the streets of the cities. At Fort Oglethorpe, Georgia, near Chattanooga, a transformation took place. Soldiers with their traditional sabers and spurs, who had for so long ridden their agile horses into the fray when wars came, now dismounted and trained for modern mechanized warfare. Incidentally, this historic military post was to become first an induction center and later a training ground for the Women's Army Auxiliary Corps. WACS in neat uniforms were seen so much on the streets of Chattanooga that one civilian remarked, "Well, the women are running the war."

In 1940 the TVA concentrated on building for defense purposes to meet the increasing demand for electric power. The program of construction which was outlined in the 1936 report was extended to include the building of several tributary dams. Among these were the Chatuge, Nottely, Ocoee No. 3, and Appalachia dams. These were completed in record time for the war effort. By the time of Pearl Harbor, the Tennessee Valley was still faced with an anticipated shortage, despite the fact that its power capacity had been doubled in eight years. Already needing a source of steady power production in order to offset the seasonal fluctuation of the river system, the Authority decided to build a steam-generating plant near the Watts Bar Dam in East Tennessee. Such measures doubled the power capacity of the TVA by the end of the war, one-fifth of it coming from coal and steam.

The Oak Ridge project necessitated a third emergency program which included a dam at Fontana on the Little Tennessee and Douglas Dam on the French Broad River. While these dams were being completed, the then-available 6-foot channel was put into use as an artery of supply for goods shipped between the South and the upper Mississippi Valley, the industrial centers on the Great Lakes, and the ports on the Gulf Coast by way of the Ohio and Mississippi rivers. Seven months after Pearl Harbor the TVA was simultaneously constructing nine dams and a steam plant.

On Labor Day, 1940, President Roosevelt journeyed to Chattanooga to dedicate a new dam. Over a national radio network the President proclaimed, "This Chickamauga Dam, the sixth in the series of mammoth structures built by the Tennessee Valley Authority for the people of the United States, is helping to give all of us human control of the watershed of the Tennessee River in order that it may serve in full the purpose of men."

Lilienthal noted that one of the early needs of the Army was a staggering amount of elemental phosphorus for chemical warfare. At Muscle Shoals the electric furnace method of providing this phosphorus had already been well developed. Plants there supplied 60 percent of this substance used by the armed forces for such things as tracer bullets, incendiary bombs, and smoke screens. The TVA also contributed thousands of tons of calcium carbide for the synthetic rubber program as well as fertilizer materials for the domestic food supply.

Meantime, the regular work of the TVA went on until the war intensified. Up on the picturesque bank of the Little Tennessee River a century-old Methodist church stood in the little town of Louisville. The Fort Loudoun Dam Reservoir was to flood the small community, and the fine old church would become a victim. Where could it be moved? Building materials were very scarce in wartime. Accordingly, the young minister and his congregation went to the TVA and asked assistance in getting materials from the War Production Board to build a new church. The TVA interceded and even helped in planning the new building. The handmade bricks from the old church were carefully saved, cleaned, and taken to the new location, where they were used to line the interior of the sanctuary. The pews of the old church were of solid cherry wood, the women of the congregation scrubbed and cleaned them, and they were placed in the new church. Now the bells of this little house of worship rang across a new countryside.

When the Japanese attacked Pearl Harbor on December 7, 1941, the TVA had 1 million kilowatts of power. This capacity was to double within three years, mainly because of the war effort. At the request of President Roosevelt and an alarmed Congress, the Authority embarked upon a construction program which was highly accelerated for the defense of the nation. Within five years the construction crews of the TVA were increased to over 40,000 in number. Plans were expanded to include the building of several tributary dams. The rate of building broke records which even their best engineers doubted could be set as the construction men worked around the clock.

On February 16, 1944, the port of Knoxville was opened with TVA and other government officials on hand. To mark the occasion more colorfully, the first commercial towboat reached Knoxville, having in its hold 70,000 bushels of wheat from St. Louis, part of another wartime necessity. A few months later the TVA Kentucky Dam lock was opened officially for navigation, and now in a vital time the Tennessee River could carry commercial cargo for virtually its entire length. Within a few days of this important event, Senator George W. Norris, the "Father of the TVA," died at the age of 83.

The Authority persistently enlarged its production of power until 75 percent of it was devoted to war uses. From 1940 to 1945 TVA power production trebled until it was producing "one-tenth of the power produced for war purposes by all the public and private power systems in the United States." This ultimate 12 billion kilowatt-hours of electricity per year was the largest production of any integrated power system in the country. One only has to stand inside the great power control room in Chattanooga, as I did, to gain an imaginatively futuristic idea of this gigantic grid of power outflowing.

The Tennessee Valley was a good supply base as well as a manufacturing area for the winning of World War II. Here among many other items are to be found iron, copper, manganese, and zinc. Nearly half of the aluminum produced in the United States is processed in the valley. Add to this explosives, rayon, sulphuric acid, methyl alcohol, and uniforms and other clothing and the impression begins to clear of how valuable was the war contribution. Control devices for planes, tanks, and warships were manufactured, along with aluminum sheets for airplanes. Thick steel plates for weapons, cargo ships, plates, rods, and bars for bombers and artillery shells were other quickly produced items.

Who worked in these wartime factories in the Valley? Some of the most patriotic people in the nation: men and women and young people who came from the hillsides and valleys and whose forebears had imbued in them the lasting idea that it was honorable, necessary, and desirable to fight for one's country. Some of them drove from their homes, as a cousin of mine did, as far as 50 miles each way to work. In the tradition of the valley, women did the delicate work on small things, filling shells and wiring planes. But a few drove trucks and handled other heavy equipment. It was a far cry from the simple work of the farm, but these hearty folks were able to meet the challenge. War-protestors were looked upon simply as traitors.

The good thing about the war effort of the Tennessee Valley was that it was lasting. Capacity was increased, but it was to carry over into peacetime. War clouds moved across the peaceful valley, but they were not to stay. Yet for awhile, it seemed so. In the cities and training camps were thousands of soldiers in uniforms. In solitary space were Axis prisoners safely behind barbed wire. The dams and reservoirs were watched over by Coast Guard personnel. And going on and on over hill and vale were the endless power lines stretching, it seemed, to infinite horizons.

That heroes are not all in uniform was evidenced by the fact that leaders in the TVA movement, although outside the organization itself, helped immensely in the progress. Some of them have gone unsung; others have been praised, but sometimes only by local historians. For example, the Chickamauga Dam near Chattanooga came to fruition just in time to take part in World War II. Fred Hixon, a local journalist, paid tribute to the men mainly responsible for this dam as follows: "The Chickamauga Dam and the beautiful lake it impounds did not just happen. It represents years of dreaming and planning. It is the realization of untiring human effort. Materially, it is a barrier of concrete, steel, stone and earth thrown across an important inland stream, harnessing a river to produce electrical energy, improving navigation and providing means of controlling disastrous floods. But more than that it is a monument to the men who conceived it, to those who paved the way for its construction and to its builders."

He listed the late outstanding Chattanooga civic leader H. P. Colvard as the one who kindled the spark which started the drive by some local citizens to place the Chickamauga Dam in the TVA program. Colvard aroused the interest of the prominent county judge Will Cummings, who got the drive started. In urging through Congress the legislation to build the dam, Judge Cummings had the support of President Roosevelt, Senator Norris, and Tennessee Senators Nathan L. Bachman and Kenneth D. McKellar, as well as the local Congressmen, Sam D. McReynolds, later, James B. Frazier, Jr., assisted by Chairman L. J. Wilhoite of the Electric Power Board of Chattanooga.

Two other dams which were fortunately completed during this period were the Cherokee Dam on the Holston River, 40 miles above Knoxville, and the Fontana Dam on the Little Tennessee River. Although the Cherokee Dam ordinarily would have taken much longer to build, it was hurried through in 16 months and began its operations just two days before Pearl Harbor. When it is realized that this dam, in the pictorial Tennessee countryside, is 6,750 feet long and 175 feet high, with a generating capacity of 120,000 kilowatts, and built at a cost of $36,300,000, it will be seen that this was a notable achievement.

The Fontana Dam has been called "the most dramatic of all TVA dams and the highest dam in the United States east of the Rocky Mountains." It is 480 feet high and cost twice as much to build as the Cherokee Dam. This dam was started and completed during a severe wartime shortage of labor, materials, and time. A beautiful structure, the Fontana Dam today is visited by many tourists.

Maps and Surveys Branch

A dynamic part of the TVA participation in World War II was its Maps and Surveys Branch. The branch was already established, but the war brought it into its fullest significance. Soon after the TVA was organized, it was concluded that engineering surveys were largely dependent upon the availability of accurate maps in order to plan the physical and economic expansion of the project.

In order to cover properly the 40,000 square miles of TVA territory, several mapping offices were set up in strategically located cities and towns. Chattanooga was selected as the best location for the central offices of the Maps and Surveys Branch. This city is logically placed in respect to the drainage basin of the Tennessee River and the system of dams and reservoirs as well as near the edge of the seven states touched by the watershed. The central branch had responsibility for the regional mapping program, river improvement work, land acquisition and disposition, and even the relocation of cemeteries.

At first the mapping branch was not large, having only some 40 experts who proved to be especially dedicated to their work. Little could they realize that within ten years they would be doing war mapping of a million square miles from the Far East to Western Europe. Their number grew by 1943 to 860 people, and a special building was required to house the branch's new military activities. Of course World War II did not bring its combat zones to Chattanooga, but aerial photography did, particularly that of enemy-held terrain. The finished maps were used for a variety of purposes, ranging from strategic planning to artillery fire control.

During the first year of the war, the assignments of the Maps and Surveys Branch were confined to mapping within the continental United States. But after the African invasion, the collapse of Italy, and the Normandy landings, business picked up for the branch. Not only were new personnel necessary, including many women who still work there, but more design, research, drafting, photography, and reproduction work were required. Cooperation was set up with the official mapping agency of Great Britain. It and the TVA undertook the mapping of certain designated areas of the world. The first bomber raids of the war brought valuable aerial photography for mapping purposes. Speed as well as accuracy were required.

For example, on Thursday, September 9, 1943, at 11:30 A.M., an urgent request was received by the TVA mapping branch to furnish the Army with five copies of maps of an area in southern France. The deadline was Saturday morning. These maps were to be prepared from existing maps, but several details had to be added: bar scales, series numbers, sheet numbers, sheet names, and a grid system. Photographic processes were used to make the deadline. The job was finished by Friday night. The copies were immediately flown to Washington, D.C., where an Army Transport Command plane was waiting. By Sunday morning copies of the maps were at the headquarters of

General Dwight Eisenhower in North Africa, ready to be used for military operations.

Showing what seemed to be a special verve for its work, members of the Maps and Survey Branch have extended their activities to include maps for selecting routes for interstate highways, neighborhood maps desired by local residents, and maps for hunters searching for a good spot. The navigation charts are prepared mainly for the use of pilots and commercial craft on the main river reservoirs. These are useful to visitors, in particular if they arc hunters or vacationers who wish to know about the local recreation with its boat docks, public parks, and wildlife management areas. Of timely interest, the branch is required to determine at least once a year how much coal is in the several piles at the TVA steam plants.

The Maps and Surveys Branch of the TVA can hardly be said to be the most modest of the Authority. According to one of its ebullient members, "Thanks to TVA the Tennessee Valley is probably the most complete, up-to-date and accurately mapped area in the world and copies of these maps are available to the public at the cost of printing."

In the midst of war there was broad interest in the possibility of new industry in the Tennessee Valley. An inquiry came from the Bowaters Paper Company in London, England, a firm with pulp and paper manufacturing facilities not only in that country but in Sweden, Norway, and Newfoundland. In 1944 a group of representatives from the English firm got in touch with the TVA. They had had inquiries from southern newspaper publishers in the United States asking about the prospects for a newsprint mill in their region. Nothing more was heard about this until 1951, after Bowaters had surveyed 33 other areas. Now it had found that the Tennessee Valley was the most likely one, especially since plentiful TVA power would be available.

Plans went forward rapidly. Over a thousand people would be employed at the plant and in the nearby pulpwood forests. The plant, to be located at Calhoun, Tennessee, would have an annual payroll of around $5 million and consume a thousand cords of pine every day, and the company would conduct a reforestation program.

In its issue of October 10, 1954, the *New York Times* reported: "the Bowaters Southern Paper Corporation dedicated its $60 million newsprint mill here (Calhoun, Tennessee) today in ceremonies attended by more than 450 newspaper publishers, paper industry representatives, state officials, and other persons. The mill is the largest of its kind to be built in the United States in more than a quarter-century. Its product is sold out through 1969."

An Individual Fatality

The war had its casualties and so did the TVA. One of these was George Fort Milton, nationally known Chattanoogan and ardent advocate of the Authority. Along with his notable achievements, he made many enemies. But biggest sacrifice of his career came as a result of his strenuous fight for the TVA.

Milton was the son of a prominent man who at one time was appointed U.S. Senator from Tennessee. In 1910 the elder Milton purchased *The Chattanooga News* and served as editor and president of the newspaper until his death in 1924. His son, George Fort Milton, Jr., then became head of the publication. Educated at the University of Virginia and with a flair for American history, the young Milton regarded graduate degrees as superfluous but held a high respect for education. He felt quite at home as head of the prosperous newspaper and enhanced his personal horizon by marrying Alice Warner of Chattanooga. She later became an ardent opponent of the Tellico Dam project.

Much of editor Milton's vibrant energy, however, was not confined to his journalistic work. For long hours in his comfortable home he devoted himself to writing books on American history, with emphasis on the Civil War. They soon became accepted by institutions of higher learning and remain so to some extent today, mainly as reference works.

The interest of George Fort Milton in national affairs was not only on paper. It was natural then that the editor develop a strong interest in the Tennessee Valley. In an article in the *Atlantic Monthly* he revealed that he had in his family files a letter from his great-grandfather, Tomlinson Fort, written to his wife in 1842 stating that "at last, I believe, the Government at Washington is going to do something about Muscle Shoals." Milton said that in regard to the TVA, it was better for people of the Valley "to eschew absolutists, and to consider the debate from the standpoint of the welfare and development of the region itself. And for us the question is not merely one of whether power shall be private or public; we are chiefly concerned about the economic development and social progress of the Valley and its people."

More than most Southerners, Milton expressed the failings of the South as well as its virtues. He believed that in the Tennessee Valley could be seen the whole Southern problem, which he described as "poverty in the midst of potential plenty. We have rivers running to waste that should be harnessed; we have rich resources needing development; we have people of low incomes with all the qualities needed to do skilled tasks and to build a civilization of high degree.'' He embraced the TVA enthusiastically and made this clear in the columns of his newspaper; so much so in fact that he incurred the hostile antagonism of local conservative leaders. This opposition was to show up sharply when the TVA acquired the Tennessee Electric Power Company in 1939, and the stockholders of the latter felt left out on a financial limb. George Fort Milton courageously stuck by his guns.

Milton did not accept the operations of the TVA in their entirety. He admitted that at the beginning some of the local people deeply resented the paternalistic attitude of top TVA officials. "These outlanders seemed to have come down here to reform an illiterate, godless lot who would not wear shoes," Milton commented. But he added that later less was heard of this zeal for reform. Now there appeared to be a growing understanding by the TVA of the good qualities of the people of the region.

In regard to the controversy over public and private power, Milton stated his position: "If I read aright the feelings of the general run of folks here in the Valley, it is about like this: First, they do not feel that the private power companies can ever do one-quarter as much for building the region as can the Federal Government through TVA, and therefore they want TVA to do the job. But in doing so they would like the TVA to take over the generation and transmission of electric power in the Valley, purchasing the area's existing private utilities' transmitting and generating facilities."

Editor Milton felt that he spoke for a number of others when he said the TVA should be more of a local enterprise. He pointed out his impression that most of the common labor was recruited in the valley area but charged that the TVA directors had filled the key posts with experts from almost everywhere in the country. He quickly added though, "We begin grudgingly to admit that they are pretty good fellows, even if some of them talk about a *crick* instead of a *creek*."

So active was George Fort Milton in behalf of the TVA that when A. E. Morgan was on his way out as chairman, it was rumored in Tennessee and Washington that Milton would succeed Morgan. This, however, did not come about. Instead the editor appeared to lose no opportunity to praise the TVA in newspaper and magazine articles as well as in numerous speeches before civic and educational organizations. He seemed to feel that he was a spokesman for the new South, telling one group that "the South has one-half of the farm population and one-fourth of the farm income in the United States. . . . Put another way, with one-third of the nation's children, the South must support them on one-sixth of the nation's income. Despite all this, the percentage of income given by the South for education is the highest of any section in the United States."

Milton was unable to conquer the growing opposition and boycott of his advertising by disgruntled stockholders of the Tennessee Power Company. (He did show some political foresight by being one of the first to encourage and sponsor a young Congressman by the name of Estes Kefauver.) And so it came about that misfortune descended like an avalanche upon George Fort Milton. In short, he lost his newspaper, and his mortgaged home and was divorced from his wife. In his last desperate efforts to save the newspaper, Milton appealed to personal friends around the nation for small loans to help tide him over. Allan Nevins, my former teacher at Columbia University, told me he sent Milton $100; David Lilienthal noted in his journal on New Year's Day of 1940 that Milton came and asked him to help out financially, explaining his dire and urgent needs. Reluctantly, Lilienthal turned him down. The unfortunate editor tried to start another newspaper in Chattanooga, but it did not succeed. He then worked for other publications and later for awhile with the U.S. government in Washington until his health failed. Within a few years he died.

Oak Ridge

The TVA has never been simply a regional or even a national institution. It was destined to play an international role, and this was most crucial in World War II. The tremendous production of TVA power helped defeat the Axis just as surely and effectively as if its great thrust had originated on the battlefields of Europe and Asia.

The most dramatic contribution was Oak Ridge. This activity did not begin in the Tennessee Valley. It started one day in the hot summer of 1942 when two generals met in Washington and launched what was called the Manhattan Engineer District, which was the official operational name of the atom bomb project. This highly important and later decisive part of the Allied war effort was located just west of Knoxville, Tennessee, because of the accessibility of the site to the matchless TVA electric power; its nearness to a dependable water source; its remoteness from the coast and therefore relative safety from air attack; its distance from large population and industrial centers; its spaciousness, which could accommodate four different plants all separated from each other by natural ridges to reduce explosion hazards; and its nearness to Knoxville, which had a large, noncritical labor supply.

The Oak Ridge locale had been a peaceful and simple community which the TVA had hitherto left mainly untouched. Now the inhabitants had to move out and many of them were angry. One reason was that the government officials would not explain why. In fact they were not allowed to. One old-timer came to the gates of the Oak Ridge plant and asked the guards what was being built. They answered that they did not know. The old farmer then said he had heard they were building a new Vatican for the Pope. When told by the guards to go on his way, he cocked his head and asked, "Well, if you don't know what is being built, how do you know it ain't a Vatican?"

Signs at the gate of the Oak Ridge plant said "Clinton Engineer Works." Soon a government-built city sprang up to house the workers. In two years Oak Ridge became Tennessee's fifth largest city, population 75,000. The entire area comprised 59,000 acres. One plant had three miles of wall surrounding 600 acres. Recruiting workers for the secret operation was no easy task. So many interviews were held with each worker and so many forms had to be filled out that a number of them quit before they got started. Each applicant had to give a detailed account of his activities for the past ten years.

The first residential dwellings within the compound were 300 units for the scientists, each with a wood-burning fireplace. These were located on an elevation which later became known as "snob hill." Thousands of trailers were parked within the outer limits of the area. Soon several smokestacks could be seen rising in the interior. By this time rumors in the communities around Oak Ridge ran wild. One was that a new rocket fuel was being made; another, that a secret, high-test synthetic gasoline was being refined; and another, that the whole project was devoted to the manufacture of silk stockings, Roosevelt campaign buttons, WAC face powder, and dehydrated water for overseas troops. The most elaborate and intriguing rumor was that they were making green paint to spread over the water so that a submarine attempting to surface would get sea-colored paint over its periscope and would continue to rise until it could be shot down by enemy antiaircraft guns! Local newspapers asked so frequently for information on the project that finally a Congressman announced from Washington, D.C., that a demolition range for planes and artillery was being built here. Some of the workers became so impatient at not knowing what they were working on that they quit, but the majority remained.

To a meeting of 5,000 foremen, Major General Leslie Groves, the Army officer in charge of the project, said: "You'll just have to take my word for it that this is a very important undertaking, the most important of your lives. All I can promise is that if this project succeeds—as I am certain it will—you will never have to be ashamed of the part you played."

An idea of the size of the plants can be gained by a brief description of two of them. The gaseous diffusion plant alone consists of 70 buildings, and its four-story main building has wings 1½ miles long. The electromagnetic plant contains 170 buildings and cost $400 million. At the time of the latter's construction, copper was so scarce that a half-billion dollars' worth of silver was borrowed from the Treasury for use as electric conductors—making it just about a billion-dollar building. Inside the plant were magnets 230 feet long with a pull so strong that it was hard for a human to walk past them because of the pull on the shoenails.

One thing which distinguished the whole operation was a lack of noise. An almost deathly quiet hung from the mystery-shrouded buildings. Men rode bicycles to get from one connected floor to another. At night the hundreds of busy buildings resembled long, giant boxes hugging the ground and honeycombed with holes of streaming light. There were 10,000 houses and apartments and dormitories with 13,000 rooms. The houses had been built at the rate of one every 30 minutes and rented for as low as $22 a month including TVA electricity and garbage collection. There were eight elementary schools and a junior high school, having in all 11,000 pupils.

Religion was a part of Oak Ridge from the start. In this fundamentalist region not many miles from Dayton, a unique institution sprang up. It was just a little chapel on a hill in the atom center, but in it 17 different religions worshiped. It was called the United Church and had no members; all of its communicants were "associate members," retaining their affiliation with churches back home.

For diversion, community services were created in the form of theaters, bowling alleys, nurseries, riding academies, a roller skating rink, an amusement park, dancing classes, a poolroom, an art school, and a junior band. There were all kinds of athletics; 25,000 persons played tennis at various times. With half the workers being native Tennesseans, the square dance flourished, and scarcely a week went by that did not include one or two hoedowns in the recreation halls.

Employment at Oak Ridge was uneven. This unique city was the only one in the country with no unemployed and no extreme wealth or poverty; nevertheless the wartime working conditions were monotonous. Because of the extreme secrecy, the workers could not see the results of their labors and consequently had nothing tangible in which they could take pride. Carload after carload of material rolled into Oak Ridge and then seemed to disappear. Much went in, but little came out.

Perhaps the most striking characteristic of this singular community was the effect of security measures upon the residents. One worker said that even those who talked in their sleep learned to keep their mouths shut so that their wives could not learn what was going on. Remarked he: "There was a time when, after coming home from work, I couldn't talk to my wife at all. I had an idea what the project was making but I couldn't tell her. We'd sit around the dinner table and the strain was terrible. A man could bust. Then we started quarreling. So we decided to have a baby."

On August 6, 1945, Oak Ridge reached its climax. The atom bomb was dropped on Hiroshima. President Harry Truman explained that the bomb had more power than 20,000 tons of TNT. He described it as "a harnessing of the basic power of the universe."

Empowered by the Tennessee Valley Authority, the people of Oak Ridge had fashioned a new age—the atomic age. The workers who had been pent up and confused for so long went around crazily shouting new words which they had not been allowed to use before: "We are making uranium here. Uranium-235!"

The *Oak Ridge Journal* ran a headline: "OAK RIDGE ATTACKS JAPAN." Signs which read "You Can Lick Japan" were taken down, and in their places were substituted others saying "You Hold the Key to World Peace." Oak Ridge people gathered in their chapel and prayed. The curtain of secrecy was partly withdrawn from Oak Ridge. Many of the workers made their way back to their former homes or elsewhere to jobs which promised more permanence. Within a matter of months the population of 75,000 dropped to less than half. Labor unions had previously agreed not to try to organize the Oak Ridge workers during wartime. Now the AFL-CIO moved in. On January 1, 1947, the Manhattan project was officially transferred to the newly formed Atomic Energy Commission. Functioning of the new commission was delayed because of the time spent in the Senate confirming David Lilienthal as chairman. His old adversaries, who differed with his viewpoint about public power, arose to confront him. In spite of this he was confirmed.

General Groves, a modest man, told me that "a generation of scientific achievement was compressed at Oak Ridge into three years." When the project began, he added, atomic energy development was at the stage where the automobile was at the beginning of this century. Three years later, it had progressed as far as has automotive science since 1900.

President Truman retained to a considerable extent the enthusiasm of his predecessor for the TVA. On October 10, 1945, Truman dedicated the huge Kentucky Dam before thousands of people gathered in its shadow. It had cost $115 million. Declaring that he had always been a strong supporter of the Authority, the President said, "Why has TVA succeeded so well? Why does it have the esteem of the people of this Valley and attract the attention of other regions of America and of the entire world? To me the answer is clear. TVA is just plain common sense hitched up to modern science and good management. And that's about all there is to it."

6. Shaping Up

As the 1930s wore on, the economic situation in the electric power business grew increasingly uncertain. Was the country headed toward public ownership of this industry as the New Deal indicated, or would these plans be struck down so that private power would reign again?

A possible remedy for this situation was the idea of a "power pool" brought forward by Alexander Sachs, former NRA and Lehman Corporation official. According to this plan, public and private electric power companies, instead of competing with each other wastefully, would pool their resources. This not only would help consumers but would furnish an outlet for the overproduction of electricity.

In the Tennessee Valley, where the plan was first to be tried, the TVA and Commonwealth and Southern Corporation instead of selling their power directly, would furnish it to a pool. This organization would then distribute the power to public and private agencies at a uniform price, something like the British system. It was estimated that this would lower the price of electricity by as much as one-fourth. Should the pool work well, it could substitute for the well-known yardstick.

This idea did not change the minds of the TVA officials who still believed that public power was the answer to the needs of the Tennessee Valley. Also, by this time (1936), the TVA was considering seriously the purchase of the Tennessee Electric Power Company. The TVA idea was to buy the company's generation and transmission facilities while the cities would purchase the distribution system. In an election year, this plan of compromise warmly appealed to FDR, although he did not clearly understand all of its technical aspects. It did seem a sensible thing to do. Wendell Willkie wrote Roosevelt that his company and the TVA were carrying on a needless warfare which he hoped could be eliminated. This concept was somewhat supported by Arthur Morgan. On the other hand, David Lilienthal was greatly disturbed about the prospects. He refused to make any definite promise until he had studied the idea of the pool carefully as well as its potential results.

Fontana Dam, North Carolina, the TVA's highest at 480 feet. Bordering the Great Smoky Mountains National Park, it is the tallest concrete dam east of the Rocky Mountains.

Fontana Dam at night.

As was his habit, Lilienthal obtained the opinions of his friends, Senators La Follette and Norris and Justice Frankfurter. There was some difference in their viewpoints, but generally it appeared desirable to approve the pooling plan, which Lilienthal did. He wanted to show up the selfish interest of the power companies and at the same time present the TVA in a favorable and reasonable light. The ideas of Arthur Morgan were another kettle of fish. He determined to support

Inside the Fontana Dam showing the widely-used TVA slogan, "Built for the People of the United States of America."

the idea and, instead of being passive in the board meetings, this time to fight vigorously. Perhaps he fought too vigorously. A TVA consultant remarked about a 22-page memorandum which Morgan had had prepared that "Dr. Morgan, throughout the memorandum, has well stated the position of the Commonwealth and Southern Corporation." It was also observed that the memorandum had been written with the assistance of George W. Hamilton, former chief engineer of Samuel Insull's Middle West utilities companies.

A conference was held on September 30, 1936, with six representatives of public power, five of private companies, and two men of neither. Roosevelt presided and in his tactful way tried to get the two sides together. But the meeting soon sank into a controversy between Willkie and Lilienthal over the fairness of the TVA yardstick and the usurpation of Commonwealth and Southern Corporation customers by the TVA. A delay was suggested, and this pleased FDR who was running for his second term. After Roosevelt's landslide victory over Landon, the liberal minds within his administration were more confident than ever about extending their ideas. Commonwealth and Southern Corporation was pictured as an arch enemy of the President, and its opposition to him in the election was held up as an example. Roosevelt was strongly advised to reject the power pool.

Soon after the reappointment of Lilienthal in May 1936, nineteen southern power companies brought a constitutional lawsuit against the TVA. Among these companies were five within the Commonwealth and Southern Corporation system. This suit was still pending when the pooling conferences were going on. The companies obtained from Federal Judge John J. Gore a strong injunction which stopped the TVA's expansion program. Lilienthal told Roosevelt that the injunction was a "breach of faith" with the government and a slap in the face for Roosevelt personally. Finally, after several months of consolidation, the power pool ceased to exist.

The long and tedious Congressional investigation of the TVA from May to December 1938 brought out vividly the issue of public versus private power. This was perhaps the most valuable result of the proceedings since both sides had an opportunity to air their differences before a national audience. With the Democratic Administration strongly entrenched, Wendell Willkie saw the handwriting on the wall. He offered to sell those parts of his southern subsidiaries threatened by the TVA. Yet in his proposals he included requirements that after such purchase the TVA must not engage in further competition. Lilienthal refused to accept this provision, but he knew as well as his antagonist, Willkie, that the purchase of the Tennessee Electric Power Company would be of mutual advantage. Such a transaction would save the capital of the investors in the power company and the TVA would have a much-needed market for its increasing power supply.

Lilienthal believed that the purchase price should be the legitimate cost of the properties, minus accrued depreciation. Willkie agreed but also referred to his properties to be purchased "as going concerns." This led to a lingering controversy and delays. Neither side would give in, but both issued strong press releases. While this stalemate was going on, Lilienthal became seriously ill with undulant fever caused by drinking unpasteurized milk. Being unable to continue, he turned the negotiations over to two of his assistants, Joseph Swidler and Julius Krug. These men, in their early thirties, carried on for their side exceedingly well. For awhile the deadlock continued, but both sides were anxious to consummate the deal and a compromise price of $78.6 million was decided upon. This permitted the payment of the outstanding bonded indebtedness of the company at face value and payment of the preferred stockholders at the face value of their shares and left about $7 million for the common stockholders. Under the circumstances, this was felt to be a fair deal.

It will be noted that the final price was in excess of the cost of the physical properties, less the TVA estimate of depreciation. The TVA did not pay for all of this. The share of the Authority in the total price was $44,949,400 which represented mainly hydroelectric and steam-electric generating plants and the company's transmission system. The share of the 33 municipalities and cooperative associations, chiefly for distribution properties, was $33,650,600.

In a dramatic ceremony in which the two main participants were not unconscious of its wide publicity, Lilienthal and Willkie formalized the transfer on August 15, 1939. The ceremony took place on a spacious floor of a New York bank, and Willkie accepted the government's check in the glare of newsreel cameras. Thanking Lilienthal for the large check, Willkie made his famous remark, "This is a lot of money for a couple of Indiana farmers to be kicking around."

Forestry

In 1939 the TVA published a forestry bulletin which covered an inventory for 18 of the 26 million acres of the valley. The data collected indicated that the drain of sawtimber was 1.10 times the rate of regrowth. It was pointed out that this condition necessitated adjustment among the wood-using industries if the employment was to be maintained and sufficient progress made in development of the forests. At this time the timber industry of the valley employed 15,000 workers with annual wages of $11 million. Related industry such as those manufacturing wood pulp, paper, and furniture doubled these figures. About half of the forest land in the valley was in farm woodlands, a third was in private industrial holdings, and the rest was under public management. Reforestation plans including kinds, mixtures, and spacing of trees were prepared by the TVA for its lands. The U.S. Park Service CCC camps had assisted in fire suppression, a little publicized part of the government activities in the region. In one year the TVA-CCC camps helped suppress 470 fires.

Millions of trees for erosion control continued to be planted by the TVA on its own and on private lands. In nut-cracking tests, commercial yields of kernels from improved varieties of black walnut trees were found to be twice as large as yields from common walnuts.

Woodland demonstrations were set up by the TVA in cooperation with state forestry services and county agents. In such demonstrations trained foresters helped the owner in determining the kind and quality of timber and its rate of growth and in marking the mature and defective trees for cutting. For example, a Claiborne County, Tennessee, farmer estimated that his 400-acre woodland contained about 2 million board-feet of timber. But before selling it, he consulted his county agent and, through him, became a woodland demonstrator. An inventory made by a TVA forester revealed that he had not 2 million but 3 million board-feet on his land, of which 1 million board-feet was ready for cutting.

Almost invariably the woodland demonstrations led to increased immediate return once an inventory had shown the amount and quality of timber available. A Monroe County, Tennessee, farmer requested $2,800 for the timber on 100 acres but received $5,800 when an inventory showed he had 800,000 board-feet on the wood lot, of which 500,000 board-feet were ready for cutting. In Houston County, Tennessee, a timber operator who had offered $1,400 for the timber of a farmer in a "boundary" sale eventually paid $3,000 for 169,000 board-feet of marked timber. A Franklin County, Tennessee, farmer received $3,500 for 435,000 board-feet at a public auction after his timber had been marked, and he still had 630,000 board-feet in his 152-acre woods to provide growth for future cutting.

The Fiscal Aspects

One of the most difficult things to understand about the TVA, at least for the layperson, is its fiscal aspect. TVA officials and the supporters of the organization claim that it is a good investment: a form of benevolent socialism. There is also another side.

The TVA claims that by purchasing reservoir lands and power installations and equipment, it has transferred much property from private to public ownership. This property owned by the federal government cannot be taxed by state and local governments. In order to compensate these smaller governments, the Authority is instructed to make to them annual contributions known as in-lieu-of-tax payments and to devise the formula by which the amount is determined. One-half of the sum arrived at in this manner is distributed among the states in the proportion that each serves as a source of the TVA's gross power revenues. The other half is distributed according to the location of TVA property associated with the production and distribution of power. The Authority pays directly to each county in the valley a sum equal to the ad valorem property taxes that the county formerly collected on the power property now held by the TVA. All payments made to counties are subtracted from the total of in-lieu payments otherwise due to the states.

County services, such as upkeep of roads and schools, are eliminated from reservoir areas when taxable property is withdrawn from the tax base. Since schools and other such properties are purchased by the TVA, the local authorities thus can build new facilities. The Authority cooperates in helping to improve such facilities. It therefore claims that this system is not only financially fair but in addition has added greatly to the welfare and happiness of thousands of residents of the Tennessee Valley.

On the other hand conservatives (even in the region itself), who apparently are sincere in their traditional and propertied viewpoint, still say that the TVA is a subterfuge for funneling taxpayers' money down a giant drain. Their chief criticism is that the TVA pays no income tax. This is true and, in a literal way, can be construed as a subsidy. Without attempting to make any magisterial judgment, it would appear that both sides have logical arguments. At the same time, the obvious benefits brought to the valley by the TVA tend to overshadow fiscal objections. As one observer put it, private agencies might have been able to bring similar innovations to this natural region, but for whatever reasons, they did *not*. Both Republicans and Democrats accept and enjoy the tangible fruits of the TVA.

In discussing the Tennessee Valley project, L. S. Kimble, writing in the *Journal of Land and Public Utility Economics* for November 1933, presented to some extent both sides of the power issue:

> The private power interests and those who desire to keep the government out of business have been instrumental, heretofore, in blocking public operation. They have continually contended that a government bureau could not operate as efficiently as private businesses with the incentive of individual profits. They have further contended that government in business is unfair competition and contrary to American practice; that government should confine its activity to controlling business practices, leaving to private interests the actual operation of business according to American traditions. However, it is thought by many that there is need for establishing standards of costs of construction and operation for the production and distribution of electric light and power.

Kimble added that it was demonstrable that many power companies were much overcapitalized and that the public was expected to pay returns on much watered stock in these valuations. He thought that the development of the Tennessee basin might be very beneficial to agriculture and that the TVA could offer possibilities of saving farmers a large sum annually if fertilizers could be furnished as cheaply as estimated.

Recreation

Some of the most shining results of the TVA program are those which have happened indirectly. Among these, recreation stands out. The main reason for this is that the Tennessee Valley is rich in recreation, especially through its lakes and mountains. Interspersed with the TVA development has been that of the Great Smoky Mountains National Park, another favorite project of Franklin D. Roosevelt. In the average summer, more visitors see this park than any other in the United States. Therefore the development of the recreation and tourist industry has assumed special significance in the region of the Tennessee Valley.

Unlike the days of my childhood, when the main roads of this region were muddy thoroughfares out of which tourists' cars were pulled for a price by designing farmers, the valley mainly has paved highways. At any rate, the principal recreational centers are now readily accessible by land, sea and air. Chambers of commerce flood the tourist with colorful literature about these natural wonders, and most of their statements are true.

One of the first realizations of the TVA was the scenic resources of the area. The Authority prepared a comprehensive report covering the opportunities for economic return from recreational development. It was found that the territory of the Authority by 1976 had 400 public access areas, 19 state parks, 91 local parks, and about 300 commercial recreation areas on TVA lakes offering sailing, boating, fishing, camping, and other opportunities for visitors. By that time over 65 million visitors had come to the lakes.

As time went on TVA studies were developed in great detail. For example, returns from tourist travel were evaluated and highway traffic was analyzed. Of course much of this relates to the use of TVA parks and reservoirs and visits to its dams and other facilities. It is the policy of the Authority to encourage the widest possible use by the general public of its recreational facilities. This is, incidentally, good public relations. However, the preference for such use is given to state, county, and local operations of the parks and other areas. Boat docks and fishing camps are usually run by commercial people.

Land Between the Lakes

As the Tennessee River nears the Ohio near Paducah, it broadens into a big lake formed by the Kentucky Dam of the TVA. Another river, the Cumberland, runs parallel to the Tennessee, and between the two streams lies a large section called Land Between the Lakes. A century ago this land was the location of large iron smelters. As the Kentucky Dam progressed, the TVA decided to make this isthmus into a recreation area. It was not long before the hardwood forest there was thinned to improve the life of the turkey, deer, beaver, bobcat, and imported buffalo which live there. A few eagles inhabit the place, and wild geese pause there on their way south.

The aim of the TVA in sponsoring the Land Between the Lakes, which is in driving distance of one-third of the population of the country, is to keep it in as natural a state as possible and at the same time offer comfortable facilities for visitors, particularly the young people who wish to know more about primitive nature. Bird watching is a natural pastime. One area is reserved for cross-country motorcyclists, although it is difficult to see why such a dangerous sport is encouraged. There is a camp education program for young people. A reproduced "Homeplace of 1850" has been constructed to show the contrast between domestic life then and now.

The TVA says that it has developed here "a vast cafeteria of outdoor recreation for the ever-increasing number of Americans who want to take the family to the great outdoors." The recreation area between these lakes is more than 170,000 acres. Primarily a place for campers, there are no motels, shopping centers, or service stations in the park proper. One has to drive about an hour to find these "modern inconveniences." Preparations have been made for at least 25,000 overnight campers.

Besides the facilities for fishing, there are some for swimming, hiking, picnicking, and limited hunting. There is a music camp where school bands and similar groups can stay and practice in the summer. The area was once known as Land Twixt the Rivers and in the 1930s was locally renowned for its moonshine activities. The "white lightning" even had a brand name. It was called Golden Pond moonshine.

Beaches around the bay are designated as such so that boats will not enter. The camps have attracted the interest of religious, civic, and fraternal organizations as well as educational groups. A special education center affords teachers an opportunity to study outdoor education methods. Facilities are available for showing films, holding classes, and performing laboratory experiments in outdoor education.

On June 14, 1963, President John F. Kennedy announced that TVA would have the mission of developing the Land Between the Lakes. Officially the project was launched in January 1964, immediately after President Lyndon B. Johnson signed the public works appropriations bill of 1964. It meant that "for the first time under Federal administration, all of the resources of an area of this size would be managed and cultivated to produce the most favorable possible environment for outdoor recreation." The southern boundary of the Land Between the Lakes is based on U.S. Highway 79 between Paris and Dover in northwestern Tennessee.

In later years other recreational facilities were added by the TVA. In eastern Tennessee a canoe shuttle service was started on the winding Hiwassee River. This service, which attracts a considerable number of users, has provided rafts and other transportation equipment for this scenic stream. A similar development is that on the Elk River in middle Tennessee. Included in the plans for this were overnight lodging facilities, marinas, shops, restaurants, public golf courses, parks, beaches, and hiking and riding trails.

In the Horseshoe Bend Recreation Area in North Alabama, a new water system was created which helped to stimulate leisure-time activities. Developments like these also took place in the Goat Island recreation section in northeastern Mississippi. Picnic tables, litter barrels, and electrical outlets were added. In such work the TVA has cooperated with state governments. Completed also were parks around Bryson City, North Carolina; Pikeville and Whitwell, Tennessee; Trenton, Georgia; and the Chatuge Shores Recreation Area in western North Carolina.

Dollars Fell on Alabama

More substantial than recreation were the changes made in the city of Decatur, Alabama. Here I found an eloquent-speaking advocate of the TVA, Barrett Shelton, whose comments about the effects of the Authority upon his community attracted even international attention. A visit with him in his attractive, modern office was like that of interviewing an official of the TVA, although he was publisher of the *Decatur Daily,* a thriving newspaper. Typical of many such publishers, Shelton was nourished on the conservative viewpoint.

In 1949 publisher Shelton was invited to speak to the United Nations

Scientific Conference in New York on the conservation and utilization
of resources. The statement he gave me was mainly included in his
speech to that organization on September 5 and was entitled "The
Decatur Story." Comprehensive in itself, it is as follows:

I am privileged to tell you the story of Decatur, Alabama, a town
that has come from "nothin' to somethin'" in fifteen years of a
working partnership between the Tennessee Valley Authority and
the people of my town. . . . In the beginning I opposed TVA. I didn't
know what it intended. I knew I wanted no government control of
my life, nor over the lives of my people. Throughout much of our
lives the progressive citizens of Decatur had tried to better conditions. And it appeared that no matter in what direction they turned,
the result was far from producing lasting good.

Then [came] 1933. Economic depression settled down on the
United States, more pronounced if possible in the Tennessee Valley
and in Decatur. The one major industry we had, which had kept
2,000 men at work, closed. This railroad shop gave way to the truck
and the bus and economic conditions. Another industry, which in
earlier years we had brought from New England with considerable
subsidy in money, went bankrupt. A third industry, manufacturer of
full-fashioned hosiery, went to the wall from poor management and
bad times. Seven of eight banks in our county closed.

Our farm situation [was that] we had only one crop in the
Decatur area—cotton—and cotton was five cents a pound. Lands
were selling for taxes, the people were ill-housed, ill-clothed and out
of hope. So you can see that we were not interested in saving a dollar
or so on our power bill. That would solve little or nothing. We
needed jobs and opportunities for our people.

Into this dismal, perplexed economic setting one late midwinter
afternoon came David Lilienthal, then a member of the Board of
Directors of the Tennessee Valley Authority. Four of our citizens
who had long been hopeful of improving conditions generally met
him in conference. We were almost frankly hostile, for he represented to us another way of thought and another way of life. And our
conversation might be summarized in this fashion, "All right, you're
here, you were not invited, but you're here. You are in command,
now what are you going to do?" Dave leaned his chair back against
the wall and the twinkle of a smile came into his eyes, as he said
gently and firmly, "I'm not going to do anything. You're going to do
it."

He went on to tell us something we never knew before. He went
on to say that TVA would provide the tools of opportunity—flood
control, malaria control, navigation on the river, low cost power,
test-demonstration farming to show how our soils could be returned
to fertility, a fertility lost through land erosion, another wayward
child of a one-crop system. He told us the river would no longer
defeat man, but would become the servant of man. "What you do
with these tools," he said, "is up to you." Dave Lilienthal had

passed the task right back to us, right back to local control. He let us know that simple economics could be applied in the Tennessee Valley and that the faith, determination and sweat of the people would bring about the result we had eagerly sought for so many years. . . .

Our first step was to form our own Chamber of Commerce, formed at a time when most people didn't believe it could be done. There was very little money. So, with considerable struggle, we got together some cash and more pledges amounting to $3,000 for the budget the first year. A man who had lost all he had in the crash of one of the industries we had brought to Decatur with subsidy, became the first secretary at a salary of $100 a month. We then decided we were going to develop a cash market every day in the year for every farm product grown in the Decatur area. We were going to welcome industry, but not wait for it. We were going to develop our own farm processing plants. We decided a packing plant would be the first venture and persuaded the local ice company to put in packing plant facilities when there wasn't as much as one wagon load of hogs in our whole county. We are now producing our own livestock to meet the demands of this market.

We then turned to milk, formed a little corporation with paid-in capital of $15,000, telling every stockholder to forget his investment, that he would never receive any return from his money anyway. What we were trying to do was establish a payroll every two weeks for the farm families of our section. The first day that plant went into operation there was a total supply of 1,800 pounds of milk. Today the production of milk pouring into this one plant peaks at 60,000 pounds and we have just started in this agricultural industry. What happened to the stockholders? Well, they never failed to receive six percent annually on their money and about two months ago that little plant paid stockholders a 100 percent dividend.

Along about that time we got some help from the outside. Navigation on the Tennessee River made it possible. Here, you see, an exciting example of what can happen when a liability is changed into an asset. The Tennessee wasn't navigable before the creation of TVA, there was no opportunity for a successful flour mill operation. Low-cost power didn't attract Nebraska Consolidated Mills Company to establish the Alabama Flour Mills at Decatur. Navigable water did it, plus the possibilities that flour could be produced at a cheaper cost per barrel owing to save on freight. The impact of this industry on our section was tremendous. Farmers could grow grains because there was now a daily cash market. They could produce corn and wheat, and all the grains with assurance that they would sell their production. They could get cash for products for which previously there had been no market.

Tennessee Valley Fertilizer Cooperative, a fertilizer mixing plant serving ten counties, was established by the people. Later, when we saw the possibility of selling seed commercially, this same organization put up a modern and efficient seed-cleaning plant. An alfalfa-drying plant has been built, another way of keeping our pledge that markets would be established every day in the year for every product grown in the Decatur area. . . .

A resident of a nearby town came into Decatur with an idea that he could build a market for poultry. We agreed with him and encouraged him to go forward. Today that market though no more than three years old in our area is doing a $3,000,000 business. . . .

Let's stop here for an illustration of the value of malaria control. Did you ever have malaria? I have, the majority of my people have. Do you know what you want to do when you have malaria? Nothing. You want to prop your feet on your desk, or if you are not an office man, perhaps you'll take a day or two off from your job in industry or take out of the fields, just to get a rest. Malaria is restful— nonproductive. Soon after the creation of TVA a nationally known manufacturer of full-fashioned hosiery bought a bankrupt hosiery plant in our community. The new company introduced physical examinations for all employees and found that 35 percent of all employees had malaria. Ten years later, after the TVA malaria control program had been in action, the figure had dropped below one percent. Today, because malaria is completely controlled, this hosiery firm does not even require the malaria test in physical examination. And what happened to the people in that plant? Why, they out-produce the employees of three other plants of this same company. That's what defeating malaria has meant just in this one illustration of how government can be helpful to people by making it possible for them to help themselves.

Industry-wise, our people have not been sleeping. Here again the pledge has been kept to never again be dependent upon any one major industry, or to seek after big industry alone. By the year 1940, there were 61 firms manufacturing a product in Decatur, Alabama, employing 2,834 people in an annual payroll of $3,159,000. By 1944 the number of industries was 68, employing 6,908 people with an annual payroll of $12,927,000. In 1948 the number of firms making a product had reached 87 and employment, off from the war peak, was 5,204, but the annual payroll was $12,605,000, just a quarter of a million short of the payroll total during the war. You see, through the years we have been putting together the industrial picture in sound fashion. We had sought after diversity of industry rather than bigness. . . .

Just a moment on the electric picture. Have the benefits of electricity been made wide-spread? In 1939 there were 3800 customers in Decatur, in 1949 there are 6933. In 1938 they burned 12,000,000 KWH annually, now they burn 120,000,000 KWH annually. In 1938 the average sales price to the residential customer was 3 cents per KWH. Today it is just above 1 cent—and our Electric Department pays taxes. Well, the private company paid $7,500 annually in 1938. The municipal operation pays to the City of Decatur $28,000. Yet we have the second lowest residential rate in the U.S.

Or let's look at this figure to prove what's happening in Decatur, Alabama, in this partnership between the people and an independent corporation of the government. In 1933 there were 7,000 property owners listed on the tax books of our county; today there are 11,000. The assessed valuation has grown from $15,000,000 to $22,000,000. The population of our town has grown from 12,000 to 24,000, and yet the most significant change has been in the thinking of our people. We have come from the status of a well-nigh beaten citizenship, merely existing, to a hopeful, exuberant, smilingly confident people, secure in the belief that given the opportunities afforded through making the forces of nature the servant of man, and with intelligent determination and sound application of the principles of economics, we could rise to heights of good citizenship, limited only by our own imposed limitations. . . .

In the words of Dr. Sen, a visitor in Decatur from the Embassy of India, who viewed TVA as an improvement in an ever-improving democracy, or in my own way of answering visitors who come into our section of the Valley and ask, "Wouldn't this all have happened without a TVA?" And my answer to one and all is, "It didn't!"

A recent drive along the Tennessee River near Decatur convinces one that Shelton had more than chamber of commerce advocacy in his speech. More than 40 industries line the banks of the river, all of which have been built since the TVA came. According to a special edition of the *Decatur Daily*, May 18, 1971, total industrial investment on the river in seven states is $2 billion. One-fourth of that is around Decatur. Products manufactured or processed here extend from aluminum sheets to automotive products, from concrete pipe to corrugated boxes, from tire cord fabric to plastic film, from poultry to plywood, and from industrial chemicals to ice.

John D. Long, traffic manager of the Alabama Flour Mills, estimates more than 260 barges are towed here annually, carrying all types of grain. "If we did not have barge transportation, our feed to farmers would be higher and products in general would cost more. The availability of water transportation keeps down rail freight rates," he said. "What it boils down to is cheaper transportation."

United States Senator John Sparkman was quoted in the same 1971 edition of the newspaper: "The improved Tennessee River waterway system has saved freight shippers about $496 million since 1933. This represents the difference that shippers would have had to pay had they used other means of transportation rather than the TVA barge channel serving western Kentucky and Tennessee, northeast Mississippi and North Alabama. The $496 million saving is nearly four times as much as the $133 million in cumulative operating costs since 1933."

Of course this tremendous growth in Decatur's industrial development was accompanied by a corresponding extension of recreational facilities. One of these is Point Mallard, a large swimming and diving complex. This billion-dollar pool and beach facility has extensive camp grounds, resort hotels, and a golf course. Needless to say, after the rehabilitation of the community, the local people felt more like relaxing and celebrating here.

About 50 miles upstream from Decatur, another small Alabama city and farmer trading center, Guntersville, faced its own problem. TVA had begun building the Guntersville Dam ten miles downstream and the local people learned that the rising reservoir waters would cover much of their farmland. The 3,000 people in the town were pessimistic. At first they wanted the TVA to buy the entire town so they could take the money and move away.

Instead the TVA suggested that a local planning commission be formed to examine the problem and see what could be done. The new commission set to work on a scheme to make the new reservoir an asset rather than a liability. It saw possibilities because of the new navigation channel in the river of making the town a recreation center for a wide area. The dam was finished, and the reservoir encircled the town. A motorboat race was sponsored, and more than 50,000 people came. Today Guntersville is a busy river port and recreation center. Automobile barges have filled the town's docks with cars for distribution throughout the South. An elevator receives Midwest grain. Instead of withering away, the town has doubled in population.

Decatur, Alabama, is an example of the earlier progress of the TVA. When the Authority was established in 1933, the seven Tennessee Valley states contributed 3.4 percent of the total income tax collections in the United States. The proportion rose until in 1960 it was 6.7 percent, almost double what it was in 1933. The trend has continued. In other words, the seven states paid $15 billion more in income taxes than they would have paid had they stayed in the same relative position as in 1933. Obviously other factors are involved besides the TVA, but undoubtedly it has been a factor. Its fertilizer had been especially significant. As one North Carolina mountain preacher declared, ''From now on, I'm going to preach less hell-fire and brimstone, and more phosphate and limestone.''

7. Postwar Regrouping

Hardly had the TVA emerged from its extensive World War II activities when it was faced with a local adversary. Within five days in the valley area above Chattanooga, 4.2 inches of rain fell in January 1946. The Authority estimated that had the runoff from this rain been uncontrolled, it would have produced the fifth largest flood in the history of the city. Instead, storage dams on the tributary streams above Chattanooga were used to store the flood waters, and the main stream dams, especially Chickamauga seven miles upstream from the city, were used to store water and to regulate the flow. These operations held the flood to a crest of 35.7 feet as compared with the estimated crest of 45.8 feet which the TVA believed would have occurred in the absence of its dams.

Industries have shown increased interest in reducing wastes poured into the streams. One company installed a new kiln which burns 75 tons daily of sludge formerly discharged into the Holston River, and another machine burns 25 tons of black ash daily. Bristol, Tennessee-Virginia, approved bond issues of $3.5 million for sewage treatment. With the recent emphasis on ecological improvement, such measures have been extended elsewhere and others are in the planning process.

In its 1946 annual report the TVA restated its problems and objectives:

> In the Southeast, of which the Tennessee Valley is a part, the situation has been acute. The reasons for this lie in history, geology, biology, and climate. Historically, the Tennessee Valley region has been long settled, as regions in the United States go, and the effects of traditionally poor farming methods are more apparent. Geologically, it is a relatively old area whose soils have been subjected to ages of weathering with resultant leeching and erosion. Biological factors, like the presence of the cattle tick for many years, made livestock raising difficult and hazardous and prevented agriculture from turning from row crops of cotton, corn, and tobacco, which do not protect the soil on sloping fields. Under these circumstances, the climate, which is relatively mild and provides plentiful rainfall, often became a liability rather than an asset. With summer crops predomi-

151

nating, the soil was usually unprotected during the heavy winter rains either by vegetal cover or by freezing as in more northern regions. As a result, the land was subjected to erosion and to loss of the mineral elements of fertility. In the forested regions, which include more than half of the total Tennessee Valley area, cutting of timber proceeded along traditional lines, with practically no attention to the replenishment and preservation of growing stock through selective cutting or to the necessity of adequate protection against fire. As a result, the productivity of the soil declined, and the forest areas grew annually less commercial timber than was cut from them.

The most significant part of the joint agricultural program conducted by the TVA, the land-grant colleges aided by the U.S. Department of Agriculture and state governments and farm organizations, is the test-demonstration farm. Here new soil mineral materials, new agricultural practices, new machines, and new farming systems are tested by farmers on their own land. The results, according to the TVA—and this has been verified—are water- and soil-conserving farming practices, better crop and livestock production, and more profitable and happy farming in general.

The test-demonstrations were originally developed as a means of carrying out the Congressional direction that TVA arrange for large-scale testing of fertilizer materials to forward a program of agricultural development and watershed protection through improved fertilization. TVA was empowered to do this directly. It elected, instead, to seek the aid of organizations already in the field, and the test-demonstrations were incorporated in the already existing programs of the land-grant colleges and are carried on under their guidance.

These test-demonstration farms have produced a pattern which develops and utilizes the resources of the sun, water, air, soil, and crops. Affected are the buildings, fences, power, machinery, equipment, and livestock. This involves labor, skills, and knowledge as well as community resources such as marketing, distribution and processing facilities, churches, and schools. Of course many such improvements through other factors have come to the farm life in other parts of the country; in this region the TVA at least helped to hasten the trend.

Following a general trend in the South, the raising of livestock increased notably in the Tennessee Valley in the 1940s. During the war years farm buildings had generally depreciated because of the lack of labor and materials. The TVA explored plans for the building of improved farm structures more suitable to the local climate than the older ones. It was pointed out to the farmers that waste had been occurring for lack of storage facilities: that increased use of artificial heat and refrigeration called for more suitable farm buildings. In addition to studies about better barns and other outbuildings, investigations were made on such subjects as sweet potato curing houses, walk-in coolers, and grain and hay-drying equipment.

TVA fertilizers are required to be used only on pastures, meadows, and crops such as alfalfa, lespedeza, and small grains which conserve soil and water. The farmer must purchase his own lime, seeds, fencing, livestock, machinery, and other such materials. Usually his purchases of commercial fertilizer are greater than the amount supplied by the TVA. County soil improvement associations, with the advice of their county agent, select the test-demonstration farmers, making the selections on the basis of the type of soil, size and kind of farm, and willingness of the farmer to undertake the task.

The farmer keeps his own records of his operations for analysis by the extension service, the land-grant colleges, and the TVA; both his farm and records are available for study by other farmers and the public.

Power Production

The TVA had wished to continue the expansion of its electric power system. A heavy transmission and distribution construction program had been started, but this had been handicapped by the wartime shortage of materials. Even so the TVA was the only single integrated power system in the nation to produce more than 10 billion kilowatt-hours annually. The load had doubled during the war years. The Authority had interconnection and interchange agreements with all the principal utility systems serving the areas adjacent to the Tennessee Valley. In fiscal year 1947, for example, the average residential consumer in the TVA area had an annual power bill of $36.51. According to the Authority's estimate, the average annual bill for the nation was $43.49. The average domestic consumer in the Tennessee Valley region thus used 60 percent more electricity at home and paid 16 percent less for it than the average U.S. consumer. Yet the TVA customer's average income was still only 60 percent of the national average.

But there is a limit to how much water streams through the Tennessee Valley from its upper mountain sources. By 1949 the TVA realized that its water power was not enough. The nature of things to come was stated by the Authority in this announcement:

It will be necessary to install additional steam generating facilities. . . . The accepted practice, dictated by the economics of power supply, calls for the installation of steam generating equipment to carry a portion of the system load during the periods of low streamflow. Secondary power—that which is available only part of the time because of variations in streamflow—is thus converted to primary or firm power.

So in its budget request for fiscal year 1949 the TVA included funds to start construction of a steam-electric generating plant, with a maximum capacity of 375,000 kilowatts, at New Johnsonville in West Tennessee. The budget request was approved by President Truman. However, apparently because of its opposition to his liberal policies, Congress did not approve this initial appropriation. Later in the year, however, funds were forthcoming, and construction of the big steam plant was started. Within ten years all of its ten units were placed in service, and it now has a capacity of 1,450,200 kilowatts. The plant cost $196 million and consumes 13,266 tons of coal every 24 hours.

By June 30, 1949, there had been a total investment of $816 million in the TVA system. The allocation of the investment was as follows: 19 percent to navigation; 19 percent to flood control, and 62 percent to power. Such allocation was called into question by the General Accounting Office, so the Federal Power Commission was asked to make "an impartial and independent review of the principles and methods followed by the TVA in making the allocations." The conclusions of the FPC were as follows:

1. The alternative single-purpose projects are justifiable on a cost-benefit ratio basis, and the use of the estimated costs of such projects in arriving at the percentages for allocating joint costs is reasonable.
2. The principles and method employed by TVA in allocating the joint costs of its multiple-purpose projects are reasonably adapted for the purpose.
3. The allocation of the actual joint costs of the multiple-purpose projects to navigation, flood control, and power made by TVA in its report dated November 13, 1945, is reasonable and should be accepted for the purposes of the Tennessee Valley Authority Act.

The Authority was further gratified by a report from Haskins & Sells, New York public accountants, at about this same time. It was made to the Hoover Commission and stated: "The Authority is presently earning more than sufficient revenues from power operations to repay the investment in power facilities with interest."

Another report by a government agency during this period heartened the TVA. It was a report of the Joint Committee on Labor-Management Relations of the Congress of the United States. The report complimented the employee-management relations of the Authority and said that "management and labor in the great Tennessee Valley Authority projects have learned to work together to their mutual satisfaction and in the interest of the people of these United States."

For more than a dozen years the several thousand miles of major power transmission lines were patroled on foot. This was a laborious, expensive, and time-consuming process. A helpful mechanical step forward was taken when helicopters replaced the walking crews. These machines are each operated by two men, a pilot and observer. The latter is equipped with a dictating machine with which to record observations and with radio equipment to maintain close contact with headquarters. This newer method of patroling not only is less expensive but makes it possible to locate quickly places in the lines where repairs are needed. Emergencies are comparatively easily located, and line crews are soon on the job to handle the situation.

Soon after the Johnsonville steam plant was under construction, another major one was started, this one at Widows Creek in Northwest Alabama. The second one was to have even greater capacity than the first. Other steam plants were to follow and cause criticism of the TVA as competing more with private power companies. To this TVA replied that since 1949 the area's use of electricity has multiplied more than six times, while additional water-generated power potential was limited. It also was pointed out that private power systems in the Southeast have from 40 to 100 percent of their capacity in steam plants.

TVA Libraries

The TVA library has been compared to that of a large corporation. Here are found, in addition to the Authority's own publications, books, government documents, periodicals, pamphlets, catalogs, handbooks, and newspaper clippings. Stress has been placed on the various fields of engineering; but in addition there are many publications on the subjects of agriculture, forestry, industry, power, public utilities, navigation, transportation, sociology, education, and related topics. Other libraries which cooperate with the TVA are those of the area universities as well as the public libraries which are located near those of the Authority. Of course needed materials are obtained from other sources through interlibrary loan services. Inquiries to the librarians are often quite technical, such as questions on "asphalt grouting, contraction joints, efficiency of hand placed riprap, freezing of soil to prevent slides, rainfall data, thermal conductivity of mass concrete, and damage done by floods.''

The TVA Technical Library plays more than an ordinary role in the operations of the Authority. The way the library service has developed has had a human as well as documentary side. In the early spring of 1933, the University of North Carolina had called a conference of community and state leaders from throughout the South. The purpose of the meeting was to find methods of carrying out the necessary functions of government in the midst of the Great Depression. Present were heads of universities and government agencies, editors, industrial leaders, ministers, and librarians.

One of those attending the meeting was Miss Mary Utopia Rothrock, chief librarian of the Lawson McGhee Library of Knoxville. She came forward with a plan to extend the scope of library service by putting libraries on a regional basis, served from a central point. Meantime the TVA Act had been passed and Norris Dam was being built. The workmen and their families living in the village of Norris needed books. The TVA hired Miss Rothrock as a consultant, and her library in Knoxville had a branch in this new little town. Other such branches followed at other TVA construction projects.

''The camp library was very flexible,'' she recalled in an interview. ''The workmen went in and out, wore their hard hats, smoked if they wanted to, and wore their overalls if they wanted to. We felt that they got, and we wanted them to get, an idea that there was not a wall built between work and books.''

The librarian remembered an occasion at Huntsville, Alabama, in which a library program was getting started. She was present at a meeting of the local library board at which some city commissioners were present, and these men appeared cool and skeptical. When the meeting was over, one of the ladies on the board invited Miss Rothrock to go home with her and have a cup of coffee. She did, and the coffee turned out to be beer. Her hostess asked her what she really wanted. ''I don't want a thing in the world except to see the library service in Huntsville strengthened.'' The board member agreed, and the library plan was worked out. It is said that this is one of the strongest library areas in the state of Alabama today.

The outspoken librarian's interest was more general than that of the library. She mentioned that former Congresswoman Helen Gahagan Douglas of California, who was defeated for reelection by Richard Nixon, stated in one of her speeches:

The barefoot people of the South had to have shoes . . . this was aggravating because throughout the South there are individuals and there are areas of education, of leadership actual and potential, and of knowledgeability in general that are comparable to anywhere else in the country and you hate to have your whole region labeled as ignorant and barefooted. H. A. Morgan knew that. A. E. Morgan accepted the barefoot theory.

Some one asked the barber in the village of Fontana Dam if he used the new library there. He replied that he did and read a good deal of the time. The questioner, thinking he probably read simple Western or adventure stories, asked him what kind of book he last checked out. He replied that it was a book of poetry entitled *A Shropshire Lad* by Alfred Housman.

A vivid example of the effects of this regional library service was brought out in 1942 when the representatives of 11 surrounding counties met in Knoxville to discuss what to do about keeping the library system operating in the face of TVA's declining construction program. Mrs. Willis Shadow of nearby Meigs County spoke up and said,

We have six thousand people in Meigs County and no railroad, no telephones and no newspapers. The tax valuation is less than a million dollars. We have no industries and the TVA dams have taken the main part of our river bottom farms. The land that is left is mostly submarginal. The bookmobile and the grapevine are the only means of communication. If we lose the library bookmobile, how will we know what is going on in the world? What chance have we to improve standards of health or living except through reading? Talk about country people not reading! In Meigs County we read four thousand books a month. There is not a family in the county that the library doesn't touch!

In 1945 a representative of the Canadian Library Council visited the Tennessee Valley and with Miss Rothrock observed several of the multicounty regional libraries. Upon her return to her country, this representative reported:

These Tennessee Valley areas are as isolated as many Canadian communities, the mountain roads are as difficult as our mountain roads, bookmobile service is not always possible in the winter, the population appeared as individualistic as our own. In short, the library service of the areas of the seven states seemed to hold an augury of what could be attained in Canada toward complete library coverage under a union for library service of provincial and local authorities.

Education

A general characteristic of the TVA has been education. This applies not only to the internal functions of learning and training but to its effects on those outside of the organization. With a new approach to social experimentation in general, it is but natural that the Authority should have used novel ways in carrying out educational processes.

If the educational system of the TVA was somewhat unorthodox, so were some of its settings. At Wilson Dam the operation of the Muscle Shoals properties and the building of Wheeler Dam brought a large number of new people into the immediate area. The TVA established a temporary school to take care of the children of its workers. The only quarters available outside of an old school building was an officers' barracks constructed during World War I. This was to be the scene of a new type of school for the community. As principal Virginia James and teacher Grace Tietje described it, "Preparations for entrance into the old war barracks revealed untold possibilities for a school in which creative thinking was to be encouraged. In the building itself resided the first challenge to such thinking."

The barracks stood on a bleak hill on which there were no flowers, shrubs, or trees and little grass. The box-like structure had long, low windows and large doors leading to the porches and yard. The lengthy and rambling building "seemed to be waiting for someone to partici-pate in an adventure of rehabilitation, particularly if that rehabilitation were concerned with delightful plans for receiving a big family of boys and girls." The interior presented handicaps. But it did have huge, inviting fireplaces which suggested a number of picturesque and emo-tional features not usually found in the schoolroom. The teachers envisaged a satisfying combination of intellectual effort and a deep feeling for experiences such as possible pioneer cooking, popcorn parties, story hours, and relaxed children just watching the flames with all their changing colors.

Such big windows were indeed not customary in Alabama public schools. The local authorities felt that they would cause eyestrain. The school staff felt differently. "These were more than windows," they said. "They were a release from school traditions. They looked like windows in our homes. . . . We were not going to remain stationary for long periods of the day. The light would not disturb us; it would work with us."

Once used by "90-day wonder" officers headed for overseas "to make the world safe for democracy," the barracks were made up of three-room apartments. The partitions were removed to give sufficient space for 30 or 40 children in each group. Naturally the bathrooms were not of the multiple type usually clustered in conventional school buildings. But it was decided that a frank and open, more individual approach to the use of such facilities would make these ample. The lobby was divided by means of beaverboard partitions, and the porches were enclosed with wide windows. These allowed more light to come in and gave a pleasant view of wooded hillsides where rabbits, chickens, and other small animals moved at will.

Old carpenter tables were remodeled to hold painting supplies, lunch equipment, and rugs. Lockers were made out of orange crates, and clothes racks were fashioned from poles and planks. Shelves were added to the closets and boxes were brought in to hold supplies in the halls.

The school building at Wilson Dam was surrounded by wide stretches of meadow crossed by a creek and bordered by the pleasant river. Within a stone's throw was a wooded hill, a delightful place for eager, growing children. Teachers and pupils made the most of this attractive and inviting setting.

Inside the improvised schoolhouse, movable furniture enabled the children to use the space effectively. Much of the furniture was built by the children, parents, and teachers. Curtains at the windows, flower boxes, window gardens, pet and insect cages, vivariums, aquariums, and garden space gave breadth and depth to the youthful gaining of knowledge. Mops and brooms were hung at a low level so that they could be easily reached. Rugs for rest time were so arranged that the children could select their own rugs without help from an adult. All the furnishings were planned from the standpoint of attractive decoration as to color and arrangement. Through the use of materials such as newsprint, wrapping paper, alabastine paints, large brushes, easels, and clay, the children had an opportunity to express their own ideas and feelings.

Animals at school, at home, and in the fields and woods were prized possessions of the Wilson Dam school. Also utilized in the educational process were the post office, the industrial buildings, stores, farms, gardens, and orchards nearby. Visits to marble quarries, coal mines, and a pottery shed extended even more the practical experiences of the children.

Miss James now looks back upon the school with some wistfulness: "Our little TVA school was in session for seven years," she said. "We averaged 1,000 visitors per year not only from Alabama but also from other states and educational institutions. Supervisors of schools came and brought their teachers. It was not in all respects the 'open school' of today. We were fortunate enough to bring together an outstanding staff. . . . Our objectives included the maximum well-rounded development of the individual child, in learning, in self control, etc. We felt strongly *our responsibility to guide* the children in the most valuable directions.''

8. Taking Stock

Born out of World War I and expanded in World War II, the TVA in midcentury was to be involved in yet another war. The year 1950 saw the participation of the United States in the Korean conflict. The Atomic Energy Commission stepped up its production levels at Oak Ridge, Tennessee, and TVA power backed it up. The Authority completed arrangements by which some 25 utility systems from Pennsylvania to the southwest would supplement the power supply to Oak Ridge.

Industries around the country increased their national defense participation, including companies which already were operating in the TVA area. There was an urgent need for basic materials such as aluminum, chemicals, and ferroalloys. The TVA was committed to supply the Atomic Energy Commission with about as much electrical energy as is used in the City of New York. TVA plants were quickly converted from production of fertilizer to large-scale output of both phosphorus and ammonium nitrate munitions. As already noted, there was a trend toward steam-electric generating capacity in the TVA power production. This was just the reverse of what happened prior to and during World War II.

In the years 1940 to 1945, power capacity in the Tennessee Valley was increased from 1.2 million kilowatts to 2.5 million kilowatts. But at this time the valley was in an advantageous position for hydro development of the plentiful stream-flow. During this period the TVA completed ten dams with power installations. Now the Johnsonville steam plant was being geared up to generate around 6 billion kilowatt-hours a year or about four times as much as the entire TVA power service area used in 1933. In virtually every dam constructed, vacant stalls were provided for additional generating units. Such units were installed, for example, at Pickwick Landing, Guntersville, Chickamauga, Hales Bar, Fontana, Cherokee, and Douglas dams.

In addition to increasing its generating capacity, the Authority slowed its transmission system construction with top priority given to carrying additional power for the Oak Ridge atomic energy plant.

These transmission lines recalled the crucial time for the TVA, when President Roosevelt decided to allow the Authority to build its own transmission line system instead of allowing private power interests to purchase the power at the dams and then sell it. The latter development would have meant a short life for the Tennessee Valley Authority.

In order to facilitate interchange operations with other power systems to obtain energy for the AEC, the TVA replaced its load control system. This change helped the Authority to secure such power from other generating systems stretching from the Great Lakes to the Gulf of Mexico. In regard to traffic on the river, with stockpiling of coal beginning for the new TVA steam plants, water traffic began to have the importance it held in World War II. Regular bargeload shipments of sulphur began to move to a new chemical plant in East Tennessee. River traffic in automobiles and scrap metals went through the terminals at Knoxville and Chattanooga, Tennessee, and Guntersville and Decatur, Alabama.

In 1954, for the first time, steam power generation exceeded that of water in the TVA operations. There were three reasons for this. First, during World War II the power requirements of industries producing aluminum, chemicals, and other essential war materials, and of the initial atomic-energy installation at Oak Ridge, Tennessee, had dictated a speedup of TVA's long-range river development plans. Second, after the war, a vigorous resurgence of nondefense economy took place. Rural electrification spread rapidly over the region, domestic use climbed sharply, and new industry took root. Third, the Cold War and the Korean conflict dictated renewed development of power capacity for atomic energy production. A strategic research center for supersonic aircraft was established in the region. Critical metals and chemicals were being produced at new and expanded plants of private industry.

A little known activity of the TVA has been its assistance to the U.S. Army Chemical Corps in connection with its program to produce nerve gas for use in warfare. During the middle 1950s, TVA was furnishing personnel to operate and maintain the Phosphate Development Works under the control of the Chemical Corps. Actually the TVA engaged under conditions of wartime secrecy in the development of this nerve gas production project for a considerable time, starting in 1950. Its assistance was requested by the Chemical Corps. Such an element of warfare has been widely criticized, but at that time the United States was fearful of military involvement with some of the major world powers. In the year 1955 federal agencies used more than half the power sold by the TVA. It delivered almost 22 billion kilowatt-hours to the Atomic Energy Commission, the Arnold Engineering Development Center of the Army Air Force, and other federal agencies.

The Korean War accentuated the importance of chemicals for defense as well as agriculture. The TVA phosphate and nitrate plants were in continuous operation making fertilizers but also capable of munitions manufacture. The Authority was called upon to supply most of the elemental phosphorus and most ammonia for military use. As a result of its research, the TVA took out a number of patents in chemicals and other fields. These patents are made freely available to industry on a nonexclusive, royalty-free basis.

In describing this research and experimental production, a distributor of fertilizer in Mississippi expressed it in the following words:

> Farmers participating in the program have possibly been the best salesmen of the soil conservation and grassland farming idea. To the layman, the sight of a luxuriant, dark-green pasture with fat cattle grazing on it in January and February probably creates a passing interest in an unusual sight. To another farmer, however, who has not experimented with winter grasses, minerals, and nitrogen, another's success with a winter grazing system will sooner or later provoke an interest in the methods, the cost, and the expected returns from the investment. The idea, therefore, is conveyed by a successful cooperator better than a platoon of salesmen or a library of books.

Historically it has been estimated that a single large furnace of the type built by the TVA can produce in a year more phosphorus than was made in the whole country from 1896 to 1918. In World War I the United States was able to come up with only about 1,000 tons for use by the Armed Forces. In World War II the TVA supplied two-thirds of the 100,000 tons of elemental phosphorus used by the Armed Forces, and its technical knowledge helped much in enabling industry to produce another 40,000 tons. The TVA furnished all of the elemental phosphorus required by our forces in Korea.

So after 20 years the Tennessee Valley Authority could look back to marked achievements in several fields, regardless of whether or not this deserved criticism. This confidence was reflected in the annual reports:

> The sum total of progress has been the result of a combination of effort in which the people of the region have begun to make good use of the new tools provided for them through the development of Federal projects. One of the assets of the region today is a new confidence and a new knowledge of the strength of its own resources.

Furthermore, the TVA announced:

> Similarly, no bookkeeping can tabulate what it was worth to the
> nation, in the early days of World War II, to have in the Tennessee
> Valley the power resources, the plans for expansion, and an organi-
> zation capable of providing the extra power needed to increase
> production of aluminum for the great air armadas that helped to
> prepare and cover D-day on the coasts of France. The same assets of
> men, management and performance supplied power to Oak Ridge to
> produce the atomic bomb. If the atomic bomb saved lives of United
> States military forces by hastening the end of the war, the nation's
> ledgers of account must enter a substantial credit under the heading
> "TVA.". . . . In 1933, less than 300,000 consumers were served; in
> 1953, the distributors were serving 1,300,000 consumers, more than
> four times as many. A part of the increase is due to the greater popu-
> lation, which has increased 19 percent in the area served by TVA
> power between 1930 and 1950. A much larger part of the increase—in
> fact, more than half of it—has resulted from the extension of service
> to rural areas.

During the latter half of 1952 a severe drought occurred in the valley
and resulted in damaging forest fires. A million and a half acres were
burned over, causing $10 million in damage. For 20 days the fires
raged, crews of fighters were exhausted, and the smoke was so thick
that fire detection was almost impossible. TVA foresters pitched in and
acted as scouts and crew leaders, and construction and maintenance
forces joined the fire fighters until rain ended the emergency.

The University of the South at Sewanee, Tennessee, is situated on a
picturesque plateau virtually covered with trees. In the earlier days of
the TVA, this institution placed its 6,800 wooded acres under intensive
forest management and was the first forest landowner in the valley to
do so. Such action dated back to the influence of Gifford Pinchot, first
head of the U.S. Forest Service. In 1938 state foresters and those of the
TVA helped the school prepare a plan which has been a model for
instruction in forestry, fire prevention especially from brush burning,
timber production, recreation, and wildlife development.

At one time there was a proliferation of small timber-cutting operations in the valley known locally as "peckerwood sawmills." These
were usually unprofitable, and efforts were made by the TVA and local
government agencies to improve the operations. The log-grading system was devised to assist the sawmillers in selecting the best logs for
the highest profit. It was found, for example, that railroad cross ties
were usually more valuable themselves than the lumber that could be
sawed from them. Experiments were conducted in the preservation of
wood posts with oil soluble preservatives. Millions of such posts were

used in the valley. Thousands of gallons of molasses were produced at Muscle Shoals using a formula for wood hydrolysis developed by the United States Forest Products Laboratory. The molasses was used in stockfeeding tests by southern agricultural experiment stations.

A Foundation Evaluation

A study made by The Twentieth Century Fund foundation of New York on the relations between the federal government and the electric power industry included the TVA in a mainly impartial but liberal-leaning attitude. The study pointed out that private power interests had previously advocated low dams in the Tennessee Valley. However, it was shown that these would have provided little flood control or power. Congress did authorize on the other hand private or public interests to substitute high dams, but no southern institution, public or private, showed interest in this proposition. Therefore the study concluded the enterprise had to be done by the government.

The TVA's price policy was described as rates being determined with regard to cost at full utilization of capacity, with the rate schedule being simple. The Authority had funds to undergo an unprofitable period and thus could test the effect of rates and sales conditions upon both demand and costs. It did not have to wait as private systems do for consumption to increase before reducing prices. Operating data were available from experience at Wilson Dam and public plants such as those at Tacoma, Washington, and Ontario, Canada, and from a three-year study by the New York State Power Authority. Llewellyn Evans, chief consulting electrical engineer of the TVA, designed the original rates along with other experts. He was formerly manager of the Tacoma, Washington, municipal plant and was to become in time an adviser to the Chinese War Production Board. He knew that it was not easy to understand the TVA power rate structure—nor is it for the layperson today. As S. R. Finley, former general superintendent of the Electric Power Board of Chattanooga said, "It is probably one of the most widely discussed and yet perhaps least understood projects which our national government has carried out. Many yet do not understand or have a knowledge of the fundamental facts concerning it."

The Twentieth Century Fund study further found that: "There is no flood protection in a full reservoir. To draw down reservoirs in preparation for expected floods often requires water releases beyond the amount which can be passed through the turbines or is needed for power. Water thus released is wasted capital investment from the point of view of power generation. . . . The Authority has taken special pains to give the ratepayer, and not the taxpayer, the full benefits of economies in municipal operation. . . . The TVA may, however, have subsidized its distributors by performing unpaid services such as legal, accounting, engineering, and organizational assistance. . . . The TVA influence is difficult to measure statistically because there is no fixed time interval between causes and effect . . . we may conclude that previous rates were not only high but often unprofitably so. . . . The benefits of many government services are difficult to appraise, and even the cost of government activities cannot be measured by direct expenditures. . . . The intangible benefits of a multiple-purpose project may even outweigh the tangible benefits. Lives saved, health improved, opportunities open, and security from flood are impressive advantages."

The foregoing study also pointed out that one of the most suggestive developments in the relation between public power projects and private companies was the contract, signed in August 1941, by the TVA and the Aluminum Company of America. Under its terms the TVA agreed to operate the five-dam hydroelectric system of the company on the Little Tennessee River. The contract further provided for the TVA to acquire the Fontana Dam site which the company had owned for 30 years. This transaction was in contrast "to the rancor that characterized TVA's early relations with private companies." It was noted, too, that "public projects enjoy advantages over private industry, such as freedom from the risk of insolvency, or responsibility to stockholders for mistakes of management."

Dixon-Yates

Although he had not had any formal political party connection to speak of, General Dwight Eisenhower was adopted by the Republican Party and soon seemed to be embracing its more conservative viewpoint. During the time he had been president of Columbia University at midcentury, he was wooed by both parties and probably could have run on either ticket in 1952. His conservative point of view carried over into the TVA.

The Eisenhower Administration was economy-minded, was watching the national debt limit, and was trying to start balancing the budget. In his budget message to Congress of January 21, 1954, the President hinted that the Administration was concerned with the TVA, which Eisenhower had described as "creeping socialism." He denied, however, any intention to change or destroy the Authority. He noted that no appropriations were contained in the 1955 budget for new TVA power generating units. He added that in order to meet new demands for power "arrangements are being made to reduce" commitments of the TVA to the Atomic Energy Commission. In a letter to the *Knoxville News Sentinel,* the President had emphasized that he had no intent to abolish the TVA.

Prior to this, Congress had refused to appropriate a requested $100 million for a proposed TVA steam plant at Fulton, Tennessee. This plant was to provide a direct source of power for the Atomic Energy Commission (AEC) plant at Paducah, Kentucky, which would have relieved the burden on other TVA facilities. Concern also was felt by the Administration, which believed that the TVA was already big enough. It also was known that for years private companies had been wanting to supply power to the TVA.

At the request of the President, the Bureau of the Budget directed the AEC to explore the possibility of getting more such power from private utilities. This led to talks with Edgar H. Dixon, president of Middle South Utilities. In the meantime, Eugene A. Yates, head of The Southern Company, another utilities firm, approached the Bureau of the Budget and AEC with a plan similar to that of Dixon. It was suggested that these two talk with each other. Critics of this idea charged that the proposal was "hatched in the dark of the moon" and was a devious path to follow.

The contract was drawn up between the AEC and the Dixon-Yates combination. It was approved by the Bureau of the Budget, the General Accounting Office, the Federal Power Commission, and the Joint Congressional Committee on Atomic Energy. The difference between it and earlier contracts was that the earlier ones were for direct purchases of power by the AEC for use in its own plants while this one was to provide 600,000 kilowatts power to the TVA as replacement for power it was furnishing to the AEC. The Authority protested that it was being involved in a contract which it had no part in negotiating but which would entail important administrative and financial responsibilities. The TVA also contended that it could build the plant, furnish the power, and save the taxpayers its entire cost over 25 years.

A new organization, the Mississippi Valley Generating Company, was formed to build the plant near Memphis, Tennessee. A ceiling of $600,000 a year was placed on profits to meet the objections of the opponents of the project. This amount would have provided a return of about 11 percent on the $5.5 million investment by the Dixon-Yates organization. Its officials, however, asserted that this profit was not at all guaranteed—that the group was taking the risk that it might not realize any profit at all if the enterprise did not succeed.

Meantime the demand for power in the area did not slacken. The controversy over the Johnsonville steam plant became an almost straight party line fight in Congress. President Eisenhower was quoted as saying in a cabinet meeting, "If ever we could do it, before we leave here, I'd like to see us sell the whole thing, but I suppose we can't go that far." Senator Lister Hill who, as a young member of the House of Representatives, had cosponsored the TVA Bill along with Senator Norris, led a fight in the Republican-dominated Senate to restore the TVA nonpower developmental funds.

George D. Woods, chairman of the board of the First Boston Corporation, which was the largest underwriter of private utility bonds in the country, suggested making available one of his vice-presidents, Adolphe H. Wenzell, to make a study of the TVA power situation. This led to the Dixon-Yates scheme. Then it was revealed that this scheme was to be underwritten by the First Boston Corporation itself. The revelation created a sensation in the Tennessee Valley and in Democratic circles elsewhere. Tennessee's colorful Senator Estes Kefauver, whose coonskin capped campaign for President in 1952 initially was a threat to Eisenhower, fought hard for the TVA, as did his colleague Senator Albert Gore.

The immediate background of the Dixon-Yates affair was localized in Memphis, which sits serenely on the bank of the Mississippi River in the southwest corner of Tennessee. Its mayor was red-headed Ed Crump, "the last of the big city bosses." For years he had denounced the "power trust." In 1938, Memphis signed a contract to obtain power exclusively from the TVA. Across the broad river Hamilton Moses, articulate chairman of the board of the Arkansas Power and Light Company, did not view the TVA development with favor. However, he did lead the way in keeping his rural rates down, and when asked why he replied, "We have given a preference to these cooperatives. They might propose another TVA over in the Southwest."

He was not the only one, of course, who was worried about the growth of the TVA. The organization of private utilities, known as the National Association of Electric Companies, was afraid that the Johnsonville steam plant would set a precedent which would "justify unlimited future expansion of electric generating facilities by means of TVA steam plants." In an effort to refute this contention, Tennessee's young governor, Frank Clement, wrote President Eisenhower on February 5, 1954, charging that the Chief Executive's advisers were hostile to the TVA. Clement was a Democrat. His state of mind was not helped by the President's refusal to see a delegation from the TVA before its budget was cut.

As early as the following month, some of the associates of Adolphe Wenzell began to be concerned about his participation. One man, E. J. Donnelly, told Wenzell that he felt the latter was getting too involved in the situation. He told him, "You are from private business and there are a lot of things about government you don't understand, probably. He asked me what I meant. I said, you are liable to go to jail for the things you are doing here."

Although Gordon Clapp had little chance to be reappointed TVA chairman, he was not without supporters. States Rights Finley of Chattanooga called on President Eisenhower on March 16, 1954, carrying a petition with 40,000 names urging the reappointment of Clapp. Apparently this did not sway the President. Another blast came from Democratic Congressman Thomas Abernathy of Mississippi, who charged that "for twenty years the Old Guard in the Republican Party has been trying to destroy TVA. Only now have they found a formula and a tool. The tool, an unwitting one, is the Atomic Energy Commission."

On the other hand, Republican Senator William Jenner of Indiana observed that the TVA was a "great show-piece of the Socialist economy." Arkansas Senators and Congressmen were inclined to support Dixon-Yates. Congressman Charles Jonas of North Carolina stated, "I do not say this in any spirit of animosity toward TVA, but rather in the spirit of an indulgent parent that asks himself when his son reaches voting age, has a family, a booming business and a heavy bank account, but still comes home to ask for a handout: 'Won't that boy ever make his way by himself?' "

Senator Estes Kefauver, who had an uncanny sense of expedient publicity, saw in the Dixon-Yates case a vehicle not only to help the TVA but also his own rising political fortunes. He told his friend, Senator Paul Douglas of Illinois, that the Johnsonville steam plant was likely to burn large quantities of Illinois coal, something which he felt the proposed Dixon-Yates plant would not do. Another Southerner, Bobby Jones of Atlanta (the famous golfing companion of President Eisenhower), was discovered by Senator Wayne Morris of Oregon to be a director of the Southern Company. Morris told the Senate during the Dixon-Yates debate, "It raises a question in my mind if what we are doing is substituting the golf stick for the yardstick. The golf stick does not protect the public."

More humor was added to the situation when Lewis Strauss, chairman of the AEC, told the National Press Club that the Dixon-Yates contract "had the misfortune to occur in a year when issues were scarce. As my friend Roscoe Drummond said, they are grasping at Strauss."

Adding confusion to the situation, Chairman George Woods of the First Boston Corporation stated that his organization would not take a fee for its part in the Dixon-Yates matter. In a hearing, Senator Kefauver asked Woods whether the considerable publicity about the whole thing had anything to do with his firm's decision not to take a fee. The chairman replied, "Who is to say it didn't? I am not." The fact that this was the only time the First Boston Corporation had refused a fee for its services contributed more to the question. There is little doubt that President Eisenhower was honest, but apparently he was either misled or misinformed. At a press conference on June 29, 1955, he said that he had no knowledge that Wenzell had had anything to do with the Dixon-Yates contract. Questioned further about it, Eisenhower stated immediately after the press conference "that his information was neither wholly accurate nor quite complete." Late that afternoon Senator Kefauver exultantly sent the President information that between January and April of 1954 Wenzell had taken part in many conferences on Dixon-Yates. "It is clear, Mr. President," the Senator wrote, "that even at this late date you have not been fully and accurately informed."

In a later press conference on this same subject, President Eisenhower, even on the basis of correct information, still insisted that the role of Wenzell was a proper one. In regard to the disclosure of information about Dixon-Yates, Eisenhower admitted that official deeds (except those involving national security) when questionable, could properly be investigated by Congress. But as to conversations between an official and his advisers, or in respect to papers which expressed personal opinions, these (the Chief Executive believed) were not subject to investigation. It is the impression of Aaron Wildavsky in his *Dixon-Yates: A Study in Power Politics* that Eisenhower felt such an investigation could wreck the government—that no business could run on such a basis. Harking back to his old Army days, Ike added, "If any commander is going to get the free, unprejudiced opinion of his subordinates, he had better protect what they have to say to him on a confidential basis."

As the complicated evidence built up, even the President and his advisers became convinced that decisive action must be taken. On the morning of July 11, 1955, a delegation of Tennesseans called on

Senator Gore and then Attorney General Herbert Brownell. Also present at the meeting were General H. D. Vogel, new TVA chairman; Raymond Paty, TVA director; and Budget Director Rowland Hughes. Within an hour this group visited President Eisenhower in his office. In 45 minutes they came out and Brownell announced that the President had ordered the Dixon-Yates contract canceled.

The ill-starred company which made the contract was even refused termination costs by the government after its contract was canceled. A lawsuit by Dixon-Yates to obtain such costs was negated by the U.S. Supreme Court because of the Wenzell conflict of interests. The City of Memphis went ahead and built its own power-generating plant but came back into the TVA system in 1965. Despite this victory the TVA received no new power appropriations for four more years. This led to the necessity for the Authority to raise its own funds in the open market.

Gordon Clapp, who had resisted the Dixon-Yates plan, of course was not reappointed as chairman of the TVA board when his term expired. President Eisenhower had typically turned to his old Army circles in choosing the new chairman, Brigadier General Vogel of the Corps of Engineers. According to Frank E. Smith, later to become a member of the TVA board, "General Vogel, within the limitations imposed by the Eisenhower administration, turned out to be a good administrator for TVA, proud of TVA's achievements and increasingly conscious of the agency's role." This sentiment has been echoed by other officials of the organization.

9. On the Personnel Side

The record of the Tennessee Valley Authority in regard to its personnel and its relations between labor and management has been exceptional. This statement is not based upon internal opinion or subjective observation but upon the impressions of many who have come in contact with the organization. The TVA has achieved an esprit de corps which in some ways has set it apart as a decentralized and different government agency.

From its inception, the Authority has emphasized good human relations within and without. The Act which created it seemed to place unusual significance on harmonious interrelationship among all the people involved in the enterprise. No other New Deal agency held quite the combination of humans working happily together and producing novel, concrete results. Perhaps it was an impelling need for a camaraderie brought on by the acuteness of the Depression which seemed to say in effect "work together or else," or it may have been a fortunate selection of personnel. Whatever the case, members of the TVA from its beginning have presented in general a public pattern of uncommon cooperation.

Organized labor as well as management appeared to sense this new idea. As early as July 25, 1933, D. W. Tracy, president of the International Brotherhood of Electrical Workers, wrote to union Vice-President G. X. Barker in Birmingham, Alabama, as follows:

> The placing of the large Muscle Shoals jurisdiction in your charge is a fitting one. You are familiar with that area of the country, its labor problems and the labor men who make up the large army of skilled workers in the seven states affected. Your appointment also indicates the desire of the International Brotherhood of Electrical Workers to cooperate fully with the United States Government to make the Tennessee Valley project a complete success and an achievement worthy of the great national plan, of which it is a part, as visioned by President Roosevelt.

It was pointed out by the U.S. Bureau of Labor Statistics that in selecting personnel for major positions with the Authority, certain

172

experience and training were required, regardless of the locality from which the applicant came. Specialists in the field were asked to recommend people whom they considered qualified for the positions. The TVA Act itself states that "all members of the board shall be persons who profess a belief in the feasibility and wisdom of this act." Therefore, the Authority has expected to have men and women not only technically qualified by training and experience for the job at hand but who also hold similar beliefs and are social minded.

Examinations for the open positions were given by the Civil Service Commission at 138 examination centers. This was the first time an examination of this type had been used in the selection of laborers. It consisted of a mechanical aptitude test, a test of ability to follow printed instructions, and a test of ability to follow oral instructions. When it was first announced, the examination was viewed with skepticism by many persons concerned. But the results have proven satisfactory to the Authority and mainly to the employees.

Opportunity was offered for personnel to work in that particular position where they can be most effective. All avenues of promotion are open within the Authority. For example, the long-time chairman of the TVA, A. J. Wagner, rose from an early position as a low-paid engineer. Transfers, promotions, and demotions provide changes from one section to another or within sections. As new positions become available, the records of present employees are reviewed to see whether someone already employed is qualified to handle the new job. One construction superintendent remarked that if he needed a man to do a special job all he had to do was to stick his head out of the door and let it be known that such a job needed to be done.

Historians J. Leonard Raulston and James W. Livingood state:

On the local scene the immediate enthusiasm for the Authority waned because unemployed men, looking and hoping for jobs, could not understand the delays in hiring workers. But such essential matters as land acquisitions, geological surveys, and the production of engineering drawings took time and had to be given first priority. As a relief agency, TVA seemed at first to these people to be another bureaucratic "slow-poke." Others were provoked by the Utopian plans and speeches of some of the directors. When a sociological inventory was circulated, many people poked fun at TVA for inquiring about where they slept, what they owned, and how much they paid for things. As one writer put it, the survey "opens the door of every bedroom, bathroom, clothes closet, refrigerator, food storage place, kitchen, living room, stable, barn, chicken house, silo, garage, linen cabinet, china closet, coal bin and pig sty in the valley of the Tennessee."

A minor interruption in the generally smooth workings of the TVA personnel occurred on May 24, 1934. At that time James W. Cooper, land commissioner of the Authority, resigned in a huff.

Although it was not quite clear as to why he resigned, Cooper was evidently unhappy and the TVA directors were at least nonplussed. Cooper, who was called "General" because he had been assistant attorney general of the State of Tennessee, had been employed to purchase land for the Norris Dam reservoir. He apparently felt he was getting along all right in his job until he heard that he was being replaced by one John I. Snyder of New York. Cooper talked to David Lilienthal but received what he regarded as a somewhat polite brush-off. Thereupon he resigned despite offers of help by prominent friends and some assurances from the TVA board.

Governor A. H. Roberts of Tennessee wired H. A. Morgan in behalf of Cooper, who was a native Tennesseean, that it "would be very discouraging to Tennesseeans for this organization to be Yankeeized."

Cooper himself had previously appealed to Lilienthal, reminding him that he (Cooper) had been instructed by the director "to buy all the land in the Tennessee Valley from the Great Lakes to the Gulf." Added Cooper, "I know I did do a good job in the Great Smoky Mountain National Park, and I know I can do it here if I am given some authority and some discretion, but I can't do it if I have to run and ask somebody every time I turn around. I despise the disposition of people who run to the teacher and say, 'Johnny Jones is chawin' wax.' This disposition has been evidenced by certain people with whom I have had to deal."

The TVA records show that Cooper had run afoul of some politicians and was accused by a number of Union County citizens of favoring a Republican for the position of circuit judge. Since the TVA board was pledged not to engage in politics through members of the organization, this situation probably did not help Cooper in his position.

In September of 1934, an inquiry from outside was answered by the TVA about its wages and salaries. The reply was that they were comparable with those in the field service of the U.S. government. The largest salary, $10,000 a year, was paid to each of the directors; the lowest salary was for an executive $8,400 annually. Most construction work was done on a 33-hour week. Foremen received from $1 to $1.25 a hour; skilled workmen, $1; semiskilled workers and helpers, from 60 to 75 cents; and unskilled laborers, 45 cents. These wages and salaries were in line with comparable ones in the surrounding areas.

Employees injured at their work were entitled to federal benefits. An office of labor relations was established which had charge of matters relating to labor conditions, wage rates, violation of labor codes, and the relation between the Authority and organized and unorganized labor groups. Serious labor difficulties could be referred to the Secretary of Labor. One objective was racial equality in employment. At Muscle Shoals, the population was about 20 percent black, and their proportion in the TVA was about the same.

The personnel policies of the TVA were designed, according to Dr. Floyd W. Reeves, director of personnel and training in its early days, to meet equal opportunity objectives both in and out of the Authority. This included personnel administration, employment, medical care and treatment of employees, labor relations, promotion of safety, and maintenance of records. The purpose was to select the best personnel possible on the basis of merit and efficiency; to cooperate with national, state, and local agencies to solve problems of unemployment; and to promote the personal, social, health, and general welfare of the employees.

In support of this idea, Arthur Morgan said: "In the building of the Cove Creek Dam, which is the first large construction job, the plan is to select intelligent and teachable young men from rural communities and to combine work with a training program. In this way twice as many workers can be taken off the unemployment lists. While half of them are working on a short week, the other half will receive training in hygiene and sanitation, in home management, and in some skilled calling they can use later. After three or four years spent in building this great dam, these young men and their wives should be far better adapted to a new order."

TVA personnel officials agreed that the group of men selected not only were efficient but also had the intelligence to enable them to receive maximum benefit from a training program.

Participation in the program was entirely voluntary, and there was no charge for it. Except in the extension classes offered by certain colleges, the training program was administered without awards of grades, credits, and degrees. The real rewards were increased skills, greater efficiency, and intellectual stimulation. Training in personal finance was given through the Norris Cooperative Credit Union, which provided investment and savings facilities and made credit available at a low cost for its members.

TVA encouraged the men to make furniture for their own homes and with their own materials. Women were encouraged to develop art depicting various phases of life, such as that portrayed in rugs, quilts, and tapestries. This was especially successful among the black employees, where the response was more spontaneous than among the whites, particularly in music and dramatics.

Arthur Morgan had taken frequent opportunities to express his philosophy of personnel relations:

> Sometimes I think that the manner in which people do things is more important than what they do. The things people do fade away, but the spirit and manner in which they do them becomes a part of the fabric of human life. . . . Here in the TVA we can have a nucleus of an American civil service. We have a group of people who are not primarily watching the clock. Our people are not constantly making alibis. I think our people feel generally that they are doing a good job and are wanting to do a good job. In this we have something that may become significant in the course of American life. . . . The saying is generally true, "An institution is a shadow of a man." Unless there are shadows of many men you will not have a very large institution. . . . We do not want an organization that has only one shadow.

One characteristic of the TVA is that its charter permits administrative decisions to be made without those detailed checks, in advance of decision or action, which have been traditionally imposed upon public agencies in the United States. In short, the TVA was endowed with some of the same kind of managerial responsibility and authority which private companies and corporations have in carrying on their business. Its headquarters, where decisions are made, are close to the area of operations. The entire organization, from the board of directors down, is subjected to the practical test of day-to-day contact with its works and with the people who are affected thereby. Thus there is a smaller gap in the TVA between plans and decisions, on the one hand, and contact with the public which uses the services, on the other hand, than in most large public agencies. This gave an added sense of reality, meaningfulness, and responsibility, both to the employees and to the top management.

The TVA board was authorized under the TVA Act to appoint, without regard to the provisions of Civil Service laws, its officers and employees. An effort was made to get away from the idea that every citizen has the right to public employment. In order to do this and to give every applicant an equal chance and eliminate politics, there was developed a system of formal testing. Appointment was to be made on the basis of merit and efficiency.

In regard to political influence, Senator Lister Hill of Alabama stated that: "There were doubting Thomases, and I must admit that I myself sometimes wondered whether we could create a Government corporation and have it operate entirely free of any politics, of any political consideration in the matter of the appointment of its employees. The record will show that the board of directors of the Tennessee Valley Authority have carried out the provision of the law. . . . If I have ever had any say or if any other Senator or member of Congress, or any politician in the Government or out of the Government has had any say in the naming of a single appointee of the Tennessee Valley Authority, I certainly have never heard of such a case.''

Even crusty old Senator Kenneth McKellar of Tennessee, widely known for his favors to constituents, placed in the Congressional Record of January 24, 1938, in response to a question, the following answer: "If the Senator wishes to find whether any of my recommendations have been accepted by the TVA and the parties appointed because of my recommendations, I assure him that I do not know of a man I have recommended who has been appointed by the TVA; not one.''

Leonard White, in his study of personnel administration for Congress, agreed that the TVA "maintained unusual freedom from political interference.'' The uniform response of the TVA to Congressmen was a polite statement that "the candidate will be considered along with other qualified candidates for any vacancies which might occur in line with his qualifications.''

Senator George Norris said that "the TVA is the only organization in the Government of the United States that has a system of civil service running from top to bottom.'' Most of the early recruitment was from the Tennessee Valley, the common laborers coming from within a few miles of the job. But recruitment of top administrative and technical personnel has been on a national basis. The idea seemed to be that anyone, anywhere, or at any time could apply for a TVA position.

Active recruitment began in 1951 of black engineers from colleges where substantial numbers of such engineers are trained. As a result, several black engineers were employed and assimilated into the working force. Notwithstanding, it was found that the custodial positions such as janitors and elevator operators, messengers, and the like became almost entirely filled with blacks and thus created a kind of unintended segregation. But it is claimed by the TVA management that black employment over the years has been close to the proportion of their population in the Valley.

Bill Pace, program manager, TVA Minority Economic Development, said in 1978, "From the economic record of the Tennessee Valley region, it's clear what an impact TVA has had . . . . TVA can make a difference in minority economic development.''

Wider recruitment of engineers was in line with an unusual statement

printed editorally by the conservative *Electrical World,* even before the
TVA began: "The times have changed and professional engineering
societies should discuss economic and social aspects of engineering."

Before the passage of the Veterans' Preference Act of 1944 there was
no provision in the TVA employment policies for preference to veterans. Of course the Authority bowed to the new law which covered all
federal employment, and it was found that there was no resulting
conflict with the principle of merit and efficiency in appointments. In
fact, by 1954 veterans constituted 56 percent of the total TVA employment. This compared with 49 percent in the overall federal service.

Given more than average authority, the TVA supervisors naturally
became subject to questions as to how they performed. Observers have
commented that people at various levels in the organization usually
make decisions confidently and without the fear which is found in many
large public organizations. Another significant factor is that TVA
supervisors are not protected from "the consequences of their decisions by an authoritarian philosophy that the supervisor is always right.
One consequence of the policy of encouraging employees to organize
into strong and independent representative associations or unions is
that we put our supervisors on the spot to be able to explain and justify
their actions to their employees. We also actively encourage face-to-
face exchange ideas."

The labor record of the TVA has not been perfect. There have been a
considerable number of work stoppages on the construction projects,
mostly of brief duration. It appears that the relationship between the
TVA and labor organizations as well as internal associations have
contributed to better than average harmony in this respect. For example, a TVA engineers' association, which has participated in the mutual
bargaining relationship, has helped. A former president of this association, M. M. Williamson, said in this connection about the organized
engineers: "They have successfully demonstrated how responsible
professional employees can combine professional ability and integrity
with collective bargaining into a joint effort of tremendous value to
both employees and management."

Suggestions by employees and supervisors for the improvement of
work and work conditions are encouraged, although no cash rewards
are given for these. Some suggestions have been found to save money
and others to make the work more agreeable. They provide channels of
exchange of information between management and the workers. Outside employment is discouraged if it interferes with the activities or
policies of the TVA. When an employee's personal activities affect the
TVA, the organization will intervene. The most common example of

this has been the matter of bad debts. It has been made clear to the employees that they will not be retained indefinitely if they are continuously harassed by creditors. According to businessmen questioned, people who work for the TVA usually pay their bills well. A comment by one merchant, however, was to the effect that sometimes TVA personnel take a somewhat snobbish attitude in making purchases and asking for discounts.

TVA is usually the largest employer in the vicinity, and the labor unions like to see TVA wages as high as economic factors can justify. A principal reason for this desire is that the unions regard TVA rates as influential factors in their negotiations with private employers. The Associated General Contractors of America protested that the unions used TVA rates as levers in their negotiations with private contractors doing construction work. Wage rates for all classes of work have gone upward since 1933. In general, rates have gone up faster in the Tennessee Valley than in other parts of the country. Of course whether "real wages" have actually increased is a matter of debate not only here but elsewhere.

TVA provides its own retirement plan, administered by a retirement board of which three members are appointed by the TVA board, three elected by the employees, and a seventh chosen by the other six. The retirement plan is open only to "indefinite" appointees and therefore excludes the hourly construction workers. These are now under Social Security. The plan is "actuarially sound" and receives approximately equal contributions from TVA and employees.

When in 1940 the Ramspeck Bill became law, it authorized the President to bring under the Civil Service those agencies which were then exempt by law. But it provided specific exclusion of the Tennessee Valley Authority. Again in 1947 the question of TVA's exemption from the Civil Service was brought before Congress. This time a bill to amend the TVA Act and place the employees under Civil Service was introduced by Senator McKellar, who had become furious because of TVA's independence of him. Although he was a powerful Senator and extensive hearings on the bill were held, it did not pass.

In July 1947 Congress created the Hoover Commission. A task force from this commission studied the personnel system of the TVA but did not recommend bringing the organization into the Civil Service. In 1953 the Senate Committee on Post Office and Civil Service, after a study of the Civil Service in operation, concluded that the TVA and some other agencies "should continue to operate their programs free of Civil Service Commission control."

Gordon Clapp found that the more common complaints made by the personnel and their representatives included inadequate compensation for work; discrimination and favoritism in connection with terminations, promotions, transfers, assignment of work, and so forth; inadequate or inconsistent reasons for terminations, demotions, rating, and disciplinary measures; supervisors being incompetent or disagreeable; working conditions being inefficient or unsafe; failure to consider requests or to recognize qualifications for transfer; layoff and reemployment procedures not giving adequate consideration to qualifications; supervisors failing to criticize work previous to termination for unsatisfactory performance; assignment of work contrary to recognized jurisdictional awards; and excessive driving and overtime, irregular hours, and too long hours.

The TVA seems to have placed some special emphasis on nepotism. The board of directors has stated that the Authority will not employ on a monthly or annual basis the husband or wife of a person similarly employed by the Authority. This applies also to all members of the same household related by blood or marriage. It has been said that the TVA policy on this point is more rigid than has been the practice in other parts of the federal government.

Three systems of service ratings are used by the Authority. This provides for three possible ratings: *unsatisfactory, satisfactory,* and *unusually satisfactory.* Although political activity on the part of employees is generally prohibited, such does not apply to the activity of personnel in this regard when it is during their off-duty hours and does not reflect upon the integrity of the TVA. Few cases have arisen where this is a problem. After all, the employees did not enter the TVA through politics, so why should they thus jeopardize their positions.

The policy of the TVA in the field of labor relations is so stated: "For the purpose of collective bargaining and employee-management cooperation, employees of the Authority shall have the right to organize and designate representatives of their own choosing. In the exercise of this right, they shall be free from any and all restraint, interference, or coercion on the part of the management and supervisory staff. . . . On the other hand, no employee or applicant can be required to join an organization. Discrimination because of membership or nonmembership in an organization is forbidden."

Not only were there changes in the requirements for organized labor movements in connection with the TVA, there also were progressive steps by corresponding management. Frank C. Wardwell, senior civil engineer on the Chickamauga Dam project, told of old contractors who, when bidding on proposed work, simply walked over the site, calculated their bids on the back of an old envelope and, when awarded a contract, computed their profit or loss by checking bank balances at the end of the year: "Most of the contractors who worked in this free and easy way are here no longer," said Wardwell. "Some have died of heart failure; some have retired by way of the bankruptcy courts; perhaps a few may be wintering in Palm Beach. Contracting—and all major construction—is being placed more and more on a firm business basis."

Wardwell illustrated his remarks by emphasizing the importance of the cost engineer whose chief function on the job should be to assist in reducing the cost of the work. Such engineers use time studies which have an important relation to cost and the individual production of the men themselves. The men were conscious of such time-study observations and usually as a consequence increased their production. This frequently resulted in a good-natured rivalry between different crews or between different shifts.

A further step toward what was regarded as internal progress was a plan adopted by the TVA to build up a pool of skilled craftspersons. This was done in association with labor unions. For example, John Crosby, a former sharecropper, went to work at Chickamauga Dam for 60 cents an hour. Because of the apprentice on-the-job training program, five years later he was working on the Cherokee Dam near Jefferson City, Tennessee, as an outside journeyman machinist at $1.25 an hour.

As the program proceeded one man out of every 20 employed in such trades in the TVA took part. On the job these men learned to be skilled electricians, ironworkers, carpenters, linemen, bricklayers, painters, steamfitters, and machinists. The training took place over a period of 54 months, totaling 9,000 hours. The program was divided into four periods, each one more difficult until it was completed. For instance, one of the four major phases of Crosby's training was machine-shop work. All told, he worked 510 hours on lathe operation; 394 on the drill press; 432 on grinders; and 193 on learning reaming, sawing, tapping, pouring metal, using pneumatic tools, fitting, keying, testing, filing, chipping, measuring, finishing and fitting bearings. In addition Crosby was required to take 144 hours a year of related technical instruction at Chattanooga Vocational High School.

The New Republic commented on August 9, 1943, that the labor-relations policy of the TVA had functioned as well in both peace and war, that the organization had had no strikes or serious labor disturbances for the ten years of its existence. Even before the Wagner Act was passed, the magazine stated, "the Authority has bargained collectively with the fifteen standard international labor unions whose craftsmen it employs, and further, that this labor policy which has produced such gratifying results was a joint affair, since it was just as much a creation of these unions as of the Authority itself.''

Bruce Bliven related his experience on a trip he made at about this time to the Fontana Dam. Along the mountain road, he observed the beautiful scenery of the Great Smoky Mountains. Then a mile before he reached the dam, he came upon an old log cabin beside the road with a young woman standing in the backyard. She was dressed in a dirty flour-sack print dress and doing her washing beside the well which supplied the water for it. A soiled baby played in the dust nearby. To Bliven the woman looked tired and dispirited, and the shack that she lived in reminded him of the stage setting for *Tobacco Road*.

Soon afterward at the dam, at that time the fourth largest in the United States, the visitor found rows of trim, white cottages with screens to keep out flies and flowers adorning the yard. Inside he saw neatly dressed women cooking on electric ranges and using modern plumbing and some of them washing their clothes with electric machines. In a cafeteria there were seven basic types of food, each identified by color, and customers were urged to take one food from each marked section so as to make sure of getting a balanced diet.

In the TVA training program for chemical plant operations, many of the men had come directly from the farms and the women from their kitchens. An average of 450 kiln operators were usually in training at one time. These employees rose through several steps to reach the desired positions. Others started as laborers and were trained and promoted to conveyor operator, graining room operator, and ammonium nitrate operator. In one classification, 209 women completed 435 steps and then worked in 37 different kinds of positions.

The TVA officials expressed their gratification when it was realized that a thousand such operators had learned new and technical jobs. Most of these had had no previous experience in operating chemical plant equipment. Of course higher salaries came with promotion along with higher standards of living for the local people who for one reason or another had not before become better trained and educated.

In the Tennessee Valley itself there were significant and related changes. In 1957 there were 936,700 persons employed and covered by Social Security, some of these in the TVA. Six years later the number of covered wage employees in the valley had risen to 1,142,000, a net gain of 22 percent. Blacks comprised only 10 percent of the covered labor force in 1957 and 8.4 percent in 1963. There was an in-migration of 39,700 persons during this period, most of whom were new workers in the labor force. Figures showed that white males who were employed in the Tennessee Valley in 1957 but who had migrated to the North by 1963 increased their income by 59 percent. Those who migrated to the West increased their incomes by 94 percent, and those who migrated to the Southeast had an increase of 43 percent. But the dollar difference in income between white and black male out-migrants was greater in 1963 after the move than when both groups were employed in the Tennessee Valley in 1957, according to a study made by the TVA in 1971. (TVA employment of over 40,000 persons had been reached in 1942.)

The study showed that for blacks as a whole, out-migration did not improve their relative income position compared to their white counterparts regardless of the area to which the migrants moved, even though Negroes who migrated experienced larger income gains than those who did not. It was found that the Tennessee Valley gained in its income-generated capacity between 1957 and 1963 through in-migration of skilled workers (particularly from the North, who filled jobs that valley residents were presumably unqualified to fill) and by the out-migration of low income people who presumably had few skills and undoubtedly worsened the economic position of the receiving area to which they moved. The study concluded: "If the income problems of the Tennessee Valley and the Southeast are to be lessened rather than shifted to other regions through migration, and if we assume that level of income is a fair proxy for level of skills, then there is a great need for improving the training and skills of the resident labor force in the Valley and the Southeast if persons from these areas hope to compete with in-migrants for high-wage jobs in the future."

In a similar study at this time by Wesley G. Smith and Roger A. Matson, it was found that between 1960 and 1965 the off-farm movement of a large group of farm operators that occurred in the Tennessee Valley region was largely offset by a countermovement of persons from nonfarm employment to farming. Transfers between the two sectors by farm operators followed the business cycle. The net contribution by farm operators to the growth of the nonfarm labor force was essentially zero. Retirement rather than off-farm transfers was a far more important factor in the decline in the number of farm operators.

The TVA retirement system for its employees appears to compare well with organizations of similar size. The retirement income is derived from pensions, annuities, and Social Security. Each pension is based on years of service and the highest average salary of three years. Pensions constitute a fixed income except when changed by a cost-of-living increase. Service derived from unused sick leave at retirement is added to the creditable service. The size of the annuity is determined by accumulated contributions and interest.

John E. Massey retired as director of personnel of the Tennessee Valley Authority in 1974. Interviewed by this writer just before he left the organization, he gave the impression of being a man of exceptional ability and dedication to his work. At the same time he spoke frankly about the TVA and made no pretense that it was perfect. He had praise for David Lilienthal under whom he had served, stating that the former director handled the personnel situation well when he initially agreed "not to raid the employee ranks of the private power companies" to get them to work for the TVA. Massey also had high regard for Chairman A. J. Wagner who, he said, exemplified the philosophy of the original board of directors and was the last highest executive of the old school of thought.

John Massey on the eve of his departure made some cogent observations about the Authority in which he had spent 37 years. He believed that the TVA involved a new kind of relationship between the people of the region and the government. "TVA was not created," he said, "as an agency to come into the region and build structures. It was to become a part of the region. The people were to be partners." Some characteristics of the organization which he felt to be distinctive were as follows: the TVA is outside the federal departmental structure; the board is directly responsible to the President and Congress; salaries for officers and employees are determined by the TVA board but no employee can be paid more than a member of the board; the TVA is "flavored with a bit of experimentation and pioneerism"; the merit system was not imposed on a reluctant management but from the beginning was built into an overall concept of management accountability; the most effective communication between employees and management is through strong representative employee organizations; and for the first time in government, top management recognized the employee organization in its affirmative and positive role and all negative values concerning unions were dropped, with union leaders participating and not as opponents.

In a perhaps lighter vein, Massey set forth rules he believed from long observation were helpful for secretaries. Some of these seemed typical of his ideas:

> Set goals for yourself that take into account your own physical and mental stamina. Goals should stretch you but not tear you. Goals set too high will discourage, even defeat you; goals set too low will stop your growth and job enrichment which we all need as a person.

Respect yourself. People who know their worth don't carry chips on their shoulders. On the other hand, they don't take themselves too seriously. To be able to laugh at yourself is one of the great gifts of life itself. An organization, like a person, is known by the company it keeps. Whether you like it or not—you represent your organization wherever you go in your life outside the office. The impressions you and your co-workers leave with people outside your organization and your attitudes toward the organization will cumulatively affect the community standing of your company and very possibly its future and yours.

The Armour Fertilizer Plant on Pickwick Lake in southwest Tennessee. In background is the Natchez Trace Bridge. Such plants using TVA power and improved water transportation have improved and increased fertilizer use in this nation and abroad.

Grain elevator and mill at Decatur, Alabama, a city which has been virtually transformed by the presence of the TVA and the numerous industries that have located in the community since 1933.

10. Resurgence

The TVA was rather prematurely launched into the second half of the twentieth century by a dramatic happening. Near Bristol, Virginia-Tennessee, on February 5, 1949, about 1.3 million pounds of dynamite tore off the top of a mountain at the South Holston Dam site. An estimated 1.7 million cubic yards of stone in the solid rock mountain flew skyward during the building of a rock-faced, earth-fill dam across the south fork of the Holston River.

This was said to be the biggest construction blast in history. Windows and dishes in homes and shelves in stores were rattled in Bristol 9 miles away. Residents of this city of 35,000 swamped newspapers and radio stations with calls. The blast was even heard in Johnson City, some 40 miles to the southwest. L. Don Leet, a geologist and seismologist from Harvard University, who measured the atom bomb blast effect in New Mexico in 1945, recorded the shock. The blast made the timer, William J. Rooney of the Carnegie Institute, a bit sad. He said, "It was a second and a half too soon."

Less explosive was a study by Walter M. Daniels published by the H. W. Wilson Company in 1950. It stated that the criticisms most frequently made are (1) that TVA has subordinated its main operating functions, flood control and navigation, to the generation and sale of electricity; (2) that it has engaged in subsidiary activities, such as the manufacture and distribution of fertilizer, to an extent never visualized by its creators; (3) that it has charged off too much of its investment to flood control and navigation in order to hold down its electric rates; and (4) that it does not provide the advertised "yardstick" for electric rates because TVA is excused from payment of interest on its investment and of local taxes, both considerable items in the calculation of private utility electric rates.

The study concluded that the TVA is democratic because it does not *command* cooperation, that it achieves results by negotiation and written agreement defining the responsibilities of the parties, and that it does not seek to coerce citizens. Its operations are of such magnitude that the task was too big for private capital to undertake, and if it had done so, this would have been dangerous to the public welfare. The benefits of the TVA, it was contended, cannot be exactly measured in dollars and cents. The setting up of a federal regional agency did not mean the undermining and destruction of state and local governments. These are stronger than ever in the Tennessee Valley today. There was a psychological advantage in using the corporate device because the corporation had come to embody in people's minds the idea of managerial responsibility. The Negro benefited because hate and fear do not flourish when families are comfortable and living side by side.

In the Daniels study, Robert L. Duffus observed the Tennessee Valley people in this way:

> The pioneer stock hasn't gone to seed. It still has character and virility. What it needed was something outside itself of which it had been robbed by unhappy circumstances. It needed hope for the future. Hope is the pioneer's mainspring. He can't keep it wound up when every year the same amount of work brings in worse returns. But if he can inch ahead year by year, get a little more corn out of the old field, increase his milk yields, get more work done because he has electricity and machinery to help him, pay off his mortgage, paint his house, put in new plumbing and other gadgets, give his children better schooling—then he will be as good as he ever was, and as good as his ancestors were, which is pretty good. . . . If the TVA had gone into the Valley with the avowed purpose of "uplifting" the inhabitants, it would have pauperized a small minority and estranged the great majority. The sober truth is that there were some signs of a rather tactless attempt at uplift in the first year or so. They soon ceased. TVA had made its way in the Valley because it took the people into partnership. . . . The Valley people were, and are, proud. They had rather be poor than dependent. The essence of TVA, from their point of view, was that it opened up to them the road to independence. . . . Private business in the Valley seemed to them better off because there was this much public business.

The foregoing expresses one of the most intelligent viewpoints about the Tennessee Valley and the TVA that this writer has discovered. But in the same study other opinion is not so favorable. Dean Russell pointed out that the TVA has been given power to force state and local officials to conform to its decrees and decisions. What he does not show clearly is that the Authority has used this power sparingly. The Southern California Edison Company's Big Creek development is cited as an example of what private power companies have done in contrast to the theory that private enterprise cannot or will not do the job such as the TVA has done. The California company built in the High Sierras a $100 million project including access railways and highways, a 13-mile tunnel, hydroelectric powerhouses, and dams. These dams are said also to provide valuable flood control for the lower San Joaquin River. They store water which is released for power production in the dry season, which is then available for irrigation in the valley below. Said Russell: "Not only do the taxpayers make no contribution to this project but also they receive contributions from all these improvements through taxes paid on them by Southern California Edison. Contrasted to the tax-supported TVA project, this job is taxed while the people get the resulting incidental flood control and irrigation benefits without charge."

The conservative Russell contended that the TVA represents a step backward instead of forward and "is an agency that sets its own course, fixes its own rates, and makes up its losses by compulsory levies on the taxpayers."

John T. Flynn in a similar vein charged that TVA "propaganda claims that the total net profit from power since the beginning in 1933 to June 30, 1944, was $38 million. But alas, this left out the fact," stated Flynn, "that $53 million was paid by the government as interest on the money borrowed to build the power plants. Hence a power deficit of $15 million."

On the other hand, Ernest Kirschten, staff writer for the *St. Louis Post-Dispatch,* stated in the same study that a corporation device such as is used in the TVA can be as useful in the public service as for private gain. It seems propitious that the TVA is largely divorced from Washington and that its work is done in the region which it serves, with all the engineering and accounting facilities which modern management commands. "Along the Tennessee," he writes, "there are none of those interdepartment battlefields that scar the valleys of the Columbia and Missouri." The president of Westinghouse was singled out as one who "went all out against collectivism." Even so, said Kirschten, Du Pont, Union Carbide, and Alcoa seemed to be convinced that the government sells its products more cheaply than do private plants, or they would not have located in the valley.

In defending the financial setup of his organization, TVA chairman Gordon R. Clapp took issue with an article in the *New York Times* by John P. Callahan based on an Edison Electric Institute "analysis" claiming $120 million "loss" for the TVA. Instead, Clapp continued, the TVA showed a "net profit" of $31.5 million for the year. In regard to the *Times* article, "By the same logic," Clapp said, "the United States Army Engineers should be charged interest on levees on the Mississippi and navigation improvements on the Ohio, and the United States Treasury Department should pay interest on its investments in lighthouses and Coast Guard cutters. . . . Incidentally, $187 million of the "loss" incurred by TVA has been spent in purchases in four northeastern states, New York, Pennsylvania, New Jersey, and Massachusetts."

What was considered a bright financial note by the TVA occurred on August 14, 1955, when the Authority announced that it would pay $14 million to the U.S. Treasury the next day to retire all its outstanding bonded indebtedness 14 years ahead of schedule. The bond issue, floated in 1938–1939, totaled $65,072,500. Redemption of $10 million of the bonds was due in 1963 and the balance in 1969.

A new note was injected into the financial picture on April 4, 1955, when the TVA board of directors unanimously recommended to the Bureau of the Budget that the Authority finance its own future power needs. Legislation was proposed for the TVA power system which would reduce the necessity of direct federal appropriations and make the agency almost self-sustaining. The Authority further stated that it would be able to maintain its present power rates and meet operating expenses, payments to states and counties in lieu of taxes, and payments to the U.S. Treasury.

Projecting a pertinent opinion about the TVA, although given from a largely local viewpoint, S. R. Finley, superintendent of the Electric Power Board of Chattanooga, spoke to the Missouri Valley Association in Omaha, Nebraska. After being invited to accept the position, he became in 1937 engineer of the power board. Although he was from a traditional South Carolina family, he was soon a devotee of the Authority's policy and said: "We do not consider ourselves a recipient of special gifts from the Federal treasury at the expense of other taxpayers in the nation. Instead, with our own money, secured from our customers by the sale of electricity at retail, we are paying to the TVA for electricity at wholesale, enough money to cover the electrical expenses of the project, with enough over to repay the Federal government, or to pay the TVA's other operating expenses of agricultural research and demonstration, recreation and use of public lands, fertilizer development, flood control, and navigation."

Now living on fashionable Lookout Mountain, in the midst of ultraconservative friends, many of whom opposed the TVA, Finley told this writer that "The Tennessee River is really not a great river anymore. It is a moderately flowing body of water subdivided into several great lakes." In reference to the human history of the region, Finley reminded me that it does not take very much to start an argument in East Tennessee: "The original settlers," he recalled, "here were pushed over into that area just after colonial times by the growth of the seaboard states. Apparently the experience made them a little objectionable to being pushed around, so they just turned in and pushed the Indians out and the bears back into the caves in the mountains. Even now when there is nobody else to fight with, we just naturally start an argument among ourselves."

He remembered that when he came to Chattanooga there were still reverberations of the fight between the private and public power interests which involved the TVA. "Even at that late date," he said, "all of the split families, broken business partnerships, disrupted church congregations and neighborhoods, had not gotten back together again." In regard to the buying by the TVA of the Tennessee Electric Power Company, Finley believed that "the purchase price paid permitted the power company to pay off in full all of its bondholders, its preferred stockholders, and even left a good many million dollars for the common stock which was of rather doubtful value. Practically all of the existing employees of the company who desired to remain in the services of the TVA and the municipalities were retained. Many of them immediately began receiving higher salaries than they had been paid."

Finley added that the Authority has paid as tax equivalents amounts representing taxes formerly paid upon the private company's property. He said that many employees of his Electric Power Board who were formerly employed by the private power company had told him that now they were "more free from attempted political direction than they were when employed by the privately owned company."

Moderate but unhesitating in his praise, Finley pointed to the boating, fishing, outdoor water sports, and additional recreational opportunities which he said had made the region around Chattanooga "a mecca for those who enjoy outdoor life. Very definitely one of the great benefits we have received as a result of our experiences so far with TVA has been the development of a greatly enlarged outdoor recreation life for our citizens. . . . TVA activity along this line has acted as a stimulant to many of us to work toward improved health conditions in the community. TVA recognized the high tuberculosis rate in the area, and for its own employees instituted a system of periodical chest X-rays made by a mobile unit. From this has come the inspiration in Chattanooga for the city to have a mobile unit for the benefit of all our citizens."

Early in 1956, Coleman Harwell, editor of *The Nashville Tennessean,* and a staff member, Nat Caldwell, went to New York City to interview Gordon Clapp, whose term as TVA chairman had expired in 1954. Apparently the two newspapermen felt that Clapp was still the most articulate source of information about the TVA. The interview appears to have been a candid discussion of the issues involved. Clapp was now associated with his old friend and former superior in the TVA, David Lilienthal, in an organization which had been formed to carry out projects like the TVA in foreign countries. It was called the Development and Resources Corporation.

Clapp still had definite ideas about his former capacity and the opposition to the TVA. He stated: "At first the private utilities, and some of those who opposed TVA in the Valley and elsewhere, said they were against it because they didn't think it would work and it would be a waste of effort. Then as TVA proved successful, the private utilities have continued to oppose it because it has worked so well. . . . No agency outside of the Federal government could do on the Tennessee River what the TVA was set up to do and has done."

Harwell reminded Clapp that a favorite wisecrack was to the effect that "TVA drains 47 states for the benefit of one." Clapp scoffed at the idea and told his interviewer that when there were floods on the Missouri River, such as the one which happened in 1951, that the whole country comes to the rescue and pours money for relief into the area, "more money than has been put into the development of the Tennessee Valley by the Federal government to prevent there the very thing that was taking place on the Missouri."

The controversy was highlighted when "America's Town Meeting of the Air," a national radio broadcast, devoted its program of May 18, 1954, to the subject. "Is TVA good for the country?" The program originated in Chattanooga, and the announcer quoted President Eisenhower's reference to the TVA as an example of "creeping socialism." Replying to this statement had been Governor Frank Clement of Tennessee who said, "There is no symbol of American democracy more persuasive to those enslaved by poverty and those enslaved by communism, alike, than TVA."

The opposing speakers were Congressmen James L. Whitten, Democrat of Mississippi, and Frank M. Wilkes, president of the Southwestern Gas and Electric Company. Congressman Whitten led off, stating that the private utilities surrounding the TVA territory had tremendously increased their sales, greatly reduced their rates, and greated increased their profits. "You will find," he said, "that the greater the distance from the TVA, the higher the rates of the private utility; and the closer to the TVA, the lower the rates and also the greater the profits."

Wilkes replied, "There is no provision in the Constitution of the United States which permits the United States Government to engage in the electric utility business or, for that matter, any business with an area-wide monopolistic obligation such as is now claimed under the TVA regime . . . . The TVA Act was passed by Congress within the first 100 days of hysteria of the New Deal.''

Not long afterward Senator Lister Hill, speaking before a Congressional committee on water resources and power at Muscle Shoals, intoned:

> I wonder if any member of this committee has ever driven along a country road when dusk is falling in this Valley. I wonder if they have ever seen the lights come on as the darkness deepens. On hillsides and in hollows, from isolated coves and friendly settlements the beacons glow. From barns and sheds, from kitchens and parlors, the lovely pattern they make is a symbol of what TVA has meant to the people. I wonder if the members of the committee have ever visited the majestic dams and steam plants built by the TVA, and if their hearts were ever stirred as mine is lifted every time I read the plaque which each one bears: BUILT FOR THE PEOPLE OF THE UNITED STATES.

Senator Hill had been defending the TVA almost from the moment he introduced the bill for its enactment into law in the House of Representatives in 1933. Now, he stated:

> In an effort to discredit TVA, the direct financial returns to the federal government are misrepresented, and the benefits accruing indirectly to the nation are wholly ignored. Nowhere is it recorded, for example, that the growing economic strength of this area is permitting its citizens to bear an increasing share of the total federal *individual* income tax collections. The fact is that individual income tax collections from the TVA area represented only 3.4 percent of the national total in 1933, while in 1953, the last year for which I have the figures, 6.1 percent of the total collected was received from this region.

Across the Atlantic, echoes of the TVA reverberated in the trenchant words of the English writer Julian Huxley. They appeared in a pamphlet entitled *TVA: Adventure in Planning* with a foreword by John G. Winant, the U.S. Ambassador. It included this interesting comment:

> The problem of intervention by government for the common good has always been the concern of statesmanship. The continuing development of the Tennessee Valley marks the advance that science, in combination with the popular will, can evolve out of a co-ordinated national and local authority; it is proof that democratic

government under wise leadership can direct our natural resources to serve present human needs. It is a unique experiment in government as well as an engineering feat of tremendous significance.

Looking down his nose from an obviously great distance, Huxley wrote that there were

the crying needs of this backward region which might largely be met by cheap electric power. Much of the rural area of the Valley was inhabited by peasant farmers, who, although originally of excellent British stock, had in their mountain isolation too often developed into poverty-stricken poor-whites. Primitive in their reproductive habits as in their farming methods, they multiplied rapidly until they presented a typical Malthusian population, pressing hard upon its means of subsistence.

But the Englishman was on surer ground when he concluded that the TVA had introduced a new constitutional dimension into the U.S. government. He felt that this had come about when the TVA, acting as an autonomous authority, entered into contractural relations with the individual states of the region which crossed and enveloped all political boundary lines—in other words, "another case of full powers for a limited function." It even benefited by its own mistakes. For instance, it was wrong in concentrating too much at the outset on its function of producing a "yardstick" in the matter of electricity, successful though this had been in certain important respects. It realizes now that achievement of any planning authority worthy of the name must be measured first in all-round development and general welfare; and it has invented new social tools, one of which is the enlistment of the educational system to induce a sense of participation in the plans on the part of the population at large.

On the whole, Julian Huxley approved of the TVA and ended his comments thus:

With all this it looks as if the TVA were now safely established as a permanent organ. But even if this should prove not to be the case, the TVA . . . will have definitely established the validity of over-all, regional, democratic planning: and this is an achievement of first-class importance in the evolution of human society.

Another Flood

Farming and other activities were interrupted in the early part of 1957 when a serious flood occurred. A TVA report best described the beginning of the deluge: "Late in January of that year the rain began. It poured down in the Holston Valley, in the Clinch and on the Little Tennessee. It fell on towns and cities, on highways and on airports, in the mountains and the hollows. Forests and winter pastures slowed the runoff for a day, or even two, in the beginning, but for twenty days of twenty-one the rain continued. More than 25 inches fell on Clingman's Dome in the Great Smokies, over 23 at Flat Top in the headwaters of the Ocoee. In the rugged watersheds of Tellico, Cheoah and Nantahala there was no respite. Gauges in the Hiwassee basin, in the French Broad valley, and on the Powell all reported the swelling volume of runoff and the relentless rise in stage as the water ran to the rivers from land soon soaked beyond its capacity to hold.''

The TVA men who managed streamflow from the central point of control in Knoxville remained at their posts all day and night throughout this flood period. They collected reports from more than 600 stream gauges, relating them to the Weather Bureau forecasts and issued orders which held back the waters of the Clinch and Powell Rivers surging behind Norris Dam. They let the rising Little Tennessee River flow through Fontana Dam and restrained the strong stream flow at the Watauga while the discharge from the Hiwassee River was allowed to move downstream to make room for the approaching downpour. "Hour by hour, the orders went out, and like a giant orchestra responding to the baton of its conductor, the rivers obeyed. It was the major test of the system, and there was no flood."

The Tennessee stayed within its banks, unlike the times when it had overflowed into its valleys and was witnessed helplessly by the Indians who gave these rivers their picturesque names. Obviously, a situation leading to a major flood was created. Runoff from soggy land was greatly increased, and still it rained. As the flows became heavier, the greatest danger grew at the city of Chattanooga. Flow of water also enlarged downstream at Muscle Shoals, where it was necessary to close one of the locks to river navigation for nine days. A delicate balancing of water control was done at Fort Loudoun, Watts Bar, and Chickamauga Dams, the three mainstream projects above Chattanooga.

Gradually the river rose to a stage of 32¼ feet on the Chattanooga gauge, the remaining flows being impounded. This was about 2 feet above flood stage, with 206,000 cubic feet per second of water coursing by the city. In the storage reservoirs above Chattanooga, 8 million acre-feet were available at the beginning of the storm. Half of this space had been used. Flood waters piled high above the dams on the tributary streams. The flow of water into the reservoirs was greater than at any time since the dams were built.

Fortunately the rainfall began to slacken and finally ended on February 10. Now it was the job of the TVA to lower the reservoirs to their usual levels. Water withheld from the main river during the flood now had to be passed on downstream. As a consequence, the flow in the Tennessee River remained high for some time. Because of steady operations, the hydroelectric units at the dams produced more power during this period than in any previous months.

When the water turmoil had died down, it was estimated that regulation of this 1957 flood by the TVA system had averted $66 million of damage at Chattanooga. Under similar conditions in the past much of the city was inundated. Industrial areas were damaged. Thousands of houses flooded, and as many families were driven from their homes. Forty years before, Rossville Boulevard, a leading local thoroughfare, in a similar flood resembled a great lake with the top portions of houses alongside it barely showing.

But if the power of nature was displayed in a stormy and violent way, it was harnassed in a more beneficial one. The need for atomic power increased after the Communist armies crossed the 38th parallel into South Korea in July 1950. The power-producing capacity of the TVA expanded to meet the demand. The Kingston, Tennessee, steam plant, the largest of its kind up to that time, was completed in 1956. Its great condensers use as much water as the City of New York, and its boilers consume a 50-ton carload of coal every 6 minutes. By this year TVA became the largest buyer of coal in the United States, burning nearly 18 million tons annually. At Hiwassee Dam in North Carolina, the Authority placed in operation the largest pump-turbine unit ever built. As a generator, it had a capacity of 59,500 kilowatts; while reversed in operation and used as a pump, it could return some 4,000 cubic feet per second of water to the Hiwassee Reservoir to maintain the power status and to be reused through the turbines.

A milestone was reached in 1956 when the average residential use of electricity in the area doubled the national average for the first time. Also, the average cost of electricity for residents of the area was less than half the national average. Interestingly, the town of Alcoa, where the largest such plant of the Aluminum Company of America is located, decided to buy the power distribution system serving the town and adjoining rural areas and contract with the TVA for the power supply.

As the TVA approached its quarter-century mark, it was greeted with cheers and jeers. Some of its opponents harped on the saying which was said to have been invented by Wendell Willkie in 1936: "The Tennessee River waters four states and drains the nation." This quipping slogan was repeated with variations. In 1945 one writer stated that the river flowed "through five states and drains the nation." The *Wall Street Journal* stated in an editorial on June 9, 1951 that "the stream ran through three states and drained the other forty-five"; and in 1958 a letter to the editor of the *Washington Post* from an official of the U.S. Chamber of Commerce commented that the "Tennessee River flows through seven states and drains forty-eight."

From another corner, Governor Frank Clement of Tennessee agreed strongly with Thomas E. Dewey, who told a Senate committee that the TVA was not socialism. Clement, who was at the time endeavoring to build national stature for himself, declared: "We in the Tennessee Valley believe TVA is the same kind of sound Federal conservation as are the flood control dams and levees, harbor and water way improvements, reclamation and other projects built elsewhere in the country. If TVA is socialism, so are the great irrigation dams in the West, the Post Office, the Panama Canal, our roads and schools, and the thousands of utilities owned by towns and cities."

As if in reply, the Chamber of Commerce of the United States issued some pungent charges. One was that the TVA had allocated $159 million to navigation improvements and that this amount was more than double the original estimate when the project was authorized. Some of this cost, the chamber argued, should have been charged to power development. Thus navigation improvement was assessed against the taxpayer while charges to power users were reduced proportionately. This the TVA denied.

Flood control, the chamber stated, was in the same category, with some of its cost belonging instead to power development. To the charge that much good land had been unnecessarily inundated by reservoirs of the TVA, that organization replied that much of that land in its original state was relatively worthless because of the constant threat of floods, while the lands now protected are highly developed and valuable, besides in many cases providing recreational assets.

According to the chamber, TVA fertilizers were sold commercially at about 10 percent below the competitive market, the difference constituting a subsidy to TVA fertilizer operations. To this the Authority replied that its research program is charged off as a developmental expense and not reflected in the manufacturing costs.

In regard to electric power, it was alleged that the TVA does not charge its power operations for interest on federal funds, is not assessed taxes or their equivalent, and pays only nominal taxes to state and local government and that all these costs should be reflected in the price of power.

The TVA replied that the chamber failed to mention TVA objectives of widespread electricity use and seeks to judge the Authority solely as a profit-making enterprise. "TVA's accounts show power is financially self-supporting and self-liquidating, earning a return of 4 percent."

To this the chamber rejoined that the "favored treatment of the TVA service area has not only resulted in an unfair shift of wealth within the nation, but also has required the taxpayer living outside of the benefited area to suffer an out-of-pocket cost of between $268 million and $470 million for the fiscal year.

Not at a loss for words, the TVA through its chairman, General Herbert D. Vogel, responded that the report of the U.S. Chamber was based on "fundamental misconceptions of Congressional policy and TVA administration. . . . For example, the phenomenal growth of Houston was due to government construction of a waterway to its front door. Pittsburgh has been able to develop and beautify its Golden Triangle because the Government built the great system of flood control reservoirs on the Allegheny and the Monongahela Rivers." Other developments such as the Great Lakes also were given as examples of important national projects receiving federal government support.

In appraising the chamber of commerce's report in general, the TVA board concluded that the attacking organization applied different criteria to the TVA than to other river developments, took statements and facts out of context and time sequence, failed to report certain pertinent facts, and minimized TVA's contributions to the national defense. It was pointed out that Tennessee Valley consumers paid about $100 million less for power during the year than they would have at regular commercial rates.

Whose Land?

Another phase of TVA operations which became highlighted in the 1950s was its policy of land acquisition. Charles J. McCarthy, the assistant general counsel of the organization, contributed an article to the *Ohio State Law Journal* in which he noted that the corporate device for carrying on governmental business was not new and in fact went back as far as the creation of the Bank of the United States in the administration of President James Madison. Leading into his discussion of the land acquisition policies, he said that the thing about the TVA which was unique was the delegation to an autonomous agency, with its headquarters in the region, of complete responsibility for the carrying out of a program of regional development: "If the program is a failure in any respect," McCarthy wrote, "TVA cannot excuse itself by saying that the responsibility for that branch of the program rests in some other agency. Congress has given TVA the necessary tools to do the work and has imposed on it full responsibility."

Two major objectives were established in the land acquisition: first, to obtain the lands needed at a cost fair to the government and, second, to leave the area in which a reservoir is built and the people who live in that area at least as well off as they were before TVA entered the picture. Where part of a county road system has been flooded, for example, it has not been the policy of the TVA to pay damages to the county or require that the county sue it for damages. The procedure has been to make a careful study of the needs of the county as they would exist after the reservoir was constructed; to prepare a tentative proposal for the relocation of the county's roads; and then to sit down with the officials of the county, go over the entire problem, and agree on exactly how the county's road system should be readjusted.

An example of this kind of problem occurred in the Fontana Reservoir in western North Carolina. Between the reservoir and the Great Smoky Mountains National Park is a mountainous area of 44,000 areas which before the construction of the reservoir was served by a narrow mountain road running east to Bryson City. The road was flooded by the reservoir in several places, and its relocation would have cost about $1.5 million. The highway belonged to the state but had been constructed by the county.

The final solution was an agreement among the TVA, the National Park Service, the state of North Carolina, and Swain County by which the TVA agreed to purchase all the lands served by the highway and turn them over to the National Park Service for inclusion in the Great Smoky Mountains National Park. The agreement was advantageous to all parties. It gave the park a border on a beautiful mountain lake and the TVA settled its legal obligations for several hundred thousand dollars less than the cost of building a comparable road to replace the one that was flooded.

The land acquisition program of the TVA apparently has worked rather well despite an occasional loud squawk from a disgruntled landowner who probably was not anxious to lose his land in the first place. "In spite of the original fears on the part of program divisions," said Ashford Todd, Jr., the energetic head of the Division of Property and Supply of the TVA, "the sales program has been developed and is being handled without sacrificing any part of these other programs, and, to the contrary, is bringing about a better and more complete utilization of lands retained, an understanding of the possibilities open for joint or combined use of land, and a consciousness of the advantages accruing from the relinquishment of lands for private use and development."

The TVA customarily disposes of its surplus land after it is of no direct benefit to the organization. There has been in general a ready market for such properties, especially the recreational, timber, and agricultural lands. A number of sales of sites have been made for the development of privately owned clubs, recreational resorts, and other commercial enterprises. Offerings of industrial and recreational sites near populous centers have brought the highest prices.

The land here is not always quiet. Berlen C. Moneymaker, chief geologist for the TVA, was sitting in his fifth floor office in Knoxville on September 7, 1956, when he felt the floor shake violently under him. "It felt like the whole building was being lifted up," he said. "Immediately I knew what it was. The telephone began ringing. The newspapers and radio stations were asking me what had happened." The reason why such inquiries were made of him was because Moneymaker was the local authority on earthquakes. He recalled that this was only one of more than 2,000 earthquakes recorded in Tennessee in the preceding century and a half.

Moneymaker stated that an earthquake in 1811 shook the state of Tennessee from one end to the other and created Reelfoot Lake in West Tennessee. "That was," he added, "perhaps the most severe earthquake of recorded time." From the beginning of the TVA, Moneymaker's job was to advise engineers on how much tremor they could expect at the site of each dam and in regard to steam plant chimneys. Naturally, attention to possible earth tremors is important in a great amount of TVA construction.

Other "sounds" related to the TVA were heard about this time, though in a different vein. The consulting firm of Walter Von Tresckow in New York City, obviously motivated by conservative interests, made a study of the TVA and recommended to the federal government that the Authority be sold to its municipalities and cooperatives which distributed its electricity. Other recommendations were that no further investments be made by the federal government for the expansion of TVA power facilities and that repayment to the federal government be made of its remaining investment in the TVA power facilities.

This strong-worded recommendation probably fell on sympathetic ears when it reached President Eisenhower. The statement went on:

The impression of TVA gained by most Americans indicates clearly that the TVA has succeeded so well and is so strongly established that the Federal government support is no longer needed for the TVA to continue the good work it has done. . . . From the beginning of TVA in 1933 until 1945, income in Tennessee grew very much faster than the average for the country. Per capita income grew from 52 percent in 1933 to 73 percent of the national average in 1945. During this period of inception, federal ownership was a distinct advantage. Between 1945 and 1957, however, the per capita income in Tennessee has dropped from 73 percent to 68 percent of the national average.

11. The Silver Anniversary

By the year 1958 the Tennessee Valley Authority had come of age, at least in some ways. And voices were not lacking to celebrate its virtues. For a time they almost drowned out the clamor of opposition.

Prominent among such voices was that of Senator Lister Hill. Pointing to a picture of a group of national officials gathered around President Franklin Roosevelt, Senator Hill noted that he was the only survivor. "Alone of all the group," he said, "gathered to witness when the President signed the TVA Act in 1933, I have seen the dreams, the hope and the faith that we wrote into the statute become a reality."

R. L. Duffus, writing in the *New York Times* of May 18, 1958—the twenty-fifth birthday of the TVA—took a somewhat more moderate approach but was still warm in his praise. He called the Authority "the world's most dramatic experiment in the use and control of a river. . . . A Pilgrim who first traversed the Valley a quarter of a century ago, between the old Wilson Dam at Muscle Shoals on the main river and the site of the Norris Dam, above Knoxville, on the Clinch, may feel like Rip Van Winkle returning to scenes that are both strange and familiar."

Duffus observed that the people in the valley were living better than they did 25 years before. "The work the TVA has done," he said, "was not being done in 1933, and there were no signs that it would be done by any other combination of public and private enterprise." The writer prophetically stated that in the years ahead it would be necessary to develop to the fullest all sources of power in the United States by whatever means. He believed that public and private power could well work together for the needs of our future. He concluded, "In the opinion of this Pilgrim, there will not be and cannot be a duplication of the TVA if only for the simple reason that there cannot be a duplication of the Tennessee Valley."

Opinion was not unanimous, however, on the TVA's birthday. In the *New York Times* of February 5, 1958, a letter from W. B. McGuire of Charlotte, North Carolina, jibed at the Authority by stating that the Duke Power Company paid federal income taxes up to 6 cents on every

202

dollar of plant investment while TVA's figures were just one-tenth of that amount. His company, McGuire complained, was one-fourth the size of the TVA but paid more than twice as much in taxes: "TVA pays no interest," McGuire charged, "and pays no income taxes to support the Federal government, although TVA is 'big business.' It pays less than one-third the local and state taxes paid by utility companies based on plant investment. It enjoys other governmental favors which reduce its costs. Without these cost advantages it would show a substantial loss, not a 4 percent return."

No such sentiment was expressed in *Labor World,* the Chattanooga publication of the AFL-CIO. In its April 30, 1958 issue, it hailed the Authority as the labor "realization of a dream." It stated that in 1932 union members turned out and voted for Roosevelt and for people who would back the Norris plan. After the President had signed the TVA Act in 1933, the publication said, union members got busy in their own localities and voted in referenda to establish municipal electric systems. Citizens throughout the country received the benefits brought by the TVA. "Truly, the TVA system was built for the people of the United States."

The Annual Report of the TVA for 1960 termed itself

> a report to the stockholders—the people of the nation who own it through the agency of the Federal government. It differs from the usual corporate report, however, in that the dividends from most of TVA's activities must be recorded in terms other than monetary profit . . . the electric power program is the one aspect of the integrated development which may be reported on in terms of financial profit and loss as well as in its contributions to the general welfare.

Indeed the report did have something new. It concerned a major change in the financial arrangements for the power system. This was the authorization by Congress in August 1959 for the sale of electric power bonds on the public market to finance additions to the power system as necessary to meet future power requirements in the region.

One of the early developments was a visit to Washington, D.C., by General Herbert Vogel, chairman of the TVA, to help formulate the legislation for the purpose of this financing. He held a discussion with Roland Hughes, Director of the Budget. In an interview some ten years later General Vogel stated:

> I can recall one conversation in particular as we were working out the details of the financing act and we had come up with the proposal that the ceiling be set at a billion dollars. The Bureau of the Budget in

reviewing this had reduced the amount to $500 million. I was discussing this point among a number of others relating to the provisions of the proposed bill with Hughes, and I told him that $500 million was really too small an amount. He said, "A billion dollars I couldn't go along with." I asked why not. "Well," he said, "It just sounds like such a lot of money." So I proposed a compromise and he agreed to split the difference. That is how we arrived at $750 million—just because a billion sounded like too much money.

The Chamber of Commerce of the United States immediately attacked the TVA financing program, charging that it was actually

a new system for feeding taxpayers' dollars into a federal power empire which serves a selected portion of the country. This new system may appear to be less painful than the present one of annual federal appropriations, but the results would be essentially the same. The proposed legislation would not relieve the nation's taxpayers of the subsidy which they continue to provide to the TVA area.

The chamber recommended that the TVA be relieved of its function of producing and transmitting electric power and be confined to the duties of conducting its authorized nonpower functions. It was also recommended that the TVA power facilities including transmission lines and steam and hydroelectric plants at TVA dams be transferred to local ownership and operation. No further federal funds should be appropriated to TVA for expansion of its electric power business. Appropriations would not be needed if TVA's power operations were required to pay their own way—and only by requiring power users to pay the full cost of power could revenues be increased and the obligation of the taxpayers eliminated, the recommendation added.

The publication of the Guaranty Trust Company of New York joined in condemning the financing proposal for the TVA. It stated that the plan raised grave questions concerning sound fiscal practice and the future of the electric power industry as a whole. The publication repeated the charge that "it is because TVA pays no Federal income tax and nothing in lieu thereof, and because it receives its capital funds from Congress and yet has never paid any interest to the Federal Government on any Congressional appropriation."

Meanwhile officials of the TVA were busy providing information needed by financial institutions and private investors. Members of the board of directors and key staff appeared before a meeting of the Municipal Forum of New York and other such groups to give information and answer questions about bond financing plans. The *New York Times* of November 13, 1960, observed that although the legislative outlook for the TVA seemed dark at times in the decade preceding, this new development was encouraging to the organization after the

eclipse in the Republican 80th Congress and in the first two years of the Eisenhower administration, when the President indicated a lack of sympathy with his now famous reference to "creeping socialism." There are probably only two of the President's ten cabinet members, Secretary of Labor Mitchell and Secretary of Interior Seaton, who would not cheerfully assent to a destruction of the agency if it could be feasibly done. But the national pride in the institution has been sufficiently asserted to warn all comers that it could not be done without attrition and to suggest that the TVA has grown beyond the reach of all but a violent swing to rabid conservatism. The Dixon-Yates battle was an excellent test of hardiness and the TVA stood up. . . . So there is double drama in the 25th anniversary of the agency in that it is a milestone marking a proud and successful past and a crossroad representing the alternative between a bright and hopeful future and the deterioration for which its enemies have long hoped.

The newspaper noted that the TVA still had special access to financial accommodation from the U.S. Treasury and that the agency was the largest generator and distributor of electric power in the United States, accounting for 10 percent of all power produced by the nation's utility systems. The new TVA bond issue of $50 million would mark the first publicly sold bonds of a major federal agency to be secured solely by revenues from a producing operation. Designated as financial adviser was Lehman Brothers of New York, and two prominent law firms there were appointed as counsel.

This bond-financing amendment to the TVA Act changed the statutory financial requirements that power operations were expected to meet from power revenues. It repealed the provision of the Independent Offices Appropriation Act of 1948 which provided that the TVA should pay into the Treasury sums equaling the appropriation investment in the power system within 40 years from the time facilities so financed went into operation. The amendment authorized the TVA to issue electric power revenue bonds up to a limit of $750 million outstanding, with debt service to be met from power revenues. The TVA should repay to the U.S. Treasury on a schedule covering up to 54 years $1 billion of the $1.2 billion of Treasury investment in the system.

The net interest cost of the $50 million was approximately 4.4 percent. Present at the ceremony marking the Authority's entrance into the capital market were Congressman Brooks Hays of Arkansas, General Herbert Vogel, A. R. Jones (another TVA director), and Paul

Clarke (partner of Lehman Brothers). Principal and interest on the bonds were to be payable solely from the TVA's net power proceeds—the net operating income of the system, plus provision for depreciation charged against power operations. The bonds would not be obligations of, nor payment of, the principal thereof or the interest thereon to be guaranteed by the United States.

Although the utilities who fought the measure lost, they did succeed in having the bill contain language restricting future expansion of the TVA's power area. As finally approved by Congress, the bill limited TVA's service area to points within 5 miles of its current one. Aubrey J. Wagner, then general manager of the Authority, in addressing a meeting of the Tennessee Valley Public Power Association in March of 1960 said: "It wasn't a perfect law when it finally passed, but it was a good one. It was workable. Now at last, after several years of uncertainty, we could see a way to meet the region's ever growing appetite for more and more electricity to light and to heat and to power the drive for a stronger and better region."

Health Care

Meantime the health and safety features of the TVA were moving in a forward direction. Dr. O. M. Derryberry, manager of health and environmental science for the TVA, retired on December 31, 1972. In an interview with this writer, just before this time, he "pointed with pride" to the achievements of his department. He recalled the work of a predecessor, Dr. E. L. Bishop, as being outstanding not only in the Tennessee Valley but in the nation. Bishop became known before his death as an outstanding malariaologist in the United States for his work in this field with the TVA.

Bishop also gave his attention to the general health and safety of the organization and told Derryberry that the work of the department could be classified into two main categories: first, the health care of the employees, including medical service, the control of preventable diseases, safety service in the prevention of accidents, and environmental hygiene, and second, the solution of public health problems inherent in a project involving the conversion of a system of flowing rivers into a chain of great lakes. There remained the necessity for preventing maladjustment to biological changes which, if uncontrolled, could offset with disaster the results of the whole enterprise. This included the problems of stream sanitation and prevention of malaria.

It was the policy, Bishop continued, of the TVA to supplement and extend existing facilities within the several states in the region instead of duplicating them. Another objective was coordination of service with that of educational and other institutions of the region. Emphasized were maintenance of employee health; prevention and control of communicable diseases among employees; the definition of occupational health hazards; providing facilities for the treatment of sickness and injuries associated with employment, including medical care of illness at points inaccessible to normal facilities; and the appraisal of medical and public health programs.

Other such responsibilities were planning and supervision of safeguarding water, milk, and food supplies; executing malaria programs, sewage, and waste disposal, including stream sanitation; protecting recreational areas and facilities; and maintaining hygiene in housing and working environments especially in regard to standards of air, light, and space. Added to these responsibilities was that for the prevention and control of hazards to human life resulting from accidents, fires, and similar occurrences on all properties and operations of the Authority. Bishop realized that in eradicating the mosquito, other factors such as water and soil control should be taken into consideration. He did not believe in wasting natural resources simply to get rid of the insect. "Economically," he said, "such a process resembles burning a home to rid it of rodent infestation."

The Authority stressed the treatment of service-connected injuries. First-aid kits and stretcher boxes were placed in the field with work crews at substations and at other locations where small groups of employees were working. Portable first-aid stations accompanied construction workers and were available 24 hours a day for emergency treatment. If a man became ill on the job, say from heat prostration or similar cause associated with his work, he was given appropriate treatment immediately in order that he might have the best chance for recovery and could go back to work at the earliest practicable time. It had been found that if an employee lacked such attention, he might never go to a physician, would certainly be off the job much longer, and might possibly suffer serious consequences or lingering aftereffects.

In his long association with the TVA, Bishop concluded:

No other area of the same size in the United States has such a diversity of climate, soil, vegetation and resources as do the states in the Tennessee Valley area. The region has an equal variety of health problems, ranging from respiratory infections in some sections to subtropical diseases in others. As earlier indicated some problems are related to activities in the Authority in connection with its general program; others have a direct impact on Authority personnel since that personnel is recruited principally from the region itself.

Another problem of the Tennessee Valley was and is stream pollution. When the TVA was only ten years old, it was charged that the paper industry was dumping into the Tennessee River system a pollution load equivalent to the raw sewage from more than a million people. This, it was said, came from a number of manufacturing plants, with more than half of the pollution load being contributed by less than a score of pulp, paper, and rayon plants. The TVA began a stream sanitation program for studies of stream conditions particularly in relation to the changes resulting from impoundment of water. W. G. Stromquist, principal sanitary engineer of the TVA Health and Safety Department, stated:

There are two extreme viewpoints on the question of stream pollution. On the one hand, there is the enthusiast who believes very strongly that all streams should be restored to their pristine purity. On the other extreme is the industrialist who thinks that a stream is there for his convenience to carry away material which he cannot otherwise utilize. To satisfy the first, it would be necessary to return to pioneer days when a man could provide his family with meat by shooting a bear or deer from his cabin door with no worry about consequences. At the other extreme, there is a flagrant disregard of national good housekeeping and common decency. There is a reasonable middle ground.

During the construction of the Kentucky Dam, a first-aid station was located on each side of the river. These simple, one-room stations were portable and could be moved by crane as the construction went forward. Some stations had wheels for this purpose as the reservoir clearance areas expanded. Three nurses and four medical corpsmen were assigned to each of the first-aid stations for each 24-hour period, with a doctor on call for emergencies. Patients were quickly carried from the clearance and construction areas to the nearby hospital.

The TVA nurses had a blend of industrial and public duties. They served on rural construction area projects at dam sites, giving first-aid care and bedside nursing in small hospitals; they conducted urban industrial hygiene programs for office workers and former employees with disabling conditions; and they offered industrial hygiene programs for employees of rural dam maintenance units and in connection with chemical engineering. Some home services were carried on cooperatively with the county health departments.

During the period from November 1933 through June 1951, over half a million health examinations were given in the TVA with almost that many immunizations against communicable diseases provided. About a million treatments of job-related injuries were administered, and half that many clinical diagnostic laboratory examinations made. Not a single case of smallpox or typhoid fever had been known to occur at a TVA construction camp or village during 18 years of work, much of it done in rather "frontier" locations. The accident frequency declined from 62.5 accidents per million man-hours worked in 1935 to 5.5 accidents per million man-hours worked in 1951. Similarly, absenteeism was reduced from 6.95 days lost per thousand man-hours in 1935 to 1.45 days lost per thousand man-hours worked in 1951. The average number of employees during these years totaled about 15,000.

In more ways than one, this was a constructive period for the TVA. Congressman James B. Frazier, Jr. arose in the House of Representatives and declared: "Nowhere in the world is a river so completely turned from destruction to the people's benefit; nowhere is an agency operated more efficiently than the TVA; nowhere is there a more striking example of effective decentralized administration."

12. Heralding Maturity

In spite of the progress which had been made, the TVA believed that more measures were needed to increase the size of the farms and make farming more profitable. There was still more work to be done to keep the people at home or at least in their home country. Accordingly there was established in 1961 a Tributary Area Development Office which was designed as a new administrative vehicle to collaborate with other branches of the TVA and attempt to make a significant contribution toward achievement of the foregoing objectives.

The last census had shown that more than 5.5 million people lived in the 200 counties of the valley region. But the increase in population was far less than that of other sections of the United States. Of the 200 counties in the region, 135 were predominantly rural and lost a total of 283,000 people while the other 65, which were urban industrial counties, gained by 387,000. In 1960 nearly half of the population in the seven valley states lived in cities. The average farm in the valley was only one-third the size of the average one in the nation. Encouraging, nevertheless, was the fact that now about half of the valley farms had tractors, a tenfold increase over the reported number in 1945.

TVA construction went ahead of dams, steam plants, and related projects. A major event was the first commercial operation of the largest steam-electric turbogenerator in the world—the 500,000-kilowatt unit at Widows Creek Steam Plant in northern Alabama. At the same time, the TVA retired from service its smallest hydroplant, an 800-kilowatt installation at Columbia, Tennessee.

A setback occurred when on June 2, 1961, at 9:20 P.M., the north wall of the old lock at Wheeler Dam fell. It was caused by an unusual thin seam of clay, later found in the bedrock. The lock was full of water at the time, and the upper gate was open. Immediately the construction area of the new lock being built was flooded. A small crew was working therein, and as two leaves of the lower lock gate were torn from their anchorages, two of the men were killed.

At once work was started to stop the flow of water through the upper lock gate by installing a horizontal girder and vertical steel beams and panels. This succeeded. The upper lock gate was closed on June 6. Next a cofferdam was built to seal off the lower end of the locked chamber. By June 14 the area was empty of water and construction officials could determine the extent of the damage, how to repair it, and what effect the misfortune would have on the building schedule. It was decided to rebuild the old lock on a fast schedule and enlarge it so it could handle two jumbo barges.

Now the question was what to do about shipping freight through the dam. After conferences and agreements with other government agencies concerned, the decision was made to build a road around the south end of the dam for this purpose. It was especially important at this time because soon there was to be shipped from the George C. Marshall Space Flight Center at Huntsville, Alabama, to Cape Canaveral, Florida, the Saturn space booster. (This was successfully done a few weeks later.)

It was not so much with water, however, that the TVA was to find its biggest problems—it was on and under the land. For some time coal had been one of the main sources of power. During 1961 the TVA

U.S. Senator George W. Norris, "father of the TVA," in front of Norris Dam, named after him, and the first such structure built by the Authority.

Aubrey J. "Red" Wagner, chairman of the TVA Board of Directors for seventeen years, longer than any other chairman. Retired in 1978, he is credited with being the most influential and innovative figure in the history of the organization.

Present TVA Chairman S. David Freeman examining a model of the $120 million office complex which the Authority is planning for downtown Chattanooga, including novel cost effective solar heating. Appointed in 1978, Freeman has stated he wants the TVA to move in new directions.

announced that it would consider accepting limited quantities of coal not meeting previous standard specifications for total moisture, dry ash, or dry sulphur content. An arrangement was worked out with the L&N Railroad to bring coal from the western Kentucky fields to TVA plants in northern Alabama. While most of such coal arrived at the plants by rail, about a third of it came by barge and truck. Near the end of 1962 the Peabody Coal Company placed in operation a power shovel it called "the largest self-propelled land machine" which could remove the overburden from coal seams at the rate of 115 cubic yards in a single "bite."

The TVA claimed that in 1962 it stepped up its effort to solve the problem created by strip mining of coal. It was resolved to bring about effective redevelopment of strip areas. A four-person task force representing forestry, coal procurement, aquatic biology, and engineering was established to review the situation. The Authority stated, as it often has since, that the regulation of strip mining and the requirements for restoration of strip areas is the responsibility of the states. In its 1962 Annual Report, the attitude of the TVA was this: "Landowners in general have done little reclamation and according to recent discussions with owners of 10,000 acres of stripped coal and iron land, few feel any compulsion to do so, despite public concern over the appearance of stripped areas, erosion, silting, and pollution of streams." Despite this statement, the Authority frequently has been accused, especially by environmentalists, of paying too little attention to the condition of the land after its coal has been strip mined.

In 1961 the Kentucky Department of Conservation and the Peabody Coal Company joined with the TVA in a strip mine reclamation test. The purpose was to discover if the use of pine seedlings thickly planted would help reclaim the spoil banks. In the Tennessee Sequatchie Valley, two strip mine spoil bank rehabilitation demonstrations were carried out in 1963. Trees and shrubs were planted. A soil test program was started to evaluate the agricultural potential of the area.

In late 1962 a survey was made by the TVA which showed that there were about 15,000 acres of stripped land in the Tennessee River watershed, primarily in Tennessee and Virginia, and another 20,000 acres in the valley counties but outside the watershed. Mining was proceeding at the rate of 1,000 acres a year in the watershed and 2,000 acres a year outside of it. The survey led the TVA to the following conclusions concerning surface mining:

1. The value of the mineral resources involved is tremendous, and their recovery is essential to the industrial economy.
2. The surfaces of areas from which minerals are taken must be restored.
3. The cost of such restoration should be included in the sales price of the mineral.
4. In the cases of coal and phosphate, in which TVA's study and experience are limited, restoration can be accomplished without an unreasonable increase in price.
5. Each state should develop a policy on strip mining and reclamation, taking into consideration its own combination of geologic, topographic, economic, and social conditions and reflect that policy through adequate legislation.

No organization is more conscious of anniversaries than this one. On May 18, 1963, President John F. Kennedy spoke before a crowd of 15,000 people at Muscle Shoals, Alabama, commemorating the thirtieth year of the TVA. "The work of the TVA will never be over," Kennedy declared. "There will always be new frontiers for it to conquer. For in the minds of men the world over, the initials TVA stand for progress."

In November 1960 the TVA had issued its first bonds under the new authority approved by Congress and the President in 1959. The issue of $50 million, bearing an interest rate of 4.4 percent, was sold competitively. The successful bidder was a financial syndicate headed by the Chase Manhattan Bank, Morgan Guaranty Trust Company of New York, Chemical Bank New York Trust Company, C. J. Devine & Company, and the Northern Trust Company. A second issue of the same amount of bonds was sold in June 1961 with a similar syndicate buying it. This was typical of other such financing which followed in the years ahead. The proceeds from the sale of these bonds was to be used only to provide capital for the power program.

In a financial commemoration of the one-hundredth anniversary of the birth of Senator George W. Norris, the TVA announced a new and lower schedule of retail rates for optional use by the distributors of TVA power. These rates were about 25 percent lower than the TVA basic rates initiated in 1933. It was called "The Norris Centennial Rate." Average use among the 1,371,000 residential customers served by the distributors of TVA power at that time was 10,406 kilowatt-hours, compared with 4,353 kilowatt-hours for the nation as a whole. The average cost per kilowatt-hour was 0.94 cents as compared with 2.39 cents in the nation.

By the mid-1960s increasing emphasis was being placed in new homes on year-round electric climate control, coupling electric heating in winter with air conditioning in summer. A popular item is the heat pump which has been improved in performance and operates at a comparatively low cost, consuming less electricity in a year than does a combination of central air conditioning and resistance heating.

The first all-electric school in the valley was constructed in 1953; by 1964 there were 75 such schools in operation, 13 of them having summer air conditioning as well as electric heating, with additional ones having been built since. Electricity in rural schools made possible pressure water systems, refrigeration, automatic waterheating, improved lighting, and convenient fuel for cooking. This aided home economic courses and facilitated visual aids.

By this time virtually every farm in the TVA area had electric service, as did most of those in the nation. But it was felt that the job of rural electrification was far from over.

According to a report at that time, experience in the TVA area is showing that the job is just beginning. The use of electric energy on the farm can be greatly increased with benefits to farm users. In the TVA area, electricity has already helped immensely in bringing about favorable and profitable changes in agriculture. Electric equipment on the farm is saving time and money, increasing productivity, replacing manual labor, and helping to bring about a more diversified agriculture as farms decrease in number and increase in size. This is a start. The possibilities for much fuller use of electricity on the farm are indicated by the cooperative Electrofarm Program which has been under way for several years in the TVA area. At the close of the fiscal year 1965, 263 Electrofarms were in operation, and they used an average of 46,000 kilowatt-hours per farm this year. This was an increase of 2,800 kilowatt-hours over 1964.
The Electrofarm Program, started in this area and still unique to it, is a joint program sponsored by the TVA, the distributors of TVA power, and the agricultural extension services of the states. It is designed to help the farm family use electricity both in the home and in farm operations as a means of obtaining the maximum of convenience and saving time and labor and increasing profits of farm operations. The Electrofarm families are assisted by the specialists of TVA, the extension services, and the distributors in planning the uses of electricity which best fit their individual needs.

A natural corollary to the availability of cheaper electric power in the valley has been, of course, that here exists one of the best markets in the country for electrical appliances. For some reason most of these have been manufactured in other sections. For many years distributors of these appliances have employed electrical development specialists who work with customers and dealers. The TVA also has a staff whose services are available where needed along this line. The work of the latter staff is largely that of planning programs which coordinate the activities of the interested agencies, conduct research into new uses of electricity, and provide services which the distributors may request. TVA power distributors in a 28-county area formed the North Mississippi Industrial Development Association which has helped to provide new jobs in industry. Similar programs were carried out by distributors in north Alabama and west Tennessee.
The TVA has been pleased to point out that since the mid-1950s, an increasing number of "utilities, trade magazines, such as *Electrical World,* and trade associations have been pushing electric heat with increasing vigor. Two developments helped to spur this interest. One

was the rapid extension of natural gas lines to all parts of the country, bringing competition not only in house heating but for other major uses, such as cooking and water heating. Another was rapid expansion of air conditioning, bringing a shift from the traditional winter peak loads for many utilities to peaks in summer, when temperature and other factors lowered the load-carrying capacities of the systems. Electric heating offered a balance to summer air conditioning.''

Tributary Development

A full-time staff was established by the Authority for the purpose of tributary area development. In its early stages, the TVA had been primarily concerned with the task of harnessing the Tennessee River and its major tributaries. Now it was recognized that with the help of state and local governments, more localized enterprises should be considered. The TVA had reported to Congress soon after its inception that ''the control of the smaller rivers should not be dominated by any single end, but by consideration of the greatest total benefit.''

Toward this end, the Bear Creek Watershed Association was organized in a 900-square-mile area of Alabama and Mississippi. The association named committees on human resources, agriculture, forestry, water control, minerals, and business and industry. These committees with help from the TVA and state agencies collected information as a basis for determining steps to be taken to solve resources conservation and to further economic development.

In the Beech River watershed in west Tennessee, an Authority was established by the state legislature for the purpose of planning multiple-purpose dams, reservoirs, and channel improvements to control the Beech River and help advance the economic life of the area. This upland once produced good cotton crops, but the land had eroded away and in some cases had been abandoned. The bottom lands remained fertile, but during the crop season they were often flooded by a stream choked with silt from the uplands and thus failed to produce an adequate income.

Landowners asked the TVA to dredge the local stream channel in the hope of reducing flood damage to corn crops in the river bottoms. Cooperation was forthcoming, and trees were planted on eroded lands and markets found for the pulpwood. Farmers diversified their crops and improved their fertilizer; dairy, hog, and poultry enterprises were established, and the output of the region increased several times in value. In the upper French Broad River Valley, the TVA prepared maps of some 40 sites which appeared to be suitable industrial areas. In cooperation with North Carolina State College a survey was made to obtain information on education, training, employment, income, expenditures, labor mobility, and other factors.

Melton Hill Dam, the twenty-first major water control project to be constructed by the TVA, was finished in May 1963 and the lock officially opened to traffic. This dam, at the head of the Clinch River arm of Watts Bar reservoir, extended the navigable waterway 38 miles upstream to the Eagle Bend area near Clinton, Tennessee. It also serves the city of Oak Ridge and the Atomic Energy Commission installations there. This was the first dam to extend navigation on a tributary of the Tennessee River and was the first such TVA project not to be financed entirely by Congressional appropriations.

A decision was made in 1963 to replace the 50-year-old Hales Bar Dam on the Tennessee River below Chattanooga with a new dam, the Nickajack, 6½ miles downstream. It was decided to abandon the old dam because of the difficulty of keeping the structure in repair for long-term service. The dam rested on a foundation of cavernous limestone, and leakage defied all efforts to stop it permanently. The Nickajack Dam, named for a nearby Indian cave, has a good foundation on a different type of rock formation.

As the TVA moved into the construction of larger units, it also moved toward automation and embarked on a program of installing electric data collecting and computer systems. For example, the Widows Creek unit with its 500,000-kilowatt machines acquired a high-speed data collecting system which keeps track of a large number of measurements, including temperatures and pressures. When measurements show up that are not normal, an alarm sounds. Digital computers perform monitoring and logging operations and make hourly computations on equipment and cycle performance as well as prepare periodic statistical reports on unit operation.

A financial consideration which had not been computed was the proposed new rate, about 40 percent of the existing level, which was announced by the Southern Railway Company to become effective in August of 1961. The Interstate Commerce Commission examined the proposal and found the rates to be "unjust and unreasonable . . . and constitute unfair and destructive competitive practices." The ICC suspended the rates and began investigation of them. The TVA sided with the ICC because the former felt that these rates were but an attempt to undercut the prices charged for shipping on the rivers of the valley. The Southern Railway contended that the drastic reduction in rates was made possible by technological improvements resulting from the use of aluminum hoppers in multiple car cuts. It was the position of the TVA that if such improvements did justify the reduction, the proposed rates should apply also to other commodities. "It is TVA's position," according to the report, "that the barge-rail route represents the low-cost mode of transportation."

Indirect benefits, disputed by some economists, were said to come from savings of something over $20 million for shippers who used the waterways of the valley. It also was estimated that at least equal savings were realized in transportation charges accounted for by reductions in rail rates made to meet barge competition. The lakes over which such shipping was made had locks having lifts of from 40 to 100 feet by which towboats and barges ascend or descend over 500 feet in traversing the full length of the waterway. The mild climate along the Tennessee River is advantageous because it permits year-round navigation. By 1965 the minimum depth in the channel was 11 feet, providing a 2-foot overdepth for vessels drawing 9 feet of water. The minimum channel width is 300 feet, with widening on bends where necessary. Water depths of 25 feet or more are found in more than half of the channel length.

In 1965, three out of every four tons of freight moving on the Tennessee River either originated outside the valley or was destined for an outside port. A personal visit to the Nickajack Dam by this writer obtained the information that sizable vessels from foreign countries now go up the river with ease to its headwaters. In 30 years the estimated accumulated benefits of the TVA navigation system were more than $300 million. Private investment in waterfront plants and terminals had passed the $1 billion mark, and virtually all of this had taken place since the completion of the 9-foot navigation channel. Besides pulpwood and metal plants, others included the manufacturing of food, petroleum products, stone, clay, glass, and transportation equipment. Also along the river now were atomic and space installations, arsenals, and TVA steam plants.

It is not easy to determine the exact attitude of President John Kennedy toward the TVA. In helping to celebrate the thirtieth anniversary of the Authority, he urged it to go forward but made inquiries as to where it was going. In 1961 Kennedy, at the request of a Senator, addressed a letter to the board of directors of the TVA strongly suggesting the location of a steam-generating plant at a site known to have been recommended by the legislator. The letter was made public and was widely interpreted as bordering on political pressure. But like the intervention of President Eisenhower in the Dixon-Yates controversy, this Presidential interference did not succeed. The board went ahead and made its own decision regarding the location of the plant.

The foregoing outcome was in accordance with the law by which the TVA was set up. In another legal direction, a publication of the Duke University School of Law carried an article which examined the financing of the TVA. It concluded that power revenues had been sufficient to meet the current operating and maintenance expenses of TVA's power program and would continue to be so. Earnings have not been sufficient, the article stated, nor is it reasonable to expect them to be sufficient to finance by themselves the cost of building new power facilities to meet load growth. In the past, earnings have been supplemented with appropriations; in the future these sources will be supplemented with bonds. It is generally expected that earnings may provide one-third to one-half of the system's capital requirements and that bonds will be required for the remainder. Insofar as nonpower activities are concerned, appropriations supplemented with proceeds from the sale of fertilizer and from other sources will continue to finance operating expenses as well as capital expenditures.

Through the 1960s the TVA continued to receive bouquets and brickbats. Yet as some wag expressed it, the latter were either caught and thrown back at the assailants or, better still, were simply incorporated into some new TVA structure.

Not everyone was happy with the TVA. A concrete worker, James P. Prater of Farner, Tennessee, wrote a letter to the Authority as follows:

> Gentlemen:
>   As an employee of the Tennessee Valley Authority, it is to my sorrow to make this statement: I am so very much disgusted and disappointed in myself and the TVA that I am asking the Authority to accept my resignation.

A search of the files of the TVA revealed no more information about why this man wrote such a letter or what happened to him after he left his job. Perhaps no more is necessary.

Broader criticism of the Authority appeared in the January 4, 1962, issue of *The Reporter,* in which John Ed Pearce had an article, "The Creeping Conservatism of TVA." In this he took the organization to task for appearing to veer from its original objectives of regional development. Pearce admitted that the TVA is always under attack and especially in each session of Congress. But the latest one was different:

It comes not from traditional foes but long-time friends, people of the Valley who for a quarter century have been the stubbornest defenders of TVA policies and practices. It is a curious attack, planned not to wreck but to reform, mounted by men who swear they love TVA more than the men who run it. It is their contention that TVA has become so engrossed in the production and sale of power that it is little more than a big utility, conservative and cost-conscious, with neither time nor liking for the tasks of regional development for which it was created.

Pearce stated that the trouble started during World War II when the TVA, called on to furnish power for government plants such as Oak Ridge, turned from hydroelectric dams to steam plants. Following the war, the great increase in demand for power left TVA no choice but to continue building steam plants to meet the demand. He charged that the TVA failed to check flooding on the Elk River, and this forced the city of Shelbyville, Tennessee, to spend much of its urban renewal funds on a flood wall. The Army Corps of Engineers planned two dams on the Cumberland River in Kentucky, assuming that part of the cost could be justified by sale of the power to TVA. When TVA declined, saying it could produce the power more cheaply in steam plants, the engineers were forced to reconsider. Pearce concluded with the sentiment that is still felt in some quarters:

Throughout the years, when critics have demanded that TVA be sold to private power firms, its defenders have been able to reply that while private utilities might make and sell power, they could not undertake the regional development and human service that are, and have always been, the prime and unique functions of TVA. But if TVA neglects these tasks, it destroys its own best reason for being.

13. Toward an Image

If those who oppose the TVA were categorized into political parties, the Republicans would certainly take first place. The fact that East Tennessee for the most part has traditionally been Republican adds to the irony of this situation. Here families were divided in the Civil War Between the States, as was the case of the grandparents of this writer. A Republican Congressman became a biennial occurrence in the district in which I grew up.

Barry Goldwater, Republican nominee for the Presidency in 1964, was flatly against the TVA. On a previous occasion he had said in the Senate: "TVA was conceived in socialism, born during a period of economic chaos and has been nurtured and expanded in deceit. The only way we can keep that agency under control is through the power of appropriations." Goldwater said that his substitute plan would save the taxpayers millions of dollars a year by returning to other appropriate federal agencies all those TVA functions which have counterparts in national programs. These sentiments of Goldwater were probably sincere, but they doubtless helped considerably in causing him to lose the South in the election.

When Lyndon Johnson was elected President, friends of the TVA hailed this as a victory for the organization and rightly predicted that its existence was now safe for several more years. Many Republicans of the area, though not elated by the national victory of the Democrats, were nevertheless relieved to feel that the organization which was benefiting them personally through cheap electric power and other means would still be around.

In the mid-1960s, when it was announced that higher interest, fuel, and labor costs necessitated an increase in TVA electric rates, this came as a shock to many people of the valley who perhaps were more interested in the power of the purse than the power of TVA. Chairman Aubrey Wagner made the announcement in words which were in various forms to ring down the years:

For the past fifteen years TVA has been able to offset steadily rising cost trends with various improvements in efficiency and economy, without increasing its wholesale power rate. However, a thorough review of all cost factors now makes it clear that greater revenues must be obtained to assure reliable power supplies for the region's needs and financial soundness for the TVA system.

Not surprisingly, one factor cited by Wagner was the trend of increasing prices of coal, the largest single TVA power expense, then costing about $100 million a year.

At about the same time there came a blast from Edwin Vennard, managing director of the Edison Electric Institute, who stated in a broadcast the low opinion his organization had of the TVA. He admitted that the Authority was often praised for its efficiency but added that after a study made by the institute they "found that if TVA and its distributors were required to pay taxes equivalent to those paid by investor-owned companies, rates would need to be raised 56 percent. When so raised, TVA's rates are no lower than the rates of tax-paying, investor-owned companies operating under similar conditions."

Adding "insult to injury," so to speak, another broadcaster, Dan Smoot of Dallas, Texas, trained his verbal guns on the water developments of the Authority. He said that the $200 million which the TVA claimed it had spent on flood control were costing the taxpayers about $7 million annually in interest. The Army engineers replied that a flood which could cover 666,000 acres of land in the Tennessee Valley could happen once each 500 years. Smoot scoffed: "In order to protect this many acres from being flooded once every 500 years, the Tennessee Valley Authority has permanently submerged almost a million acres under TVA man-made lakes or emergency reservoirs. In other words, every 500 years the Tennessee River might have flooded two-thirds as much land in the Tennessee Valley as the TVA has permanently flooded or set aside in its flood control program."

Taking a rap at the navigation developments, Smoot charged that while the 650-mile-long waterway created by TVA was free to shippers who use it, it actually costs taxpayers over $8 million a year in maintenance. "If people who ship freight," he said, "on the government's 'free' waterway in the Tennessee Valley were charged freight rates just high enough to pay for the cost of operating that waterway, the rates would be considerably higher than those which private railroads charge in the same neighborhood."

Tellico

If the TVA's head was bloody, it also was unbowed. It had another dream, this one being ideal to its advocates and preposterous to its opponents. About 25 miles southwest of Knoxville on the winding Little Tennessee River there is an especially beautiful place known to the Indians as Tellico. Here the stream flows languidly past wooded hills and peaceful meadows. Here the Indians fished and hunted and built their mounds, some of which still remain; and here the white settlers have come to love this land for its picturesque beauty, its restfulness as a retreat, and what they fondly call "a fisherman's paradise."

So a sensation was exploded in the valley when the TVA announced in 1965 the purchase of 5,000 acres of land in the Tellico area for the purpose of building a new dam and creating a model town nearby. The Authority explained that such a project would not cause great harm to the natural features of the region. It argued that the Tellico Dam would be a worthwhile addition to the TVA water control system and would add significantly to the economic development of the area.

The Authority insisted that this dam would be unique in that it would provide millions of dollars worth of navigation benefits without requiring construction of a navigation lock. It also would provide electrical energy, but the water flowing from the Little Tennessee River, already regulated by Fontana Dam and those of the aluminum company upstream, would continue through a connecting canal and then over the Fort Loudoun turbines.

The TVA embellished its announcement by a reminder of the beauty of the land with its clear water and mountain background:

> Fishing will be good in the reservoir and its embayments. Indications are that trout fishing will continue in the upper reaches. The topography of the shoreline, the network of local roads, and the short distance to metropolitan Knoxville can be expected to produce major subdivisions for permanent homes as well as summer cottages. With headquarters of the reservoir adjacent to the Great Smoky Mountains National Park, the most heavily visited national park; with the Cherokee National Forest forming a portion of the shoreline; and with north-south flow and east-west interstate highways passing nearby, ideal opportunities will be created for extensive recreational development.

This idyllic-sounding announcement may have been pleasing to the public information office of the TVA, but it was not to the national headquarters of private industry or to ardent conservationists. In a stinging speech at Mankato, Minnesota, Robert P. Gerholz, president of the Chamber of Commerce of the United States, accused the Authority of a "flagrant assault on free enterprise." He said the organization was proposing to speculate in land and sell it to favored business firms. "The idea of a Federal community is taking form," he cried, "a community laid out and developed by Federal blueprint, with local industries handpicked by Federal planners, and free enterprisers excluded from the community if they don't fit into the plan."

Striking back in defense, Frank Smith, TVA board member, replied:

> Anything the U.S. Chamber states about the TVA should be accepted with the knowledge of its long history as a national opponent of virtually all TVA programs from the beginning and throughout the years. On Tellico, the Chamber appears primarily concerned with our purchase of 5,000 acres of what is certain to become prime industrial land. This land on the Little Tennessee River lacks industrial site potential for a number of reasons. One of its deficits is the lack of water transportation. Another is the lack of the often immense water supply requirements of chemical and related industries.

Director Smith admitted that the TVA could be making a profit on the land but wondered what would be wrong if the national treasury should receive back part of the original cost of building the dam. He felt that the local government could handle the zoning and development pattern and provide the best possible use of the land for local citizens. TVA chairman Wagner estimated that private industry would invest some $265 million in the Tellico project and provide 6,600 new jobs for young people of the area, many of whom would otherwise go elsewhere.

Another phase of the Tellico Reservoir problem was its archaeological side. Suddenly the Cherokee Indians on the other side of the Great Smoky Mountains seemed to arise as if they were on the warpath against the project. They remembered their ancestors and their temple mounds along the Tellico, and some of their leaders decided to try to preserve these former "happy hunting grounds" even though modern landmarks had already made inroads. The TVA itself, in it Progress Report of the Division of Water Control Planning, stated that the University of Tennessee was conducting archaeological explorations around the site of the Tellico Reservoir. "This area along the Little Tennessee River," said the report, "is a veritable storehouse of archaeological material; it was frequented by all cultures from the Paleo through the Historic."

Sydney Izlar, a former TVA official, was incensed. He told this writer:

The recent controversy over the inundation of the areas of the Tellico project, and the objections of the week-end trout fishermen can hardly be heard above the noise created by the instant archaeologists who suddenly have decided that the Tennessee Valley is a treasury of Indian artifacts. They remind me of the little one-year old who has suddenly discovered his navel. He has found something he never before has seen.

Construction went ahead on the Tellico Reservoir project, and for awhile it seemed to be proceeding on an even keel, despite some strong objections. However, aroused environmentalists eventually became so active and organized that they went into court and obtained an injunction to stop the construction, even after more than $119 million had been spent on the project.

Rumors had gone around while the TVA projects were under construction that the wide lakes created by the high dams would endanger boats because of wind and wave action. Captain Donald T. Wright, a river pilot and editor of a publication devoted to furthering inland waterway development, was one who made such criticism. However, after making a trip by water from Paducah to Knoxville, he admitted that his criticism was not well founded. While the TVA agrees that its slack-water lakes are not suitable for rowboats, the records do not show many sinkings. It may be that some of the veteran river pilots had little taste for the changes in the navigation channel.

Navigation had been referred to by some in the formative period of the Authority as a constitutional peg on which the whole TVA program was hung. When Pickwick Dam was being built, an observer remarked that it would be cheaper for the TVA, instead of building a navigation lock in the dam, just to buy every boat that came up the river and wanted to get through. Stuart Chase, who still believes that the Tennessee Valley Authority was one of the New Deal's best assets, thought little of the navigation purpose. "As a matter of fact," he said, "and I trust the Supreme Court is safely asleep as I whisper—navigation is probably the least important aspect of the cycle, from the point of view of the well-being of the people of the Valley."

A prime example of the effect of the TVA navigation improvements is the Chattanooga district. This city was a manufacturing center for years before, but since the Tennessee River has had 9-foot navigation, industrial growth there has greatly increased and diversified. Like sites on the river in Alabama, Chattanooga has become a feed grains and flour milling center. One of the largest such firms in the world, Combustion Engineering, Inc., is located in Chattanooga and produces soil pipe and atomic reactor vessels. The General Portland Cement

Company has a large plant there, and a huge nylon factory is there as well as firms producing chemicals and iron.

Water transportation was considered in locating these plants. Between Chattanooga and northward to Knoxville, the river front is less industrialized. Exceptions are the huge plant of the Bowaters Southern Corporation at Calhoun, the Olin Mathieson Chemical Corporation plant across the river, and the Tennessee Products and Chemical Corporation's ferroalloy plant in the old iron furnaces site at Rockwood.

In Knoxville itself, the industrial space is comparatively limited, while the tendency has been for big new industries in the valley to locate on large plots of land, thus leaving room for future expansion. But the general picture is different. William J. Hull, chairman of the legislative committee of the Ohio Valley Improvement Association, stated: "Industries in the Southern States have long been handicapped by higher rail freight rates than those their competitors in the North have to pay. This has been one of the factors contributing to the retarded economic growth and lower income levels in some of these states. Partially offsetting this, water transportation has been the foundation of much of the industrial growth in the South since the end of World War II."

Grain from the Midwest had begun to move up the Tennessee River before World War II. With the improvement in navigation on the river, the shipments increased rapidly until by 1961 the tonnage of grain being shipped on the waterway was around 2.3 million tons. A grain distributor at Guntersville, Alabama, reported that in one week in 1959, the port there handled more corn than the Chicago Board of Trade did in the same period. Besides corn, wheat, oats, soybeans, and flour are among the other grains shipped. Such a supply has led to the establishment of new processing industries and increased poultry and livestock production and created new grain distribution centers in the region. It was not only the navigation but the behavior and quality of the water which continued to hold the attention of the TVA. Some 600 gauges provide the records of rainfall. They confirm that this averages for the valley as a whole 52 inches in a typical year. The highest precipitation is in the southeastern mountains. At one location, near Highlands, North Carolina, 93 inches of rain falls in an average year. Yet not far away at Asheville, only 37 inches of rain descends annually. Just as the rainfall is not equally divided among areas of the watershed, it is not evenly distributed throughout the year. More than half of the annual total is received in winter and early spring, from November to mid-April. March is generally the wettest month, although in some places midsummer sees the highest precipitation. The driest season is usually in September and October. On the average, 22 inches of the valley's rainfall moves somewhere in its rivers.

The most conspicuous increase in the use of streamflow by the people of the watershed is involved with their recreation. The TVA reservoirs have about 700,000 acres of water surface and 10,000 miles of shoreline. In 1965 use of the impounded water for swimming, water skiing, boating, and fishing and of adjacent areas for camping, picnicking, and such resulted in a total of over 40 million visits. In the decade following, the figure approximately doubled. The number of summer homes and commercially operated services and concessions related to this recreation has greatly multiplied, and their total value has been estimated at around $300 million.

One commercial activity, however, has had disappointing results. For awhile mussel shell harvesting was a sizable and profitable enterprise. But for some reason, as yet uncertain, the supply of mussels has been decreasing. The TVA and other agencies have been investigating the situation as to what causes the lack of plentiful reproduction. Some of the states in the valley have taken protective measures for the supply of mussel shells, most of which are exported to Japan to be used in the production of buttons and cultured pearls.

Another problem confronting the Authority is that of the discharge into the streams of waste from industries, from the sewerage systems of municipalities, and from floating craft. As the economy has expanded, here and elsewhere, pollution of streams has increased and preventive measures have not kept pace with it. The TVA urges that waste should be treated at its source and thus make certain that the quality of the valley streamflow "is protected from impairment, and that this ancient use of water does not frustrate the growth of others."

The tremendous use of steampower generation causes the withdrawal of about 5 million acre-feet of water from the streams of the Tennessee Valley. Nearly all the water used at the coal-burning plants of the TVA is used for cooling and condensing the steam. It passes through the condensers once and returns to the stream with little loss in the quality of the water but with considerable rise in temperature. It can easily be seen that this can affect the life of the fish and other creatures which come in contact with this water. Attempts are therefore being made to solve this problem, with thus far varying results.

A J. Wagner predicted that economic growth will not be hampered by a scarcity of water in the Tennessee River basin. An expert on the use of water, Wagner can wax poetic about it. "It is nature's constant gift to man," he says, "delivered in abundance to use as he chooses."

He believes that the valley's future growth does not depend on progress in the art of converting saline waters into fresh. He believes there will be enough water for all purposes.

The TVA recognizes that owners of cottages and managers of resorts on the upper tributaries complain because seasonal or emergency drawdown of water levels reduces their year-round enjoyment of the lakes. Here is a basic conflict between the use of water for recreation and that for flood control, navigation, and power generation. In regard to the use of the shoreline, Dr. Guy T. Vise of Meridian, Mississippi, animatedly told this writer that although he was impressed with the early progress of the TVA, he believes that it is "now hamstrung by antiquated rules and regulations. TVA needs a model change as Henry Ford did with his cars."

The TVA is a fine thing, said Vise, a propertyowner himself. But he pointed out that many areas of its shorelines are below flood stage: "These gradually erode and in case of very high water are thus ruined. Many acres of land are made useless for farming by many inches of sand deposited at flood time. Silt from the hills gradually fill and diminish the storage capacity of the reservoirs. This will worsen with time unless we take measures to compensate," he declared.

Vise had a plan for improvement of the situation. He suggested: (1) elevate the shorelines along the lakes above the high water line and (2) keep the water storage capacity the same by excavating the soil back of the elevated shorelines, thus keeping all water levels and flood control levels identical to the present standards and computations. This would add billions of dollars of taxable lands to the tax rolls of our cities, counties, and states.

In commenting on the foregoing suggestions, Chairman Wagner said that the TVA appreciated it and saw some merit there but doubted if Dr. Vise fully realized the magnitude of such an undertaking. "Such a construction effort would be larger than the Tennessee-Tombigbee Waterway project. The accomplishment would be so complex and expensive as to be virtually impossible," Wagner concluded.

More concerned about pollution, the TVA has felt encouraged by continuation of programs carried on by municipalities in the valley to lessen water pollution. Not so encouraging is the problem of controlling industrial pollution. "Long established plants are generally the worse offenders," a TVA report said:

A single industry in the French Broad River basin, for example, discharged waste which in biochemical impact on the stream is equivalent to raw sewage from an urban population of over 600 thousand. . . . The rivers of the French Broad River basin receive the greatest volume of industrial wastes in the Valley. The Holston River basin comes next, and the Tennessee River from Knoxville to Guntersville ranks third. The resulting pollution varies in kind and degree, and different conflicts are created on different rivers. In a few stretches of the watercourses the value of the streams for recreation is destroyed as unsightly color, foam and boiling gases offend the senses of the visitor. In other areas water is unfit for swimming, and aquatic life is menaced by the toxic wastes of industrial operation. In some places new industries are limited in site selection because establishments already operating upstream arc polluting the naturally excellent water supply at desirable locations.

Irrigation is usually.considered to be a blessing. Here, however, it is a mixed one. The reason is the possibility of conflict between the use of water for irrigation and for power generation. In other words, local conflicts of this nature may develop between farm and factory. So far this has not been a big problem in the valley, with most of the TVA water being used for irrigation in the dry years, which have been few. Some creeks were pumped dry, and the amount of hydroelectricity available was reduced.

Nature has introduced some problems such as when the winter rainfall carries forest debris into the water. More serious is the task of eliminating noxious plant growth such as Eurasian watermilfoil, which has invaded a number of TVA reservoirs. It is believed that this began when someone dumped the contents of a single fish bowl into a small embayment of Watts Bar Reservoir. Also, a fisherman introduced it into the water near his dock in an effort to catch more fish. Milfoil spreads rapidly and is carried by the wind or by boats as well as by the current. If not checked it disastrously reduces the recreational value of the stretches of the river where it becomes established. It can clog water intakes and provide a breeding place for mosquitoes. The TVA is engaged in a major effort to control its growth by manipulating reservoir levels, undertaking extensive research, consulting with technicians working in other areas where milfoil has appeared, and experimenting with chemicals designed to eradicate it.

The TVA is convinced that what it has done in the valley in the development of water resources had to be accomplished by the federal government. On the other hand, the Authority believes that the value of this achievement to the region will be limited or expanded by the degree to which state and local agencies promote full utilization of the assets which have been provided. "The future is in their hands," the TVA states. "Decisions of communities on the waterfront will affect the extent to which the navigation channel is used for commerce between regions. Local agencies of distribution are responsible for promoting the effective use by their consumers of the electricity made available by streamflow regulation. Town by town, stream by stream, municipalities must move to reduce the remaining flood hazards and by zoning to limit the growth of the area's damage potential.''

It has been found that any disturbance of the cover of the soil adds silt to the streams as rainfall washes sediment from the earth which has been strip mined. Mining for coal adds another serious threat to water quality. When the coal itself or sulphur-bearing rock is exposed to weather, the runoff from storms carries polluting acid to the valley's streams. Such pollution usually occurs in creeks and branches located immediately below mining operations. To combat this the TVA has conducted experiments in cooperation with coal producers and land-owners. It has been proven that if adequate provisions for drainage and spoil disposal are made in advance of mining, acid pollution from strip coal mines can be sharply lessened. The TVA feels that ''no producer should be permitted to engage in stripping if he fails to adopt acceptable mining procedures and effective reclamation measures.''

However well such aims have succeeded, the Authority points out that thousands of people are presently employed in new industries which use the navigation channel or rely on a dependable supply of water. The labor of the valley's youth is no longer so much needed on the family farm; instead, it is utilized in such places as modern chemical plants, pulpmills, factories that make furniture, and plants that process food.

Some of these people of course work for the TVA, and none of its activities seems more interesting than that of its electronic computers. Those in Knoxville and Chattanooga transmit information back and forth in a matter of minutes. In this way the TVA can calculate the amount of water which will be flowing into each of its 32 reservoirs.

By 8 A.M. each day, rain gauges are read at more than 200 key locations in the valley area; by 8:45 A.M. all these rainfall readings have been transmitted to Knoxville. These readings are punched onto IBM cards along with factors taking into account current river and reservoir conditions. Other equipment ''reads'' the cards and sends the information quickly over a telephone line to Chattanooga. Here similar equipment turns out identical cards that are fed into a big IBM 705 computer. This process was formerly done more slowly by hand until mathematicians devised a set of formulas by which the big computer could be used.

A unique situation had occurred in the March 1963 floods in the Tennessee Valley. This gave the TVA valuable experience in demon-strating the importance of obtaining adequate information on the distribution of rainfall in successfully regulating a flood. Also, the importance was learned of not discounting the possibility of a second flood, because twin floods occurred then less than a week apart. Such a situation makes it imperative to release surplus stored floodwater as soon as practical so as to be prepared for a second flood when it comes. Much of the heaviest rain fell on the area downstream from the tributary storage reservoirs. This produced a heavy flow into the mainstream reservoirs, requiring careful operation of these reservoirs based on adequate knowledge of rainfall and streamflow.

Floods are sporadic, but the need for continued development of the watersheds of the Tennessee River goes on. The work along the tributaries has been called "Little TVA Ventures." As an example, in Henderson County, Tennessee, dams have been built in a water control system that will regulate crop-destroying floods, supply water for municipal and industrial use, provide for irrigation, and create new outdoor recreation. In the Sequatchie Valley, a downtown plan for improving Dunlap was put into effect and was called "Operation Townlift."

In broader efforts to improve and restore the land, the TVA continued to cope with the specter of strip mining. In a speech in Lexington, Kentucky, Chairman Wagner pronounced that coal produced by strip mining must carry in its selling price the cost of reclaiming the land and indicated that TVA expected to pay its share of this cost. (Little did he realize how much coal would eventually cost.) He did point out that the haul roads to the mines over which the coal is removed provide access to areas which have otherwise been virtually inaccessible.

In the same state in which Wagner spoke, another voice was thundering opposition to such mining operations. Harry M. Caudill, a Kentucky leg. writer, stated in the *Atlantic Monthly:*

By a process which produces huge and immediate profits for a few industrialists, the southern Appalachians are literally being ripped to shreds, and eventually every taxpayer from Maine to Hawaii will have to pay the cost of flood control and soil reclamation in this strip-mining belt, Compounding the deepening tragedy is the fact that the TVA, which the Congress established for the benefit of one backward Southern region, has become a full-fledged partner in the devastation of another.

Caudill said that until about 1953, the TVA

was a benevolent agency whose administrators gave every evidence of a wide dedication to public service . . . but . . . a change has come

over the TVA. [By] degrees it changed direction, converting itself
into a mammoth corporation. . . . It was calculated that the steam
plants would burn millions of tons of coal annually, and the coal
industry was delighted by the prospect of such a fabulous new
customer. . . . The TVA, mighty benefactor of the Tennessee Valley, is subsidizing the destruction of the southern mountains. . . .
Inspired by the success of TVA, other large consumers have re-
sorted to the same methods. Already both Bethlehem Steel and
United States Steel are stoking their furnaces with coal ripped from
the southern hills.

Other critics agree with this eloquent Kentuckian and add that the
TVA is performing too little and too late in remedying the situation. Its
spokesman urged patience: "Nature's processes," said Wagner,
"even with man's best help, are sometimes discouragingly slow. Even
though we have walked in space, we have not been able to produce
'instant trees.' But I am sure that no thoughtful person will contend
that we have exhausted our ingenuity."

14. Into the Atom Age

At 5:16 P.M. on November 9, 1965, I was in a classroom on the tenth floor of the main building of New York University's Washington Square Campus in New York City. My 60 graduate students were more or less listening to a lecture on early American history. Everything seemed to be proceeding well until, right in the middle of a sentence, I mentioned "The Enlightenment"—and the lights went out.

Thinking it was a routine such interruption, I made some comment about my previous remark not being entirely appropriate, and the students laughed. But it was no laughing matter. The lights did not come on. I looked out of the window across Washington Square and saw that there were no street lights on either. After some mumbling and fumbling, we realized that the situation was serious, that something big had gone wrong.

After gathering up books, briefcases, and topcoats, the students and I felt our way slowly but calmly through the darkness into the hallway. There we encountered hundreds of other students and professors talking excitedly and edging carefully towards the elevators, only to find that they were not running. It was then that we made our tortuous way to the stairs leading to the ground floor. By this time a few candles and flashlights had appeared and, held upright, gave an eerie, irregular glow to the serpentine procession of humans which inched its way almost imperceptibly downward. As we slowly descended in increasing wonder, we were joined on each succeeding floor by many other students filing out of similar classrooms and thus making the process of descending even more crowded and slower.

Some 50 minutes later we arrived on the street floor, there to find a milling mob of NYU people, some of whom could be seen outside in the glare of automobile lights and a few emergency lanterns. Out of the clamor of voices one gathered that there had been a massive blackout not only of the city but of the surrounding area as well. I had never realized before how dependent we are upon the marvel of electric power.

Out across the square I could see, as I made my way through the

234

crowds and mainly halted traffic, the lights of a bus rapidly filling with people. I made a frantic dash toward the vehicle, bumping off of other pedestrians as I ran, and reached the bus just as the front entrance door closed. Desperately, I glanced toward the rear and saw that the side exit door was still open. A reckless lurch and I was inside, having to pull my briefcase through as the door closed upon it. I was the last one to enter the overcrowded bus.

Two hours and 40 blocks later, I arrived at my club uptown, which I found filled with nonmembers as well as our own group, seeking shelter and lodging. There was no way to get home. After staking out a place to sleep on a lounge, I hastened into the already-filled dining room and was barely able to grab one of the last-remaining sandwiches for dinner, the only thing left to eat in the club. It was thus that I encountered the "great blackout" of 1965.

It was the largest power failure up to that time. Affecting most of the northeastern United States, the interruption lasted from a few minutes in some localities to more than half a day in others. It encompassed about 80,000 square miles, approximately the same size territory as that serviced by the TVA, which was called upon to help. Although this did not work out practically, TVA personnel did become involved in the crisis. The blackout directly affected an estimated 30 million people in the United States and Canada, and it occurred at a time of day in which there was a maximum need for power in an area of great population density, so it held the greatest potential for chaos.

The territory in which the power failure took place included most of New York State, Connecticut, Massachusetts, Rhode Island; small parts of northern Pennsylvania; and northeastern New Jersey. Large portions of Ontario also were without power from 15 minutes to 3 hours. New Hampshire and Vermont experienced similar spotty failures. Some 28 electric systems were affected in the United States and Canada. Each system checked its equipment, and no faulty items were found. The mystery of why it occurred was unique in that there was no external evidence.

This was the worst outage, or interruption of electric power, in the nation's history in terms of number of people involved. It caused one of the most widespread and terrible frights of any event since 1938, when Orson Welles produced his shocking radio program based on "The War of the Worlds" by H. G. Wells. People of the country were alarmed, from the President on down. Lyndon Johnson ordered a full-scale investigation. Said he in a memorandum for Joseph C. Swidler, chairman of the Federal Power Commission and former TVA official: "Today's failure is a dramatic reminder of the importance of the uninterrupted flow of power to the health, safety, and well-being of our citizens and the defense of our country.''

In answer to a Presidential directive, the Power Commission stated in its report:

That panic was averted during the blackout is a tribute to the courage, poise, resourcefulness and faith of the millions of Americans who were left in darkness. There was much successful improvisation by individuals and agencies. Among the reasons the situation did not develop into a disaster was the prompt and efficient action by the President and by local government bodies, the effective dissemination of news by the radio industry, and the willingness to assist on the part of many volunteers. The dangers were alleviated somewhat by mild temperatures and a bright moon. There was no widespread looting, and reports indicate that crime rates throughout the region fell below normal.

When the outage occurred in New York City, it was a peak hour on the subway system and about 600 trains were in operation. More than 600,000 people were stranded. Over 10,000 people were still on the stopped trains at midnight, and 1,700 passengers were stranded for five hours on the Williamsburg Bridge above the East River. All of the 720 miles of subways had to be patroled before service could be restored at 6 A.M. the next morning. Within 2½ hours, all these trains were back in operation, but some of them were still behind schedule into the following day. The subway system in Boston, on the other hand, continued to operate throughout the blackout because it has its own generating facilities.

Railroad service in the New York City area was out until 5 A.M. except for the Pennsylvania Railroad, served by the Public Service Company of New Jersey. Even this road lost power for switching. At the airports, tragedy was averted only because of the bright moonlit night and the operation of the main control towers which had auxiliary power. About 250 flights were canceled or diverted to other airports. Radar and navigation aids in the metropolitan area were out of service for about six hours.

As a result of the failure, 855 hospitals were without commercial power, but nearly all of these, with the exception of those in the New York City area, had some form of standby power available. At many of the hospitals in New York, police and fire officials were called upon to furnish portable units for maintaining essential facilities and to help in the movement of patients. Although a number of radio stations were out of commission for a few minutes, many of them resumed broadcasting by using their emergency power and thus were able to keep up an almost continuous flow of important information to the public, which could receive it through battery sets and on automobile radios. Most television stations were out of operation for the full blackout period because they depended on commercial power, as did the receiving sets in the home. The national television networks were able to switch their broadcast operations from New York to other cities outside the blackout area and continued broadcasting.

Telephone communications remained operative in most places by the use of auxiliary power. But delays in placing calls took place because of the overloading of local and long distance lines, especially in New York City. Telegraph service was delayed up to 14 hours. Fortunately, however, most of the important intergovernmental services, including those for overseas, either remained in service or were quickly restored. Throughout the region big traffic jams occurred in the cities because of the failure of traffic control signals. Gasoline pumps did not work, and this left people stranded and out of gas.

One of the most frightening aspects of the whole situation was the feeling fed by rumors that some foreign power, even an invasion, was involved. However, when the Department of Defense checked major military installations, including the Strategic Air Command and North American Air Defense, it was found that communications were intact. Emergency organizations at state and local levels were activated within 5 to 15 minutes after the power failure. Civil Defense personnel were used in many cities to assist fire and police departments. Even so, at the Walpole Massachusetts State Penitentiary, 320 prisoners took advantage of the darkness to riot, resulting in $75,000 in damage.

The blackout was caused by the failure of a relay operation at a hydroelectric plant on the Niagara River in Ontario, Canada, which disconnected the transmission lines then moving power from that plant. No evidence was found of any sabotage being involved. "The prime lesson of the blackout," said the Federal Power Commission Report, "is that the utility industry must strive not merely for good but for virtually perfect service."

At the beginning of the trouble, the Federal Power Commission telephoned the TVA to ask if it had power to spare. It did have the power, but the nature of the blackout and the connection of the intergrid systems made it impossible to transmit power northward at the time. Steps were taken to remedy this situation.

Top power authorities from the TVA—including G. O. Wessenauer, manager of power operations, and C. P. Almon, Jr., power systems operations director—were called immediately to Washington, D.C., to help investigate the northeastern blackout. They knew something of such a happening because on January 19, 1964, high winds blew some sheet metal into the big substation at the Paradise steam plant of the TVA in Kentucky, causing a short-circuit and separating the plant from the system. Within 4½ mintues, other parts of the TVA power system picked up the generation lost at Paradise.

Flash Floods

As a result of these and other control activities, a report was submitted to Congress by the President entitled "A Unified National Program for managing Flood Losses." This report was prepared by a task force organized by the U.S. Bureau of the Budget with a TVA staff member as one of a panel of eight. It reviewed the national flood problem and recommended a program much in line with the experience of the TVA in the Tennessee Valley. The report stated in part that despite a big investment by the federal government in flood control there was an "estimated annual loss from floods showing an upward trend since 1936." It recommended steps to determine the urban areas where flood hazards exist and action by all government agencies to regulate the development of flood plains and floodproof structures vulnerable to floods.

The foregoing report noted that there was a tendency for builders to invade flood plains with new structures, even after knowing that a risk existed and that dams and reservoirs for protection against floods had neither been planned for or built. The recommendation: control and guide new developments in such a way as to avoid or minimize future damage. The TVA had previously recommended to the President that its flood control program be expanded on a national scale. A result, an executive order was issued requiring that flood hazards be evaluated by all executive agencies in planning new federal facilities, in disposing of federal lands or properties, and in the administration of programs supported by federal grants, loans, or mortgage insurance. The order directed the agencies to request necessary flood information from the TVA for areas within the valley and from the Secretary of the Army for other areas of the nation. The TVA and the Corps of Engineers jointly sponsored a pamphlet, "Introduction to Flood Proofing," which was published by the University of Chicago in 1967.

After virtually a lifelong study of water control and development, Chairman Wagner concluded:

> We have the science, the methods, and the experience to enable any city in the region to make itself virtually invulnerable to flood damage, if, together, we wish to make it so. It is a goal worth

working for. But it involves more than protective works to keep the water away; it involves as well as willingness on the part of the community to keep its structures out of areas where the flood hazards are greatest. . . . In the Tennessee Valley we are—and we should be—working toward complete flood control. This will be when the greatest rainstorms sweep over the Valley and their waters pass out of the smallest streams and through the mighty Tennessee itself without damage, leaving the people unaware of the flood that might have been. I believe this day can come—though only after a long period of time and with the patience, willing efforts, and fullest cooperation among TVA, state and local governments.

The period was not without its extraordinary deluges, particularly flash floods. An extreme one occurred on August 7, 1947. Four girls were sunbathing on the rocks of the West Prong Little Pigeon River just below the Chimneys in the Great Smoky Mountains National Park. Although little rain fell at this point, a cloudburst in the mountains above them produced a "wall of water" that carried one girl to her death while the other three were barely able to climb out alive.

The flash flood on November 18, 1957, inundated much of the business and residential portions of Spring City, flowing 9 inches of rain in 2 hours over a portion of the Piney River watershed. The water rose 8 feet in 30 minutes according to an account by R. E. Looney:

> We went home for dinner at 6:40 P.M., and then returned to the cleaning plant at 7:20 to work a short time. At 7:30 the water had risen to a height of eight inches in Maner's Garage which is diagonally across First Street from the laundry. We continued to work in the plant and at 7:45 P.M. a "wall of water" about thirty inches high struck the front of the building, breaking the door. The water rose rapidly to a height of eighty inches in the building. By means of a ladder, we climbed out onto the roof at 8:15 as the flood approached its crest at 8:20 P.M.

The little town of Clinchmore in the headwaters of the South Fork Cumberland River was literally wiped off the map on July 24, 1965, when 12 inches of rain fell in two hours. Stony Fork Creek rose 20 feet, the rate of rise exceeding 10 feet in one 15-minute period. Five persons lost their lives. The force of the water was so great that a 24-inch I-beam was carried downstream from a bridge and wrapped around a stump into the shape of a hairpin.

Oliver Springs, with a population of close to 4,000, is located at the foot of the Cumberland Mountains about 25 miles went of Knoxville. This is only 1 mile west of Oak Ridge. The town was once a center of coal mining activity, but with the decline of deep mining, it suffered widespread unemployment. Like similar Appalachian communities, it has become a home for retired coal miners and people on relief. Many Oak Ridge employees also live here. In addition to unemployment, low income, and declining population, Oliver Springs has been blighted by unsightly railroad tracks which crossed the town, heavy coal trucks lumbering down the main street, and the administrative inconveniences of being located in three counties. But most depressing has been frequent flooding by its Indian Creek. This stream rises on the steep slopes of the nearby mountains and is especially subject to flash floods resulting from thunderstorms. The TVA has long been concerned about this situation.

On July 6 through 12, 1967, two floods struck Oliver Springs. The first caused by 6 inches of rain which fell on July 6. The property damage was not great, but two persons were drowned. Approximately the same amount of rain fell on July 11 on ground already soaked by the previous rain. With the stream now up to its banks, the community was virtually inundated. Flood waters were 3 feet deep in the city hall, fire hall, public library, and post office. The high school and railroad station were flooded with 2 feet of water. Also flooded were 68 residences, 30 business buildings, and two churches, one church being completely destroyed. Roads and streets were heavily damaged, and power, telephone, and water services were disrupted. The greatest damage was to the high school.

TVA board members and other officials visited Olivier Springs during the flood and offered assistance. This led to meetings with officials of the town regarding action that might be taken to reduce such catastrophic events in the future. In their efforts to find a solution, the TVA officials saw an opportunity to revitalize the whole town and its business. It had already organized a local housing authority to provide improved housing for workers from Oak Ridge. A full-time TVA community planner was assigned to the job and worked with the local leaders in an earnest action to bring about broad-based community development. A plan of stream improvement to alleviate the flood problem was worked out in cooperation with the State Highway Department to accelerate road improvement and coordinate it with related plans for urban progress.

TVA flood control engineers were worried in the early spring of 1969. Rain fell from April 3 to 5. The Ohio River rose, causing some concern. By April 11 a crest of 40 feet was predicted for Cairo, Illinois, because snowmelt had swollen to record stages in the tributaries of the upper Mississippi River. By April 14, Cairo was slightly above the

40-foot flood stage and the engineers, TVA, and Army watched nervously. If it got much higher, steam plant operations would be hampered, camping areas at Land Between the Lakes would have to be closed, and other activities would be affected in like manner. In consultation with the Army engineers, the TVA decided to try to limit the Cairo crest to 45 feet. Discharge from the Kentucky and Barkley Reservoirs was reduced and an estimated $117,000 in flood damages was averted. Someone in the River Control Branch of the TVA remarked, "The engineers prepared for the worst and hoped for the best. This time the best happened!"

The largest Tennessee River flood in nearly five years occurred at Chattanooga in late December 1969. Flood control operations held the crest there to 28.5 feet, 1.5 feet below flood stage. It was estimated that without TVA regulations, the crest would have reached 39 feet, would have flooded 7,000 acres within the city (more than 500 homes), and would have caused over $21 million in damages.

Thus it is seen from a century of records that the major floods in the valley occur between late December and early April. Nearly 12 million acre-feet of storage space is reserved at the beginning of each year for the regulation of floods. Water is stored during the drier months of summer and fall to maintain streamflow for power production and navigation and to lower the reservoirs for the next flood season. The TVA emphasizes that the priority of flood control over power production is strictly observed. The lands completely or partly protected from flooding in the Tennessee Valley and along the Ohio and Mississippi rivers amount to 15 times the reservoir areas that are used for this control, according to TVA estimates.

In March of 1979 heavy floods struck the Southeast, including Tennessee, Alabama, and Georgia. Whereas there were millions of dollars of damage in parts of the Deep South, there was virtually none in the TVA region, where an estimated $20 million of flood damage was prevented.

Outdoor Recreation

The recreation facilities in the valley continued to grow, highlighted by more and more pleasure craft visible on the lakes. In the ten years preceding the mid-1960s the estimated value of recreation and development increased threefold. National legislation including the Appalachian Regional Development Act promised a further stimulation to recreation programs. All of the seven Tennessee Valley states received approval of the Bureau of Outdoor Recreation for their comprehensive outdoor recreation plans as a prerequisite for obtaining matching grants under the Land and Water Conservation Fund Act.

The TVA acquired seven acres along the Virginia portion of South Holston Reservoir to provide public access to the upper part of the lake; previously TVA had only flowage rights on the reservoir rim, and private owners had posted much of the land. Heavy use began as soon as the new access areas were cleared and marked. A change was made in the operating procedures for TVA's Hiwassee River reservoirs to provide improved recreation opportunities for Chatuge and Nottely Lakes in years when normal or above-normal rainfall permits. Two public access areas were licensed to the states of Mississippi and Alabama for development as a part of adjoining state parks, and 31 acres on South Holston Reservoir were leased to Washington County, Virginia, which immediately began to improve the area for recreation use by road improvements, grading a temporary boat-launching ramp, and clearing.

The increase in canoeing and other types of stream recreation intensified the need for better public information on access points, scenic stretches, and facilities available on streams suitable for these activities. The TVA began to identify and inventory the scenic streams in the valley as well as to assist several groups which sponsored canoe and kayak races and canoe training schools.

There was an interruption in the pleasant outdoor scene in 1968 when more than a half-million dead fish were found on the shores of the Watauga River in upper East Tennessee. Later in the year, on the nearby South Holston River, more than 2 million fish also were found dead. After a thorough investigation by the TVA and state and federal agencies, it was determined that the cause of the killing was the leakage of a mercury compound from a discarded metal drum found along the shore of Boone Lake. This lake area was found to be littered with hundreds of derelict drums, used to float docks and boathouses and set free after they began to deteriorate. Later the TVA announced that metal drums could not be used for flotation on any new structures on TVA lakes.

Wildlife increased in the Land Between the Lakes recreation area. Now there could be seen more deer, raccoon, opossum, wild turkey, geese, and bobcat. In 1970 a herd of 19 American buffalo arrived from the Theodore Roosevelt National Memorial Park in North Dakota. They were believed to be descendants of the woods strain of buffalo which once roamed through this part of the country.

A large amount of algae was found in Pickwick Landing Reservoir.

The plants covered about 6,000 acres; interfered with recreation, navigation, and water supply; and also increased mosquito production. So extensive was the algae that it was named "The Green Tide" by a local newspaper. More than 30 chemical formulations were tried in an attempt to destroy it, but none was successful. Finally it just began to disappear on its own.

The TVA looked forward and backward in its thirty-fifth year. At Muscle Shoals, nucleus of the TVA idea, the 200-millionth visitor, represented by Vern E. Pearson of Minneapolis, Minnesota, was welcomed. Half of those visits had taken place in the past decade. Not far away was another interesting situation: a man who generated his own electricity. He was Russell Cain of Moulton, Alabama, near the city of Florence. Cain had his own dam, turbine, and grist mill on a creek beside his home. Everything in his home requiring power used electricity. For 15 years before he retired to farm, he was an employee of the TVA.

"I started generating my own power before the TVA came in here," Cain said. "I still have TVA power because sometimes in the summer the water gets too low to pull the turbine."

Power Use Increase

All-electric apartment buildings increased in number in the valley. The sale of electric appliances was encouraged by low rates, local and national advertising, and active campaigns by the distributors. Virtually every home in the area by now had an electric refrigerator, and most of them had ranges, water heaters, and clothes washers electrically powered. Soon to come were more freezers, air conditioners, and automatic dishwashers.

An indication of the growing bigness of the TVA power generation was the Bull Run Steam Plant in East Tennessee. At the time this plant was the largest in the world, having a capacity of 950,000 kilowatts. Coal was carried to the plant by trains from the east Kentucky coalfields; when it reached the plant the coal was automatically weighed, sampled, and unloaded by electronic devices while the train was still in motion. In one timed operation, 7,200 tons of coal were unloaded from 72 bottom-dump cars in 20 minutes. Only 50 minutes lapsed between the time the train arrived at Bull Run and the time it left on the return trip.

In a move which, if extended earlier, might have alleviated the great blackout of 1965 in the Northeast, the TVA by the next year was making seasonal exchanges of power with other systems. Around half a million kilowatts were supplied to the Mississippi Power and Light Company in the warm weather months. This was to be returned to the TVA in the winter when it was more needed. Such an exchange to fill in mutual power requirements made substantial savings, it was said, in capital investment in generating facilities and made more effective use of facilities idle during offpeak months.

The seasonal exchanges between the TVA and the South Central Electric Companies reached 1.5 million kilowatts in the summer of 1968. The TVA and the American Electric Power Company, the nation's two largest power systems, placed a major new extra-high-voltage transmission interconnection in operation in June 1970 in the exchange of power. This initial connection between these two giants provided greater strength and operating flexibility for both systems, which together provide electric service in parts of 11 states from Michigan to Alabama. The new interconnection, near Bristol, Tennessee-Virginia, has a capability of enough power to meet the needs of 750,000 average homes.

A cloud appeared on the financial horizon as the 1960s neared their end. Unlike earlier times, the TVA claimed it was having difficulty making ends meet. So as the fiscal year 1970 ended, an official statement went as follows:

> TVA and electric systems across the nation were caught in a mighty struggle against other forces largely beyond their control—forces which pose grave threats to the country's energy supply and indeed to its economic future and national security. Sharply rising prices are at the source of the struggle. Everything required to generate electricity is costing more—labor, equipment, money, and particularly coal. A rapidly increasing demand for coal, while coal production has remained relatively stable, has caused skyrocketing prices which go far beyond the normal impact of an inflationary spiral. The cost of coal is the prime factor forcing TVA to increase power rates substantially, as it is forcing rate hikes on other systems throughout the nation.

An electric power rate increase was announced. A previous one had been announced in 1967. This increase came in two stages, on August 1 and October 2, 1970. This was said to "reflect increases in the cost of fuel and money and will provide about $15 million of revenue. Coal was one of the increasingly expensive items, its cost having doubled within a year. Coal transportation was also more expensive, and in 18 months the cost of money used by the TVA had increased an estimated $18 million.

The U.S. Forest Service and the TVA jointly established a wood chemistry laboratory at the National Fertilizer Development Center at Muscle Shoals. Its purpose is to explore thoroughly the chemical and related uses of valley hardwoods. A progress report was made on the 7,000-acre demonstration forest of the University of the South at Sewanee, Tennessee, in 1967. The school has pioneered in forest management, fire protection, forestry education, and multiple use. Here lakes have been built for recreation and water supply. Scenic trails and overlooks attract many visitors, while much timber is still harvested and the wildlife has been improved. The next year the TVA took action to stop pollution by toilet waste discharges from boats and floating structures on the TVA lakes in North Carolina, Tennessee, and Georgia. Under the program, the owner of each boat or floating structure on which there is a toilet of any kind must have it equipped with a waste treatment device meeting the standards already set by the state pollution control agencies.

In the same year the Hiwassee River Watershed Development Association and the TVA, cooperating with state and local school officials, sponsored a pilot project in high-school level adult education in Bradley and Polk Counties in Tennessee. The object was the upgrading of educational qualifications for people. Enrollment was 130 adults, ranging in age from 18 to 56. For ten weeks they went to school two nights weekly and received instruction in standard high-school subjects, and at the end of the period they were given an opportunity to take a test for a high school equivalency diploma. The school was a success, and plans were made for continuation of such special education.

At the same time the Authority issued a timely and sobering statement:

> Man, through *use* of his ever more refined machines, and not the machines alone, has brought on the deterioration of air and water, created mountainous garbage heaps, clogged and congested cities. People—in ever-growing numbers demanding ever-increasing amounts of goods and services—have asked for and received the material blessings of a high-technology society. Now they must call on that same technological competence to deliver them from the byproducts of that society—the miseries of pollution, blights, and waste.

This observation is also of timely appropriateness today.

15. "The Last of the Old Guard"

According to General Herbert Vogel "One of the most remarkable things about the Tennessee Valley Authority is that over the years the Directors have all been good and honorable men. One may comment on their personalities, their training or backgrounds, but there has never been a rascal among them. All have been men of high principles, who have worked as they could for the organization, developing the highest esprit de corps. As you look back you wonder how in the world this could have come about, because by the law of averages there should have been a bad egg somewhere—and there simply has not been one in this case."

Succeeded as chairman by Aubrey Joseph Wagner, the general said about him, "I think it is a wonderful appointment. He has a wealth of experience based on background knowledge. He has the best interest of the organization at heart and should provide excellent leadership." A veteran official of the TVA who was associated with the chairman for many years used his nickname—as do most others—and told this writer, " 'Red' Wagner represents the best ideals of the TVA. He is the last of the old guard."

Wagner was appointed chairman of the TVA board by President John F. Kennedy in 1962. Eight years later and at the other end of the political spectrum, President Richard M. Nixon reappointed Wagner to the board and also to continue as chairman, authorizing him "to execute and fulfill the duties of the office according to law until 1978."

Wagner was born on January 12, 1912, at Hillsboro, Wisconsin. From his German Lutheran parentage he inherited and has developed strong religious convictions. One of his distinguishing characteristics was his red hair.

With his family he moved to Madison, Wisconsin, at the age of 15 and, after finishing high school, entered the University of Wisconsin, being graduated with a bachelor of science degree in civil engineering, magna cum laude, in 1933.

Young Wagner held four odd jobs during his first year out of college, but they were not promising as to the future, so he was glad when he had an opportunity to go to work for the TVA. His acceptance, however, included the provision that he would take the job "if it looks like it will last more than a year." The reply of the TVA was, "This job should last a year. After that it depends on whether you can hold it."

H. R. Johnston of Knoxville, longtime associate and friend of Wagner, recalls "hearing Red say that he arrived in Knoxville in mid-July, 1934, in a worn-out Dodge, a wife and a two-week old baby, and with less than $25 in his pocket."

The first year with the TVA, Wagner was an engineering aide in the General Engineering and Geology Division. He was assigned to the navigation program, and one of his primary duties was to develop and install buoys, lights, and markers for the channels on the Tennessee River and its tributaries. These duties kept him out in the field for considerable period of time, especially during the impoundment of the reservoirs.

David L. Brooker, in the Lutheran magazine *Correspondent*, said that "TVA was a dream job for Wagner. He has an affinity for the outdoors and the outdoor life. An avid boater, hiker, and fisherman, he walked and boated down the great river both as a professional engineer and as a sportsman in his ideal environment."

In 1948 Wagner was named chief of the Navigation and Transportation Branch of the TVA. In that post he was responsible for the general planning of the navigation program, including both engineering matters and economic studies involved in the growing commercial use of the improved Tennessee waterway. In 1950 he was appointed a member of the Committee on Domestic Water Navigation Projects and National Policy of the President's Water Resources Policy Commission. His star was now rising rapidly. He was appointed assistant general manager in 1951 and general manager in 1954. In this latter capacity he was the chief administrative officer of the TVA, holding this position until he was appointed to the board of directors in 1961.

In more ways that one the story of Red Wagner is, in microcosm, the story of the TVA. On September 29, 1961, while Wagner was a TVA director but before he was appointed chairman, he spoke to the Brainerd Kiwanis Club at Chattanooga. He was already becoming a spokesman and a rather effective speaker. Alert on his feet and quick with answers to leading questions, he spoke not only of the past but of the future of the Tennessee Valley. Said he:

The generation now growing up and the generation after that and the countless generations to follow will depend, as do we, on this Valley, its land, its water, its minerals, and its forests to furnish them with the base for useful, productive and satisfying living. The tools of growth and development can never be laid down.

In the development of needful areas, he said that there is a common denominator—the desire and need for economic improvement and the feeling that the area is not realizing the full potential of its resources. The TVA, he said, sees three requirements for a program to get underway on a sound basis:

First, we urge that the total, not just a fragment, of the resource base be inventoried before a decision as to the priority of activities is undertaken. You might call this the "clinical diagnosis" to find out what is wrong with the patient so that the basic trouble can be cured, not just the symptoms;

Second, we urge that the organization should include representatives of all parts of the area and of all sectors of the economy—farmers, businessmen, bankers, forest and sawmill owners, representatives of towns and villages and rural areas, of labor and employers;

And third, we urge the participation of the state government, for we believe that governments of the states should share increasingly in responsibility for developing the resources of the Tennessee Valley, that they should not be bypassed by an agency of the Federal government.

Dedicated to the value of electric power in modern life, Wagner usually compared this energy to the influence of that exerted by humans. He has always been proud of the wide use of TVA-generated power in the valley and that the number of homes there heated entirely by electricity is about a third of the total for the entire United States. In recent times, however, this is not entirely an untarnished blessing because of the rising rates for electricity. This applies also to the low-cost rural power which TVA brought to the farms of the valley, a problem made more acute by fluctuating farm income. Said Wagner:

The importance of low-cost electric power to industrial processes like chemical production, electrometallurgical operations and paper-making can be seen in major plants employing thousands of workers up and down the Tennessee Valley but the value of electricity to industry goes beyond production processes. Healthy employees work efficiently through the summer in air-conditioned comfort today, in communities where forty years ago the summer season meant energy-robbing heat and malaria. Even electricity in the home, by helping to broaden the outlook of the people who live there, has been an element in creating the kind of progressive climate in which industry can grow more readily. Low-cost power played a part in the location of the vast atomic installations at Oak Ridge and near Paducah, Kentucky, as well as the big Air Force wind tunnel research center at Tullahoma, Tennessee. TVA power was used at the Huntsville, Alabama, space center to build the rocket that put the first U.S. satellite into orbit.

It is perhaps little realized that the REA cooperatives which sparked the electrification of most of rural America had their prototypes in the Tennessee Valley prior to REA. . . . I have told you a good bit about the activities of the TVA, and I can assure you it is a busy organization. But I want to be sure that you keep it in perspective. It is no "do-gooder" enterprise, determined to do for people what they should do for themselves. Quite the contrary. Its function is to provide the tools with which the people of the region can shape a better future. Viewed in one way, it is a very small potato in the total economic life of the region: for example, it expenditures over its lifetime have been about one-tenth of the total Federal expenditures in the region. And Federal expenditures in this region, on a per capita basis, are only a little over a half what they are for the country as a whole. The Tennessee Valley is no favored region in this respect.

On May 18, 1963, Chairman A. J. Wagner of the Tennessee Valley Authority stood before a large audience assembled outdoors at Muscle Shoals, Alabama. It was a memorable occasion for it was the thirtieth anniversary of the TVA. Said Wagner: "We are gathered here today at Muscle Shoals—the cradle of the TVA—to commemorate the day of TVA's beginning. We are here to honor the past, in a sense to render an accounting, and to rededicate our energies and talents to meet the challenge of the future."

The future held more of a challenge than Aubrey Wagner could realize, because the man he was going to introduce had appointed him chairman and had only six months to live. He was President Kennedy, making a youthful bid for recognition as a chief executive. Harvard-trained Kennedy was in good speaking form as usual. His sense of history was also present. He paid tribute to President Franklin D. Roosevelt, Senator George Norris, and Congressman Lister Hill as founders of the TVA, which he himself regarded as a fine thing. "There were many, moreover," he said, "who still regarded the whole undertaking with doubt, with scorn or with outright hostility. Some said it couldn't be done. Some said it shouldn't be done. Some said it wouldn't be done. But, today, thirty years later, it has been done—and there is still more for TVA to do."

So those who head the TVA "walk with kings" and, it may be added, do not lose the common touch. With the President, appearing before Congress, entertaining visiting heads of state, or associating with people in the valley, the chairman has more responsibility than the average member of the President's cabinet.

As if to answer future criticism, Wagner pointed out during this same period that members of the TVA Board are required to "be persons who profess a belief in the feasibility and wisdom" of the TVA Act. No member can be engaged in any other business. Conflict of interest is forbidden by the provision that directors cannot have any financial interest in a public utility corporation or in any corporation having an interest in fertilizer production. TVA receives a lump sum appropriation. Wagner explained that "the legislative body usually does not undertake to say what shall be spent where or for what purpose, specifically. This is with knowledge that, as circumstances change, the corporation may shift its employment of funds."

What does not seem to be widely known is that an accounting as to performance and finances is combined in the annual audit of the TVA by the General Accounting Office. The GAO, an agency of Congress, not only examines the account books of the Authority but also looks at the main activities of the organization in order to determine whether they are within the law. TVA directors are appointed by the President for nine-year terms which expire at staggered intervals of three years. As a consequence, there are usually on the board at least two members who are well acquainted with the policies and programs.

Before pollution became such a popular subject, the chairman was aware that industrial growth in the valley was bringing some adverse results. He discerned that one of the most obvious and potential limitations was stream pollution. But at the same time he believed that the Tennessee Valley would have a plentiful supply of water for all foreseeable needs for years to come. Although the rainfall for the area for each year is usually around 52 inches, it is obvious that any water supply can be curtailed or even destroyed when cities and industries fail to provide adequate treatment of wastes prior to discharging them into the streams. The TVA contends that the quality of the water in the area is better now than it was in 1933. This appraisal is important because the shoreline of the TVA lakes is now more than 10,000 miles long, equal to the shoreline of the northern Great Lakes.

The chairman felt that the difficult situation of the farm youth who must choose whether to remain or migrate could be eased in major degree if, in a search for industrial plants, they acquired higher skills and responsibilities. Vocational training programs, if they are both effective and widespread, can make an important contribution here, assisting not only in taking up the slack of unemployment and under-employment but upgrading skills and incomes at the same time. High skills demand high wages and salaries. High incomes are the generating force for greater trade and commerce, and it is in the field of trade and commerce that the economy of the Valley region is most deficient. The greatest source of additional employment in the future is in such fields as retail and wholesale trade, service industries ranging from laundries to television repair, insurance, warehousing, and hundreds of satellite functions that make up the essence of a prosperous economy. A society is not truly free if a young person must farm because the parents farmed or must mine because the parents mined. Freedom is achieved only when a combination of achievable education, adequate income levels, and variety of employment opportunities permit our youngsters to select and move into the field of opportunity which best suits their talents and ambitions as they appraise them.

The chairman and his associates have numerous occasions in which they defend the financial structure and operations of the Authority. The contention is that the public investment in the TVA has paid off in ways that defy strict financial measurement. How, it is asked, does one put a dollar value on the topsoil saved by a million acres of pine seedlings planted on gullied hillsides? Or on the fact that one and a half acres of woodland which once burned over every year now are free from the scarring effects of fire?

Norton E. Long is quoted from the *Harvard Business Review* of July-August 1958:

> The failure of regional planning, with the notable exception of TVA, is largely due to lack of muscle behind the planning and frequently to lack of realism concerning the basic nature of land-use planning. The real protagonists of effective economic development must come to a large extent from the ranks of business. . . . To put muscle into regional planning, "Private-enterprise TVAs" are needed—for example, public utilities or banks with interests concentrated in the region and capable of thinking ahead about the territory as a whole.

A New York City official recommended in early 1975 that such a bank be established to handle that city's financial transactions.

Chairman Wagner was quite proud that the TVA pioneered in rural electrification. He said this before such a cooperative association in Las Vegas, Nevada, in February 1966:

> Congress made it clear in the basic TVA legislation that this agency should start the massive job of bringing electricity to rural America. Soon after TVA was founded in 1933 our engineers were

working out cheaper ways of running power lines down the country roads. Our lawyers were drafting charters and bylaws and state legislation necessary for the operation of rural electric cooperatives. TVA funds were the first sources of financing for rural electrification on an area-wide basis. This experience was the foundation for the National Rural Electrification Administration, set up initially by President Roosevelt under Executive Order and later by Act of Congress. TVA's direct financial interest remained until 1952 when the last of the TVA loans were paid off.

The chairman expressed himself to the effect that more important than electric power is the devotion of the TVA to the ideals of service to consumers, to the maintenance of more pleasant and comfortable living, and to national goals for economic growth. TVA power will live and remain vigorous only so long as this nation continues to recognize that freedom in business enterprise encompasses service enterprise in the consumer interest as well as profit enterprise in the private interest. He believed that the greatest test of the TVA is in its performance, its dedication to this consumer interest.

At the twenty-fifth anniversary of the founding of Fairleigh Dickinson University at Rutherford, New Jersey, Wagner brought up the question of an all-electric city. Is it possible by using electricity widely to fashion a community free of air pollution, he asked. His expressed belief was that with electricity used to heat not only home but churches, schools, and public buildings, a major source of pollution in most cities would be eliminated. Could we encourage the use of electric cars and trucks to the same end? Could this be the place to dispose of domestic wastes electrically on a citywide scale? Could we build a city that would not pollute the water? Complete undergrounding of electric distribution lines in an entire city would be worth demonstrating, he concluded.

He pointed to examples of industry locating large new enterprises in the rural countryside of the Tennessee Valley in current years. Among them were Revere Copper and Brass establishing a new aluminum plant at Scottsboro, Alabama; U.S. Plywood-Champion announcing a pulp and paper plant at Courtland, Alabama; Goodyear Tire and Rubber, one of its largest tire plants at Union City, Tennessee; Firestone Plastics, a tire cord plant at Bowling Green, Kentucky; General Electric motor plant at Hendersonville, Tennessee; and Eli Lilly Drug Company's bulk antibiotics plant at Murray, Kentucky. These plants involve initial investments ranging from $10 million to over $100 million, often with plans already announced for doubling or tripling. Each makes a substantial impact on the small communities near them.

Referring to the book *The Urgent Future* by Albert Mayer, Wagner formulated what he felt that in a capsule sentence is the basic long-range objectives of the TVA: first, a strong natural resource base, steadily improving by conscious effort of the people; second, improved incomes and living standards, fostered by growing industry and commerce; and finally, an environmental character that combines beauty with utility, cultural quality with commercial prosperity, and freedom of the individual with opportunity to use freedom fully.

At the age of 57, on May 23, 1969, Aubrey J. Wagner was confirmed by the U.S. Senate for his second term as chairman of the TVA. This time, of course, the appointment came from President Nixon and was to extend for nine years more until 1978. The appointment was announced by the White House about 12 hours after Wagner's term had expired, thereby leaving the TVA with only two directors to carry on its work. Technically, Wagner's $40,000-a-year salary stopped during this period in which he smilingly remarked that he was out of a job. But job and salary soon resumed, and his pay was about ten times as much as when he started with the TVA 35 years previously. Later his pay was raised to $52,500.

Writing to the *Chattanooga Times* later on, a man named John "Hoss" Holt stated that Senator Howard Baker was responsible for the reappointment of Wagner. Holt added:

> TVA served Tennesseans well when we needed flood control, production of electricity, and lake recreation; but Mr. Wagner doesn't seem to understand that it is possible to have too much of a good thing. Flooding is no longer a problem, in the future most electricity will be produced by nuclear power plants, and we already have more lake frontage than the Great Lakes. But Mr. Wagner keeps right on building dams as if free-flowing water were an unforgivable sin. He is destroying the natural environment, flooding much valuable farm land which will be needed in the near future to feed a hungry world, and adding to a tax burden which is already too heavy. I am not suggesting the abolition of TVA, but I am saying that TVA needs to move in new directions. There are many worthwhile projects which TVA could be engaged in, other than the building of dams. A new day is dawning, but Mr. Wagner and his assistants are living in the past.

Wagner himself admitted that there was criticism of his organization. Speaking before a meeting of public utility representatives in Seattle, Washington, on December 11, 1969, he explained that the scheme to develop a whole river system as a unit had never been tried before the TVA. "There were plenty of skeptics who said it was plain nonsense and would not work. They said that 'those hillbillies' could never build dams or tame a river. They said the same system of dams could not

both control floods and generate power. They said barge navigation
was a farce, a constitutional peg on which to hang a wild scheme of
doubtful legality. And they said a region so poor could not possibly use
all the power that the mighty Tennessee River could generate."

"Well, they were wrong. They were all wrong. Wrong on every
count!" cried Wagner:

> The river has been completely harnassed—a world-wide model of
> multiple-purpose water resource development. "Those hillbillies"
> not only did a superb job building dams but they have gone on to
> build some of the world's largest thermal generating stations, both
> coal burning and nuclear, and to build billions of dollars worth of
> new factories that are now the lifeblood of this once impoverished
> region.

Many of those who lived for years in the Tennessee Valley feel that
the word "impoverished" is too strong a general term for the region as
a whole, even in the dark days of the Great Depression. In New York
City there are many displaced Tennesseans. Some of the more enter-
prising ones years ago formed a lively group which came to be called
the Tennessee Society in New York. By invitation, Chairman Wagner
addressed this society on January 23, 1970, and took the occasion to
throw out a challenge to the organization, most of whose members held
positions of leadership in the city and nation. Wagner declared:

> Many of you came to New York because opportunity was greater
> here than in Tennessee. In the future, many of your children and
> grandchildren will take the reverse path to find, as you did, a more
> rewarding and satisfying way of life. The Tennessee Valley today is a
> land of new opportunity, and the long exodus from the area is ending
> with jobs at home. The region has achieved a balance between
> outmigration and inmigration, reflecting the wide economic and
> social opportunities for its people. Tennessee today hums with the
> sound of busy industries. TVA has been a proud partner with the
> people of Tennessee and the rest of the surrounding Valley.

Back in Knoxville some months later, the chairman did not sound
quite so sanguine. He told the Knoxville Technical Society that people
are always at a crossroads of one kind or another, facing a continuing
series of decisions about the direction in which to go. He believed that
always there are those who urge single-mindedly that we must take the
lefthand fork or we court certain disasters. Just as positively and just as
single-mindedly others are sure we must take the fork of the road to the
right or we move toward our ultimate and certain destruction. As a
matter fact, he felt, there is usually a third choice at the crossroads. It

may be less clearly marked, less distinct. It may even require building some new road. But often it is the *only* road to a secure future.

At the World Conference of the Society for International Development in Washington not long afterward, Wagner expressed what appears to be his underlying philosophy:

> Functions whose successful performance is vital to the public interest and which will be performed not at all or inadequately by private enterprise, must be carried out by public enterprise. But they should be so controlled as to free and expand opportunity for local and private initiative and enterprise which, in the final analysis, carry the heavy load of development. . . . I think that every public enterprise should be imbued with a great deal of what I might call "the wisdom of self-restraint." Its greatest failure might arise from the assumption that, given broad authority in a wide-ranging field, its powers are sufficient to accomplish its objectives through self-contained action. Perhaps the greatest potential of the public enterprise is its ability to implement the enthusiasm of the people. The people must understand the goals toward which they work, and approve those goals.

The northwestern part of the United States has had a special interest in the developments of the TVA, partly because of similar movements to utilize the headwaters of the Missouri River. So it was natural that Red Wagner speak before the South Dakota Farmers Union at Huron on October 12, 1971. He did not endeavor to paint a perfect picture. He was in favor of developments in their area such as the one he headed, but he set forth some of the difficulties to be found in the mammoth effort to effectuate proper usage of our national energy. Said he:

> Electric heat, of course, doesn't completely *eliminate* air pollution and the other environmental effects stemming from thermal power generation. But it does lessen them and it moves them to a location where they are more manageable—the point where the power is generated. Where coal is burned there is fly ash. Where either coal or oil is burned there are sulfur gases. Where thermal generation is involved there is potential danger to aquatic life from the heated water discharged into nearby streams. Where coal is mined underground there is danger to life and health of miners. Where it is mined by stripping methods, there is the threat of damage to forests and streams and to the wildlife they support.

But he added in a later interview that "anybody who says TVA is only trying to perpetuate itself by building new dams and power plants has rocks in his head."

Chairman Wagner stated on television's "Today" show on May 18,

1972, in response to the inevitable question about strip mining, that TVA buys only about 15 percent of the strip-mined coal in the states where TVA purchases it. He added that in the Tennessee Valley in recent years, 80 percent of the industrial growth has taken place not in the large cities but outside of them, thus providing an opportunity for people to work in an atmosphere where they can see green trees and in ten minutes they can be home by their automobile and soon have a boat attached to it and spend the evening fishing.

The realism of Wagner came through in a speech before the National Rural Electric Cooperative Association at Savannah, Georgia, on September 18, 1972. He revealed his conviction that our country has a dilemma: "Everyone wants a clean environment but no one wants to pay for it. Our prayer for common sense will have to be liberally answered if we are going to solve the problem. . . . Common sense should tell us that, in the last analysis, all of us must pay for the cost of the cleanup. We will pay for it either through taxes or in the cost of the things we buy and use every day. There is no magic source of funds that can be painlessly tapped to do the job."

If one had to select, in a study of the TVA, its two most important tangible products, power and fertilizer would seem to be the choice. The chairman emphasized the importance of both. He explained that the TVA had pioneered a rapid switch from powdery fertilizer to granular products, from low to high analysis mixes. Partly as a result, one American farmer now produces enough food to feed 50 people, while as recently as 1950 his single production fed only 15 people. Among other reasons for this gain are improved crop varieties and new pesticides and herbicides as well as efficient farm machinery. But fertilizer was given credit for nearly half of the gain in agricultural production in the preceding quarter of a century. Wagner asserted: "Our capabilities, however, did not emerge by chance. They came about because wise leaders down through our history insisted that a productive and prosperous agriculture is essential to our national well-being. Our system of land-grant universities grew out of this philosophy. National research programs have fought and won battles against plant and animal diseases, pests, and weeds. And an essential part of this mosaic has been the work of the National Fertilizer Development Center and its association with the fertilizer industry, cooperative industry, the universities, and the farmers themselves."

In a later pronouncement before a Public Power Association group in Memphis, Tennessee, on October 2, 1973, the TVA chairman again sounded a warning that changes in the power supply situation would necessitate corresponding changes in power utilization policy. In other words, conservation was stressed along with the concept of efficient power use. One step taken in 1969 was the elimination of what was called the "promotional" block in the TVA retail power rate structure, a four-mill block used to encourage wider use of electricity in the interest of lower unit operating costs. Two years later the TVA published a booklet entitled *Ways to Use Electricity Efficiently,* which told consumers how to conserve energy and save money on their electric bill by following tips on the efficient use of their appliances.

The executive stated that there was a challenge for architects and designers to devise space for all-electric living which would require less energy and still keep construction costs within reason. (Whether costs for electricity and construction are within reason at this writing is another question.) Some advances in this respect have been made in the form of reflective glass which saves on air-conditioning loads by reflecting the rays of the sun. Recessed windows in some new buildings utilize the sun for heating in winter when it is low in the sky but provides shade against the sun in summer when it is high. There arc ways to use more efficiently the heat generated in lighting, it was added. The current TVA chairman, S. David Freeman, is an ardent advocate of the use of solar energy.

Since the energy crisis has developed, the TVA has strongly recommended the heat pump as being "essential to the energy picture of the future. It is an energy conservation device unsurpassed by any other heating system. It generally extracts heat from outside air and pumps it into the home or office. Thus, it is, in effect, a device to use solar energy. A residential heat pump system can usually realize a seasonal performance factor of 2 or higher. That means 2 Btu of heat output for 1 Btu of energy input." In connection with urging wide use of the heat pump, it was announced that all certified dealers would be required to meet certain requirements, among them adequate insulation and adequately ducted airflow systems. Each heat pump installation would be inspected by power distributor personnel.

The TVA, it was stated, is also urging manufacturers to produce more efficient appliances. "We are working toward the labeling of appliances," Wagner said, "because the consumer should know more than just the first cost of that appliance. The purchaser should know the "life cost"—the cost to purchase plus the cost to operate. Choosing the inefficient model, although the Btu outputs are the same, can cost the consumer over $100 in extra operating costs over the life of a small window air conditioner."

In April of 1973, Red Wagner was elected to the National Academy of Engineers. In announcing the election, the Academy noted

Wagner's "leadership in unified resource development of a major river basin, including waterway navigation." According to the *Chattanooga Times,* "Election to the Academy is the highest professional distinction that can be conferred on an American engineer and honors those who have made important contributions to engineering theory and practice or who have demonstrated unusual accomplishments in pioneering new and developing fields of technology."

At the meeting of the Rotary Club of Chattanooga on July 19, 1973, Chairman Wagner answered questions about the TVA put to him by club members, many of whom were on the conservative side. He presented to them the informative chart shown.

Forty Years of Change in the Tennessee Valley Region

	1933	*1973*
Population	4.9 million	6.7 million
Per capita income	$168	$3,365
Navigation on Tennessee River	940,000 tons	28 million tons
Employment		
Agriculture	62%	9%
Manufacturing	12%	33%
Trades and services	17%	33%
Average residential use of electricity	600 kWh at 5.5¢ per kWh	15,000 kWh at 1.3¢ per kWh
Flood damages prevented, 1933–1973: $874 million		

16. "As Long as the River Shall Run"

The opponents of the Tellico project fought as vigorously as did the white forebears against the Indians of the region. But like the indigenous red men, the modern protagonists lost a battle. The United States Sixth Circuit Court of Appeals, meeting in Cincinnati on Washington's Birthday in 1974, gave the TVA the go-ahead to complete the Tellico Dam project on the Little Tennessee River below Knoxville, Tennessee. This decision, however, was later reversed by the U.S. Supreme Court.

The environmentalists had claimed that the project would flood "the most singificant archaeological area of Tennessee," but their fervent plea fell upon deaf legal ears. The objectors charged that the project would obliterate historical Cherokee Indian land, including the village of Tenasi, from which it was said the state of Tennessee derived its name. Fort Loudoun, the restored seventeenth-century English fortification on the south bank of the river, is named after John Campbell, the Earl of Loudoun, whose chief distinction seemed to lie in his indecision and loss of battles in the French and Indian War. Built in 1756, the fort was abandoned in 1760 and most of its members were killed by the Indians after surrendering to them.

The three-judge panel said the project "admittedly entails considerable ecological damage and disturbance," but added that there were "many "offsetting economic and social benefits." The Cherokee Indians living on a nearby reservation let out a war whoop of protest, so to speak, and said again that their rights had been violated. They recalled that in many treaties between their former tribes and the United States, the binding expression was "as long as the river shall run and the grass shall grow." Now such an agreement was no longer being kept.

In the 1750s, the early English settlers at Fort Loudoun had found the Cherokees living contentedly in towns along the Little Tennessee River. Within the lush valley, the braves hunted and fished for food while the women worked in their gardens raising vegetables. This agrarian life was not to last. By 1838 there were so many white settlers

259

in the region that nearly all the Indians were run out by a previous order of President Andrew Jackson. Thousands of Cherokees perished on the notorious "Trail of Tears" which led to Oklahoma.

Although some scholars are uncertain, it is generally believed that the Tellico vicinity was the last important settlement of the Overhill Cherokee Indians. "This is the last place that the Cherokee's history remains," said Noah Powell, chief of the Indians of Cherokee, North Carolina. "The Little Tennessee and Tellico Rivers were once the heartland of the Cherokee, the birthplace of Sequoyah who perfected the Cherokee language and its alphabet."

Among the various government officials who received this written appeal was the then-Governor Winfield Dunn of Tennessee. His ears were sympathetic. He protested to the TVA that the Tellico project entailed loss of fertile soil, a productive trout fishery, and historical sites. The governor, who at that time was attracting some national interest, stated, "The Little Tennessee could best serve all Tennesseans by remaining a scenic river gateway to the wilderness lands beyond. I will do all I can to stop this dam."

The Indians also protested that the archaeologists were plundering the graves of their forebèars. A team under the supervision of Dr. Alfred K. Guthe, head of the anthropology department of the University of Tennessee, had been digging at the site for five years after 1967. More than half a million Indian artifacts were recovered, and Dr. Guthe said that the digging project had been progressing with the blessings of the Cherokees. In addition to the artifacts, the remains of scores of Indians were uncovered, and this brought even more emotional protests from Indian leaders. Said Jonathan L. Taylor, one of their councilmen, "If Indians were doing that to the remains of white men, we would be tried in the white man's court and sent to his prisons. And they call us savages."

This project holds more significance than sentiment or sports. According to Aubrey Wagner, the project has unusual economic implications. Said he:

> It will create an extensive area having exceptional qualifications for waterfront industry sites, water transportation, rail connections, good highway access, excellent water supply and several thousand acres of land level enough and otherwise suitable for large plants. In addition, the site is in an area having a naturally superb living environment; it lies at the foothills of the Great Smoky Mountains and is adjacent to the Cherokee National Forest. With pleasant climate and with lakes, woods and mountains nearby, its potential for good living for industrial workers is great.

The area is now completely rural. Income levels are low and typical of the Appalachian region, unemployment is high and job opportunities limited. Here then is a rare opportunity, starting from scratch, to plan and build a whole new complex of working places, living places, recreation and leisure-time facilities. We estimate, based on developments at other points of the Tennessee River, that within a reasonable development period, private investment in waterfront industries should reach more than $250 million, providing as many as 6,600 new jobs. Satellite industries, away from the waterfront, will add substantially to these figures.

The Tellico Dam was scheduled for completion in 1975 but, because of the delays, two years more would be required for its completion, according to the TVA estimate. The proposed city of Timberlake there was admittedly a dream. One of its wise-cracking opponents asked, "Timberlake or Limberlost?" But the plan were certainly pleasant. According to the Authority, it would be a city where children would roam and play in the outdoors without danger from traffic, where individuality rather than conformity in housing and life-styles would be encouraged, where modest income "and affluent families of all races will live in the same neighborhood, and where man's presence will blend easily with nature's splendor."

It was planned that some 3,000 acres of sites served by highway, rail, and barge facilities would be available for industrial development in Timberlake. Industries would be required by the TVA to conform to a land use plan which would be developed so that plant sites would be compatible with the rest of the community. Here would be an opportunity to study the relationship between community development and energy use and to test and implement specific energy technology in designing the community. Energy conservation techniques would be incorporated into the designs and construction of all public buildings and studied as to effectiveness and consumer acceptibility.

This part of the plan drew a retort from Ernestine Lyle, sprightly columnist of the *Hamilton County (Tennessee) Herald*. Wrote Lyle:

"TVA could save money by going out of the new town-planning business and dam-building business on small rivers which happen to run free through scenic valleys providing fine trout fishing and watering dairy farms and cornfields along its banks. . . . Government bureaucracy knows best, of course, just what man's desires and destinies should be. The people who move into Timberlake—if and when it gets built—may not know it but they are going to be TVA guinea pigs. They will be subject to environmental control. . . . Which translated means: they will have no say in matters which TVA says is best for them.

Mark H. Harrison wrote to the *Knoxville Journal* about what he called, "the Little T Valley. This valley was already ahead of much of Tennessee without their intrusion. . . . Why so little manufacturing on the older reservoirs in East Tennessee? If they were lined with factories, this would give legitimate excuse for a well-managed Little T. . . . If they are so good at getting new industries, why save them all for the Little T? . . . Is this bureaucracy making its own rules? Is our government the boss of its creation?" Miss Beulah Davis, from the same community of Loudon, Tennessee, wrote to the same newspaper and had this comment: "TVA has told a grand story of the benefits our 'deprived' area will receive from the Tellico Project. It is a story of fantasy that rivals the fairy tales of Mother Goose and Hans Christian Andersen."

Such objections did little to faze TVA planners. Three distinct units were planned for the new lakeshore. One was a novel town residential area, providing homes, shopping, and cultural activities for its citizens. Next a major waterfront industrial area was expected to offer barge, rail, and highway transportation and furnish thousands of manufacturing jobs. Also, in the upper part of the reservoir, a recreation complex was planned—to be related to the lake, the mountains, and Cherokee history.

Different kinds of housing ranging from high-density apartments to single dwellings would be grouped in clusters in the villages and neighborhoods. Trees and open space would surround these clusters. Automobile traffic would be isolated from the pedestrian and play areas. The TVA hoped that the private sector would make large investments in homes, shops, and factories. Various other agencies of government were hopefully expected to invest in roads, schools, waste collection and treatment, and public recreation.

The Tellico project was regarded by the TVA as a bright new direction in which it was going. After all, it was reasoned, there are just so many dams which can be built and so many conventional things that can be repeated. The idea was expressed by Aubrey Wagner when he said, "The Tellico story is a story of new opportunity for the young people of East Tennessee. It is a story of the use of natural resources to provide new jobs and new economic horizons for the years ahead."

Apparently the project represents an extraordinary example of where the three modes of transportation—rail, highway, and water— are available at the same site and where substantial acreage of level land suitable for large-scale industrial plants is available. "There is a danger these days, in our 'back to nature' quest for an idyllic physical environment, that we may forget that if a man is to enjoy his surroundings it is necessary for him to have an income, for him to have a job," Wagner said. "We need to have a balanced view of the entire environmental problem. We need to keep our perspective as to the basic needs of our economy and our society."

In the presentation of the advantages of the project it is pointed out that the Tennessee Valley now possesses a strategic central location with respect to the rest of the nation. The impact of the waterway brought about by the TVA has been more than was predicted. The situation has applied particularly to Knoxville, according to the Authority. The completion of the interstate highway system has brought this more sharply into focus. It brings this city closer to other strategic economic points. While Knoxville has prospered as a trade and service center, "from wholesaling to medical care, from banking to entertainment, surrounding counties have many more manufacturing jobs. Knoxville's economic future depends in large degree on its ability to sustain healthy business activity in the nearby communities. Its physical limitation of terrain and geography which precludes large waterfront industrial development can be made up in the surrounding area, as at Tellico," said Wagner. "Another factor of change is the increase in tourism. With the national parks, state parks, national forests, game management areas, and commercial recreation on the lakes and in the mountains, Knoxville is the location which can best serve all this development."

Specifically, the Tellico project was estimated to have a flood storage capacity slightly larger than the Fort Loudoun Reservoir, thus affording flood protection to downstream sites, principally Chattanooga. The flow of the Little Tennessee River normally would be through the canal to be constructed and into the Fort Loudoun Reservoir where the water would run through turbines. These would generate an average of 20 million kilowatt-hours a year without having to build a powerhouse or buy additional coal. The Tellico River arm of the reservoir would extend up to and into the Cherokee National Forest, adjacent to the Great Smoky Mountains National Park, thus affording additional recreation.

It was planned that colonial Fort Loudoun would be on an island to be developed by the state of Tennessee, along with other adjacent land, as an historical and recreation park. The TVA announced in early 1975 that another historic site here had been nominated for inclusion in the National Register of Historic Places. It is the Tellico Blockhouse which was established in 1793 by the federal government as a principal point of communications with the Indians of the frontier and served as a military and trading post until 1807. The blockhouse was also a center for educating the Indians in the agricultural and domestic arts. Its major features have been identified through archaeological investigations conducted by the University of Tennessee and funded by the TVA.

One of the chief objections to the Tellico project has been by fishermen. To this another fisherman, Red Wagner, replied: "This is a manmade trout fishery, as you know. The water there is cold enough to support trout only because it is cooled in the deep reservoirs of the dams upstream. The trout fishing is dependent on stocking by the State Game and Fish Commission. Hatchery trout will grow well if placed in the river, but they do not reproduce to any extent because the small feeder streams are too warm. After the reservoir is impounded, trout fishing still will be feasible on the same "put-and-take" basis in a shorter stretch of the upper reaches of the reservoir. Some 105 miles of trout streams on the Tellico River and Citico Greek—both tributaries of the Little Tennessee—will be unaffected. In addition, there are many hundreds of miles of trout streams in the mountains nearby."

As dissident voices spoke, the *Chattanooga News-Free Press* devoted a full page to the controversy in its February 6, 1972, issue. It contained pictures and quotes. Said Lynn Seeber, TVA general manager, regarding the power aspect of Tellico, "Considering the long-range cost of construction, operation and raw materials or fuels, hydraulic plants still remain the cheapest and cleanest means of converting nature into electrical resources."

But Kirk Johnson, an engineer, retorted, "The part of this project that really sticks in my craw is the fact that the majority of the land TVA is condemning will not be affected by the rising waters but will be a part of lucrative land development plans."

On the other hand, Loudon County Judge Harvey L. Sproul was quoted as saying, "Ninety-five percent of graduated high school students leave this area to make their lives simply because there aren't enough opportunities to entice them to stay. We cannot build and improve this community unless we can keep the young people home."

Brody Harrison, a Loudon merchant, commented, "I certainly can understand why land would be condemned for the building of highways or necessary reservoirs, but it's pretty hard to swallow when a branch of our Federal government can legally take a farm to build a model city or actually get into the real estate business. You can build a lake anywhere, but man can never create what God has given us here."

Ray Carpenter, owner of a farm on the banks of the Little Tennessee River, said, "The wife and I sorta like our life here on the place. I've farmed this land for thirty years. A man puts a lot of himself into the land when he works it that long. My wife's family got the farm from the government in a land grant six generations ago and now they are taking it back."

Seeber seemed to be unmoved. He commented, "People are getting emotional about the families who are losing their homes. Well, I get emotional too about the way most of these people are living in this area. I am convinced that this project will enhance the standard of living in this area considerably."

And Gilbert Stewart, Jr., TVA official, in reply to the charge that the Tellico project would cover historic sites, rounded out the printed fuss by stating, "The sites are unmarked and you can't see them, they've been plowed for years. The Tellico project has provided thousands of dollars for systematic excavation which has yielded over half a million artifacts. Prior to the Tellico project there have been no funds available for this research which has given the public knowledge of the true Cherokee heritage."

A bizarre note was sounded in the discordant symphony when 97-year-old Arthur Morgan thrust himself into the Tellico picture. He came from his home in Yellow Springs, Ohio, to attend the Knoxville wedding of a Cherokee Indian named Hawk Littlejohn. Afterward, Morgan and his son Griscom called on Chairman Wagner and TVA engineer-retiree and old friend Harry Wiersema. The Morgans told Wiersema that the Tellico project was a good one and said that they would support it. Wiersema told the Morgans he thought the dam was justified despite the opposition from conservationists and environmentalists.

Thus all seemed harmonious in this situation until a short time later when Wagner read in the *Knoxville Journal* a letter from Arthur Morgan to Wagner asking the TVA to shelve the Tellico Dam project and turn the sites over to the Cherokee Indians. Wagner of course was astounded, since he himself had not received the original letter. Later on he did. It was then learned that Littlejohn had released his copy of the letter to the newspaper.

Soon came a second letter from Morgan, this one apologizing for the first and admitting that Littlejohn and Griscom Morgan had drafted the first letter. Wagner spent the 1972 Labor Day weekend drafting a reply and then decided not to make it public. "How can one respond," Wagner said, "to an old man like Morgan in a kind way and yet be firm about a position adopted in 1967 that is still valid today." So the TVA took the official position that the elder Morgan actually favored the dam but had been involved in a farce.

The TVA went ahead with its plans for the ambitious project, certainly aware by now that there was still much opposition to this new course on which it had set out. An elaborate three-volume environmental statement was prepared and made available to the public as well as to various other governmental agencies. The statement admitted that the creation of a 16,500-acre reservoir at Tellico was expected to result in changes of the land from agricultural and timber use to industrial, commercial, residential, and recreational development use. The portion of the waterway suitable for trout fishing would be reduced from about ten to four miles. The use of about 33 miles of the stream for canoe and raft float trips would be eliminated or greatly diminished. These expectations were in addition to the changes in the environment already discussed.

The TVA stated that between 1950 and 1970 the three counties affected by the Tellico project lost a total of 19,000 people. Per capita personal income in the three counties ranges from about 50 to 80 percent of the national average. The name Timberlake was proposed for the community in honor of Henry Timberlake, an early British explorer who provided the first useful maps of the area. Since the area adjoins national parks, the lake was expected to be visited by millions of the people who annually come there. Tellico Dam and Reservoir would provide an estimated 126,000 acre-feet of stored water for flood control which should help Chattanooga in this regard. The only large industrial employer in the area is the Aluminum Company of America.

As time has gone on the TVA has become more and more concerned with environment. Much of its research revolves around this subject and, in order to handle it effectively, the Office of Health and Environmental Science was set up as a separate division. In the 1970 TVA Annual Report is a statement emphasizing this problem:

> More than any other single aspect of technology, electricity has made a mighty impact on our changing environment. It has alleviated the backbreaking suffering of millions, serving as a prime force in lifting living standards to levels once thought impossible. It has helped clear the winter skies above Valley cities, skies once thick with the black smoke from thousands of coal-burning furnaces. But what of the side effects—the tons of ash and gaseous discharges from coal-burning power plants; the return to lakes and streams of heated water in large amounts from plant condensers?

For several years the TVA, in cooperation with the National Air Pollution Control Administration, has been conducting a variety of sulfur removal tests. As new plants have been added to the power system, special equipment has been installed so that in some cases 99 percent of the fly ash from burning coal is removed before it reaches the chimney. The new stacks are 1,000 feet high, and these mainly defuse the gases high in the atmosphere. The effort to control such pollution is both time-consuming and expensive. In this connection, Michael Kenward writing in the *New Scientist* for May 18, 1972, said: "Britain has taken more than half a century to clean up its rivers, and nearly twenty years to get its air to a reasonably clean state. Neither job is finished and both certainly could have been done a lot quicker. The U.S. is trying to do the same jobs in as many months."

In the *Chattanooga Times,* Martin Ochs in his editorial column took a humorous swipe at the Authority as follows: "From their pleasant offices in the old-looking New Sprankle Building, which is not an Andy Griffith pronunciation for fire control but the headquarters of the Tennessee Valley Authority, the TVA directors wrestle with developments that tend to raise the consternation count." Examples of how the TVA has dealt with the difficulties are found in its stated program of environmental technology development:

TVA operates 287 static and 37 dynamic air monitoring installations; it also operates 21 meteorological stations. TVA conducts a program of water quality surveillance to obtain and update information on all aspects of water quality in reservoirs and principal streams of the Tennessee Valley. In a typical year, 75,000 field and laboratory analyses are made to characterize the physical, sanitary, chemical and bacteriological qualities of the Valley waters. This program includes yearlong surveys on streams and reservoirs, weekly monitoring at key stations downstream from all TVA impoundments, assistance to EPA in the operation of a national network of water sampling stations, and special studies to determine the specific and overall effects of waste discharges on water quality throughout the Tennessee Valley.

Water temperatures have been collected at hundreds of sites in the Tennessee Valley since 1936; this is in addition to USGS and state monitoring.

Since the 1950s temperatures have been recorded at six depths in streams near power plants. Near nuclear and conventional power plants now under construction, more extensive and sophisticated monitoring networks are under installation.

Since 1951, data have been collected on the occurrence, severity, and extent of air pollution effects to most plant species growing in the vicinity of each of TVA's eleven coal-fired steam plants. Community noise data, both preoperational and operational, relating to gas turbine generators and air blast circuit breakers, have been collected. Preoperational data on nuclear power plants and associated 500-kv switchyards have also been collected. Environmental radiation monitoring—direct gamma radiation, airborne radioactivity, particulate fallout, surface water, water supplies, soil, vegetation, milk, fish, clams, bottom sediment, plankton, and river water—is being carried out near TVA nuclear facilities prior to operation.

Eight Tennessee River reservoirs and eight tributary reservoirs are sampled quarterly for radiological activity.

Since the 1950s annual inventories have been conducted of the standing crop and species composition of fish in various TVA reservoirs. Standing crop data in each reservoir have been compiled and species means for all sample years since 1960 are kept current.

Each year since 1968, one or more watersheds tributary to the Tennessee River are surveyed at numerous locations for fish and bottom organisms. Data on standing crop, species composition, and diversity of aquatic life in relation to the physical environment are determined. Since 1968 six watersheds have been surveyed.

Not long before he retired, Dr. O. M. Derryberry, manager of health and environmental science, presented a paper before a valley-wide conference in Chattanooga on the role of the Authority in environmental protection. He declared that the TVA had strengthened environmental protection by developing a comprehensive report on water quality conditions throughout the valley by more stringent provisions in licenses and leases of TVA lands:

> And then along came environmental fever. I distinguish between environmental fever and environmental concern by a process which in medicine is known as differential diagnosis. Concern is characterized by a sincere interest in and quest for the facts about environmental conditions, what causes them, what are the effects, what are the probabilities of the effects occurring (risks), and what are the benefits and costs of changing the conditions. *Fever* is characterized by a zealous regard for ecology *with man left out,* by frequent outbursts of hysteria in which technology is blamed for environmental degradation, and by heated doomsday-type pronouncements usually based on half-truths, distortions, or just plain error. I espouse environmental concern. I don't know how to cure environmental fever.

In regard to the emission standards at the steam plants, Derryberry added:

> the expense of changing the environmental condition at the stack exit without producing commensurate benefits where real life goes on is a subject greatly in need of more environmental concern and less environmental fever. . . . I sometimes feel that the deep preoccupation with the environment so widely evident these days may lead us to overlook an important point: *environment is for people.* [In a Biblical reference, he added] I have good authority for this point of view. It says, ''. . . and let them have dominion over the fish of the sea, and over the cattle, and over all the earth, and over every

creeping thing that creepeth upon the earth." I'm glad TVA's nearly four decades of resource development and environmental concern has been people oriented.

In agreement with this point of view, the Decatur, Alabama, *Daily* stated in an editorial headed "EPA Needs Dose of Common Sense" in its issue of January 3, 1974, "One of the biggest ecological problems the nation faces is the Environmental Protection Agency (EPA) itself. That's just opposite the reason for its creation."

New standards for the control of both fly ash particles and sulfur dioxide gas were established by state air pollution control agencies, acting under terms of the 1970 Federal Clean Air Act and under guidelines set by the Environmental Protection Agency. The TVA is willing to conform to these as much as is practicable, but it stated there were obstacles in the way of complete conformity. The Authority stated that some phases of the work could not be completed before 1978 if sufficient generating capacity was maintained in operation to meet expected electric power demands. It also was estimated that complete compliance with the EPA air quality standards would cause an increase in residential electric rates of 12.9 percent per year by 1979.

Sulfur dioxide, unlike fly ash, is an invisible, colorless gas. It results from a chemical reaction of oxygen and sulfur during the burning of coal. When released into the atmosphere through tall stacks, it mixes with other gases in the atmosphere and is quickly disbursed. Only under unusual weather conditions, according to the TVA, is it likely to concentrate near ground level. If such concentrations are allowed to occur, plant and animal life may be adversely affected. No workable method of reducing sulfur dioxide emissions significantly has as yet materialized. The TVA is working on the problem. Its biggest question surrounds the standards which seek to limit the quantities of sulfur dioxide emitted high into the atmosphere from the top of power plant stacks. This is a tough one to solve.

One of the techniques recommended for reducing sulfur dioxide emissions at power plants is called the "scrubber" system. This consists of complicated installations in connection with the emission outlets of the furnace gases. This has meant a sobering consideration for the TVA.

Chairman Wagner recommended another method. He pointed out that the waste created by a power plant using the scrubbing process requires four times as much land for disposal as fly ash. For the TVA this would require disposal areas totaling 20,000 acres in the next 20 years. The TVA-recommended method employs a combination of five scientific and engineering approaches simultaneously, costing about

$100 million to install and annual costs of about $17 million. The approaches were:

1. Very tall chimneys, which aid in the dispersion of sulfur dioxide gases in the atmosphere high above ground level.
2. Weather observations and measurements made daily at the plant, including the use of light aircraft and pilot balloons, which enable plant personnel to determine when atmospheric conditions are likely to produce unacceptable concentrations of sulfur dioxide near the ground.
3. Computers, which quickly process data on weather conditions and plant operations to determine when there may be unacceptable ground-level concentrations.
4. Reduction of sulfur dioxide emissions by reducing plant generation or other means while these atmospheric conditions exist, thus avoiding any violation of ambient air standards.
5. Sensitive monitors strategically located around each plant which report automatically the ambient concentrations and thus check on the effectiveness of the control operations.

The state of Kentucky filed a suit against the U.S. Environmental Protection Agency, the Atomic Energy Commission, the U.S. Army, and the Tennessee Valley Authority, charging that the agencies were not obtaining air pollution permits from the states in which they are located. A federal district court ruled against the state of Kentucky, and on June 5, 1974, the Sixth U.S. Circuit Court of Appeals upheld the lower court and ruled that federally owned facilities are not required to obtain air pollution permits from the states in which they are located.

The relationship with coal was a continuing, rocky one. An editorial in the *Louisville Courier-Journal* on June 12 contended that "TVA should spend more time monitoring the coal shipments it is receiving. A Knoxville television station recently reported that coal operators have been layering their truckload shipments to TVA's Kingston plant—first coal, then rock, mud and slate, then more coal, then more rock, mud and slate. The layers apparently are strategically placed—like strawberries, with the better ones on top—to foil TVA's inspection system. TVA conceded that is an age-old problem, but says it's tough to prove."

Several environmental groups challenged the TVA in court. This time it concerned a policy statement which the Authority had made about its sources of coal. The plaintiffs charged that the Authority's policy statement was vague and legally inadequate. TVA attorney

Thomas Pederson grew sensitive. "We don't like to be put in the role of an outlaw," he retorted. "The practical facts of life are that TVA is simply another purchaser of coal and has no regulatory powers whatever to reform the coal mining industries." Later a three-judge panel of the appeals court denied the appeal brought by the environmental groups. The TVA had disclosed that costs of new antipollution devices would be passed on to customers.

Not long afterward an EPA official, Roger Strelow, said that "Private companies look at TVA and say 'As long as the Federal government's own utility can get away without installing scrubbers, then why should we be expected to?' Because of what they are and who they are, they have a major effect on the attitude of private industry." The TVA hit back by claiming that its air pollution control efforts at steam generating plants would represent an investment of more than $300 million. This cost would be greater, it was stated, than the combined cost of all dams and reservoirs the TVA had built between World War II and 1975.

Meantime at the Kingston, Tennessee, steam plant on the winding river not far below Knoxville, two 1,000-foot chimneys thrust upward into the sky like giant fingers. Each contained large electrostatic precipitators designed to provide 99.68 percent efficiency in removing the fly ash particles discharged from the furnaces of the plant's nine generating units. The Kingston plant has a turbine hall the size of three football fields placed end to end. The two new chimneys replaced nine former stacks that were about one-fourth of the height of the 1,000-foot ones.

South of Greeneville, Tennessee, there is an old dam on the Nolichuky River, built by a private company over 60 years ago. Having a small hydroelectric station, the dam by 1973 had become obsolete. The TVA planned to develop there an environmental study center. The plans included a nature trail with a 30-foot overlook for students and teachers to view the waterfowl below, a walk-through tour of the old powerhouse, an open-air shelter, and an outdoor meeting area for classes. The dam reservoir is known as Davy Crockett Lake, named in honor of the colorful character who was born not far away in this eastern Tennessee region. He represented part of the state in Congress and then went to Texas, where he died fighting at the Alamo.

Strip Mining

Of all the problems facing the TVA, perhaps the most pesky and publicized one is that of strip mining. Although the Authority officials reiterate that the TVA strip-mines only a fraction of the coal thus obtained, the organization seems to get credit for doing most of it. It has been explained that the coal deposits which underlie much of the Appalachian region extend through parts of eastern Tennessee from the western end of Virginia to northern Alabama. Of course there is much coal in Kentucky and "west" Virginia.

Strip mining uses huge earthmoving equipment to strip overlying earth and rock from shallow coal seams so the coal can be dug from open pits. This method of mining dates back more than half a century, but with modern machinery such production has increased generally. Seams close to the surface make possible a more complete and more economical use of coal resources. Obviously, in regard to the safety of miners, strip mining has a wide advantage over deep mining.

Just as obviously, strip mining has serious disadvantages, especially if steps are not taken to minimize them. As the land is turned upside down to expose the coal, ugly scars are torn in the landscape. If not properly treated, these scars remain, exposing the bare earth to erosion and causing the coal wastes to pollute streams with acid. However, with careful mining and reclamation, such damage can be checked and controlled. Planting trees and other vegetation are helpful, and now hydraulic seeding by a modern machine can establish a cover such as that of sweet clover more effectively.

As early as the mid-1940s, TVA foresters began to try to encourage mining companies and landowners to reclaim and replant strip mine land voluntarily, but they had only limited success. Most such mining in the valley was in remote mountain areas where it was little noticed. In a competitive coal market, mine operators were reluctant to pay reclamation costs, often higher per acre than the land itself brought. So it seemed that laws to require reclamation after surface mining were required. Kentucky was the first state of the region to enact this kind of legislation. Since the idea was somewhat unfamiliar, other states were slow to follow, but now the other states in the valley have done so.

In the meantime the TVA was rapidly becoming the nation's largest user of coal and felt a responsibility to also take the lead in reclamation after strip mining. In 1963 it issued a report entitled "An Appraisal of Strip Mining in the Tennessee Valley" which was used nationally. A series of demonstration projects along this line were carried out in the valley. In 1965 the Authority began including reclamation requirements in its coal contract awards wherever the coal was to be produced by strip mining. These provisions have been strengthened as the need arose. Other requirements include water runoff and erosion control measures, immediate revegetation with grasses through hydraulic seeding, planting of trees and shrubs for the planned land use after mining, and other such measures. Part of the payment for the coal is placed in an escrow account until satisfactory reclamation is completed. Strip mining is prohibited in certain wilderness or scenic areas and wherever adequate reclamation is not forthcoming.

The Penn Virginia Corporation signed an agreement with the TVA and state agencies in 1969 for the establishment of a 10,000-acre wildlife management area in southwestern Virginia. This agreement combined wildlife development with timber management and strip mining reclamation. Other TVA research includes studies on the adaptability of various plant species to strip mined land; the value of fertilizers, soil conditioners, and mulches in speeding the growth of strip mine plantings; and the effects of reclamation of water quality, aesthetics, and wildlife.

From Harry M. Caudill in Whitesburg, Kentucky, came testimony before a Congressional committee about strip mining:

> I was born in 1922 in the very heart of the Appalachian Mountains and have been surrounded all my life by coal mines, coal miners, and coal companies. . . . I lament the utter ruination of the hills of my homeland and the assault surface mining has made on people of my blood and name. I have seen once-clear streams choked with mud, and lawns and gardens layered with foul sediments from the spoil heaps. And I have seen wells that once brimmed with crystaline water filled to the top with yellow mud flecked with coal.

Caudill urged that Congress adopt legislation which would outlaw strip mining in such areas as southern and central Appalachia and some parts of Ohio and which would authorize strip mining only where total restoration of the land can be carried out promptly and effectively. He also recommended that the federal government commence a massive program to purchase and restore lands already stripped.

Aubrey Wagner took issue with such remarks, stating to the Associated Press:

> In these national debates we of course always have those who advocate the easy answers. Their answer for shoreline oil pollution is to stop offshore drillings. Their answer to the ecological damage to strip mining is to stop strip mining. Their answer to the problems of aquatic environment is to stop building dams. But the answers are not that simple if we are to continue to meet the needs of society. . . . A complete and immediate ban on strip mining would turn off 40 percent of the lights and other electrical equipment in the Tennessee Valley region. Other coal-dependent regions would experience similar effects.

How serious the question of mining coal is need not be dwelled upon here. The United States has nearly one-half of all the recoverable bituminous coal and lignite believed to exist in the world. It has been estimated that this is enough fuel to meet all U.S. energy needs for about 600 years at the current rate of use. But on the environmental side it has been recognized that if we are to use the 45 billion tons of strippable coal without destroying our environment, strict laws are needed. At this writing, Congress has passed such regulations. How much they will be implemented remains to be seen.

Three national conservation groups filed a suit in federal court in New York City on March 3, 1971, against the TVA. It was accused of ignoring new government environmental protection standards in contracting for supplies of strip-mined coal in the Appalachian Mountains and hastening the desolation of the region. The suit came at an unfortunate time for the Authority, which was just recovering from an acute shortage of coal reserve. Joining in the suit as supporters but not plaintiffs were Harry Caudill and another Kentuckian, Elvis J. Stahr, president of the National Audubon Society. The largest strip-mining contract challenge in the suit concerned the remote mountain counties of Leslie, Knott, Perry, and Breathitt in Kentucky. The TVA denied the charges.

Adding fuel to the fire of controversy, the U.S. Geological Survey published a 90-page technical report on April 11, based upon an 11-year field study of ecological effects in a 25-square mile creek basin in McCreary County, Kentucky, a strip-mined coal region along the Tennessee border. The conclusion of the study was that between 1955 and 1960 such mining killed or reduced fish in the streams by filling them with acid and mineral poisons, caused the fall of hundreds of thousands of tons of stream-filling silt, and killed or stunted trees.

Later in the year James Branscome, a conservation leader, told a U.S. Senate subcommittee, "If strip mining is not abolished in Appalachia, it will be the most dangerous occupation in America. I cannot emphasize too greatly to this committee that people will use arms." Within three weeks the TVA issued new and tougher rules under which the companies supplying the agency with 16 million tons a year of strip-mined coal were required to reclaim the scarred earth. The Authority at the same time denied that strip mining had contributed to the poverty and depopulation of five coal-producing states in the Appalachian area.

An incident of doubtful merit occurred in some surface mining which took place on Limestone Ridge, following the awarding of a contract by the TVA in 1970. The contract called for the mining and delivery of approximately 725,000 tons of coal reserves by the W. B. Spradlin Coal Company. According to a memorandum from James L. Williams, Jr. (TVA director of purchasing), to Lynn Seeber dated May 1, 1972:

> During the course of the contractor's mining operations, it was found that the portion of the leased property lying on the eastern slope of Limestone Ridge is visible from Interstate 75, and, in accordance with present TVA policy of not permitting mining for TVA contracts in areas visible from major highways, the contractor was stopped from mining further in that portion of the property.

It would appear from the foregoing that the contracting parties were not open and above board in doing the strip mining and keeping the operations away from the public view. The impact on outsiders may have been softer but certainly not more convincing of genuine motives being involved.

In the June 19, 1973, issue of *World*, Roger M. Williams took the TVA to task somewhat in regard to strip mining. Said he:

> TVA is caught between its old way of doing business and the new concerns for the environment and the rights of the under-privileged. . . . TVA is the world's largest consumer of strip-mined coal. Approximately 4 million of these tons came from the mountains of eastern Kentucky, which received none of the benefits that TVA bestows. . . . TVA is at the center of the reclamation issue because of its position as the leading consumer and because it alone among America's major coal users includes reclamation requirements in all coal-purchase contracts.

On the other hand, Professor Lee W. Saperstein of Pennsylvania State University wrote to the *New York Times* as follows:

> Tacit in all arguments for the abolition of strip mining is the presumption that no real harm will be done to the economy of coal-producing regions or to the continued supply of fuel for energy. I disagree with these presumptions . . . your suggestion that four times as many men as are employed in the strip-mining industry could be employed in underground mining seems to be akin to Marie Anoinette's solution to the bread shortage. On the basis of exposure—man-hours expended—the fatality rate in underground mines is approximately twice that of surface mines . . . My premise is that strip-mine land can be restored beyond the state where it is possible to identify the past mining activity.

The General Accounting Office said in a report made public three days later that the TVA should stiffen its requirements for the reclamation of strip-mined lands even though its latest requirements were a "significant improvement" over earlier requirements. The GAO said that even though TVA had slope restrictions in its latest contracts, some slides had occurred. It said TVA should consider further limiting mining on steep slopes and that 8 of the 25 mining sites visited had revegetation problems because of acid-bearing soil, loss of topsoil, or improper planting techniques.

The next year the TVA was pleased to report that more than 5,000 acres of strip-mined land were seeded within a 12-month period. Also it reported a novel approach to the problem of reclaiming the land. In late 1972 some landowners in the Chattanooga and Sequatchie Valley areas asked the TVA about the possibility of using strip-mined land for growing grapes. The result was a one-acre research vineyard on a strip-mined area atop Sand Mountain near Fabius, Alabama. The outcome is promising but still uncertain at this writing. Some apple trees planted there, however, have borne fruit.

An eloquent voice about strip mining was raised by the conservationist James Branscome of Kentucky. Writing in the *New York Times Magazine* of December 12, 1971, he painted a lurid picture. He said that the process of extraction of the coal is frightening in itself and described how the strip miners cut a road through the timber so that they can haul to the site their heavy equipment such as bulldozers, earth movers, power shovels, and front-end loaders. The overburden of trees, plants, earth, and rock is blasted loose and pushed down the hillside. Slowly it slides downward, sometimes uprooting trees, blocking streams and roads, and even covering homes or farms. After the overburden has been removed there is a kind of dirt platform like a roadbed standing out along the side of the mountain. Above it is the high wall which has been cut and which with the platform forms a terrace-like ring around the hill, in other words, a great encircling gash.

Branscome told of a Kentucky woman, Mrs. Bige Ritchie, who stood on her front porch and watched bulldozers rip up her family's graveyard to get coal for the TVA. She said the miners paid no attention to her shouts, and she saw the coffins of her children "come out of the ground and go over the hills."

The writer concluded: "Long the pride of politicians who viewed it as a benevolent, people-serving agency, TVA is, in effect, stripping away the birthright of the people it was created to serve."

The estimate of the TVA is that about one-third of the nation's coal comes from strip mines. About one-half of the coal the Authority uses comes from such mines in Alabama, Illinois, Kentucky, Tennessee, and Virginia, although it is quickly added that TVA purchases less than 20 percent of such production. The TVA position on strip mining is set forth as follows:

It is the most economical and in many cases the only practical way of producing coal. The potential harmful effects can be prevented at reasonable cost, and this cost should be included in the price of coal. Responsibility for regulating the industry should rest first with the states, and failing that, with the Federal government.

So under the ground, on the land, in the water, and in the air the TVA is involved. Along with criticism progress has been made. In 1969, the *St. Louis Post Dispatch* carried this little article:

What city has the most electrically-heated homes among all the cities of the world? New York? London? Tokyo? Los Angeles? None of them or others of the very largest cities. It is Nashville, Tennessee, with a population of 170,000. Twenty-two years ago Nashville had only twenty-nine electrically-heated homes. Today it has 75,000. The reason: low-cost electricity supplied wholesale by the Tennessee Valley Authority and promoted vigorously by the city's distribution system. No smoke. No soot. No residues.

MONTHLY RESIDENTIAL ELECTRIC BILLS
1,000 Kilowatt-hours

OCTOBER 1978

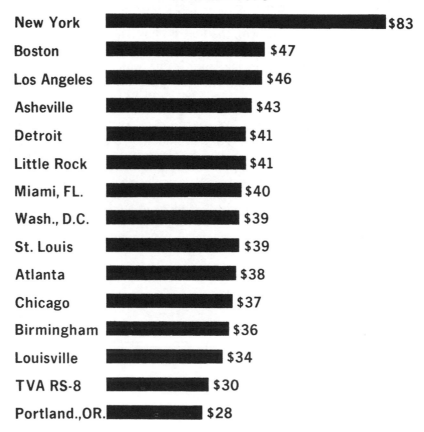

New York	$83
Boston	$47
Los Angeles	$46
Asheville	$43
Detroit	$41
Little Rock	$41
Miami, FL.	$40
Wash., D.C.	$39
St. Louis	$39
Atlanta	$38
Chicago	$37
Birmingham	$36
Louisville	$34
TVA RS-8	$30
Portland., OR.	$28

NOTE: Bills for others are based on residential rate information obtained directly from the utilities. Bills include all currently applicable adjustments and charges except local and state sales taxes. TVA rate level RS-8 is typical of basic residential bills in TVA service area; amount may vary in particular locations due to rate level difference and application of special charges.

17. The Power and the Cost

Irrespective of its other phases, the Tennessee Valley Authority brought money and jobs to this region of the South, which had one of the lowest economic conditions in the entire nation. So in a temporary way, the TVA was a relief measure; but in the long run, its greatest impact has been the production of electric power at a comparative low price to the people.

Ironically, the problem of the TVA now is the price of the power which it produces. This has brought the organization to its greatest crises, and many who have praised the improvements which the TVA have brought to them have changed their tune to one of criticism, since they have been hit in the pocketbook. With its increase in power production, its position of leadership in the national power industry, and its immense plans for new kinds of power in the future, the Authority stands in a unique position. It has an incomparable opportunity to establish a criterion and set the pace.

Surprisingly few people, including this writer, understand exactly how water creates electricity. One learns that from behind a TVA dam water falls down a big steel tube and turns a water wheel. Thus the energy from the water is transformed into electricity. Then it continues on its course through ten other lakes and as many other water wheels, creating more electricity each time.

Regardless of the merits in the argument between public and private power, the average electric rate in the United States dropped 23 percent within seven years after the TVA was established; in the previous seven years, these rates had dropped only 2 percent. Private power companies still made money.

The TVA explains that it makes payments in lieu of taxes on its power properties and operations even though it is not subject to taxation in the usual sense by state or local governments. This arrangement is provided for in the TVA Act. Except for fixed yearly payments to the states of Arizona and Nevada by the Boulder Canyon Project (Hoover Dam), TVA is the only federal agency which makes payments in lieu of taxes to state and local governments on account of its power activities.

TVA sells power directly to about 200 customers. These include 110 municipal electric systems, 50 rural electric cooperatives. and one small privately owned electric system which purchase their supply of power at wholesale from TVA. The rest are industries and federal agencies which are served directly by TVA because their power requirements are very large or unusual. To serve these bulk power customers, TVA owns and operates power properties consisting almost entirely of generating plants and high-voltage transmission facilities. Most of these properties are located in open country outside urban or built-up areas.

The ownership and operation of the region's electric distribution facilities are in the hands of the 160 local distribution systems. These systems sell TVA power at retail rates to more than 2 million ultimate customers. They pay state and local taxes or make payments in lieu of taxes which are larger in total amount than the TVA payments. Section 13 of the TVA Act provides for TVA to pay annually to states and counties 5 percent of its gross revenues from sale of power in the preceding fiscal year, excluding revenue from power sold to federal agencies. The annual payments grow as power sales and revenues grow, and they are continuing to grow steadily. The 1970 payment of $16,098,463 was 78 percent higher than the $9,048,337 paid five years earlier, in 1965.

One-half of the annual payment is divided among the states in the same proportion that the investment in TVA's power property in each state relates to the total investment in TVA's power property. The remaining half is divided in the same proportion that TVA's power revenues in each state relate to TVA's total power revenues. In addition to the $16,098,463 paid by TVA in fiscal year 1970, the municipal and cooperative electric systems distributing TVA power paid $24,170,334 in state and local taxes or tax equivalents. The combined payments of TVA and the distributors of TVA power to state and local governments for fiscal year 1970 totaled $40,268,797.

According to Charles M. Stephenson, a TVA official:

> In all its 42-year history there have been only 2 really significant amendments to the original TVA Act; the rewriting of Section 13 in 1940, relating to payments in lieu of taxes; and the self-financing amendment of 1959, which provides for issuance of our own revenue bonds to finance construction of additional power facilities. The latter amendment also set up a schedule for the repayment of $1 billion of appropriated funds then invested in TVA power property,

with an annual interest return to the Treasury based upon the going average interest rate payable by the Treasury on its total marketable public obligations. Thus the TVA power system is said to be self-supporting in respect to the current cost of capital, and self-liquidating in terms of repayment of the original capital investment from the U.S. Treasury.

That is how the TVA describes itself. But there is another story. In 1965 the Edison Electric Institute of New York City published what it called "A Study of the TVA Power Business." Its conclusions were as follows:

1. Today 83% of TVA's investment is devoted to the electric power business. During fiscal 1964, 77% of TVA's electric generation was produced by steam plants while only 23% was obtained by using falling water.
2. About 33% of TVA's power revenue is received from the sale of power to the Atomic Energy Commission (AEC). The rate that TVA charges for this power is about the same rate that groups of power companies charge on the sale of similar blocks of power in AEC.
3. TVA has invested over $2½ billion in power facilities. Prior to the passage of the TVA Bond Bill, Public Law 86-137, TVA was not required to pay interest on the money appropriated by the Congress for the building of power facilities. TVA pays no Federal income taxes, but makes payments to state and local bodies in lieu of taxes. These payments are considerably less than the non-Federal taxes paid by companies.
4. Return on investment is influenced by the cost of money. Money costs and taxes are necessary costs of business. In all business enterprises these costs are reflected in the prices charged to customers. About eight out of ten retail electric customers purchase their power from investor-owned electric utilities. These people pay in their electricity bills the cost of money and taxes. The other two out of ten purchase their power from government power projects, such as TVA. These people do not pay in their electricity bills equivalent costs of money and taxes.

In his book *TVA the First Twenty Years,* Roscoe C. Martin has summarized that the "TVA is subsidized" theme rests upon four major charges: (1) TVA has allocated too high a percentage of its investment to navigation and flood control; (2) TVA does not pay taxes, (3) TVA does not pay interest on the government's investment, and (4) the government will never recover its investment. Martin goes on to say, however, that in Ohio and Pennsylvania, for example, the rates charged by the power companies are not required to reflect the government's investment in navigation locks and flood control in the Ohio and Monongahela River basins. "The essential differences between TVA and the private utilities," Martin stated, "are in their objectives, not in the arithmetic surrounding their accounts."

Robert H. Knowlton, executive vice-president of the Connecticut Light and Power Company, wrote an article for *The Hartford Times* in January 1946 in which his anti-TVA views were unmistakable:

> To my mind two of the most important reasons why the TVA should not be expanded into other authorities are (1) the TVA is a financial failure, and (2) the TVA autocracy constitutes a serious threat to democracy and private enterprise. While it has taken more than $800,000,000 from the nation's taxpayers since 1933 it has not yet returned any of that money to the government, except in very minor and inadequate interest payments (eight one-hundreths of 1 percent of the total investment in 1944).

Knowlton added that the TVA is free from all restrictions and regulations imposed on business-managed utilities, such as the Securities and Exchange Commission, the Federal Power Commission, and the state regulatory authorities and is no uncertain challenge to states rights and local autonomy. He observed that the TVA had no need for obtaining franchises, licenses, and other permits for water power development.

Professor A. J. G. Priest of the University of Virginia Law School took a dim view of the TVA situation. He said he found it difficult to comprehend "why the very possibly charming citizens of Tupelo, Mississippi, and Nashville, Tennessee, (TVA consumers) should enjoy all the benefits of tax-subsidized, virtually tax-free electric energy while my Virginia neighbors and I, and many others, pay electric rates which properly reflect the substantial local, state and federal taxes paid by the investor-owned companies which provide our service."

The professor stated that if the TVA were to pay local, state, and federal taxes on the same basis as the Southern Bell Telephone and Telegraph Company, the TVA tax bill would increase from the current $3,418,110 to more than $76,000,000, and its net revenue of $19,294,109 (for the 12 months ended June 30, 1953) would become a dificit exceeding $53,000,000. The deficit of $53,000,000 would become $57,000,000 if the TVA were to pay taxes on the same basis as five investor-owned utilities operating in Tennessee. Priest contended that electric power rates were reduced more rapidly in the period from 1912 to 1932 than in the period from 1932 to 1952.

Fulton Lewis, Jr., headed one of his columns, in February 1953, "TVA Worthless as Tax Producer." He stated that TVA paid no taxes.

In regard to payments in lieu of taxes, he suggested "Send the Bureau of Internal Revenue a crate of eggs in lieu of your income tax, and see for yourself what happens." However, Section 13 of the TVA Act as amended in 1940 by Senator Norris and Congressman John Sparkman apparently was designed as an answer to such a charge. For example, in 1953 TVA payments in lieu of taxes, totaled $3,418,000. Of this amount $1,150,000 was divided among 135 counties representing the equivalent of former county property taxes on power properties acquired by the TVA. The remainder was allocated among the seven Tennessee Valley states and paid directly to the state governments.

Hershal L. Macon of the TVA explained in this regard:

> The whole story isn't covered by TVA payments in lieu of taxes. TVA power is essentially a wholesale operation in so far as it serves domestic consumers. The TVA sells power to the municipal and cooperative distribution systems. These municipal electric systems are not subject to state and local taxation. TVA has no control over that, as you will understand; but in order to have a power system operating on a self-supporting basis TVA has considered it desirable that these municipal systems make payments in lieu of taxes. There is a permissive arrangement to that effect written into the power contracts. Basically the municipal distribution systems are permitted and do make property tax equivalent payments. Usually the amount is calculated by applying the prevailing local property tax rates to the book value of the power property. Book value is used in place of assessed value against which regular property taxes are levied.

Dean Russell, in a publication of The Foundation for Economic Education, took the TVA to task in 1949. He contended that the taxpayers' money used to build the TVA would have created as much work and more happiness if the individual taxpayers had been permitted to spend the money themselves. In that case they would have bought something they preferred instead of TVA navigation, fertilizer, electricity, and other products.

Russell quoted (in substantiation of his statements that the TVA is subsidized by taxpayers' money) Senator Norris as saying in substance, "If the TVA is taxed it will go out of business in three months." Also pointed out as special tax privileges enjoyed by the TVA but not by private utilities are the franking privilege in the use of mails, tax-free gasoline, exemption from various license fees, etc. In addition, Robert E. Lee, chairman of the House Appropriations Committee in 1947, is quoted as saying: "In general, federal power is not cheap, but can be made to appear so by allocating substantial portions of the investment and expenses to other than power. Also, our studies indicate that if the federal projects pay taxes at the levels paid by the privately-owned utilities, the federal rates would, in general, be higher than the rates of the privately-owned utilities in the contiguous areas.''

In continuing his surgery on the TVA, Russell wondered why the Tennesee Valley states did not choose to do the job themselves. Then he concludes that they either didn't want to or considered the cost greater than the benefits or were led to expect the federal government would do it for them—or a combination of all three reasons. The TVA, he argued, is a federal agency with all the powers of the federal government behind it and therefore can *force* state and local officials to conform to its decisions.

Lilienthal is cited as stating that private interests must be subordinated to the Authority; and among those who were reluctant to cooperate were the farmers who did not want to be moved, the landowners who did not want to sell, the private electric companies that wished to stay in business, persons opposed to government production of electricity, and those who objected to the use of federal taxes for local projects.

Russell even predicted that sooner or later TVA would have a chairman who would be ''corrupted by the tremendous power at his disposal.'' This has not come true.

Chairman Gordon Clapp seemed called upon to defend the Authority at numerous times. Lecturing at Florida State University in February 1953, he said that the TVA found it necessary to explain itself at times to New England. The reason: some people in New England were saying that the TVA should not build any more steam plants because a greater abundance of electricity in the Tennessee Valley was luring industry away from New England. Clapp denied this. He said that his organization was ''encouraging the development of industry in the Tennessee Valley and must continue to do so; its experience is available for study on the part of New Englanders interested in revivifying the industrial strength of that great region. Here TVA speaks as a representative of the region.'' He explained why TVA was not popular among some other Federal agencies. ''They think,'' he concluded, ''we are working the other side of the street. The tragic fact is that the country does not have enough power.''

In the same series of lectures, O. S. Wessel of the TVA Office of Power discussed the reasons it should not have been desirable for TVA to undertake the job of local distribution of power and why he felt that function could be handled more effectively by local agencies. Regarding its control over local rates, Wessel said that ''Congress did not intend that TVA should sell power at wholesale to municipalities and cooperatives without attaching any conditions with respect to its resale."

John Gunther in *Inside U.S.A.* indicated he was impressed by the TVA. He noted that it was the biggest job in American history from the viewpoint of sheer size; the TVA dams as a whole used 10 times the amount of material in Grand Coulee and 35 times that in Hoover Dam. TVA director James P. Pope told him that the amount of concrete, earth, and rock the TVA dams contain would fill a hole 10 feet in diameter straight through the earth from the United States to China. The concrete alone is about three times more than was used in the entire Panama Canal.

Gunther felt that the quality of TVA personnel is high, as high as that of U.S. Steel or Harvard University. He was impressed by the fact that TVA makes its own decisions, subject to general control by Congress and that TVA is very big but also very small because of its decentralization.

The author observed about the cries raised that TVA does not pay taxes and so has an advantage over private power companies: "This is not true, though it is true that TVA pays no Federal taxes as such since it is owned by the Federal taxpayers and its entire income is the property of the Federal government. In 1950, its net income represented 44 percent of its gross power revenues. This income went of course to the government, exactly as if it were a tax, and an additional point to make is that this percentage of return to the government is considerably greater than the average return of the private companies."

As early as 1961, Aubrey Wagner became the principal spokesperson for the TVA. He has not hesitated to state his convictions both for his organization and against its opposition. He had not been a director long when he struck back at the argument that the TVA is a socialistic, subsidized enterprise. He stated in a speech to the Knoxville Kiwanis Club that the private utilities have received subsidy benefits from the American taxpayer that far outweigh the sums invested in the TVA. Wagner said regarding the private companies, "The amortization certificates they obtained in the past decade, in effect interest-free loans from the government, represent a net subsidy of nearly $5 billion—enough to build three TVA power systems. . . . This past year, TVA itself was the largest single "taxpayer" to the Tennessee state government. For nearly thirty years the power companies have been telling the American people that public power is the first step toward crowding out private enterprise entirely, and so the existence of TVA inevitably means the Tennessee Valley is being socialized. Meanwhile, private industry in the region served by TVA has grown so rapidly that jobs in manufacturing have increased 111 percent, twice the national increase in the same period. Private investment in new industrial facilities amounted to $850 million on the waterfront alone."

A few years later, however, the tenor of Wagner's remarks necessarily changed to the defensive. On March 16, 1967, the TVA announced the first rise in its rates affecting residential customers. He explained that this decision had been made reluctantly and was because of rising cost trends, including the major factor of higher prices for coal. The chairman added that under the TVA Act, the organization was required to charge electric rates sufficient to cover all of its power program costs, payments in lieu of taxes to states and counties, debt service on bonds and notes, and payments to the U.S. Treasury. An increase in power rates had been made in 1952, but this change affected only industrial power rates. It was pointed out that the average residential rate among homes served by the TVA power distributors was still less than half of the current national average.

The increase meant an additional return to the Authority of about $27 million. The range of residential consumers added 22 cents a month to the bill of small users up to $1.43 a month for large users. Residential customers using 1,000 kilowatt-hours a month paid from $6.78 to $8.90 under the former rate, these increasing under the new rates from $7.68 to $9.93. The national average in 1967 for 1,000 kilowatt-hours was $18.36.

The new TVA rates of course were not greeted with welcome. Some comments were acrid. Commenting on it editorially, the *Knoxville Journal* stated that the advantages "of operating a socialistic enterprise may be counted on the plus side, but of course do not compare in importance with the basic advantage one has over all privately-owned enterprises in the same field."

The *Wall Street Journal* in an editorial entitled "The Twisted Yardstick" commented, "At least two major firms which had planned major expansions in the TVA area already are seeking alternate locations in areas of lower power costs. If TVA persists in subsidizing municipal and residential consumers at the expense of industry, the effects on business activity and employment are not hard to foresee."

Some other publications seemed more sympathetic, for instance, the Hopkinsville, Kentucky *New Era:* "But the time comes in just about every business operation when costs increase to the point they can no longer be absorbed. In case of power rates, any boost is regrettable because the consumer can't turn anywhere else to trade."

The Murray Kentucky *Democrat* observed, "TVA undeniably has done a magnificent job of bringing prosperity to the area. However low-cost power for industry is a critical part of this program."

More favorable still toward the TVA decision was the *Chattanooga Post,* which pointed out that private companies, too, including Consolidated Edison of New York, had announced rate increases. Said an editorial, "The *Wall Street Journal* reminds us of the Arab nations. Like them in their attitude toward Israel, the newspaper just refuses to admit TVA has a right to exist and continue to perform superbly its assigned task of regional development. Instead, the *Journal* just beclouds the issues and raves at the success of what has come to be known as one of the world's best examples of public enterprise."

All across the valley region comments were written and heard, many to the effect that such a rate raise by the government darling of the region seemed unbelievable; other opinions appeared to be more understanding and receptive. It was pointed out that some large publications in the nation had previously charged the TVA with purposely having low industrial rates in order to lure industries from other parts of the country. Now these same publications were saying such rates were too high. From Knoxville to Memphis, from Atlanta to Louisville, and elsewhere newspapers took up the cry. They reflected to a great extent the sentiments of their readers and publishers, both conservative and liberal: regrets that such inflationary action seemed necessary and hopes that such would not be a harbinger for the future.

Their hopes were not to be realized. Within two years the TVA announced its third increase. The causes were the same. The TVA said in a statement that its escalator provisions of rate schedules called for "automatic increases or decreases in charges for electric power with changes in TVA's interest and fuel expenses. Even after the sharp rise in our operating costs, the average kilowatt-hour cost here for residential use is only 1.06 cents, or about half the national average."

A hitherto friendly voice, perhaps surprisingly, was heard from on a different note. It was that of Congressman Joe L. Evins, Democrat of Smithville, Tennessee, and ranking member of the House subcommittee which recommends funds for the TVA. He expressed disappointment at the rise in TVA electric power rates and said that the Authority ought to, "if at all possible, reduce rates rather than increase them. As a longtime friend and supporter of the TVA, this development disturbs me. I want TVA to maintain its image as the yardstick of economic public power. TVA would do well to review this entire matter and its decision to increase rates." It goes without saying that the sanguine desire of Congressman Evins was not to materialize.

The TVA divulged that its rate increase of March 1969 was expected to provide approximately $30 million in additional revenue over the ensuing year. It was glad to announce at the same time that the number of all-electric homes in the Tennessee Valley region, which had more than any other area of similar size, increased by 35,000 to a total of 561,000. Industrial growth continued, as reflected by a 12-month increase of 595 new industrial plants, 8 percent over the previous year. But one company operating in the area was far from happy. The Reynolds Metals Company issued the following statement:

> As a result of previous rate increases, the TVA electrical power rate charged Reynolds for its Listerhill Reduction Plant is the second highest among the seven reduction plants we operate in this country. Obviously, another increase would lessen the competitive capability of our Alabama plant as well as other industries in which power is an important cost factor.

In a nearby Alabama city, however, the reaction, editorially at least, was less critical. The *Huntsville Times* said:

> TVA will have to pay the U.S. Treasury $83.4 million from power revenues under an annual repayments program set up by 1959 amendments to the TVA Act. Cost of TVA bond financing, authorized in 1959, has gone up steadily. The first interest rates paid by TVA were 4.44 percent. The latest issue of bonds, as of last month, costs TVA an interest rate of 9.25 percent. The times make victims of us all, perhaps.

Other public commentators pointed out various angles from which to view the situation. One observation was that in the case of most price and wage increases that seem unreasonable, consumers do have a choice: they can shop around and see if they can do better elsewhere. But there is no choice when public utilities start hiking charges. The *Nashville Tennessean* pointed up a different factor, namely, that fuel industry officials had been claiming that one reason coal could not be delivered to the TVA economically and in sufficient quantities was a shortage of railroad cars for transporting the coal. The editorial continued that if anyone in Washington "is seriously interested in learning what happened to all the railroad coal cars, all he has to do is drive about 100 miles down to Norfolk, Va. There, in the Norfolk & Western railroad yards, are parked hundreds of hopper cars loaded with c waiting for ships to come and transport it to foreign market."

Although its territory was not so much affected by the TVA, the *Atlanta Constitution* stated on August 9, 1970, "Shooting at TVA in Tennessee is much like shooting at Santa Claus, but with or without a long beard, TVA is being shot at from all angles because of a proposed price increase." One of the "shots" was the sharp comment from some quarters that the TVA did not have to get anybody's permission to increase rates nor was even compelled to explain. It was pointed out that the Authority simply notifies the power distributors of the various communities about the increases, and these distributors then put the increases into effect on the consumer. This is because the Tennessee Valley Authority is an independent organization, whereas if a private company finds its costs rising to the point where an increase in rates is indicated, it must go to a public utilities commission and ask permission to do so, giving figures to substantiate its request.

Growing attention was also being paid to what was felt to be increased domination of coal companies by the oil companies. It was claimed that eight out of ten major coal companies were by the 1970s owned by oil or metal companies. Tupelo, Mississippi, which had signed the first contract with the TVA for electricity, became conscious of the growing significance of the power question. Said its newspaper, the *Journal*:

> As much of the heavily populated part of our country is increasingly threatened by periodic power shortages, a strong and expanding TVA thus becomes one of the most important factors in American economic growth. Within the TVA region we have become so spoiled by the exceedingly low cost of electricity that we are disappointed and perhaps at times inclined to be critical when the power agency has to increase its charges for electricity to local distributors.

It was also charged that much of the coal in the hands of oil companies which were demanding a higher rate of profit made it an unjustified sellers' market—that these companies made higher profits than did the mining companies. Other factors were higher transportation costs, mines closed because of new safety regulations, and strip mine reclamation. All of these had driven the price of coal upward.

Laffitte Howard, writing in the Knoxville *News-Sentinel,* pungently observed that a number of Congressmen had taken issue with "Red Wagner, the twinkly-eyed chairman of the TVA," because of the rate rise. Wagner had explained that such an increase was required because of the way the TVA Act was written. Said Howard:

> But despite all Aubrey J. Wagner has said in person and through TVA spokesmen, there are still protracted polemics and even calls for an investigation by some of our Congressmen.
> Fortunately most of these gentlemen are unopposed for reelection this week and are merely making a little political hay with a welcome new topic, the pros and cons of motherhood and sin being pretty well worn out, no matter which side you take. And if the gentlemen so

disturbed about TVA following the law had serious and bitter opponents, it's feared that said opposition might be so unkind as to
compare a 23 percent rate hike with a 41 percent increase in
Congressional pay.

The Authority was also criticized for its wage scales, which were
thought by some private employers to be too high. In an otherwise
rather sympathetic editorial, the Fulton, Kentucky *Leader* stated:
"And now TVA has fallen victim to inflation it helped to create and to
other rising costs. Its already over-inflated wage scale is beginning to
work on its budget, and the sky-rocketing cost of coal for its steam
plant is sending costs soaring out of sight."

It may be well to examine the development of the TVA rate
schedule. In the early years there was but one level of retail rates, and
all distributors used it. But by the early 1940s it was evident that the
financial operations of many distributors would allow them to reduce
rates. In 1944, TVA designed two additional levels of retail rate
schedules, each progressively lower than the original level, and in 1961
another level was designed, making four in all. Distributors reduced
their rates by adopting one of the lower series of retail rate schedules.

In July 1952 the retail rates to commercial and industrial users,
especially the large users with high load factors, were revised to reflect
the changing cost characteristics of the TVA system resulting from the
increasing proportion of steam generation. The wholesale rate to the
distributors was modified at the same time so that much of the increase
in industrial revenues would be passed on to TVA to compensate for
the higher cost of steam generation. Fuel adjustment clauses were
added to the wholesale and industrial rates, the first time such adjustments were included in a TVA rate. Because of the stability of TVA's
fuel cost at the time, this adjustment was operative during only one
year—1957.

In August 1967, after 34 years of operation, TVA had initiated its first
general rate increase "to meet rising costs of fuel, money, and labor."
TVA redesigned and raised the wholesale rate. The four retail rate
levels also were revised and were supplemented with five additional
levels, making nine in all. Automatic adjustments were incorporated in
the wholesale and the commercial and industrial rates to compensate
for future changes in the cost of money as well as for the cost of fuel.

In March 1969 rising costs necessitated another general rate increase
and TVA again raised its wholesale rate and redesigned and added a
level of retail rates, making ten in all. The money and fuel adjustment
clauses were modified to make them more responsive to changing costs
and, for the first time, they were included in the residential rates.

Adjustments upward occurred in August 1969, and again in August 1970, and also in October 1970. At this time the automatic money and fuel adjustments were replaced by a contractual arrangement with the distributors for a quarterly review by the TVA and the distributors of the Authority's revenue and expenses, followed by a determination by the TVA board of directors whether a rate adjustment, upward or downward, was necessary. By absorbing some of the higher costs, some distributors adopted lower levels of retail rates and others adopted higher ones.

What is a proper rate for electric power? This is a still unanswered question as the energy crisis mounts and energy costs soar. It was a government attempt to answer the question that brought about the birth of the TVA. In the first half-century of the electric industry, many municipalities provided electric service for their people. Private power companies in most instances either could not or would not furnish this essential service. So by the early 1920s over 3,000 cities in the United States had their own municipal systems. But after World War I, as capital became more available to private companies and as cities directed their civic interests toward such things as streets and schools, the number of municipal systems began to decline and private companies took over the service. This trend was interrupted in a large manner by the corruption and financial manipulation discovered in the big utility companies in the late 1920s and early 1930s.

The liberal *New Republic* commented:

> When the TVA's new dams were complete, it began negotiations with Tennessee Valley cities and power districts for the sale of current. The Commonwealth and Southern subsidiaries, especially the Tennessee Electric Power—Tepco—fought these negotiations with courthouse-gang wiles. In the Valley's chief cities Commonwealth and Southern subsidiaries took an active, scarcely disguised part in local elections where municipal ownership was at issue. The utilities won in Birmingham but lost in Chattanooga and Knoxville.

The Chattanooga News carried an item about the resistance of some people to the efforts of a private power company to obtain more of the rural market. According to this newspaper:

> With a loaded .22-caliber rifle in her hand, Mrs. A. M. Tate faced a group of Georgia Power Company linemen in her front yard one day last week.
> "Come down out of that tree," she called. "No one gave you permission to cut those limbs off."
> She waved her gun and a lineman scurried down the trunk. Another who had been standing at the foot of the big hickory hopped

over the fence out of the yard. That was in Catoosa County, Georgia.
In the same place, farmers burned two miles of spite lines put up by
the power company.

William T. Zumwalt, director of power system operations for the
TVA, recalls the early days. In an interview with him and Paul H.
Shoun, chief of the power dispatching and protection branch, Zumwalt
said that in those early days of the power industry, his father worked 12
hours a day, seven days a week, moving coal in a wheelbarrow. The
son says the biggest problem of the organization is keeping a balance
between power requirements and its generation. He called attention to
the growing interdependence of utility companies upon each other.

An examination of a few distinguished characteristics of some of the
TVA installations should give an idea of the physical side. For example, the Gallatin Steam Plant, on the Cumberland River near Nashville,
Tennessee, was placed in operation in 1956, the TVA's seventh steam
plant in seven years. One of its innovations was soon apparent from the
outside, that is, the free use of large sheets of heat-resistant glass in the
generator wing and glass walls in the office building. The John Sevier
plant on the Upper Holston River, is unique among TVA plants in that
it receives no coal by river barge. The coal is brought in by rail.

The huge Johnsonville plant in western Tennessee was constructed
in the early 1950s, and the TVA found that because of its size it was
necessary to abandon the single-structure concept and deal with each
of the plant's components separately. These included the boiler wing,
the generator room, office wing, shops, laboratories, and control office.
One steam plant like Johnsonville can produce more power than the
combined peak production of Hiwassee, Norris, Fontana, Douglas,
and Cherokee dams.

The greatest of all TVA dams, Kentucky Dam, backs up water for
184 miles and has a storage capacity of more than twice that of the next
largest lake, Norris. Unlike any other TVA dam, the Kentucky one
supports both a highway and railroad. Statistics in these cases often do
not mean much because each year the TVA builds something bigger
than it did the year before. Some of its tasks have been virtually
completed, especially in the fields of conventional construction and
navigation. So it has turned to newer directions.

By 1970 the power requirements of the region were 60 times as great
as in 1933, so new directions have been required to operate the nation's
largest electric system, the TVA supplying power for about 6 million
people in an 80,000 square-mile area of the southeastern United States.
Based on the figures of the organization, employment in the major

types of manufacturing industry in the region grew faster in the 1960s than the national trend for those industries.

An indication of its own growth, the TVA system interconnects at 26 points with neighboring power systems for what is believed to be economical reasons and to further safeguard the reliability of power supply. As has been stated, the Authority has agreements with an interconnected group of systems to the south and west for the exchange of power on a seasonal basis. At the peak, around 2 million kilowatts are exchanged.

Of environmental as well as practical interest is the recent disclosure by the TVA that over 25,000 residential power consumers throughout the valley are served with underground facilities. In addition to these, over 2,000 industrial and commercial customers are receiving the same kind of service. The trend is expected to be even more pronounced in the future as underground wiring for homes, mobile home sites, apartment buildings, industrial and commercial customers, college campus additions, schools, hospitals, and urban renewal projects are equipped with the same kind of effective but less visible connections.

A Congressional subcommittee reported some recommendations to expedite certain trends in the valley. It was the Subcommittee on Special Small Business Problems chaired by Joe L. Evins of Tennessee. On August 7, 1972, this committee made a report which contained the following:

> Based on the analysis and evaluation of testimony, evidence and other available information, the subcommittee makes the following recommendations:
> That the Tennessee Valley Authority:
> (1) Retain and strengthen the yardstick concept of electric rates to the Tennessee Valley by formulating and implementing procedures designed to halt the escalating costs of electric power generation.
> (2) Initiate an in-depth coal production cost analysis in order to acquire the data necessary for determining the reasonableness of prices paid for its coal supplies.
> (3)Strengthen its small business assistance program to induce and encourage small coal operators to supply a greater proportionate share of TVA coal needs.
> (4) Enforce the reclamation provisions in TVA's coal purchase contracts with surface mine operators in order to insure a proper restoration of the land in mined areas.
> (5) Take the appropriate steps necessary to encourage the location of business and industry in the Tennessee Valley by providing abundant electric power at reasonable rates.
> (6) Expedite the TVA-Commonwealth Edison liquid metal fast

breeder reactor program in order to provide the Tennessee Valley and the Nation with a reliable and economical source of electric power.
(7) Closely scrutinize electrical equipment procurement policies to assure that full consideration is given to factors other than price.

The price was certainly a factor in the use of electricity in the valley during 1971–1972. Residential customers served by TVA power distributors paid an average of 1.28 cents a kilowatt-hour for electricity during that period. This was 57 percent of the national average cost. These customers used 47 percent more power than was the average ten years previously. During that time the growth rate in home use slowed down in areas where use was already high, while growth continued at a more rapid rate in areas where use had been low.

The use of TVA power had not been confined to the valley area. In the summer of 1970 the nuclear power plant at Indian Point on the Hudson River had to be shut down for the summer. To add to the situation, the Ravenswood plant of New York City suffered a great loss when its million-kilowatt generator burned out, reducing reserves to the edge of disaster. The interconnected grid system came in handy. TVA plants at the time had more power than they needed or at least enough to supply some to New York. It was different from the blackout of five years before, and for the first time the TVA filled in a crucial gap.

One of the most timely and significant viewpoints about the energy crisis has been that of S. David Freeman. In the summer of 1972, five years before he joined the TVA board, he made a pertinent comment which if not easily understood seems worthy of consideration. "Rate of return is basically cost-plus," Freeman said. "There should be incentives to conserve power, shave peaks, and meet needs as efficiently as possible." In a penetrating article in *Public Power* for March–April, 1973, Freeman stated:

In a way, it all began with the Big Blackout of the Northeast in 1965. I can still remember the shocking impact of that evening in November. No one really thought the lights could go out. But they did. In a sense, it was a freak—a failure to readjust trip-out devices in Canada. In reality, it was a warning signal of deeper trouble. . . . Thus far, the energy crisis is a self-inflicted wound. It is not Mother Nature but Uncle Sam that is to blame. . . . There is no doubt that the price of energy should reflect its true cost to society. But we must not forget that the consumer still has to pay the bill and that higher prices will impose real hardships on lower and middle income families for whom energy represents a significant part of their cash outlay.

In looking toward the future, Freeman believed:

We need to buy time by demanding more efficiency in the use of energy, that unless we start examining how wastefully the nation is consuming energy and begin to practice conservation that we are headed for a genuine energy crisis. The energy demand has grown five times faster than our population for the past hundred years. [He pointed out that only about half of the energy content of our fuels finds its way to the consumer.] The nation can keep warm, get to work, and keep industry humming with about a third less energy than is presently consumed. . . . Energy is needed to sustain a society that improves the lifestyle of the people. But we can avoid a crisis by curbing our appetite and investing in the technology for abundance.

In an article of analytical interest in the publication *Lithopinion*, Summer 1973, Robert Sherrill gave a novel definition of the Authority:

TVA is no fairy tale—it comes closer to being our longest playing Political Melodrama. All the ingredients are there: the public-power waif excapes from the clutches of several evil old men (among them Henry Ford), is reared by kindly uncles (George Norris and Franklin Roosevelt). She soon falls into the hands of city slickers (like Wendell Willkie and Dwight Eisenhower) who try to fleece her out of her birthright; but she escapes once more to achieve lasting virtue triumphant. . . . Private industry had its eye on the Tennessee River, all right, and was constantly ready to take over those portions that would return a fat profit—but it wanted to invest a minimum of money for this profit. Most of the major banks had interlocking directorates with the major railroads, and the railroads—gouging Southern shippers with rates 40 percent higher than in the North— had no interest in developing the navigational side of the Tennessee. The major money sources of private enterprise refused to invest in flood-control projects, considering this the domain of the public purse.

Sherill pointed out that the idea of "national defense" by which the original TVA Act was passed turned out to be authentic because of the major part which the Authority played in World War II. It was largely because of the availability of electric power that the Atomic Energy Commission set up its laboratory at Oak Ridge in the eastern Tennessee hills. Three-fifths of the incendiary and smoke-screen bombs used in the war were produced from the TVA-manufactured phosphorus. The goal of 50,000 airplanes per year which President Roosevelt set (and many thought was impossible) was met, according to Sherrill, because of the availability of aluminum produced by TVA electricity.

The issue which gave promise of staying alive was the continuing rise in power rates. In the closing days of 1973 the area was hit by another one ranging from about 10 to 20 percent, or $2 more a residential customer. Again there was a hue and cry; again there was an explanation. *The Chattanooga Times* as usual took an understanding view and referred to the law which requires the TVA to charge rates high enough to provide a return sufficient to exceed costs and to meet covenants with bondholders. Its operating figures, properly compiled, are on file with the Federal Power Commission. The newspaper also reminded its readers that since 1970 the TVA had engaged in a quarterly review to determine the necessary rate level.

The same newspaper remarked editorially that the item of $52.6 million in "retained earnings" was really not profit but a reserve from which to meet emergencies. The system had an investment of more than $4 billion and power revenues of $750 million with which to undertake capital expenditures instead of having to borrow funds at a steadily increasing rate of interest: "TVA raised its rates to compensate for what it could foresee happening in the year ahead—higher fuel, labor and money costs," the paper stated. "It figured as closely as it could what these increases would be, permitting it to operate in the black as the law demands while sufficient for accumulation of a reasonable level of "retained earnings." Private utilities are making upward rate adjustments."

It was said that apparently many people believed the TVA's power could always remain at the low rates of 20 or 30 years ago, no matter what happened to the cost of fuel, labor, and money in the meantime. At about the same time the *New York Post* conducted a survey after a storm of protests arose over residential electric rates charged by Consolidated Edison in New York City. It was discovered that users of 250 kilowatt-hours a month there were being charged $22.08, while at the same time TVA customers were paying $7.45 for the same amount of power.

A consumer information pamphlet issued by the TVA stated that any slowdown in electric rate increases in the future will depend on national economic trends that have caused costs to climb in recent years. More stable electric rates will be possible in the future if the nation as a whole can achieve a better balance in fuel supply and demand, lower interest rates, environmental regulations that allow alternative approaches for meeting environmental goals, and development of more efficient technology and potential low-cost energy sources.

This high-sounding explanation contained a lot of truth but did little to soothe the ruffled spirits of many customers paying approximately twice the rate for power than they had a few years before, even though such rates were still lower than in most areas of the country.

One of the most unique and talked-about sources of power in the Tennessee Valley operations is coming about on a picturesque mountain six miles west of Chattanooga. The name of the project itself is colorful, suggestive of the days of Davey Crockett or Estes Kefauver. It is the Raccoon Mountain Pumped-Storage Hydroelectric Plant of the Tennessee Valley Authority.

The object of this extraordinary enterprise is, according to the TVA, "To help maintain the reliability of the Tennessee Valley region's supply of electric power." The Authority began a study of the project when its officials were convinced that the agency's system would need additional "peaking" power to meet the fluctuations in power demands at different times of the day. These require a plant that can respond almost immediately to sudden increases in the demand.

Since the opportunities in the valley for increasing the supply of conventional hydro power is limited, this new kind of plant was felt to be highly desirable if not necessary. It has been estimated that 14 dams with the capacity of the nearby Chickamauga one would be required to supply as much peaking power as the maximum generation planned at Raccoon Mountain. Nuclear and coal-fired units are normally not suited for short-term operation to provide peaking power. The project includes a large dam on top of the mountain, creating a storage reservoir to be filled with water pumped up from Nickajack Lake at the foot of the mountain a thousand feet below. This water is then to be available to generate electricity when it is needed most in periods of highest demand.

A visit by this writer to the project was revealing and impressive. From the foot of the mountain and near the edge of the lake, about all one could see first was a gaping 40-foot wide hole being bored into the bottom of the mountain and on into its center. Rocks and dirt strewn around the outside of the opening made walking difficult. For over five years a work force of up to 1,500 men blasted its way into the limestone center of this wooded mountain. On the top, they hollowed out a 528-acre reservoir and built an embankment dam along the curving mountain crest which is more than 8,000 feet long. Walter R. Dahnke, the project manager, said they were building the TVA's largest earth and rock dam, "different from anything the TVA has undertaken."

The operation's plans include four reversible pump-turbine units, among the largest ever made, housed in a chamber carved out of solid rock deep inside the mountain. This man-made cavern is 490 feet long and 72 feet wide. It has a capacity of 1,530,000 kilowatts, twice as much power as the 21-unit Wilson Dam. The Raccoon Mountain plant works this way: during hours when the power demands of the area are lowest, mainly at night, generating units at TVA steam-electric plants, otherwise idle, continue in operation to provide power for pumping water up to the mountaintop reservoir. When peaking power is needed during the day, the pump-motor units will be reversed to operate as turbine-generators, driven up to a half-million horsepower each by the force of water falling from the reservoir high above. The reservoir holds 37,000 acre-feet of water, and the turbines can operate at full capacity for a 20-hour period if necessary before emptying the reservoir.

The powerhouse is underground and the transmission mechanism on the mountaintop is screened by forest, so only the discharge structure and tunnel portals are visible at the river's edge. The cost of the project is more than $192 million and is financed by the issue of power revenue bonds. The Raccoon Mountain project is expected to become a popular one for visitors. The TVA plans to maintain a public access road to the mountaintop, which offers a sweeping view of the Tennessee River gorge on one side and the city of Chattanooga on the other. A nature trail is being built for hikers, and picnic areas are planned for the mountaintop and along the lake shore below. An overlook will be located on top of the mountain, and an elevator will carry visitors from the overlook a thousand feet downward to the underground powerhouse.

Some of the most prominent citizens of Chattanooga have estates on top of Raccoon Mountain, and their homes have been shaken by the blasting below. But one of them, Dudley Porter, Jr., a former insurance executive, takes a stoical view of the project and hopes for the best. One good feature, he says, will be the lack of pollution. According to the TVA, the plant does not consume water, disburse gases or particles into the air, or add heat to the river. So the spry little animal which gave his name to this mountain can in all likelihood reside comfortably in his chosen tree.

As the year 1974 wore on, the situation became somber. The TVA notified its 160 local distributors in the seven states that when its coal stockpile dropped to 3 million tons, it might cut their electrical allocation by 30 percent. The fuel supplies were then, in late November, down to 4.3 million tons and could dwindle to 3 million tons within three weeks, depending upon how the current nationwide strike of the coal miners ended. The strike had cut off about two-thirds of the 500 thousand tons of coal the TVA was receiving each week. It was no wonder that Chairman Wagner said, "As a nation we are burning far more coal than we are mining each year." This dire prediction caused an uproar of alarm in the valley. Santa Claus there seemed to be far off that Christmas.

Seemingly carrying out the expression, "when it rains it pours," it was announced at about the same time that the TVA planned to purchase the Peabody Coal Company for around a billion dollars. Also in the announcement was the supplementary plan that the Authority would sell off most of Peabody's properties except the coal fields in Tennessee, Kentucky, and Illinois and thus recoup two-thirds of the purchase price. The coal company was a subsidiary of the Kennecott Copper Company which had been directed by the federal government to divest itself of Peabody.

Aubrey Wagner told Congressman Evins that such a purchase would provide the TVA with a 40-year coal supply at lower prices and thus slow down the upward spiral of the TVA's electric power rates. Evins sympathized with this idea and the fact that the TVA by now was paying as high as $27 per ton, hoping to cut it to about $10. Said he, "TVA has made nine rate increases in seven years and two recent reductions that were imperceptible. I hope to see a rate reduction that is perceptible."

Congressman Richard Fulton of Tennessee thought it was a great idea. "This is the first really innovative action taken by anybody in the Federal government or in the private sector to do something about coal costs, consumer needs, inflation, monopoly, and a host of other problems which afflict wage earner pocketbooks," Fulton said. But Senators Howard Baker and Bill Brock, Republicans of Tennessee, demanded a Congressional investigation, stating that such a step and such a purchase of a coal company was of the first magnitude of importance. The National Independent Coal Operators Association opposed the proposed sale. The *Nashville Banner* commented in an editorial:

The TVA now employs more people than does the government of the State of Tennessee. It has become, in its 41 years, a commercial power company operated almost entirely by coal and steam plants and is raising its rates faster and higher than private companies, despite liberal tax breaks as a Federal agency. If the TVA is allowed to enter the coal business, then it can seemingly enter the mining equipment business, the steel business to furnish raw materials for the making of that equipment, and even the land from which comes the ore for the steel. What could stop the TVA from buying whatever it wanted?

By contrast, the Tullahoma, Tennessee, *News and Guardian* expressed itself thus:

> The danger signals are out. It is crisis time in the Tennessee Valley. The Tennessee Valley Authority is once again under attack. . . . The drumbeat messages that TVA is dangerous, that it cannot be trusted, that it is a socialistic agency leading us down the road to slavery, that it is answerable to no one—all are the same messages that anti-TVA interests have been beating out for forty years. TVA's friends must start beating their own drums to send the message throughout the Tennessee Valley and the nation, a message of the great progress, resource conservation and regional development that have made the TVA area the envy of the world.

In a published effort to let the public know what it considered to be the facts in the case, as well as its own viewpoint, the TVA put out a brochure of answers to frequently asked questions. Although some of these statements have been touched on before, a few of the typical ones help to point up the position of the TVA which it has striven to maintain over the years, sometimes with difficulty.

It was emphasized that TVA is not a utility company, and its purpose in producing electricity is not to earn a profit. It is a federal agency established for regional development and assigned to produce electric power as part of that regional Program. Power generated by TVA is distributed to local consumers in parts of seven states by 160 municipal electric systems and rural electric cooperatives, not operated to earn a profit. Under the law, the TVA board of directors is responsible for establishing rates for TVA power that will provide adequate revenues to cover financial requirements. With family income rising and with lower electric rates than most other areas, families here increased their use of electricity at a rapid rate over the past three decades.

A second major factor emphasized was that even though electric rates have risen all over the country, TVA rates are still lower than elsewhere except for a few locations, such as the Pacific Northwest, which still get most of their power supply from dams. Again people were reminded that the biggest single problem was the rising price of coal; other factors were the increasing interest cost of borrowed money and expenses incurred in solving air and water pollution. The last-named costs also had discouraged some of the private coal industry from opening more new mines in recent years.

No business can be built on borrowed money, it was explained, and TVA as a federal agency cannot sell stock to private owners to offset the rise in indebtedness. If TVA did not reinvest money from revenues to help build power facilities, the power system financial structure would become top-heavy with debt. In the past, the system's indebtedness and interest costs were small, but today more than half the investment in the power system represents borrowed funds. The TVA power system is not operated for profit, in the usual sense of earning dividends for stockholders.

Supplying electric power, it was stated, is not the same as supplying shoes or soap or most common goods. In a pinch, most industries can cut back some production or delay expansion plans to avoid added costs. An electric system, whether it is TVA or a utility company, does not have these choices. It must make sure that when the consumer flips the switch the light goes on. Nuclear power plants appear to offer the best chance of offsetting part of the rapid rise in fuel costs. Nuclear plants cost more to build than plants burning coal, but they offer a much lower fuel cost for each kilowatt-hour of electricity produced. Environmental protection does not show up as a line in power expense tabulations. Indeed, its costs are spread throughout the expense picture, many of them with an indirect impact. But that impact is substantial and growing.

These official statements were accepted by many, but some scoffed at the reasoning. This latter sentiment reached an explosive point when Chairman Wagner announced that the TVA area might have to cut back sharply on its use of electricity. Cities were urged to limit their use of power in order to avoid emergency brownouts or blackouts. The *Chattanooga News-Free Press* reacted with a sharp editorial which, it said, was based on a survey. Commented the editorial:

1. Chattanooga seems to be the only major city in the TVA area that has taken sharply restrictive measures to limit the use of electric power.
2. The TVA is the only major power source in this section of the country that is unable to supply its customers the desired quantity of electric energy.

These situations raise the question "Why?"
Chattanooga businesses are hurting because of limitations on the hours they may be open.

TVA responds that it resisted coal prices that have risen out of proportion to the rising costs of mining, making a effort to keep the general price level low. As a result, its supplies were short when the coal strike came and when prices rose even higher. What might have been applauded as a sound business move in the beginning has turned out to be a bad bet, producing shortage while prices have

gone up even more. Now we face higher electric rates for less power
to cover higher prices and lower volume.

Mayor Robert Kirk Walker of Chattanooga issued a blast accusing
the TVA of "deceitful, irresponsible leadership." He charged that he
and the city had been misled into thinking there was a real power crisis,
when actually there was not. He quickly called together a meeting of
business and civil leaders on the eve of Pearl Harbor Anniversary Day,
December 7, 1974, and delivered a haranguing, somewhat political
speech. Walker stated that because of the TVA request, Chattanooga
had restricted its power use, while other Tennessee cities had not.
Attacking statements of Chairman Wagner as "contradictory and
self-serving," he called for a Congressional investigation of the TVA
and said that citizens should demand a "Truth in Energy Law."

By late 1979, however, the city of Chattanooga had reason to be
grateful for TVA assistance. A $15 million project, mostly funded by
the Authority but partially by the city, was nearing completion, designed to give flood protection to its Brainerd area where the South
Chickmauga Creek has often overflowed its banks and inundated a part
of the municipality.

From another viewpoint, Mayor John T. Reid of Scottsboro,
Alabama, in a city council meeting criticized "a big city mayor for
attacking the TVA and for calling for an investigation of the agency."
Mayor Reid said that "other than our mothers, TVA is the best friend
we ever had."

John S. McQueen, Chattanooga Electric Power Board manager, was
quoted as saying about the parties to the dispute, "They have talked out
of both sides of their mouths."

Writing in *The Chattanooga Times,* Mary Reynolds commented
about those who favored and those who opposed the TVA: "Between
these two groups of hotheads are cooler heads who say that because of
TVA's magnificent past, they've expected more of it than of private
companies and are sorely disappointed in TVA."

Soon afterward, Chairman Wagner "poured oil on the troubled
waters" by announcing that especially due to the end of the current
coal strike, any drastic reduction in the supply of electricity for the area
would be unnecessary.

In its 1974 Power Annual Report, the TVA took a calm approach and
"pointed with pride" to its record. This revealed that the TVA system
had generated an all-time record of 18,110,000 kilowatts in June when it
met the region's highest-ever summer peak and sent some 2.4 million
kilowatts of power to systems in the South and West in exchange for
power delivered to the TVA in the winter. In April tornadoes had

toppled a number of transmission lines, for a time cutting all lines feeding Huntsville and Decatur, Alabama. Construction crews hastily restored power service.

Another rate rise was made in July. More than 10,000 persons were reported to have attended 164 programs and demonstrations on energy conservation sponsored by TVA and power distributors. Most of those attending were civil groups, teachers, limited-income families, professional groups, consumer groups, students, and builders. Rising costs continued, and fuels for power generation reached their highest levels; employees' wages increased in line with those in the communities; and new equipment was higher priced from transmission tower steel to substation transformers.

Meantime the TVA could take some comfort from the report of an investigation started by then-Congressman Lamar Baker, Republican of Tennessee. The report stated that the investigation showed "TVA has done an outstanding job of restraining the price of electricity in face of the most adverse economic conditions." It was pointed out that the price of coal had increased from $4.35 a ton in 1967 to more than $30 a ton in November 1974. The report concluded that the TVA had taken steps to meet its power requirements while reducing coal consumption.

Opposing winds had not died down, however. On December 16, 1974, *Barron's* financial weekly carried an article by Shirley Scheibla which fired a verbal barrage at the TVA for proposing to buy the Peabody Coal Company. The writer questioned the authority of the TVA in making such a bid and stated:

> Despite an ambitious program for 13 nuclear power plants, TVA has completed only one and expects its annual coal consumption to go from 40 million tons at present to 46 million by 1980. At the moment, however, TVA doesn't know where its supplies will come from. It's now abundantly clear that TVA originally failed to realize the seriousness of the coal shortage and to take adequate steps to cope with it.

The article poked fun at the request the TVA had made to its customers, which called for "setting thermostats at 65 degrees and limiting commercial business hours to a maximum of sixty hours per week, cooking fewer hot meals, avoiding staying up late, and forming the habit of longer hours of rest at night."

John Van Mol, director of information of the TVA, replied to the publication's article, stating:

> The facts belie the charge. With a good reserve—9 million tons—in its stockpiles, TVA did make a conscious management decision early

in the summer of 1974 to resist paying spiraling prices for coal, prices which had no relationship to increased costs of production. To protect its consumers TVA dug in its heels, and into its stockpiles. It is true that in the years since electric rates began rising, the percentage increase in TVA rates has been higher than the national average, because TVA rates had been held at such low levels. The article concludes by calling for a Congressional investigation of TVA. Fine. Perhaps that could bring out some of these facts that seem to get lost in Ms. Scheibla's kind of dissertation about "mismanagement."

In the leading article in its business and finance section of Sunday, March 2, 1975, *The New York Times* revealed that along with the TVA there were two other bidders for the Peabody Coal Company. They were the Cities Service Corporation and the International Carbomin Corporation. The article further said:

Peabody, up for grabs by the bidder with the right price, the best terms and perhaps holding a stamp of approval from the Government, is the nation's largest coal producer. With some 9 billion tons of minable deposits scattered throughout seventeen states, Peabody has been the major supplier of steam coal to the electric utility industry for many years. It produced 69 million tons of coal last year, more than 10 percent of the nation's total.

Chairman Wagner is quoted as saying:

In view of the problems we're having getting coal, and in view of the prices of coal and our further dependence upon Peabody, we felt like we had to make an offer for it. Our intention was not to get into the business of selling coal to someone else or getting more than we need, but to insure an adequate supply for our needs at a cost to us that would make sense.

Nevertheless, a Congressional investigation was forthcoming. It was announced on February 7, 1975, that the U.S. Senate Public Works Committee would conduct a full investigation of the TVA and that a major target would be its proposed purchase of the Peabody Coal Company. The announcement was jointly made by Chairman Jennings Randolph, Democrat of West Virginia, and ranking Republican Howard Baker of Tennessee. Their statement said that "Recent questions about some aspects of its activities and the national concern about energy and the economy require that we exercise our responsibility of Congressional oversight review." Partly as a result, the TVA dropped the idea of purchasing the Peabody Coal Company.

So a time of real crisis had come. The *power furnished to the people* was more and more involved with *the power of the people*. A challenge lay ahead.

18. Energy Crisis Time in the Valley

In 1952 William S. Paley, head of a Presidential commission and chairman of the Columbia Broadcasting System, warned that shrinking resources raised the strong possibility of "an arrest or decline in the standard of living we cherish and hope to help others to attain." How prophetic he was need not be emphasized here.

Almost at the same time we were reminded that the future energy picture depended almost entirely upon technology. Just by reducing the heat which is wasted when energy is consumed could extend the abundance of the latter. The most efficient plants generating electricity convert less than half of their fuel to power. The remainder is lost heat which is dumped into bodies of water or spewed into the air. Similarly, automobile engines convert only a tenth of their fuel into transportation, a problem also being wrestled with.

Waste has not only become increasingly objectionable but extremely alarming. In the United States the demand for electrical energy doubles about every ten years. Measured in British thermal units, it is estimated that there is enough coal to meet all U.S. energy needs for some 650 years at the current rate of usage, although unforeseen conditions could change this. Nuclear plants being built will do away with some of the air and waste pollution problems of coal, but they will increase the problem of waste heat. Most of such heat goes into condensing water, and very little escapes directly into the atmosphere.

There has been a rather general impression that we have a plentiful supply of uranium. Some justification for this belief exists, but all too many estimates have been made without taking into consideration the increasing demand for energy. Since 1970, for example, substantial uranium ore discoveries have been reported in Australia and South Africa. But L. W. Boxer told the United Nations that "Notwithstanding the improved position on reserves, these are insufficient in themselves, and production capacity must obviously be expanded to keep pace with anticipated demand. It is estimated that uranium production capacity in the non-Communist world can be doubled fairly easily from its present annual level. . . . Given adequate effort in the development

305

of resources, low-cost uranium reserves may be expected to be sufficient until fast breeder reactors can assume a substantial share of electricity production from nuclear sources."

According to Paul Kruger of Stanford University and Carel Otte, vice-president of the Union Oil Company of California, in an article in the publication *Aware* (September 1973), it was only where fossil fuels began to be employed that civilization was released from the con-

Profile of a unique TVA project which is hailed as a brilliant engineering feat. It is the Raccoon Mountain Pumped Storage Plant near Chattanooga designed to pump water up to a man-made reservoir at night when power requirements are low; then release it downward during periods when the water beneath is at a low level and power is needed more.

straints of subsistence agriculture and home industry and began its breathtaking growth in both population and per capita standard of living. Coal mining began about eight centuries ago, the production of petroleum as an important fuel was started just over one century ago, and the use of natural gas on a large scale has occurred even more recently. The United States leads the world not only in per capita income but also in per capita consumption of energy. With 6 percent of the world's population, America consumes 33 percent of the world's

Energy Sources for the U.S. Economy
(Trillions of Btu)

Energy source	*Actual 1971*	*Forecasted 1985*
Coal	12.6	21.5
Oil	30.5	50.7
Natural gas	22.7	28.4
Nuclear power	0.4	11.7
Hydroelectric power	2.8	4.3
Total	69.0	116.6

Source: U.S. Department of the Interior, "United States Energy: A Summary Review," 1972.

energy production. Yet human labor in the United States constitutes far less than 1 percent of the work performed in factories, refineries, and mills. Said Kruger and Otte:

> It is becoming increasingly evident that the United States has supported its population expansion, its economic growth, and its high standard of living by means of an accelerating utilization of low-cost energy—energy derived chiefly from a bountiful endowment of domestic fossil-fuel resources. But fossil fuels are finite in amount and nonrenewable in periods less than millions of years. Sooner or later the limits of supply of all of our energy supplies are going to be reached.
> It was pointed out [that] unlimited supplies of low-cost energy have been taken largely for granted in the United States, and long-range projections of increases in the real gross national product and improvements in the quality of life have been based on assumptions of a continued abundance of energy. Yet it is a fact that the United States is falling from a position of relative energy self-sufficiency into dependence on other countries to meet its requirements. . . . The increasing awareness of the exponential growth of energy consumption, the rapid depletion of our natural resources, the lagging development of new energy resources and technologies, the strain on the dollar in world markets, and the growing public and institutional demands for energy and materials conservation and environmental protection have forced the Federal government to look toward a more rational plan for the nation's energy economy.

The U.S. Department of the Interior has published a table summarizing by type the energy sources expected to provide the gross energy input for the next several years (see table).

A former official of the Tennessee Valley Authority, David Lilienthal, had entered the more general power picture after he left the TVA in 1946 to become chairman of the Atomic Energy Commission.

Following his service in this capacity and other work, Lilienthal, to the surprise of many, came out against the commercial future of atomic power plants in 1960. He told a news conference in Honolulu that there are still innumerable economic and safety problems to be solved before electricity can be produced commercially from atomic energy. Ironically, he blamed the lag on government control and secrecy.

Following up his contention, Lilienthal stated that (1) he had concluded that the peaceful atom had had a fair trial but that the original hopes for it had collapsed and (2) despite the investment of billions of dollars, power from atomic sources had not been produced at cheaper rates than from conventional sources. In addition, the project had shown that the use of atomic energy and power production creates serious hazards both in the handling of the material and in the disposal of the atomic wastes.

The House Government Operations Subcommittee on the Environment, Energy and Natural Resources reported on April 10, 1978, that radioactive waste generated by both military and civilian reactors was a "significant and growing problem" for which there was no demonstrated method of handling. "Congress and the executive branch," the subcommittee said, "should consider requiring that further licenses for nuclear power plant construction be conditioned upon the timely and satisfactory resolution of radioactive waste and spent nuclear fuel permanent disposal and storage problems."

On the other hand, when appearing before the Joint Committee on Atomic Energy of Congress, Lilienthal seemed rather vague. When asked to square his views with facts and figures on the nuclear power program, he replied that he was not speaking on the basis of detailed information but rather on reflections.

In a series of lectures at Princeton University, the former AEC chairman praised what the Commission had done and indicated that atomic power had proved feasible. He was concerned with the high cost of atomic power, when at that time the cost of coal had gone down. He indicated that where it was needed, it would be done without help from the government. Instead, he believed that the need would be met by private industry. This seemed a far cry from his views when he was with the TVA.

On March 3, 1963, Lilienthal frightened many people when he told the Senate-House Atomic Energy Committee that he would not live in Queens in New York if a proposed nuclear power plant were built there. He was referring to a plan of the Consolidated Edison Company of New York City to construct such a plant in this borough of the city. He felt that the plan was a risky one for the people of Long Island because of the problems of atomic waste disposal and the possibility of accidents or sabotage. These views of Lilienthal were challenged by some of the committee members and utility officials also testifying.

Several years later Alvin Weinberg, Director of the Oak Ridge National Laboratory, agreed to some extent with what Lilienthal had said but was more hopeful. "The moment of truth has arrived for nuclear power. We are victims of our enormous success," said Weinberg. He saw nuclear power as our greatest possibility but felt that considerable advance planning is necessary to minimize the risks to human life and the environment which necessarily accompany nuclear energy. "It is only by scrupulous attention to detail, and exertion of great care that we can expect to maintain the safety of nuclear power plants. So far we have been highly successful. The serious problems will arise when and if all the world's energy demands are met by nuclear power."

Weinberg liked the breeder reactors, which generate more fuel than they expend. He favored the U.S. plan to store the radioactive waste in abandoned salt mines. He told the *New Scientist* that "the underlying motivation for the development of nuclear energy is valid, despite noisy criticism which is being leveled at the enterprise."

Admiral H. G. Rickover, the outspoken "father" of the U.S. nuclear Navy, made two typically novel suggestions along this line. He pointed out that electrical space heating has a maximum total efficiency of less than 50 percent, while there is no theoretical limit on system efficiency for obtaining heat directly from a combustion of fuel. The use of electricity for heating should be prohibited unless the situation uniquely requires such practices, he said. This was directly opposite to the views of the TVA management. Admiral Rickover said that air conditioning should be prohibited except for required industrial or medical purposes, giving as a reason that about 16 percent of the increase in electrical generating capacity is caused by air-conditioning requirements.

In an increasingly urgent search for new sources of energy, scientists have even examined the wind up to 80 meters above the ground, and some samples are estimated to contain five times the energy that we now use. Temperature differences in the ocean also are believed to hold a potential reservoir of energy. Private industry in this country carries on a considerable amount of research on energy technology, but the amount of this activity is largely undetermined in view of the financial risks and uncertain length of time required. So the government has stepped in to urge more research for new energy, including the building of many more nuclear plants.

The year 1972 seems to have been a busy one for research, at least in the compilation of figures resulting from energy research. For example, the August issue of *Mechanical Engineering* contained the information that our population is currently increasing at the rate of about 1.3 percent per year, while the total energy consumption is increasing about twice that much. The conclusion was that energy consumption is closely related to the total value of all goods and services produced in the United States and that it is related to and is a vital ingredient of our economic growth, our per capita income, and the enhancement of our standard of living.

The conclusions agreed with others that as the availability of fossil fuel decreases and the cost of fossil fuel increases, it will become more economical to use nuclear energy for electric power generation. Water power will become a less important source of electric power, simply because our more advantageous hydro sites have already been utilized. Total energy consumption is related to population growth and in the United States is increasing at a rate of about three times that of population. Consumption of energy, in all forms, is a vital ingredient in our economic growth, in the continuing improvement in our standard of living, and in increasing income per capita. Consumption of energy presents environmental problems, but means will be found to control the environmental impact without having to reduce our appetite for energy. The energy sources that will be used and the form in which energy is used are related to technological developments, the availability of fuel resources, and consumer preferences.

Not loath to set forth definite opinions, *Fortune* Magazine in its September 1972 issue apparently felt that it had found an answer to much of the energy crisis. It stated that the fast breeder reactor "might take care of mankind's electricity needs for a thousand years. . . . Of all the advance sources of power, the fast breeder is closest to our grasp. Its scientific feasibility was demonstrated, in effect, back in 1942 when Enrico Fermi achieved the first sustained fission reaction. Experimental breeder reactors have been operating since the 1950s, and Milton Shaw, the tall, athletic-looking director of the AEC's breeder program, says the development of a reliable commercial model "is solely an engineering problem."

There are opponents of the fast breeder who worry about the possibility of an explosion which would scatter radioactive substances in the vicinity of the reactor. They expressed the fear that some deranged person might steal the plutonium fuel of the reactor and make atomic bombs to blackmail society. It has been pointed out that in 1966 the Enrico Fermi reactor in Detroit, cooled with liquid sodium, incurred a partial meltdown and was incapacitated. A GAO report in support of the Clinch River Breeder Reactor was released on May 8, 1979. The two-month study contended that the project was not the technological turkey President Carter had called it.

If it were to move ahead in its search for new sources of energy, the Tennessee Valley Authority unquestionably had to make decisions as to what direction it would take in its quest. It decided to build nuclear plants. Construction on the first one began in 1967, about ten miles southwest of Athens, Alabama, and is called the Browns Ferry Nuclear Power Plant. It was announced that when completed it would have a capacity of nearly 3.5 million kilowatts in three generating units. The first generating unit was scheduled for operation in 1972, but delays attributed to late environmental requirements and slowness on the part of manufacturers in the fabrication and delivery of critical components, as well as other things, caused a deferment. Unit 1 at Browns Ferry began commercial operation on August 1, 1974; Unit 2, on March 5, 1975.

The site of the plant is on a 840-acre reservation on the north shore of Wheeler Lake. The powerhouse itself covers an area larger than a city block. Three reactors are now operating, housed in a rectangular building on the lakeshore side. Largest structure in the complex is the turbine building, its main floor the size of three football fields. On the northwest shore of the lake, six cooling towers have been under construction. Also in the plant area are an office building with administrative and engineering offices as well as a visitors' section on the first floor.

The project was estimated to cost $750 million, although with overruns that are customary, it seems useless to forecast what the final figures will be. Most of the work is being done by the TVA's own personnel, and more than 3,000 have been employed there during the peak construction periods. However, only about 175 persons are expected to be the permanent operating force. Excitement ran through the region when the Browns Ferry plant was first announced. Alabama state officials said the estimated investment would be the largest single expenditure for any one industrial project located in Alabama. Governor George Wallace stated that the site selection was "a tribute to this fine section of the state."

Congressman Bob Jones of Alabama predicted that construction of the facility would be a boon to the economy of the area. He praised the TVA for "joining in pioneering this energy source for low-cost power."

A local city official said simply, "We're tickled to death."

Chairman Wagner explained that the TVA had decided in favor of the nuclear plant after an exhaustive study showed it would be more economical than a coal-fired plant. He estimated that about $100 million would be saved over the 12-year period in which the cost of the nuclear fuel was to be guaranteed by its supplier, the General Electric Company. The construction of the plant was authorized by the Atomic Energy Commission, which later revised upward its environmental requirements.

Project Manager W. T. Kelleghan assured the local people, "A nuclear plant is a real good neighbor. There is nothing to worry about in this scare propaganda of a power plant being the same thing as an atom bomb." He said the only possible malfunction could be a leak in a steam line which computers would automatically shut off. Time was to show that he was somewhat overoptimistic.

The TVA explained that the basic elements of a nuclear power plant are similar to those of a coal-fired plant. The nuclear reactor and the coal-burning furnace are both sources of heat for producing steam. The force of the expanding steam drives turbines, which spin a rotor inside a magnetic field to generate electric power. The difference between the two kinds of plants lies in the method and fuel used to produce heat at the start of the generating process.

At Browns Ferry heat is created by the controlled nuclear fission of uranium fuel in the core of a boiling water reactor. This uranium fuel is in the form of pellets that are small enough to fit in a thimble. The fuel is a ceramic material something like firebrick. The pellets are put inside metal tubes about a half-inch in diameter and 12 feet long. These tubes are assembled into bundles containing 49 rods each. The bundles, in groups of four, are separated from other groups of control blades which have to be withdrawn before any usable amount of fission can take place. The bundles, about 800 of them, are installed in a large steel vessel containing water. As the control blades are withdrawn, the fission process generates heat which boils the surrounding water and makes steam. This steam leaves the reactor vessel through pipes to turn a turbine to produce electricity.

After passing through the turbines the steam goes to a condenser, where it is converted back to water by circulating it around tubes carrying cooling water from Wheeler Lake. The water formed when the steam is condensed is pumped back to the reactor vessel to continue the steam-making cycle. The water in the power system and the cooling water are separate and distinct. The lake water that flows through the plant's condensers never enters the reactor vessel and the water in the reactor vessel never comes in contact with the lake water.

Efforts have been made by the TVA to make the Browns Ferry plant "clean, quiet, and attractive in appearance. There will be no smoke, no large coal storage and handling facilities, no ash disposal areas," according to the Authority. Some concern has been expressed by people of the community about the heated water of the plant harming fish and other aquatic life. It is the position of the TVA that there is little danger of this because of the elaborate cooling system. In order to reinforce the idea of safety, biological monitoring activities are carried on by stations which measure the temperature and radiation levels of the lake.

Favorable results regarding the preservation of fish were found in connection with the water drawn from another lake. This is Pickwick Reservoir, the water from which is used to cool the steam condensers of Colbert Steam Plant, a coal-fired TVA power unit in northwestern Alabama. Here heated water is returned to the reservoir through a 3-mile-long portion of Cane Creek, where it is diluted and cooled by the natural flow of the creek. A biological survey detected no damage to the fish there.

Construction on the second nuclear plant of the TVA was started in 1970. It is the Sequoyah Nuclear Plant and is located on Chickamauga Lake, 18 miles northeast of Chattanooga, near the town of Soddy-Daisy. Although not as large as the plant at Browns Ferry, this one will also be a major source of electricity. Its two generating units are designed to generate 20 times as much electric power as the hydroelectric plant of Chickamauga Dam. The projected cost of the former plant was $552 million—and one can safely add "plus." The nuclear reactors and turbogenerators, as well as nuclear fuel for the first ten years of operation, are being supplied by the Westinghouse Electric Corporation.

According to the TVA; "The plant site, a peninsula extending into Chickamauga Lake, was chosen because it meets several requirements for this type of plant—good foundation conditions, a large supply of cooling water, and access to the TVA transmission system in an area where the power supply must be increased. In the tradition of several TVA projects with names of Indian origin, the Sequoyah project was named for the famous Cherokee scholar of the early nineteenth century who developed the only written language of any Indian tribe."

As the project takes shape, people have expressed curiosity about it. "The first thing people ask me," said Jere Ballentine, plant superintendent at Sequoyah, "is 'What are you building? Are you producing material for atomic bombs?' We will produce ordinary garden variety electricity. Two pounds of nuclear fuel can generate as much electricity as one hundred tons of coal. We need this facility to meet the forecast of our electrical power needs of this area."

It is estimated that a neighbor of the Sequoyah Nuclear Plant will receive less radiation exposure from plant operation than the additional amount he would receive if he were to move to a home on top of Lookout Mountain at Chattanooga—where there is slightly more cosmic radiation from the sun because of the higher elevation. Lookout Mountain is a towering elevation overlooking Chattanooga and a lovely bend of the Tennessee River. Here was fought "The Battle Above the Clouds" during the Civil War.

Other nuclear plants have been planned by the TVA, and steps have been taken including some construction. At this writing these are the Watts Bar Nuclear Plant, near the Watts Bar Dam in East Tennessee; the Bellefonte Nuclear Plant which was started in 1974 in northern Alabama; those at Hartsville Phipps Bend, Tennessee; and Yellow Creek, Mississippi. These facilities have run into the same difficulties in relation to environment and the economy that previous ones encountered. The big question about the future of nuclear energy in general is involved.

A background event which has led up to a major new development of the TVA occurred more than three decades ago. On December 2, 1942, the eminent scientist Arthur H. Compton made a telephone call from the project on which he was working in Chicago to his colleague James B. Conant at Harvard University. "The Italian navigator has landed in the New World," said Compton.

"How were the natives?" asked Conant.

The reply: "Very friendly."

This was the first announcement in code of the first self-sustaining, controlled fission reaction by Enrico Fermi and his associates working in the squash court underneath Stagg Field at the University of Chicago. Such secrecy, of course, was due to World War II which was then going on, and the nuclear weapons which resulted eventually led to nuclear power plants. The Atomic Energy Act of 1954 gave industry access to nuclear technology which had previously been a military secret. The Atomic Energy Commission was given the responsibility of developing this technology, helping to introduce its commercial application and regulating its use.

By mid-1977 the TVA had spent some $50 million to obtain uranium rights in five western states in order to assure that it would have adequate uranium supplies for future years. The element is used to fuel the agency's $13 billion worth of nuclear power plants. News of the purchase brought a caustic comment from South Dakota Senator

George McGovern, who was concerned about the impact of the development upon supply and quality of water.

A signal step in a further direction was announced on August 7, 1972, by James R. Schlesinger, then Chairman of the Atomic Energy Commission. It disclosed the signing of a memorandum of understanding providing for the construction and operation of the nation's first liquid fast breeder reactor demonstration plant to be located in the Tennessee Valley Authority system near Oak Ridge, Tennessee. The memorandum was signed in Knoxville by Schlesinger and the heads of the two principal utilities participating; Thomas Ayers, president of the Commonwealth Edison Company of Chicago, and Chairman Wagner of the TVA. Two special corporations were formed to carry out the project, the Breeder Reactor Corporation and the Project Management Corporation. The plant was funded jointly by utilities across the nation, and the government and was designed to produce some 400 megawatts of power. At the same time it was to demonstrate breeder reactor technology permitting more efficient use of uranium.

In making the announcement, Chairman Schlesinger called attention to the fact that in his energy message to Congress the previous year, President Richard Nixon had urged new efforts to assure the nation an ample supply of clean, economic power. Added Schlesinger. "This is a unique joint venture involving participation by the utilities of the United States, both privately and publicly owned, and the Federal government. I think we have assembled the optimum team. Both Commonwealth Edison and TVA have broad nuclear experience, and both organizations have strong innovative management. We look forward to a successful demonstration program."

The AEC chairman pointed out that this was to be a demonstration plant rather than a full-scale facility, because future breeders were expected to produce at least twice as much electrical power as this first American one. Other countries had already carried on such experiments. Schlesinger predicted that the breeder reactor would furnish "electrical energy for tens of thousands of years to come. There is less waste heat than existing nuclear and fossil fuel plants and no air pollution." The Commonwealth Edison Company of Chicago apparently was selected to take part mainly because it has the most experience in nuclear power production.

In the selection of the site, TVA officials were torn between the one which was agreed upon and another at the John Sevier steam plant near Rogersville, Tennessee. Although the latter site in some respects would have represented a lower investment, there was the problem of using existing turbogenerators and hooking on the steam source from the breeder reactor. So the location near Oak Ridge, a 1,360-acre tract on the Clinch River about 25 miles west of Knoxville, was decided upon. The first estimated cost was $500 million, with private utilities across the country pledging $240 million, the TVA $22 million, and Commonwealth Edison $11.4 million. AEC agreed to supply the rest of the funds which would undoubtedly be much more. The TVA was to take the energy from the plant during the demonstration period and pay a price based on the value of the net output computed at the going rates.

With typical enthusiasm, Chairman Wagner told the American Public Power Association meeting in San Francisco that there were three basic and interrelated reasons for developing the breeder to commercial usefulness: (1) it is an essential conservation move in terms of both uranium and fossil fuels, (2) it is environmentally cleaner than present methods of generating electricity, and (3) it holds the promise of reducing the cost of generating electricity.

"The nation's known, economically recoverable reserves of uranium will be used up in perhaps thirty years if we rely solely on light water nuclear reactors such as are now being built," Wagner said. "It is estimated that the breeder will extend their life by perhaps 100 times." He pointed out that light water reactors capture only 1 or 2 percent of the energy potentially available in uranium:

> The breeder, on the other hand, is estimated to capture from 60 to 80 percent of the potential energy. Seventy percent of the energy in 1.5 million tons of natural uranium (the present estimate of economically recoverable uranium in the U.S. alone) is comparable to that released by burning three trillion tons of coal, which is more than half of the world's estimated coal supply. From a pure conservation point of view, the breeder's advantage is thus obvious: it wastes much less of a valuable and limited resource. [Coal, gas, and oil can be saved for] uses for which they may be better suited.

An editorial in the *Tennessee Valley Public Power Association News* stated:

> The Tennessee Valley should give full credit to TVA executives, primarily TVA Power Manager James Watson and TVA Chairman A. J. Wagner, for a crucial leadership role in bringing the breeder demonstration plant nearer to reality. But the Tennessee Valley must also realize that its power systems and power consumers are picking up a sizeable piece of the tab for this project, and it must be aware of the hazards and obstacles involved in this pioneering effort.

Thomas G. Ayers, chairman of the board of the Breeder Reactor Corporation, observed that as a nation we no longer have the luxury of competition among fuel resources, that all sources of energy are needed and that all must be developed to their full potentials. The best source, he believed is nuclear power enhanced by the fast breeder, which he also believed is safe.

Breeder reactors operate in this manner: they use a small, central core of plutonium-239, a substance turned out as a by-product by current atomic energy plants, "surrounded by a much larger blanket" of uranium-238, which is taken from the ground or stockpiles. When the plutonium undergoes fission, the product has at least 1000 degrees heat and in addition many fast-neutrons. By "bombarding the blanket," these neutrons change most of the uranium-238 into new plutonium, thus converting the uranium's energy, about 70 percent of it, into usable fuel.

As time passes, increasing alarm is being felt about the danger of plutonium. Some commercial airline pilots have protested they do not wish to have it in their cargo. Others fear breeder-plant explosions which might scatter plutonium over wide areas, causing death to millions and inflicting genetic mutations on those who survive. In defense, those who advocate breeders say that such fears are groundless. While admitting that plutonium is the most poisonous of all radioactive matter, they argue that the Atomic Energy Commission handled large amounts of plutonium for use in atomic weapons for more than a quarter of a century, with virtually a perfect safety record.

Ray L. Copeland, official of the Project Management Corporation of Chicago, buttressed the defense. He predicted in 1973 that a working experimental fast-breeder reactor would be developed by 1980 and that by the year 2000 a large number of such plants will be in operation. The new type of reactor, he said,

is just as safe or more safe than the light water reactor (conventional) which I have already said is one of the safest pieces of equipment ever produced. Many persons who oppose and fear nuclear reactors do so because they associate them with nuclear bombs. Such persons do not realize that reactors are constructed on an entirely different principle from that used to build bombs. A primary purpose of the breeder demonstration is to show that a relatively large breeder reactor power plant can be designed, built, operated, and maintained in a utility system framework.

Nuclear power is still in growing pains, the November 1, 1972 issue of the *Battelle Research Outlook* admitted. There was an initial surge of reactor orders in the mid-1960s, a paucity of orders in the late 1960s, and a resurgence of interest in the 1970s, the publication says. This pattern can be attributed to reactor siting, construction, licensing, and scheduled startup. Also involved have been environmental, safety, and radioactive waste-disposal concerns. It was predicted that by 1980 the liquid-metal fast-breeder reactor, with its inherent fuel-conserving advantages over the thermal reactor, would be brought out in prototype. Before the end of the century, predictably, fission reactors will be proven in engineering concept to the point where the transition from fission to fusion will become a national goal for the early 2000s.

Herman H. Dieckamp, president of North American Rockwell Corporation's Atomic International Division, has hailed the new type of breeder. He told the American Geophysical Union in April 1971:

> The reasons for the emphasis that is being placed on the development of the fast breeder reactor in both the United States and Europe as the energy source of the future include: savings on power generating costs, establishment of a premium market for plutonium generated in light water reactors, protection of today's investment in light water reactors, and to the consumer an abundant supply of low-cost electricity. What is more remarkable, the fast breeder reactor can achieve these economic goals while protecting the environment better than any other alternate method of generating electric power currently available to meet rapidly growing power needs. Its potential environmental benefits include: conservation of natural resources, lack of air pollutants, and reduced thermal pollution. The fast breeder reactor can meet the growth requirements of electricity and at the same time provide increased protection on the environment.

Obviously the nuclear breeder reactor is not something easy to understand. This was recognized by the publication *Mechanical Engineering* in its November 1974 issue. It set forth some helpfully explanatory statements as follows:

> Everybody's talking about the Clinch River Breeder Reactor Project. For those of you who know little about it we offer herein a few essential facts on the project to keep your cocktail party (or business lunch) conversation up-to-date.
> CRBRP is the nation's first large-scale demonstration breeder nuclear plant. It is a joint industry-government effort. Major participants are the Tennessee Valley Authority, the AEC, Commonwealth Edison Co., Burns & Roe, Westinghouse, Atomics International, General Electric, and Homes and Narver. Large electrical associations—Edison Electric Institute, American Public Power Association, and National Rural Electric Cooperative Association—

have backed it. Congress has provided $100 million in base funds support and is funding up to 50 percent of the capital cost. Industry has pledged $254 million. The total cost for the system is estimated at $1.736 billion. [A later estimate was near $2 billion.] The possible completion date is late 1981. [Later revised to 1983, if at all.] The plant will generate between 350 and 400 megawatts of electricity. Fuel will be a mixture of plutonium and uranium oxides.

The plant has a breeding ration of 12 plutonium atoms produced for every ten consumed. . . . Design features assure safety. One of these is the number of barriers that must be breached before radioactive materials can be released to the environment. The first barrier is the fuel material and its stainless steel metal cladding which retains radioactive materials. A second independent barrier—the reactor core and sodium coolant—is contained in a high-integrity steel primary system, which in turn is surrounded by a guard vessel. The third barrier includes the inerted equipment cells surrounding both the primary system components and the low leakage containment building.

Meanwhile warnings as well as encouragements continued to be issued. "We could well go through a period during which energy would not be available, rationing would be introduced, jobs would be lost, and production would be cut back," said Gerald D. Gunning, an energy economist of the Chase Manhattan Bank of New York. He was quoted in *Industry Week*, which observed:

> For decades the United States has ignored its utility bills. We have had a national energy policy: keep it cheap. We implemented that policy through regulatory distortion of free market relationships. Energy *apparently* cheap and abundant was the result, and it played an important role in U.S. industrial growth. But we bought that cheap and abundant energy by borrowing against the future. Now our accounts are past due, and they will fall most heavily on industry.

James R. Schlesinger was more optimistic. He noted that the enemies of nuclear power state "quite correctly that a power reactor in the course of a year will produce as much radioactive fission products as 150 atomic bombs." But he said there was equal logic in the fact that one automobile in a year produces as much combustion as five tons of TNT or that all autos in the United States generate enough carbon monoxide each year to kill three billion people. This, he said, is like saying there is enough water in the Atlantic Ocean or even in Lake Erie to drown every man, woman, and child in the world.

The U.S. Department of the Interior has estimated a threefold increase in energy consumption by the year 2000. Given as the cause of the nation's energy bind is the reliance on three basic fuels for 95 percent of its energy needs. These are petroleum, 43 percent; natural gas, 33 percent; and coal, 20 percent. The rest comes from hydroelectric and nuclear power. Hollis Dole, Assistant Secretary of the Interior, said that "oil, gas and coal are the easiest forms of energy to utilize, and we have been using them up like the little boy who sticks his hand in the candy jar and thinks the bottom will never be reached."

"Well-qualified people could have predicted this crisis long ago," said John O. Logan, an oil company official. He felt that the situation sneaked up on industry, which felt it had no reason to question the source of supply. The Department of the Interior cited the rapid growth of air conditioning in homes and automobiles, greater use of home appliances, more cars, processing of raw materials, and the lack of applying known technology to increase efficiency in the use of energy as prime causes of the great growth in energy use. As the then-Secretary of Commerce Peter G. Peterson told some businessmen: "Few predictions I am likely to make will more likely turn out to be right than this one—namely, that the price of energy over the next decade will go up much faster than the cost of goods and services in general."

While the talk of the energy shortage continued, the supply of uranium increased. This caused some firms to reassess their commitments despite the looming need for more energy. Among these firms was the Getty Oil Company of Los Angeles, which announced in August 1972 that it was temporarily discontinuing its uranium mining and processing operations in Wyoming. Officials of the company, however, expressed a strong belief in the future of nuclear power and said the firm will continue its uranium exploration program in this and other countries. The problem was given as too much uranium being available.

In the meantime the TVA was commemorating its fortieth anniversary and trying to keep its collective head above turbulent waters. James E. Watson, manager of power, said "I am convinced that nuclear power plants are today our most attractive power supply alternative, both in terms of economics, conservation of national resources, and protection of the environment. But even so, nuclear power plants are being delayed for a number of reasons. Across the nation, the reasons include the normal run of development problems in a new technology, unforeseen labor and component production problems, and delays caused by the requirement to meet a continually changing set of regulatory standards. We engineer safeguards into plants so that if an accident should occur, which is unlikely, the radiation will be contained within the plant. For every nuclear plant that is built, the worst possible accident that could happen is postulated, and then the plant is designed to give adequate protection in case of such an accident."

Lynn Seeber, TVA general manager, said that the great body of the scientific community favors nuclear power as a means of generating electrical energy in the years to come, despite the criticisms of some who question its safety. Seeber said that people who are against nuclear power for safety reasons and who advocate coal, do not realize that deep-mine coal production is the single most dangerous industry in the country. Robert Davidson, chief of TVA's nuclear power program, commented that radiation releases from a nuclear power plant would be less than five units, which is the amount a passenger on commercial jet flights is exposed to each time he travels. James Hill, AEC assistant manager at Oak Ridge, added that a group of scientists who had studied the dangers of nuclear power plants came to the conclusion that if proper safety devices were used, a worker in a nuclear power plant has only a one in 300 million chance of being injured or killed.

The United Press International said that the year 1974 was one of irony for the Tennessee Valley Authority. The news service recalled that at the start of the year the TVA raised electric power rates from 14 to 20 percent, and by the end of the year it announced another 13 percent increase. The Authority was averaging the burning of 110,000 tons of coal per day and was pushing a program of nuclear power generation. Meanwhile, it had moved ahead on the Duck River projects and that of the Tellico Dam in Tennessee.

In its sensitivity to environmental demands, the TVA was giving more consideration to the visual aspects of its transmission system. Substation sites were selected to fit in more with local topographical conditions. More of them were landscaped with trees and shrubs enclosed in decorative walls or fences, painted in harmonizing colors with low profiles and unobtrusive lines. When transmission lines parallel highways, they are set back from the road to allow trees and ridges to screen them from view. Line crossings of major roads at intersections and interchanges are avoided where possible, and necessary highway crossings are made at a right angle to minimize visual impact.

In furtherance of improvements, at TVA's Norris Engineering Laboratory, there was built inside a quonset hut a concrete scale model the size of a basketball court showing a five-mile-long stretch of Wheeler Lake. This model provided a way to measure and predict the effects on lake water temperatures of the heated water discharged from the

Browns Ferry Nuclear Plant's condensers. The results of the study were used in meeting the water temperature limitations for this location and were expected to add to the general knowledge about controlling waste heat from large power plants in general.

The TVA is becoming by necessity increasingly conscious of the importance of proper demonstration of the ways to use electricity wisely and efficiently. Consumers are being given information about the proper use and care of home appliances. Lighting, cooking, and laundry workshops are held at various times throughout the region. The value of adequate insulation and wiring is discussed with home owners and builders.

Government as well as industry seems to realize more and more that research is essential to intelligent decisions and planning. This has been known to the academic world from time immemorial as a prerequisite to ultimate achievement. The main difficulty is that all too often the realization comes after the necessity becomes a crisis. Toward the latter part of 1972, the Ford Foundation set up a grant of $190,000 to "analyze future energy supply patterns, assuming a continuation of current growth rates in energy consumption and different energy supply sources."

John W. Simpson, an official of the Westinghouse Electric Corporation, urged more use of the heat pump which TVA advocates and suggested that every possible system of power should be converted to some kind of electricity. He recommended an electric battery for automobiles but admitted that the production, distribution, and maintenance of such batteries are not ready. A car with such power may not go more than forty miles an hour, but he said that "compared to walking it is not bad."

The experiments of the TVA branched out in various directions. In a small, plastic-enclosed chamber in a greenhouse on the TVA reservation at Muscle Shoals, agriculturists planted tomato and cucumber seeds in wooded troughs. They created artificial conditions of high humidity and studied the plants' growth and disease rates and measured the fruit they produced. This experiment was the beginning of a research project designed to explore and demonstrate the feasibility of using heated water, a by-product of electric generating plants, to grow scarce winter vegetables in the Tennessee Valley.

"From our studies so far, we believe the day will come when a significant portion of the Valley's demand for certain winter vegetables—particularly tomatoes, lettuce and cucumbers used in salads—can be met from such greenhouse production centers," said Billy J. Bond, assistant director of TVA's Division of Agriculture

Development. "The heated water discharged from condensers at nuclear plants lowers operating costs and improves the economic feasibility of such production," he noted.

The TVA has been accused of meddling in local affairs, and with some justification it has replied that its efforts were all for the common good. After the Authority began planning the Watts Bar Nuclear Plant, it was given credit for helping to establish a new Rhea County planning commission, a consolidated high school, new housing, a sanitary landfill in place of an old dump, a labor training program, and local flood control. This assistance was based upon experience in other communities and was admittedly needed in this rural county. Similar projects were in the Sequatchie Valley.

The TVA has joined with other electric utility systems both public and private throughout the nation in pledging support for the Electric Power Research Institute (EPRI). Headquartered in Palo Alto, California, its purpose is to find new technologies which will enable the nation to meet its future electric energy needs in an environmentally acceptable manner. "We have a pressing need for coordinated national planning of all energy services and of electricity supply in particular," explained EPRI president Chauncey Starr. "Because of the long lead time for altering and improving these systems, we now must plan decades ahead."

Research projects supported by the EPRI include inquiry into fusion and solar energy, the underground transmission of electric power, fossil-fuel power generation, new and economical ways of removing impurities from coal, and nuclear power plant safety. James E. Watson of the TVA was chairman and chief executive of the EPRI in 1973 and emphasized that research was one of the most important tasks facing the electric industry.

The research of Ralph Nader and his staff was not in agreement. Nader made a statement at Vanderbilt University in April 1974 charging that nuclear plants were not safe or necessary. Responding to this, J. R. Calhoun, chief of TVA's Nuclear Generation Branch, stated:

It is unfortunate that Mr. Nader apparently ignores the remarkable safety record of the nuclear power industry. Nuclear power plants have been operating commercially in the United States for more than sixteen years. At present there are forty nuclear-powered generating units producing electricity for public use in the United States. Yet not a single life has been lost as a result of a nuclear accident at any of these plants. . . . Mr. Nader is attempting to lead the public down the primrose path to much higher electric rates and ruinous power shortages.

Chauncey Starr also took issue with Nader. The former dean of engineering at the University of California at Los Angeles said that the routine operation of nuclear plants results in a much lower public health hazard than the effluents from fossil fuel plants. He added:

Mr. Nader seems to be unaware of the active worldwide programs for the use of nuclear fission plants for the generation of electricity. The issues of comparative public safety have been studied by every industrial nation in the world, with the same conclusion that the public benefits of nuclear power far outweigh the relatively small risks involved. Quite independently of U.S. programs, these nations are moving rapidly to expand nuclear power. In the development of the advanced fast breeder, they are ahead of the U.S.

A different viewpoint was expressed by Joseph Bistowish, health director of Nashville, Tennessee. He and other local residents questioned the plans for a TVA nuclear power plant at nearby Hartsville. "In the event of an accident resulting in a substantial release of radioactive materials into the environment, the likelihood of a substantial number of deaths resulting therefrom to the citizens of Nashville and citizens in surrounding counties who commute to Nashville is substantial," Bistowish said.

The TVA hit back. John Van Mol, director of information, issued a release to editors quoting a statement on energy problems made by 32 eminent scientists including eleven Nobel Prize winners in Washington on January 16, 1975. Highlights of their joint statement are as follows:

Conservation, while urgently necessary and highly desirable, also has its price. One man's conservation may be another man's loss of job. Conservation, the first time around, can trim off fat, but the second time will cut deeply.

Our domestic oil reserves are running down and the deficit can only partially be replaced by the new sources in Alaska; we must, in addition, permit off-shore exploration. Natural gas is in a similar critical condition; in the last seven years new discoveries have run far below our level of gas consumption. Only with strong measures could we hope to reverse this trend.

The U.S. choice is not coal *or* uranium; we need both. Coal is irreplaceable as the basis of new synthetic fuels to replace oil and natural gas.

However, we see the primary use of solid fuels, especially of uranium, as a source of electricity. Uranium power, the culmination of basic discoveries in physics, is an engineered reality generating electricity today. Nuclear power has its critics, but we believe they lack perspective as to the feasibility of non-nuclear power sources and the gravity of the fuel crisis.

All energy release involves risks and nuclear power is certainly no exception.

We can see no reasonable alternative to an increased use of nuclear power to satisfy our energy needs.

A few weeks later, however, an incident occurred which again raised the specter of doubt. On March 22, 1975, Larry Hargett, a TVA electrician, held a lighted candle near some insulation to find out whether air was leaking into an area under the control room of the two huge nuclear reactors at the Browns Ferry plant in Alabama. About eight hours later a fire caused by the candle brought the reactors and their turbines to a standstill. It was expected to require perhaps three months to repair the damage. It took longer.

The two reactors affected cost more than $500 million and were built by the General Electric Company. The Nuclear Regulatory Commission, which replaced the Atomic Energy Commission, dispatched a bulletin to other utilities and said that the fire in this world's largest nuclear generating plant near Athens, Alabama, had "made several safety systems inoperative." The commission asked the utilities to look over the design of the walls and floors of control rooms "with particular attention to flammability" and to examine controls of construction work where it might affect operating reactors. A governmental commission appointed to investigate the incident reported that precautions taken to prevent such occurrences were "essentially zero."

Jack R. Calhoun of the TVA admitted that the emergency core cooling system, which would ordinarily be used in such emergencies, had not functioned because the control cables had been destroyed. "We could not use this system Saturday, so we used another one that kept the reactor flooded," Calhoun said.

David D. Comey, director of environmental research for Business and Professional People for Public Interest, sent a telegram to the Nuclear Regulatory Commission demanding that all reactors not complying with the latest fire prevention standards of the Institute for Electrical and Electronics Engineers be required to close down and rebuild their electrical control systems. Even though the fire did not cause the release of any radioactivity, Comey stated that the avoidance of a major accident—the meltdown of the reactor core—was "largely the result of good luck."

Daniel Ford, director of the Union of Concerned Scientists, commented: "These safety systems are supposed to work during an emergency and they did not work. One electrician with a candle may have refuted in an instant the industry's fundamental and long-standing claim about the reliability of reactor safety systems." By early 1979, the Browns Ferry Nuclear Plant was back in full operation.

The New York Times soon took stock of the general situation. In a feature article by David Burnham in Washington, D.C., on March 30, 1975, the question was raised of whether nuclear reactors would become a major source of electricity in the United States during the next 25 years. This may depend upon how Congress decides some key issues before it. Gus Speth, an attorney in the Washington, D.C., office of the Natural Resources Defense Council, is quoted as saying, "The key issue is whether Congress is going to embrace the nuclear future despite the risks or take a long second look before it is too late."

The United States now has 68 reactors which produce about 12.5 percent of the nation's electricity. Gerald Ford, while President, called on the country to have by 1985 a total of 245 reactors capable of producing 30 percent of the electricity needed. Attention was called to the demonstrator breeder reactor being built on the Clinch River in Tennessee. By this time the cost was said to be $1.74 billion (later estimated at 1.95 billion dollars). The overall costs of the breeder research program had already jumped from an original estimate of $3 billion to three times that amount.

What lies ahead in this vital yet sensitive field, not even the best scientists know. Whether they or lawmakers or others decide, one thing is certain: the outcome will surely affect every American in one way or another.

19. Summing Up

As the TVA proceeded into the 1970s, it was certainly coming of age, even if it had not reached complete maturity. After four decades it had carried out many experiments, most of them received as being successful. From some expeditions into new fields, the Authority had to turn back; in others it made rapid progress. At any rate, there was no lack of activity in the Tennessee Valley.

The results were almost everywhere to be seen. The river once had been spotty in its navigational use. Now the Tennessee River waterway, a 9-foot commercially navigable channel extending 650 miles from the Ohio River to Knoxville, Tennessee, had been completed soon after World War II. TVA researchers pointed out that civilizations thrive on the banks of great rivers, giving as examples Babylon, Alexandria, London, and New York. "As migrants pushed beyond the Appalachian range, the rivers and the Great Lakes became prime routes of travel and commerce, giving birth to such cities as Pittsburgh, Detroit, Cincinnati, Chicago, Minneapolis, and St. Louis."

The oil companies were first to utilize to a substantial extent the new Tennessee River waterway. They built terminals along the banks, and their towboats began pushing cargoes from Houston and Port Arthur up the Mississippi River to customers in the Tennessee Valley. Grain companies, recognizing the new agricultural needs in an area which could not produce all its own feed, built mills and brought in large cargoes of corn, soybeans, alfalfa pellets, and other crops. Coal, forest products, chemicals, iron, and steel traversed the channel in increasing quantities. With the increase of commerce, larger additional locks had to be built at some of the dams.

Farming interests in northern Georgia, Alabama, and southeastern Tennessee saw that with lower cost feed supplies coming by barge from the Middle West, and with modern mass production methods of raising chickens, a successful broiler industry could be established. So grain cargoes became the fastest growing item of traffic on the waterway, and Georgia frying chickens were shipped throughout the country and also were shipped frozen to Europe. Freight cars were adapted to huge grain loads. High volume, multiple carload shipments became the pattern. To the great relief of the South, freight rates were reduced. Then more grain began to move to the broiler centers by rail. More than 65 companies operate barges on the Tennessee River waterway.

By 1971 the cumulative private investment in waterfront plants and terminals went above $2 billion. Direct employment in shoreline industries was nearly 40,000, and an equal number of new jobs was estimated to have been created in related trades and services. Freight traffic on the Tennessee River reached about 30 million tons by 1975, and the TVA calculated that shippers using the waterway saved more than $70 million in transportation costs. About 80 percent of the river traffic either originated or terminated outside the valley.

As an example of the shipping, the Bowaters Southern Paper Corporation plant at Calhoun, Tennessee, said to be this country's largest newsprint mill, in 1972 barged its one-millionth ton of newsprint shipped by such means since its beginning in 1957. The company had also barged about 4 million tons of pulpwood into the plant. The du Pont Company built a $10 million expansion of its titanium dioxide facilities at New Johnsonville, Tennessee, and constructed a new river terminal to receive chlorine shipped by barge. TVA construction work was completed in 1974 on the Yellow Creek Port on the Tennessee River in northeastern Mississippi at the Pickwick Reservoir. This included a terminal and railroad spur and was turned over to the Yellow Creek State Inland Port Authority to operate. This port is planned to be the northern terminus of the Tennessee-Tombigbee Waterway which will connect the Tennessee River with the Port of Mobile.

Freight traffic each year on the Tennessee River totals about 4 billion ton-miles (tons of freight times the distance it travels). This is more than 100 times as much as river traffic was in 1933. A single river towboat can haul as much as 400 freight cars holding perhaps steel from the North, grain from the Midwest, or petroleum products, chemicals, or ores from the Gulf Coast. There are nine dams in the 650 miles between Paducah and Knoxville. Vessels are lifted more than 500 feet in the locks at these dams. The channel is wide and deep and in the dredged sections, comprising only about 8.5 percent of the total channel length, a minimum depth of 11 feet has been provided—2 feet of overdepth for vessels drawing 9 feet of water. For about 65 percent of the length of the channel, the depth is more than 25 feet.

On the Tennessee River and its tributaries, however, there are 33 major dams, 23 of these built by the TVA and four others acquired. Six belong to the Aluminum Company of America but are operated by agreement as a part of the regional system. The Authority also has built a water control system of smaller dams and channel improvements on west Tennessee's Beech River and is constructing a similar system in the Bear Creek watershed of northwest Alabama. The channel, locks, and safety harbors are open for use without charge. The locks on the main river are in service 24 hours a day for all vessels. There are 20 public-use river terminals and about 115 special-commodity private terminals on the river. The private terminals are designed for the specific traffic of their owners and, for the most part, take such bulk commodities as petroleum, coal, grain, chemicals, sand, and gravel. The TVA steam plant terminals are not included in the foregoing and are designed only to handle coal for the plants.

Chattanooga is an example of an industrial center having older plants which utilize the waterway. Since the availability of improved navigation, several new processing and distributing facilities have been established there. Combustion Engineering Inc. uses the waterway, and its 1,000-ton-capacity crane can transfer atomic reactor vessels, too large for land transport, from its plant to barges for waterway shipment. Three public terminals at Chattanooga handle a variety of products which include iron and steel articles and chemicals in both liquid and dry bulk form.

In regard to electric power, design work began in the summer of 1971 on the first full-scale sulfur-dioxide control installation in the TVA system, to be installed on a 550,000-kilowatt generating unit at Widows Creek Steam Plant. Such modern installations are a far cry from the early years of the TVA when the reverberating rate reductions and increased use that came with TVA power, the new lights and running water in rural areas that had been without electricity, held the spotlight. Although this was to change, the average residential rate for electricity dropped from about 5 cents a kilowatt-hour in 1933 to less than a penny in the 1960s. Typical home use of electricity grew twentyfold. Lower rates seemed to be taken for granted.

Accordingly in 1970, when the TVA announced that rate increases averaging about 25 percent would be necessary to meet financial obligations, there was a furor of public protest. During the same period, serious interruptions in scheduled coal deliveries reduced reserve stockpiles in TVA steam plants to such low levels that there was concern about maintaining power supplies in the event of a threatened national rail strike. There was a general slowdown in industrial growth nationally, but this was not equally reflected in the Tennessee Valley. Much of the business continued to move forward, especially in the fabrication of metal products and the activity in chemical plants, rubber and plastic products, food products, electrical equipment and machinery, paper and allied products, primary metals, textiles, and apparel products.

New power facilities continued to be financed largely from borrowings made through the sale of power bonds and notes and in part from power revenues. Congress in October 1970 increased to $5 billion the amount of borrowings that the TVA may have outstanding. Coal-fired steam plants supplied about three-fourths of the total electricity input. Unit size increased, as exemplified by those at the Paradise Steam Plant and the Cumberland Steam Plant, both with a combined capacity of about 2.5 million kilowatts. The Federal Power Commission reported that the TVA had the most efficient multiple-plant steam-electric generating system in the United States. Construction was underway of an experimental pilot installation at the Shawnee Steam Plant to test three types of gas-cleaning scrubbers using powdered limestone to control sulphur dioxide emissions from coal-burning power plants. It was stated that the amount of fly ash particulates emitted from the stacks of TVA's coal-burning units had been cut in half.

In 1978 there came an end to the automatic monthly variation in power charges used since 1974. Now these were treated as power costs rated and requiring specific approval of the TVA board of directors. In this year TVA comptroller Willard R. Stinson reported that all the 110 municipal systems and 50 cooperatives informed TVA that their financial statements for that year had been examined by independent certified accountants.

The Authority reminded its public that since 1933 the region's power requirements had increased more than 60 times, and overall employment in the valley increased more in the five years preceding 1970 than in the previous 31 years. In an 80,000-square-mile area of the southeastern United States, the power needs of 6 million Americans were thus being supplied. During 1972 the TVA placed in service 668 miles of transmission lines, including a 23-mile long, 500-kilovolt line from the Sequoyah Nuclear Plant site to the Georgia border for a connection with the Georgia Power Company. Seven new substations were placed in service during the same period, and power capability was increased in 28 others already in service. With these additions the TVA transmission system had grown to 16,000 miles of lines and over 600 substations. In that fiscal year the TVA paid into the U.S. Treasury $75.8 million, bringing the total amount the Authority had paid to the Treasury to over a billion dollars.

The formation of new families in the region with the resulting increase in new homes added to the use of electricity. By 1973 about half of the homes in the valley were all electric. Now, with a potential power shortage, the TVA urged the elimination of wasteful uses of electricity. The Authority and its retail distributors offer advice to power customers, architects, contractors, and engineers on efficient ways to install and use electrical equipment and appliances. Industrial customers are asked to conserve energy and save power costs in a similar manner.

During the spring of 1973 record rainfalls brought the highest amount of hydroelectric generation yet recorded at the dams on the Tennessee River. It amounted to 24.5 billion kilowatt-hours for the year, 15 percent more than the previous year and 36 percent greater than that normally expected. The program for upgrading fly ash collection systems at its older plants was accelerated by the TVA at a forecast cost of $120 million. The TVA submitted to the air pollution control agencies of Alabama, Kentucky, and Tennessee—the states in which its coal-burning steam plants are located—a construction plan and timetable for bringing all its plants into compliance with state air pollution emission standards for fly ash and ambient standards for sulphur dioxide.

The matter of handling sulfur dioxide gases which result from coal combustion has been a more difficult problem. State standards divide the requirements into two categories: (1) ambient standards, defining levels of air quality near the ground with an appropriate margin of safety to protect people, crops, animals, property, etc., and (2) emission standards regulating the amount of sulfur dioxide emerging at the top of the stack of a power plant without regard for the amount which actually reaches ground level.

In its submission to the states, TVA discussed the technological, economic, and financial aspects of each set of standards. One way to meet sulfur dioxide emission standards would be to burn coal with a low-sulfur content. This alternate is not open to the TVA because significant quantities of this coal are not available in the Appalachian and midwestern fields from which TVA plants are supplied. Western coals are sufficiently low in sulfur, but their disadvantages outweigh their advantages. Not only would the transportation of this coal over long distances be very expensive, but experimental use at the Johnsonville Steam Plant showed that western coal would reduce the plant's power generating capability by as much as 15 to 30 percent. The sulfur dioxide emission limitation (SDEL) program of the TVA has been tested for several years with satisfactory results in the opinion of officials of the Authority.

An innovation in this fortieth year of the TVA was construction of an underground power system control center near Chattanooga. This center is designed to monitor, control, and activate as necessary all generation and transmission facilities. Here computer technology solves in less than a second mathematical problems it would take a man forty hours to do. Every five minutes the computer "reads" the generation in order to select the proper power source, determining the need for a generation change and sending control signals to the generating plants to bring about the required change.

Probably as clearly as anything else, the TVA Annual Report for 1974 sets forth its attitude and analysis of the current situation. Included in the report is this section:

> The TVA power system, and indeed the nation's electric utility industry, entered one of the most critical periods of its history in fiscal 1974 because of the short supply and rising cost of fuels, particularly coal. Briefly, here are the conditions which faced TVA and the region at the end of the year:
> 1. There exists a growing demand by the public and industry for electricity. Inquiries by industry on the future availability of TVA power in the region were received at a record pace.
> 2. A nationwide shortage in coal production coupled with increased demand limited the amount of new coal TVA was able to purchase during the year. As a result, coal stockpiles at steam plants dwindled well below their normal contingency reserves, and prospects for rebuilding supplies appeared dim.
> 3. The coal TVA was able to purchase was bought at record prices, with the prospect of even higher prices on the horizon.
> 4. Rising power costs, particularly for coal, required rate adjustments in January and July, 1974.

In the same report, it states that the region gained nearly 100,000 nonfarm jobs during the year, about one-third of these being in manufacturing. Industry announced new projects amounting to a billion dollars in investment and calling for 700,000 kilowatts of additional electricity. In fiscal 1974 the TVA power system generated 109.8 billion kilowatt-hours of electricity. The test operation of the Browns Ferry nuclear unit 1 provided nearly 2 billion kilowatt-hours additional to the system. Coal was the burning question, the TVA plants using about 37.4 million tons of coal during the year. The consumption rate is expected to go even higher.

Statistics show that the TVA paid $31.1 million in 1974 to state and local governments in lieu of taxes, nearly $4 million more than in 1973. As provided by law, these annual payments represent 5 percent of the previous year's power revenues, excluding sales to federal agencies. The distributors of TVA power also paid $33 million in taxes or tax equivalents to state and local governments in the region. Local governments ultimately receive about two-thirds of the combined TVA-distributor payments of about $64 million. Most of the amount paid by TVA to state governments is retained by the states, but several of the states redistribute part or all of the money to counties and cities. Local governments receive most of the taxes paid by the local electric systems.

The Authority reports that independently or in cooperation with others, it has more than fifty different energy-related research and demonstration projects under way, aimed primarily at developing new energy sources, converting fuels to more usable products, increasing system efficiencies, and improving the environment. Uranium and coal development is also emphasized. The TVA entered into an agreement with two firms to conduct a study of uranium enrichment through the use of new centrifuge technology. Enriched uranium is the fuel used in the nation's new power plants.

The TVA speculates:

> The future of coal as an energy source could be severely restricted in the United States by environmental concerns, and TVA is investigating possible ways to solve this problem. TVA has joined with the Department of Interior in a program to develop commercial technology to produce a clean fuel gas from coal for generating electricity. Plans called for designing, installing, and testing two or more large coal gasifiers with desulfurization systems at a TVA power plant if initial studies show such a process is feasible.

The TVA has stated that for the next decade it is committed to the most massive generating plant program in its history which is expected to double its generating capacity to close to 50 million kilowatts:

> It is not a construction program undertaken simply for system growth or to have excess power available for some undetermined potential user. Rather it is additional capacity that is necessary and essential for very basic reasons—to meet the electric needs of people living in the region—needs that include new industry, new jobs, new homes, and a better quality of life for all who seek it.

General Manager Lynn Seeber defended the TVA by admitting that there are rivers in the area which the organization has decided not to impound, such as the Hiwassee, the Obed near Harriman, Tennessee, and the Buffalo River in the western part of the state. Seeber struck out at environmentalists who oppose every means of producing electric power, and asked, "What are we supposed to use—squirrels running in cages?"

The general manager, however, did not leave a good impression with a group of twenty people from the northern part of the valley, who came to visit not long afterward. The group opposed strip mining and had asked to meet with Chairman Wagner. He was not able to be present and the visitors agreed to meet with the general manager. The day before the meeting the general manager also found he was unable to attend, according to the account. The assistant general manager came and told the group he was sorry that he was too busy to talk, but that they were welcome at the TVA.

In Washington, D.C., S. David Freeman, then director of the Ford Foundation's Energy Policy Project, told a House Government Operations Subcommittee:

> The time has come for TVA—which initially provided a yardstick for low-priced, abundant use of electricity at a time when making electricity more generally available was a prime national purpose—to change to another yardstick, one which measures success by how efficient and how cleanly it can produce electric power. This would mean a reversal and reordering of TVA's priorities. Instead of striving to dam up the last remaining stretches of rivers in the Valley and building more and more power plants, the management would be addressing itself to meeting consumers' needs with the minimum possible expansion of power plants. One major step would be a complete revamping of the TVA rate schedules to stress conservation rather than promotion.

From another direction also came criticism. Paul Tidwell, general manager of Meriwether Lewis Electric Cooperative and former president of the National Association of Rural Electric Cooperatives, was asked what he thought about the TVA area sharing in the benefits of the Tennessee-Tombigbee canal. "I am delighted," Tidwell replied:

> But I am not so sure there will be an area still proud to call itself the TVA area when the waterway is completed. I am not sure how long TVA can survive once it loses the favor of a majority of the people it serves. I am disturbed at a gradual slip in popular affection for the agency that supplies us with electricity and so many other services. People need to be informed of the many good and new things their agency is doing, and there must be an understanding about the environment.

Encouragement came to the Tennessee Valley Authority in its power operations when on March 31, 1975, an announcement was made by the National Society of Professional Engineers. The organization named the Raccoon Mountain Pump Storage Plant among the top ten engineering achievements of the nation for 1974. Cited were the conception, planning, design and resourceful imagination by the TVA engineering staff embodied in the project.

Still the Floods

Looking back over its eventful past, the TVA is proud of its flood control. After all, developing the human resources of a region is one thing; saving the lives and property of those humans by harnessing a river is at crucial times more important. The fact that floods in the Tennessee Valley were not effectively controlled before the TVA came along speaks for itself.

In 1971 Tims Ford Dam and Reservoir on the Elk River in middle Tennessee was added to the water control and power system. By this time reservoirs in the system had a combined storage capacity of 15 million acre-feet, equivalent to a water depth of about 7 inches over the entire valley. Flood damage prevention reports were being furnished to some 150 area communities situated on the upper tributaries of the river and beyond the full control of the TVA reservoir system. These reports furnish basic information which communities need to establish zoning ordinances and subdivision regulation to keep developments out of the flood plain or above specified flood levels. After such reports are prepared, the TVA continues to assist the communities in planning for flood damage prevention.

In cooperation with the National Academy of Sciences, TVA hosted the first "International Symposium on Man-Made Lakes—Their Problems and Environmental Effects." The symposium was attended by 550 registrants who represented 30 nations, 36 states, and the District of Columbia. The purpose of the weeklong meeting was to assess experience in a variety of environments and to encourage international collaboration in dealing with regional and global problems involved in the planning and management of man-made reservoirs. The TVA joined the Water Resources Council, the Corps of Engineers, the Soil Conservation Service, and the Department of Housing and Urban Development in financing the first of two studies planned on the regulation of flood hazard areas to reduce flood losses. The work was completed by the University of Wisconsin.

In two volumes it explores selected issues in regulation of private and public land uses as a tool of flood plan management. The exhaustive study also contains model statutes and zoning ordinances as well as a discussion of legal considerations involved in the regulation of flood hazard areas. The second volume deals with subdivision and coastal regulation.

A momentous occurrence took place in early 1973. Alfred J. Cooper, chief of TVA's River Control Branch in the Division of Water Control Planning, was awakened at 3 A.M. on March 16 by a phone call from one of his river control engineers. "It looks like we are getting some unexpectedly heavy rainfall across the Valley," Tom Mayer, the engineer said. "We may have a problem on our hands."

This was probably the regional understatement of the year. Mayer then recited the rainfall and lake elevation information just given him by the personnel at each of the mainstream TVA dams. What he said foretold the most eventful night in the flood control experience of the Tennessee Valley Authority.

At this time a whole series of devastating tornadoes ripped across northern Alabama and middle and eastern Tennessee. Besides killing about 30 people and injuring scores of others, the storms left the TVA power transmission system in shambles and shut off electric power for thousands of people for periods of twenty-four hours or more.

In the meantime Alfred Cooper had reacted quickly. He picked up the telephone and issued orders: "Close off Fontana and Douglas [Norris and Cherokee Dams were already closed off]. Call out the gate crews at all main river dams. Increase the discharge at all mainstream dams from Chickamauga through Pickwick by 10,000 cubic feet per second." He hung up the phone, dressed hurriedly, and drove through a downpour to his office in downtown Knoxville, where he was joined by some of his staff. They summoned other river control engineers to their preassigned emergency posts, and now the full-scale flood control operations of the TVA were underway.

Within a period of 48 hours, 5 to 10 inches fell over most of the valley, the greatest amount in areas downstream from the large tributary storage reservoirs. The result was widespread flooding. Some of it swelled streams such as the Duck River, which had no flood control reservoir. The greatest concentration was in the Huntsville-Decatur area of northern Alabama, where the storms criss-crossed repeatedly for some six hours.

Back in Knoxville, Cooper and his staff augmented by others worked around the clock for most of a week to manage the waters from the biggest rainstorms since the TVA began. Often they went without lunch and even dinner, eating doughnuts and drinking coffee at their desks. They knew that the greatest threat lay at Chattanooga. In order to help ease the dangerous situation there, tributary storage reservoirs were closed tight and mainstream dams between Knoxville and Chattanooga were operated at maximum capacity.

It worked. The Tennessee River at Chattanooga was held to 7 feet above flood stage—15.5 feet lower than it would have been if there had been no TVA dams and reservoirs. The TVA estimated Chattanooga's damages at $35 million. Without the regulation provided by upstream dams and reservoirs, half of the city, including much of the central business district, would have been flooded. Estimated damages then would have totaled $500 million. On the tributary rivers upstream, ten major dams furnished storage capacity for the TVA to hold flood waters from the large watershed above Chattanooga. Fortunately the reservoirs behind these dams were at low winter levels when the March storm struck. As it was, much of the eastern suburban area of the city was inundated, especially a shopping center in the Brainerd section.

The eight-man Decatur line crew of the TVA was called out when the storms first struck and later reported that they spent a hair-raising night as they attempted to repair damage to the transmission lines while trying to stay out of the way of the newly developing tornadoes. The men had left home just as the storm began, and some of them worked throughout the night to help restore power service without knowing whether their own homes had been struck or whether their families were safe.

Of the 11 large power lines serving the Huntsville-Decatur area, only one was left in service, tall transmission towers sprawled across the ground like fallen giants. From this one line remaining, service was restored in four hours to the Huntsville hospital, where most of the dead and injured had been taken. By late the next day, the crew had completed a temporary tie, restoring power to both cities in less than 21 hours.

The storm ceased and the skies cleared, and when the tired crew men looked up they saw welcome stars above. Then the Salvation Army came along and gave them hot coffee and doughnuts.

Commented William Zumwalt, director of power system operations, "It was an extraordinary effort and we are proud of all our men for the job they did. The storms pretty well split our system in two and left it hanging together by a shoestring."

This March flood helped to bring the rainfall across the valley to 70.5 inches for 1973, the highest in the 83 years of record and 35 percent more than the long-term annual average of 52.4 inches. The water runoff was also the highest of record, being 67 percent greater than the median. A smaller flood the previous December had perhaps given some warning of what was necessary in such emergencies. This flood was the first real test for the Tims Ford Dam, which was completely shut off and averted much damage. The floodway at Oliver Springs also functioned well. Knoxville was hit hard by local flooding but suffered no significant damage from that of the Tennessee River. Floodways at Sevierville, Tennessee, and Coeburn, Virginia, operated according to plan and prevented extensive damage.

As if to compound the watery impact, a heavy rain in late May 1973 averaged between 3 and 9 inches in the eastern mountain areas. The result was another flood that pushed many of the tributary storage reservoirs to their highest levels of record, especially those near Oakdale and Oliver Springs, Tennessee, and again at Chattanooga. Again heavy damage was forestalled. Storms of such intensity are rare in late spring through the valley. The TVA therefore expressed gratification that it had reserved some storage space in the reservoirs in advance for just such an unexpected happening.

How the system works may be gained by a glimpse at some of the daily routine. At 7:30 each morning in the TVA River Control Branch at Knoxville, a facsimile machine begins to hum as it reproduces sheets placed on a similar machine in the Office of Power in Chattanooga. These sheets are filled with data on rainfall, reservoir elevations, and discharges at each TVA dam. Then a teletype begins to click out the weather forecast from the U.S. Weather Bureau at the Knoxville airport. Through a cooperative agreement the TVA is furnished two special complete forecasts daily.

At 8 o'clock the telephones ring, and for the next 30 minutes a steady stream of information comes in from 200 rainfall stations and 50 stream gauges scattered throughout the Valley. Observers have read their gauges and phoned the readings to nine TVA collecting offices at central locations. There field engineers assemble the data along with measurements received from automatic radio gauges in remote areas, and phone the composite picture over scheduled long-distance calls. At 9:15 preliminary estimates of TVA's expected operation at Kentucky Dam are sent to the Corps of Engineers at Cincinnati and the U.S. Weather Bureau at Cairo. In return the TVA receives observed stages and flows on the lower Ohio and Mississippi Rivers.

Reservoir elevations and discharges are determined for the next several days and are relayed to the dams. Flood warnings are issued. Final data on the operation go to Cincinnati and Cairo. If the rains are falling significantly, quick telephone calls are made to see if the operating plan needs to be changed through the day or in the evening. Meantime other calls are coming in if people are affected by a flood, for example, industries at Chattanooga ask how long they will have to remove pumps and equipment. A towboat approaching one of the locks can get through with the existing discharge of water but not if there is any increase—can the increase be delayed for an hour? A farmer below Guntersville Dam has a number of hogs on an island. Another 1-foot rise will drown them. Can the TVA stop further increases until the hogs are removed? A cotton warehouse at Florence needs more time for sandbagging before the water level goes higher. And so on. Next morning at 7:30 the sequence starts again. Since 1944 over 50 floods on the Mississippi River with a flood stage of about 40 feet at Cairo, Illinois, were lowered by TVA's regulation of the Tennessee.

Gauge observers for the TVA report their daily readings to the river control engineers. Since their monthly pay has ranged from $3 for reading the nonrecording rain gauge daily and recording the data to about $25 for the daily reading and reporting of stream stages from a gauge located remotely from the observer's home, one wonders why some of them do this. It seems to be somewhat of a hobby, and many of the observers are retired people who are conscientious about this job.

The observers must read their gauges every day—rain or shine, hot or cold. Their readings are more important when conditions for obtaining them are at their worst. During storms some observers are asked to read the gauge several times throughout the day. The readings are telephoned to the nearest field office of the Hydraulic Data Branch of the TVA, which in turn collects the reports from several observers and transmits the information to the River Control Branch in Knoxville. In winter, water freezes in the rain gauges and must be thawed before it is measured. This evidently caused a problem for one of the observers as shown in the following letter he wrote to a TVA official:

Mr. Guy S. Block,
This morning I made 4 trials to get gage house door open. Rain water gathers on top of door & I have to get hot water to thaw out, so, I most scalded myself. Then most froze—almost fell from ladder, and Guess I better resign Feb. 1-48—Thanks—

Sam J. Alexander
Observer

Many of the gauge observers have reported for more than a quarter of a century or more. Typical of these was Henry Burleson of Plumbtree, North Carolina, who at the age of 81 had been keeping these records as an observer since he was 50 years old. The TVA presents to an observer after 25 years of service a certificate of appreciation, and Burleson was among those recipients.

In April 1977 torrential floodwaters engulfed the little town of Clinchport, Virginia, near the Tennessee line. So many homes and other structures were destroyed, the TVA agreed to help. The result: Thomas Village nearby, which includes homes using solar energy.

Fertilizer Impact

Of extremely widespread import is the fertilizer program of the TVA which has continued since the inception of the organization. Interestingly, the physical center of this program is where the TVA and it began. Commenting on this beginning at Muscle Shoals, one of its sponsors, then-Congressman Lister Hill, explained perhaps with tongue in cheek, "The fertilizer people came to us and suggested that the best thing to do would be to make it a power project and the power people suggested that the best thing to do would be to make it a fertilizer project. So we took the advice of both and made it both a fertilizer and a power project."

The heart of the program now is the National Fertilizer Development Center at Muscle Shoals, which is accepted as the nation's major source of new fertilizer technology. Educational programs with industry and land-grant universities in nearly all the states and Puerto Rico have sprung from this center. It takes some justified credit for the statistic that American farmers are producing about 40 percent more than 30 years ago and that much of this has been due to the greater use of fertilizers.

Studies to determine the amount and effects of nutrient levels in water runoff in valley watersheds have continued. So far these studies have shown that these levels have little effect from the application of fertilizer. In 1971 a four-year period of experimental operation of a compost plant to evaluate composting as a method of utilizing municipal solid wastes was completed. The plant was built and operated by the TVA at Johnson City, Tennessee, for the U.S. Public Health Service as one of a series of projects over the country to test various methods of solid waste disposal. The Authority has also tested compost to see whether it can be used to increase production of tomatoes, flowers, and shrubbery.

TVA research goes on regarding the potential fertilizer value of phosphate rock for direct application. This should help in developing countries having phosphate deposits. About 4,130 acres of TVA-owned Florida land was sold in 1971 as real estate after being declared surplus because it was no longer needed as a phosphate reserve. Some 244 acres were transferred to the U.S. Army Corps of Engineers, with 400 acres retained for forest fertilization experiments.

More than 1,500 small-scale demonstrations were used during this period to investigate or show crop response to various nutriments. The reaction in New York of corn to zinc prompted a series of trials to find the zinc deficiency. In Arkansas it was found that zinc applied with a nitrogen fertilizer can correct bronzing of rice caused by zinc deficiency and thus increase yields in many fields. Demonstrations in Kentucky and Alabama showed the potential for growing two crops a year on the same land. In Wisconsin, alfalfa on sandy or shallow soils low in organic matter responded to sulfur. On the Crow Creek Indian Reservation in South Dakota, TVA fertilizers proved to be a helpful new ingredient for a wheat crop. To improve the diets among low-income black families in Livingston County, Kentucky, 20 families grew home gardens for the first time. More than 2,500 quarts of food were canned, and some vegetables were frozen. It was found that the TVA pilot project to improve living standards in rural Madison County, North Carolina, had brought substantial improvements in community services; had resulted in increasing employment opportunities; had strengthened education, including countywide consolidation of schools; and had brought about the replacement or modernization of several substandard houses.

The increasing emphasis on livestock production in the valley, of special interest to the TVA's agricultural program, has brought into focus the desirability of the best use of manpower. Less of this is needed for raising livestock than in the traditional row crop farming. Blending part-time farming with employment in rural industry and service jobs has become the objective of many valley farmers, more than one-third of whom are engaged in part-time agriculture. Such diversification fits in with the TVA idea.

A study of the costs of feeding beef cattle showed that the area producers need to take advantage of high quality roughages and seasonal price variations in grain buying to be competitive with other regions. This relates to the need for continued promotion of improved forage and silage crops. A recent study of soybean production and processing led to the decision by a company to build one of the nation's largest soybean processing plants at Decatur, Alabama.

Several distributors cooperate with their state universities in special fertilizer research and demonstration projects. Among such TVA projects in 1972 were trials of suspension fertilizer-pesticide mixtures on tobacco in Georgia, use of partly acidulated phosphate rock on soybeans in Louisiana, and range fertilization in South Dakota and Nebraska. At Muscle Shoals, scientists and engineers pursue the development of promising new fertilizers and processes. The search begins in laboratories and moves to greenhouses and pilot plants and finally to larger demonstration production units. A potential fertilizer must equal or exceed today's products in some way. TVA fertilizer improvement methods have been studied and usually adopted in a number of countries throughout the world.

Needless to reiterate, the national and world food situation has centered much attention on shrinking stores of grain, shortages of some farm products, and generally higher food prices. Adverse weather reduces some harvests. Large exports to other nations dig heavily into reserves. The nation's own growing population consumes more food. All these conditions highlight the importance of modern productive agriculture. Behind this process is improved fertilizers, and the TVA is and has been deeply involved. Strong efforts have been made to make the Tennessee Valley a prime example of increased productivity. It is generally agreed by agricultural scientists that doubling of the nutrient content and the expanded use of fertilizer are the biggest single factors in the great increase in our national farm production over the past forty years.

A cooperative study by the University of Georgia and the TVA has indicated that the number of cattle and hogs produced in the Upper Hiwassee area—about 100,000 cattle and 30,000 hogs—will probably increase by one-third next year. A market facility is needed to handle the sale of these animals. Cooperation with the Southwest Virginia Growers Cooperative aided in expanding vegetable production and marketing. Although studies by the Authority indicate that potential catfish consumption exceeds current supplies, the situation would appear to be changing. Catfish farms are springing up and the possible use of waste heat in growing them may well shorten the time for the delicacy to reach marketable size.

So the American farmer not only produces food for this country but for much of the rest of the world. Increasing pressure on U.S. food supplies has pushed the country's food reserves to near zero levels and pushed grain prices to record heights. The international food crisis stimulated fertilizer use in this country and abroad, with the result that demand outstripped production. This has led to increased requests for TVA help in developing programs and providing technological assistance in many parts of the world. The TVA proudly points out that in 1934 farms in the valley produced an average of $15.25 per acre, compared to the national average of $21.50, whereas 40 years later, valley farms produced $417 per harvested acre compared to a national average of $262. Emphasis of the organization is on the shift from nitrate to urea as the base for nitrogen fertilizers. Urea can be produced more economically and with fewer pollution problems than ammonium nitrate, according to the TVA.

Batches of fertilizer were tagged with radioactive phosphorus or sulfur or agronomic use and were sent to several U.S. locations as well as to Austria, Australia, Columbia, and New Zealand. Under consideration because of the current shortage is the possibility that fertilizer applications could be omitted or reduced on some lands of special interest. Greenhouse pot tests showed that with adequate nutrients, especially nitrogen, rice well watered but not flooded can yield as much as flooded rice. TVA's forest fertilization research has resulted in the establishment of research cooperatives that are run jointly by forest industries and universities. Demonstrations are held at the TVA forest fertilization research area near Holder, Florida. By 1974, 571 licenses were issued to 345 companies for use of the pipe reactor process for making high-polyphosphate liquid fertilizer from wet-process superacid. These were used in 516 plants in 39 states.

The Authority has set up rapid adjustment farms to evaluate new practices and combinations of enterprises in practical operations. The results are then used by other farmers. Considerable emphasis is placed on home garden demonstrations among low-income rural families. This project furnishes information on the basics of food and nutrition as well as supplying foodstuffs for the families. Grapevines and apple trees which were planted on regraded strip-mined land in northeast Alabama in the spring of 1973 continued to show good growth.

In the Tennessee Valley the fact that today's farming brings greater harvests from much less land is notably exemplified. In 1933 the average size farm in the region was 70 acres; in 1974 it was 114 acres. At the earlier time the products of a year's work on an average farm brought about $300; today the average is over $6,000 per farm—20 times the level of the mid-1930s. The total annual sales of farm products here is over $1 billion. Even with inflation and other such factors this comparison is impressive to a one-time farmboy in the valley.

A novel organization with potentially far-reaching effects came into being in late 1974. It is the International Fertilizer Development Center, headed by a former TVA official. The idea for the new organization grew out of a speech by Secretary of State Henry Kissinger before the United Nations General Assembly the preceding April. The suggestion was supported by the Agency for International Development and gained funding from the United States and Canadian governments. The purpose is to try to find answers to the world food shortages.

The managing director is Dr. Donald L. McCune, former coordinator of international fertilizer development projects for the TVA. The center is planned to be a research center concentrating on improving the effectiveness of chemical fertilizers, especially in tropical agriculture. Another aim is the development of better methods of producing fertilizers from nonpetroleum resources. Technical assistance is provided developing countries utilizing the center. McCune said that tropical areas have over one-half the world's crop producing potential but are only producing 25 percent of the world's food.

Life and Land

Literary attention was given the TVA in an article entitled "The Southern Agrarians and the Tennessee Valley Authority" by Edward Shapiro in the Winter 1970 issue of *American Quarterly*. In the article it is pointed out that Agrarians believed that society, if it is to be free and prosperous, must have a majority of its people owning productive property. Therefore they hated modern large-scale industrialization because it centralized the ownership of property among a small percentage of the population and created an insecure and subservient proletariat.

From the vantage point of the Vanderbilt University campus, this small literary group predicted that the TVA, by providing "the means for a decentralization of productive wealth would be a solid contribution to the economic life of the Valley." One of the Agrarians, Herman C. Nixon, was especially impressed by the Industrial Division of the TVA in behalf of economic decentralization. In 1938 Nixon wrote that the TVA "is the greatest movement in the South for modernizing agriculture, conserving rural manhood, and facilitating village development. It should prove a godsend to hillbillies."

Some of the Agrarians, however, suspected the TVA of endeavoring to uplift and modernize the inhabitants of the valley. Allen Tate, though favoring its economic impact, attacked the Authority for its reformist spirit. "When the TVA tries to go into the mountains and change ways of living followed by the mountaineers for 150 years," he stated, "it is all wrong. It tries to make them play the radio instead of pitching horseshoes. They've been pitching horseshoes for 150 years and they ought to go right on pitching horseshoes." The major misgivings of the Agrarians regarding the TVA were sociological rather than economic.

Donald Davidson registered the most dissent among the Agrarians regarding the TVA and also was the one who wrote most about it. In 1934, Davidson stated that the TVA was an "ideal regional undertaking. It seems to. promise a controlled and reasoned development of ways of life and institutions that are adapted to the soil wherein they grow." But Davidson later took a negative view. He wished to know whether the TVA was "to continue indefinitely under the paternal wing of the Federal government, like some gigantic Berea College which distributed humanitarian benefits, but in an external missionary way; or whether it is finally to be integrated with the section of which it is a natural part."

Any major agricultural scene such as that in the Tennessee Valley is of serious significance, because a virtual revolution has occurred. Since just before World War II, more than 30 million people have left their rural homes for the towns, and this migration has continued at the rate of almost a million people a year. It has been estimated that about two thousand farms go out of business each week. The movement corresponds in many ways to the industrial revolutions which occurred in England and the United States in the nineteenth century. There has been some movement back to farm and to small urban communities since the beginning of the recession in the 1970s. Spokespersons for the Tennessee Valley Authority repeat that the TVA idea lies somewhere between the city and farm, hopefully in between the two extremes, and ideally representing a happy combination of both.

One of the subjects of more-than-average public concern has been that of the acquisition, utilization, and disposition of land by the TVA. The general policy has been to acquire sufficient land for the execution of the Authority's projects and then to dispose of whatever land is not needed. For several years there has been an active review of the landholdings. As a result, the TVA has sold more than 150,000 acres and has transferred to federal, state, and local agencies around 175,000 additional acres of reservoir lands. These disposals represent about 70 percent of all reservoir lands acquired above the maximum shoreline of TVA lakes.

The method said to be used to determine that properties are being put to the best use is a continuing active review of landholdings in view of current and anticipated program needs, coordination with program interests of request for use of TVA lands by other public agencies and private interests, and an effort to accommodate requests which will contribute to area development and which are not detrimental to TVA's statutory obligations and program requirements. The remaining lands around TVA reservoirs are used specifically for the project purposes.

At the same time they are being used for many other compatible purposes such as hiking; picnicking; fishing; agriculture, mostly pasture and hay crops; timber production; wildlife management; and public hunting. Some 48,000 acres of lands in TVA custody are being managed and used by federal and state wildlife agencies for programs pursuant to formal agreements between these agencies and TVA. Such agreements are in effect with the U.S. Fish and Wildlife Service covering some 10,000 acres in the Tennessee National Wildlife Refuge, the Tennessee Game and Fish Commission for use of some 10,000 acres in addition to lands transferred for wildlife management, and the Alabama Department of Conservation and National Resources for use of some 28,000 acres for wildlife management.

The Authority encourages suitable secondary uses of its retained land. Land which can be utilized for agriculture is offered for rent on a competitive bid basis. For example, in 1971, 1,011 licenses authorized the use of 24,511 acres of TVA land for agriculture. Rental income was over $100,000, bringing the cumulative income from agricultural licenses to almost $4 million. Although lands are not retained solely for such production, the timber resources on these lands are protected, improved, and harvested by selective cutting.

The increasing timber production indicates that the annual harvest from forests in the valley will more than double in the next 25 years. In order to do this, private landowners, who own more than 80 percent of this forest land, must see that the woodlands are properly developed and retained. It is the policy of the TVA to encourage and promote multiple-use land management programs among private landowners across the region. The owners are shown how they can increase timber growth as well as income and also increase the wildlife habitat.

In this regard the TVA began a new approach in 1971 to managing lands under power transmission lines. These lines stretch over more than 15,000 circuit miles and cover thousands of acres, most of which remain in private ownership but on which the TVA holds easement rights. Included in this program is a cost-sharing arrangement. The land is cleared by mechanical rather than chemical means and seeded to provide ground cover and food supply for game. Initial seeding is done by the Authority. The forest industry in the valley, which once was confined mainly to rough lumbering operations employing few people, has become the region's fourth largest employer. Predicted employment in the woods and wood-using industries is 100,000 by the end of the century.

Forests cover approximately two-thirds of the Tennessee Valley and support a $1 billion wood products industry. Some 850 wood-using plants employ 50,000 workers with a combined annual payroll of $250 million, and expansion plans are underway. The TVA forecasts that in forthcoming decades the southern forests will provide one-half of all the wood used in the United States. The valley forests produce only two-thirds of their capability. Some open land should be reforested, it is said, and certain sites that are not suited to hardwoods should be planted to pine. However, most areas can and should be managed for hardwood products. The potential for such gains in production is important in view of the continuing pressures on the total forest area for conversion to other basic uses in an urbanizing society.

Where 40 years ago forest fires were a major problem in the valley, involving considerable annual loss, this has been brought largely under control. In 1935 less than one-half of these forests were under fire protection. Presently, through the work of the state divisions of forestry, the TVA, the U.S. Forest Service, and industry, over 21 million forested acres in 124 of the 125 valley counties are protected. Only 77,000 acres in Bedford County, Tennessee, are unprotected. The annual burning has decreased from 10 to 0.12 percent.

Wildlife

Wildlife and forestry management enabled visitors to experience an abundance of game and to hunt under certain conditions throughout most of the fall and winter seasons. Feeding and watering places are provided in the heavily wooded areas, and grain crops are planted to provide food for the winter season. The latest estimate showed that about 100,000 geese migrate each year from their breeding grounds on Canada's Hudson and James bays to the Tennessee Valley. The Tennessee State Game and Fish Commission, the TVA, and the Bureau of Sport Fisheries are working together "to make some of these geese and other waterfowl year-round guests of the Valley."

Ten thousand families in the Southeast were interviewed personally during 1972 by a survey team asking questions about their enjoyment of wildlife. The interviews were part of a study being conducted by an environmental research group at Georgia State University under the joint sponsorship of the various state fish and game commissions, the Southeastern Association of Game and Fish Commissioners, and the TVA. The purpose was to evaluate the social and economic benefits from wildlife and determine the need for more wildlife-oriented recreation opportunities. Findings from the survey are used by the government agencies to plan future programs for protection and conservation of wildlife in the southeastern states.

In order to attract waterfowl, 30,000 acres of TVA lands are planted with waterfowl food and 200,000 acres of land and water have been licensed by the TVA to federal and state wildlife agencies for waterfowl management areas and refuges. One of the latest waterfowl land transactions involved 900 acres that the TVA added to the Big Sandy Wildlife Management Area on Kentucky Lake in western Tennessee. The state is developing this area's hunting and recreational opportunities for the general public.

The Tennessee Game and Fish Commission and the U.S. Fish and Wildlife Service along with the TVA are developing a trout management program on the Clinch River below Norris Dam. Fishermen there have reported catching rainbow trout up to 16 inches long—grown from 4-inch fingerlings stocked in these waters the year before. Studies show that the Clinch River has an abundance of organisms on its bottom surface on which the trout can feed. Officials believe that better trout fishing is in the offing for the Norris tailwater. A half-million acres of new fishing habitat has been added in the valley in the last four decades.

The Tennessee River has 182 species of fresh water fish, the most of any river in the southeastern United States. When the TVA dams turned the river into a series of lakes, the fish population multiplied at least 50 times. Each year sport fishermen catch from 15 to 20 million pounds of crappie, bass, walleye, and other game fish. Commercial fishermen take another 3,500 tons of such varieties as catfish, buffalo, and carp. In 1971 a total of 6.1 million pounds of marketable catfish valued at $3 million was produced. Between 7,000 and 10,000 tons of game fish are caught in the valley each year, but most still remain uncaught. Fisheries biologists have found that more fish are caught in and around underwater cover. As a result, little Bear Creek, near Muscle Shoals, Alabama, was scheduled to be the first TVA reservoir where tree stumps are intentionally left standing to attract fish.

For four years the TVA has helped the growing of catfish at its Gallatin Steam Plant. A commercial partner in this research project is helping toward answering the question: Can heated water discharge from steam electric generating plants be used in a commercially successful catfish farming operation? Ten concrete raceways, each 50 feet long, are stocked with fingerlings and use plant's warm discharge water to grow the fish to commercial size of about 1 pound each. The results in 1974 showed definite progress. It was said that fish grown here have milder and better flavor than those found in the natural river or in a farm pond. This experiment thus holds a double significance. TVA biologists at the Browns Ferry Biothermal Laboratory use electro-shocking gear to collect fish in the channels to study their growth, survival, and reproduction in waters of varying temperature.

Both by choice and necessity the Authority has increasingly turned its attention to cleaner streams. In mountainous southwest Virginia, for example, the streams are often choked with domestic refuse, natural debris, and sediment. Homes and neighborhoods along these streams often are not only unsightly but have frequent flood damage. These very people are usually those who can least afford to move to a new location or solve their environmental problems individually. So the TVA and other government agencies are helping to improve the area, with local residents assisting in the planning and implementation of the work. The improvements reduce the danger from small floods but this still does not eliminate the threat of damage from larger floods. The U.S. Weather Bureau has developed a flood warning system which is valuable in this area.

In this same region, industry has been encouraged to locate. The first company to establish a plant in the local Duffield Industrial Park, in 1971, is a manufacturer of mine-shaft support bolts. One reason for its choice of this place was the level land available, something rare in this Appalachian mountainous section. The TVA helped with the planning for this and subsequent industries and, in addition, completed flood protection work for the industrial area which is expected to have thousands of new jobs as a result. A similar project was carried out in northwestern Georgia in cooperation with the Georgia Institute of Technology. Examined were 16 sites containing 1,600 acres.

After several years of planning, the construction of a two-dam water control project on the Duck River near the towns of Columbia and Normandy, Tennessee, got underway in 1972. The multipurpose project was designed to promote sound economic and environmental development of the area by reducing flooding on urban and agricultural lands, meeting a critical need for more and cleaner water for municipal and industrial use, creating new recreational and fish and wildlife opportunities, stimulating higher and better land use, and creating opportunities for more productive employment of local labor.

Along the Duck River water problems are complex. Floods are an important consideration, for instance, the uncontrolled river crested 9 feet above flood stage at Columbia during the March 1973 flood and caused an estimated $700,000 in damages. But the area is also faced with a shortage of water during some periods of the year, and many of the rural communities have been dependent on undependable and unsanitary wells.

Town Planning

A major new town planning effort is in the Lower Elk River Valley of middle Tennessee and northern Alabama, where TVA and local officials and residents have worked on plans to develop an alternative to urban sprawl. The project is designed to demonstrate how a planned community in a rural area can meet the demand for services generated by increased population growth while preserving open space and forested land. Key to the proposal is a system of rural villages planned to incorporate a high level of urban-type services, along with opportunity for outdoor activities in the natural environment.

The site of the first village is near the small community of Elkmont, Alabama, north of Athens and within commuting distance of the larger job centers of Decatur and Huntsville. According to the plan the demonstration project will provide homesites and small farms for about 4,000 people. This should accommodate part of the population growth expected in coming years in the lower Elk River area along the Alabama-Tennessee border. The area is about 350,000 acres in size and is a triangle-shape tract. The population is now about 20,000 and, if plans materialize as expected, the number of people would increase to around 100,000.

Joe Sir, chairman of the Lower Elk River Development Association, said that the principal physical features of this concept are as follows:

Industrial water would be returned to streams clean enough to drink.
No gaseous poisons would be emitted into the atmosphere.
All industrial and residential waste would be collected for re-use or rendered harmless.
There would be a minimum of hard-surface pavements.
All structures would blend with the nature of the region.
A wildlife restoration and enhancement program would restore many species of animals, birds and fish now vanished from the land.

Social features of the plan include:

Training centers to train the unskilled or teach new skills to area residents.
Enlargement of the functions of the county governments so they can oversee the development.

Involvement of area residents by providing them with technical assistance and loans.

Revitalization of the community life of the small towns in the three counties, some as industrial and business centers, others as recreational, residential and cultural centers.

According to a report from Washington, D.C., in the *Nashville Tennessean* of May 31, 1970, by Elaine Shannon, Sir stated that he was finding "universal acceptance for this principle of creating a new industrial and residential community in a resort environment." By 1975, TVA Townlift assistance had helped the citizens of Athens, Tennessee, improve the downtown by adding a canopy and brick sidewalks.

Leisure-Time Facilities

Recreation spills over into many phases of the TVA. In 1971 rules were adopted to prevent nonnavigable houseboats and residential-type boathouses in the lakes. It had been concluded that concentrations of these structures permanently moored away from shore were usurping hundreds of acres of public waters in some lakes and becoming hazards to safe navigation. Houseboats and boathouses already located there before these rules were made were permitted to remain provided they were moved within the established limits of commerical harbors or to the shoreline where the owner holds landrights.

In the same year the Authority sold the last of more than 4,000 vacation cabin sites available from subdivisions it had established on its lakeshore lands. There are more than 16,000 permanent or seasonal homes and cabins along the shores of TVA lakes, enough to house a city of 50,000 people. The sale of these lakeshore sites began in 1946 as part of the disposal of shorelands which had been purchased for reservoir projects. This last available lot was in a subdivision near Kentucky Dam.

There are over 200,000 acres of shorelands for parks, access areas, group camps, and wildlife areas. These TVA lakes and shorelines continue to be the focal point for much recreation in the region. Private citizens, commercial enterprises, and public agencies have invested more than $450 million in recreation facilities and improvements on and around the lakes.

A canoe shuttle service on the rugged Hiwassee River in eastern Tennessee has received considerable attention and participation since its inception in the early 1970s. The service provides rafts, assorted equipment, and transportation on this and the scenic Ocoee River. A new kind of canoeist appeared called "white water enthusiast." They liked, instead of paddling around in placid lakes, navigating swift-flowing streams and shooting over rough-riding rapids.

These canoeists found that the natural streams of the valley often receded to a trickle during the dry summer months. Also, on a stream regulated by a dam and reservoir, the turbines might be shut down, leaving a practically dry streambed for miles below the dam. Often they were disappointed after a long drive. As this sport increased in popularity, the white water canoeists banded together in clubs and assigned one member the job of telephoning weekly for the desired streamflow and of disseminating it to the others. This relieved a burdensome telephone load.

Club members came to the TVA and asked for man-made white water for some canoe races they wanted to stage. The TVA complied. The Division of Water Control Planning arranged with the Power System for the desire flows to be discharged from the Nantahala and Appalachia powerhouses at the times requested. This happened to fit in with the water release schedule anyway, and the racing occasion was a sprightly success.

The current rate of visits by people to the TVA recreation areas is about 20 million. Other sports activities have been added, including the construction of the first outdoor ice skating rink in the Deep South, at Point Mallard Park on Wheeler Lake near Decatur, Alabama. A $2 million hotel complex is being built at the Fontana Village Resort on the lake in North Carolina. A recreation complex featuring tennis and basketball courts is being constructed at the Bear Paw Resort on Hiwassee Lake, and a large park is being built at Chatuge Reservoir near the North Carolina-Georgia state line. A report entitled "The Tennessee Valley Outdoor Recreation Plan" was issued by the Authority in 1974 concerning the nature and scope of the recreation facilities therein.

Paramount among the individual entities of TVA recreation appears to be the Land Between the Lakes on Lake Barkley in western Kentucky. Its facilities and emphasis on it by the Authority continue to grow. During the last decade some 25,000 students and 2,500 teachers have taken part in a resident education program at its outdoor school called the Youth Station. An unusual characteristic apparently welcomed by visitors to this recreational enterprise is the fact that it has no commercial facilities. Over the past ten years over 12 million visitors from 50 states and several foreign countries have come to the Land Between the Lakes.

A supervised recreational program is carried out here by summer intern students from nearby colleges and universities. Students majoring in outdoor recreation and conservation education earn college credits while planning and supervising recreational activities in the campgrounds. Other college students work with the forestry and wildlife management staff in program planning and public service. The TVA states that "Here recreation and education blend to create an awareness within the visitor of the importance of conserving, restoring, and developing our natural resources so that this generation and others to follow can enjoy the out-of-doors." About 85 percent of the Land Between the Lakes is forested, primarily in oak and hickory-type hardwoods. Forestry and wildlife management are practiced on 145,000 acres of forestland and 17,000 acres of open land.

Looking Ahead

An official TVA publication stated:

> people of the Valley have achieved extraordinary gains in economic opportunity and overall quality of life. Their experience is a living refutation to those who would place economic growth and environmental quality on a collision course. For the Valley today— while certainly not problem-free—is a giant step ahead of most other areas of the nation in the quality of its environment. It offers great opportunity to serve as a pilot plant, developing and demonstrating new ideas to combat environmental deterioration even as it sustains its rate of economic advance.

This situation takes on added importance when it is considered that the population of this nation has been collecting mainly into four major areas. One of these reaches from Boston to south of Washington, D.C.; another extends outward from Chicago along the Great Lakes; two others are on the east coast of Florida and the coast of California.

In the Tennessee Valley the small and medium-sized cities and towns are the key elements. These are the communities of the region's greatest population growth. When the TVA first began, only a dozen communities in the valley fell within the 10,000 to 50,000 population range. At the latest count, there are 42 within this range. As recently as 1950, only half of the region's counties contained any urban population. Now the figure approaches 70 percent. An official statement from the organization states:

> As TVA itself was established as a national demonstration, so the urbanizing Valley is today the setting for a national demonstration.

At hand is the opportunity to show that urban growth can be healthy and functional while avoiding the congestion and confusion of uncontrolled metropolises.

Internally the TVA is administered under multipurpose management. A single director of personnel supervises employee relations for fertilizer development, power operations, and hiring of scientists and engineers as well as typists and clerks. A single office of purchasing does the buying for the entire agency. A single transportation office manages the fleet of automobiles for all official travel in the valley region of 92,000 square miles, as well as trucks and other equipment used in constructing transmission lines. Now the Authority operates over 500 vans and buses to take 5,000 of its employees to and from their jobs, thus saving an estimated 3½ million gallons of gasoline a year.

The TVA general manager administers programs of the Authority and its operations in behalf of the board of directors. The decision of the TVA to do its work with its own forces accounts to a great extent for the fluctuations in the total employment over the years, the figures varying with the status of major construction projects. The alltime low employment level, 10,755, was in March, 1938, the conventional peak employment 41,801 in September, 1942 when national defense predominated. In 1979, total employment was over 47,000, many being temporary construction workers. By 1973, the total number of individuals who had worked for the TVA during its life time was 257,072. Training programs help supervisors become familiar with organizational drug-alcohol policy. The TVA helped establish the first multicounty emergency medical service program in Tennessee. This involves pooling medical resources and ambulance service in four rural counties.

The TVA has been studying a plan for recycling solid wastes. Burnable material from the region will be extracted and mixed with coal to help fuel power plant furnaces. Such things as iron, glass, and aluminum will be separated from the rest of the trash and garbage sold. The proposal provides for the TVA to build, own, and operate the processing plants and market the recoverable materials. Local governments would be responsible for collecting the waste and bringing it through various transfer stations for shipping to the processing plant instead of burying it in landfills. North Carolina has not been as enthusiastic about the TVA as have some other states, but the *Asheville Citizen* hailed the idea and expressed the desire that it be put into practice there if feasible.

This idea of waste disposal grew out of the problem which American towns and cities are facing regarding finding sites for the growing volume of solid waste material produced by an affluent society. Many rural areas have increasing roadsides despoiled by trash dumping. The experimental plant at Johnson City, Tennessee, to make compost from the city's garbage and sewage has shown promise of such improvement elsewhere, although this method has proven to be expensive.

More than 50 counties in the valley have asked the TVA for assistance in helping locate suitable landfill sites. In Humphreys County, Tennessee, 60 percent of the people live outside of incorporated towns, and officials counted 150 open garbage dumps in the county before a TVA-instigated plan was put into effect of having trucks pick up the garbage and place it in sanitary containers.

Probably the most striking aspect of the clean-up campaign which the Authority has introduced is that of recycling thousands of old automobiles cluttering the valley countryside. The way this project has developed has attracted wide attention and resulted in many requests for information about it. Some legislation along this line also has resulted. The principal problem was found to be bringing enough of the junk vehicles together in one location to make it economically practical for commercial salvage. From that point on the value of the steel in the vehicles usually makes the operation financially self-sustaining as the car bodies are crushed, shredded, and recycled to a foundry.

The TVA program shows local governments how they can carry out this key operation. The Authority loans special collection vehicles in order to get these programs underway. One of the vehicles was loaned to the city of Philadelphia, Pennsylvania, and officials there reported that autos abandoned on local streets were collected at a rate of more than 350 a week. Writing in the *Tennessee Magazine* for January 1973, Tony Holmes stated, "Exactly when junk cars became a tradition in the Southeastern region nobody seems to recollect. Like good food and football, they seem to have always been a part of the regional character. Part of growing up in the South." Needless to say, this does not add to the beauty of the Southland.

Junk and abandoned automobiles are causing serious problems throughout the United States. About 6.5 million cars are removed from the state registration lists each year. About 80 percent of these enter the salvage cycle. The remainder, amounting to hundreds of thousands of cars, are either abandoned in scattered or isolated locations or accumulated with other rusting derelicts. It is estimated that 325,000 cars have been abandoned outside commercial salvage yards in Tennessee alone. In other parts of the Tennessee Valley, windshield surveys indicate that each county contains between 2,500 and 4,000 junk cars.

Rural Appalachia, particularly its low-income sections, has larger numbers of junk cars than most other places. Old, dilapidated vehicles are frequently sold and resold, patched and repatched. They are then cast aside, deserted, and abandoned wherever they stop. Persons trying to dispose of them frequently find that auto dismantlers will pay little or nothing for the hulks. The owners must bear the cost of towing the old cars to the dismantler. But recent design improvements and the growing use of the portable auto crusher have enabled auto salvage operators to purchase and process large concentrations of junked cars in areas as distant as 300 miles from major processing centers. The portable auto flattener reduces the standard automobile body to a slab 7 feet wide and 7 to 10 inches high. These uniform slabs can be stacked on trailers or railway cars and economically transported to a recycling plant.

The ever-recurring problem of strip mining hangs over the TVA and will probably never be solved to the satisfaction of extreme environmentalists. The Authority has responded to the pressure, whether enduringly or not. One example is in Campbell County, Tennessee, where three separate seams of coal that ribbon along a mountainside have been mined by the "back-to-contour" method. Silt basins have been constructed along the slope to catch eroding soil before it reaches a creek at the base of the mountain. Toxic materials are buried. The area is contoured to a resemblance of its original appearance, topsoil is replaced, and grasses and trees are planted. TVA's surface mine demonstration on Massengale Mountain in eastern Tennessee has become the nation's first comprehensive, multiple-seam, back-to-contour example of surface mining techniques in mountainous terrain.

Another method has been tested. Spoil from the initial block cut is placed in an offsite storage area. As mining continues along the contour of the mountain, each block cut is backfilled with spoil from succeeding cuts. The site is reclaimed by layering and compacting acid-forming residue at the bottom of the pit and reestablishing the original contour.

Years ago this writer visited Briceville, a little town in the mountains of Anderson County in eastern Tennessee. It is in the narrow valley of Coal Creek. This coal mining town was never an attractive place, and became less so. The creek, like thousands of others in the region, has been poisoned by acid wastes from the coal seams for which it is named. Cross Mountain, just west of Briceville, shows on its scarred face the heavy cuts of strip mining.

Briceville was once prosperous; at least the company store showed profitable receipts. But in the early 1950s the underground coal mines which were the economic backbone of the community began shutting down. And when they were gone, no other industry came to take their place, so poverty set in. Much more could be said about the low state into which the little mountain town sank; enough to say that it became a sad, forlorn community. Into this dreary picture, the TVA helped importantly to establish a health center which was badly needed. Some of the elderly people had never had a physical examination, some of them never having been to a doctor in their whole lives.

Behind this helpful project was a retired coal miner, Byrd Duncan, with an idea whose time had come. He was president of the parent-teachers association and got in touch with some officials of the TVA. They agreed to come to Briceville with medical students from Vanderbilt University to put on a health fair. Duncan agreed and talked the local people into complying, and the visiting group came in the summer of 1970. Some 1,200 people showed up for the free physical examinations during the week the fair was in progress.

That was just part of the story. A Knoxville newspaper carried a story about the health situation in Briceville and, as a result, a plumbers' union volunteered to do the plumbing for the health center, a supply firm provided the equipment for the job without charge, the widow of a Knoxville physician gave her late husband's office equipment and X-ray machine, and pharmaceutical companies donated a large amount of drugs.

"People have been awful good to us," said Byrd Duncan. "And we sure do appreciate everything they have done. This health center is the best thing that ever happened to Briceville, and we'd be plumb ruined without it."

Dams

There are presently 58 dams which make up the integrated control system of the TVA, categorized as follows:

Major dams in the Tennessee Valley water control system—total 33

23 built by TVA: (Main River) Kentucky, Pickwick Landing, Wheeler, Guntersville, Nickajack, Chickamauga, Watts Bar, Fort Loudoun; (Tributary) Norris, Hiwassee, Cherokee, Apalachia, Nottely, Ocoee No. 3, Chatuge, Fontana, Douglas, South Holston, Watauga, Boone, Fort Patrick Henry, Melton Hill, Tims Ford.

1 taken over from the War Department: (Main River Wilson.
3 purchased from TEP: (Tributary) Ocoee No. 1, Ocoee No. 2, Blue
   Ridge.
6 owned by ALCOA, water releases directed by TVA: (Tributary)
   Calderwood, Cheoah, Thorpe, Nantahala (in addition to the main
   dam this project includes two small dams diverting Dicks and
   White creeks into the penstock), Santeetlah, Chilhowee.

Minor dams in the Tennessee Valley system—total 9

2 purchased from ETL&P: (Tributary) Wilbur, Nolichucky.
7 owned by ALCOA: (Tributary) Mission, Queens Creek, Tuckasegee,
   Cedar Cliff, Bear Creek, Wolf Creek, East Fork—the latter two
   comprise the Tennessee Creek project which has a single powerhouse supplied through converging tunnels from the two dams.

*Major dams in the Cumberland Valley contributing to the TVA
power system*

1 purchased from TEP: Great Falls.
7 operated by the Corps of Engineers: Dale Hollow, Center Hill, Wolf
   Creek, Old Hickory, Cheatham, Barkley, and J. Percy Priest.

Dams under construction

Tellico (on Little Tennessee River, by TVA, halted by court injunction). Action reversed by Congress and President. Gates of dam
   closed and water started filling the dam, Nov. 29, 1979.
Racoon Mountain (by TVA)—this dam forms an upper pool for a
   pump-storage hydro power installation, with Nickajack Reservoir
   providing the lower pool.

20. Whither the TVA?

Entering its fifth decade, had the TVA been personified, it might not have been able to recognize itself. The changes which have been wrought were hoped to be for the best, but time, like the waters through the dams, flowed on inexorably. Edwin J. Best, a TVA official who grew up in the region, commented incisively: "TVA is 40 and, like most persons at the approach of middle age, can rejoice at having gotten safely through the perils of childhood and the temptations of youth. The past 40 years have been perilous and full of pitfalls. TVA has faced the threat of death, disability, and deformity. We have suffered from malnutrition, have faced kidnapping, and have been the object of murderous plots and mistaken judgments. At 40, we are still threatened, only this time by hardening of the arteries, by psychoses, and by the possibility of becoming fat and lazy, all ills to which middle age is heir. That TVA is 40 is something of a miracle. Other New Deal agencies have been cut down, have been transformed, or have been swallowed up. TVA remains essentially as it was created, the hardiest of the lot. That TVA was created is not remarkable. That it survived is providential."

On the other hand, William L. Russell, president of the Tennessee Citizens for Wilderness Planning, charged that the TVA had become "public enemy number one in the fight to save Tennessee's remaining rivers." Speaking to a luncheon of the Chattanooga Chamber of Commerce, the Oak Ridge conservationist suggested that the name of the TVA be changed to "Tennessee Valley Arrogancy." He asserted that the Authority had completed most of its major reservoir building programs in the 1940s with emphasis on flood control, power, and navigation, and he alleged that the TVA is only proposing additional reservoir projects for industrial expansion.

For the defense, Marguerite Owen, for years the TVA representative in Washington, D.C., said she was grateful that she had the good fortune to work for the TVA for 35 years. In a book, *The Tennessee Valley Authority*, she wrote:

359

The controversial Tellico Dam in the **foreground** *with its embayment which stood empty for five years because environmentalists contended that a three-inch fish, the "snail darter", would become extinct if this small river, its native habitat, was dammed up. The U.S. Supreme Court agreed with the delay until a study could be made. Then in late 1979, Congress and the President gave the go-ahead to finishing this dam on which over 100 million dollars had already been spent by the TVA. Fort Loudoun Dam is at upper* **left.**

For TVA, there never has been and it is unlikely that there ever will be one moment of triumphant affirmation that everything has been done just right. Probably there never will be a single occasion when all the battles in court and in Congress will be vindicated, when without a doubt the wisdom of the Act and the fidelity of management to its principles will be validated by consensus.

In a more middle course, Stuart Chase later told this writer:

It would be fine if the TVA would now take the lead of U.S. power companies in ways and means to meet the energy crisis. Here is a wonderful opportunity, both in operating and conservation. Most power companies, of course, are driven by the demands of their stockholders for maximum profit, but the stockholders of the TVA are the citizens of the United States.

The *Chattanooga Times* took note of the fortieth anniversary. Editor Norman Bradley, in a featured column entitled "TVA's Battles Recounted," commented:

> Gone is the generation of Valley dwellers who viewed TVA as a daring experiment in form and purpose. Generally, they recognized that what it undertook was to their benefit and they marvelled at the steady pace with which it calmed the turbulence of a great river, restored green to denuded hillsides and extended the labor-saving and light-giving powers of electricity to the far reaches of the region.

About 850 miles to the north, the newspaper which Adolph Ochs went from Chattanooga to publish 77 years before, *The New York Times,* in a story by Reginald Stuart presented a more clinical viewpoint. Observing how far the TVA had come, the article stated that the Authority "created four decades ago as a brave experiment in regional development of resources, has fallen victim to the energy crisis." Cited were the TVA's issuance of contingency plans for energy conservation without consulting state and local energy officials.

Other complaints had been the resistance of the Authority to federal requirements for "scrubbers" to control pollution at some of its coal-fired steam plants; the admission by Lynn Seeber that he had deleted unfavorable information from a TVA environmental impact statement about construction of two dams; and the contention by citizens of Appalachia that the TVA, the biggest buyer of strip-mined coal, was neglecting to enforce its land-reclamation standards. The description was not brightened by the quotation from Senator Howard Baker that "TVA continues to operate like a cartel." On December 14, 1978, the TVA agreed to invest over $1 billion to clean up air pollution at ten of its power plants.

In reply to such criticism, Chairman Wagner said, "We still have a long way to go. There is still much to be done. As we look to the next forty years, TVA will continue to serve usefully as long as we remember that our ultimate goal is to continue to help the people of this region find a rewarding and satisfying way of life."

John S. McQueen, Manager of the Electric Power Board of Chattanooga, described the 40-year effect that the TVA had had on his area: "The difference between daylight and dark."

The *New Republic* called the TVA "a mixed blessing." In an article by Peter Barnes in the November 10, 1973 issue, it was stated that

"There's been good and there's been bad, with the former far out-weighing the latter, but there has not been any marching on to other regions." Referring to the interest of foreign countries, the article concluded, "Only in its homeland is TVA an overlooked relic of another era. It was, it now seems, a product of unique circumstances (the Muscle Shoals controversy), unique times (the Depression) and unique personalities (Norris and FDR)."

There were encouraging reports about the population of the valley. For the first time in three decades, more counties in the region showed growth rather than decline. More than two-thirds of the 201 counties gained people between 1960 and 1970, in contrast to the preceding decade, when the proportion of gainers and losers was almost exactly reversed. There was a decided westward shift between 1960 and 1970 in the location of the growth counties. In contrast to previous decades, growth was extensive in western Tennessee and an adjoining part of Mississippi, largely as a result of the industrial development occurring in that whole area.

TVA activity in general moved on. Visual evidence of this is varied. Travelers see along the river or creek bank a small shelter with a U.S. government sign indicating these are stream gauging stations to measure and record the water level; an advertisement in a Chattanooga newspaper including the information that electric power residential rates had increased from $8.03 to $21.50 for 1,000 kilowatt-hours since 1967. Two women in hard hats could be seen working with construction crews of the TVA. Owners of Watts Bar Lake resorts complained that the TVA was driving them out of business by "taking campers in large numbers that should be using our facilities."

An announcement stated that TVA procurements for a fiscal year reached over $75 million and brought to over $1 billion the amount spent in the state for goods and services since the power agency was created in 1933. Patrons of restaurants near the Kentucky Dam sampled buffalo meat, many of them for the first time. According to a report, they liked it and asked for more. The meat came from the TVA's buffalo herd at Land Between the Lakes, which had grown too large for the available pasture and had to be thinned out.

After William Jenkins was appointed to the board of directors of the TVA, there was considerable sentiment toward having open meetings of the board. Stating that the group had nothing to hide, Chairman Wagner agreed, and the first such open meeting in its history was held by the TVA Board in mid-January 1975. The meeting could scarcely be called sensational. The chairman announced that power rates might have to go up as much as 50 percent if coal costs continued to rise. He admitted that even his wife had complained about rising rates. That was the end of the board's first open meeting.

Later it was pointed out that someone believed that the TVA's records showed over $800 million in "retained earnings, and that such was in effect money in the bank that might have been used to avoid increased rates." The TVA strongly denied this, adding that there were no such funds in the bank, but that the money accumulated each year was used to build new generating plants or transmission lines, obviating the need otherwise to borrow money for that purpose.

Aside from the financial situation, the TVA was still in the national limelight. On April 20, 1977, in his nationally televised energy message and in earlier correspondence with Chairman Wagner, President Jimmy Carter singled out the TVA for a special role. The idea was that of devising and testing a wide range of initiatives which, if successful in the Tennessee Valley, could be applied on a national scale.

"TVA's history of innovation and its unique institutional position make it an obvious leader in dealing with our energy problem," said Carter. Included in the suggestions were exploration of more private home weatherization, waste heat utilization, power pooling, coal mining technology, and solar heating and cooling.

Still not cool was the issue of the Tellico Dam. As has been seen, the project was stopped by the courts. This was mainly because of a tiny fish called the "snail darter," which had been found in the Tellico River and which environmentalists vehemently insisted would become extinct if the dam were closed and the free-running water stopped. The TVA transferred some of the darters to a nearby river, and they lived. David Freeman later stated that the dam might be completed if the fish could survive in the other stream. But even though $119 million had already been spent on the dam (it was 90 percent completed and would cost only an estimated $1.8 million to finish), other obstacles loomed. The House of Representatives passed a special bill allowing the dam to be completed. But the one introduced in the Senate by Howard Baker of Tennessee in June 1979, was defeated by a vote of 52 to 43. In September, the Senate reversed itself and approved the completion of the dam, 48 to 44.

Senator Baker had moaned, "This two-inch fish, which surely kept the lowest profile of all of God's creatures until a few years ago, has since become the bane of my existence." The Senator was relieved, however, when President Carter on September 25 signed the bill into law and work on completing the dam was resumed.

Meantime, Aubrey Wagner had retired as chairman on May 18, 1978. Two weeks before, William L. Jenkins, another board member, had resigned in protest against David Freeman's new environmental policies. Bob Clement, son of a former Tennessee governor, was named to the board. Wagner also differed with Freeman over the expected settlement of the TVA's six-year battle with the Environmental Protection Agency over air pollution standards. The outgoing chairman cited the $450 million a year cost as a "staggering burden on the consumer." The Tellico Dam delay was among his greatest regrets. His absence is felt keenly by many.

Simon David Freeman was appointed to the TVA board of directors on July 19, 1977, and was designated chairman on May 19, 1978. Prior to his appointment he was a member of the White House energy staff under President Jimmy Carter. Before that time he was director of the Ford Foundation's Energy Policy Project. From 1961 to 1965 he was assistant to the chairman of the Federal Power Commission.

Born in Chattanooga in 1926, the son of an umbrella maker, Freeman was graduated from Georgia Institute of Technology with a degree in civil engineering in 1948. For the next four years he worked for TVA as an engineer, designing steam electric power plants and hydroelectric stations. Later he earned a law degree from the University of Tennessee in 1956, finishing first in his class. For the next five years Freeman served as an attorney with the TVA.

Freeman has vowed to give the TVA a new direction. "The Valley is changing and so are the problems it confronts," he said. "When power costs began to go up, TVA's popularity began to go down. We have done a great job along the river, but we need to move into other areas as well." The new chairman believes that the fundamental answer to the problems of rising rates is to get costs under control and bring nuclear plants on line. "I believe that people today want a decent job," he added. "They want decent recreation and clean air, and a chance to go to and from work without having to travel endless miles." Perhaps he anticipated the dire gasoline shortage which came not long after he had made the last statement. Memphis residents were excited about the projected solar water heating experiments there, as were those who anticipated wood stoves.

Many people, especially those of the Red Wagner era, differ with Freeman regarding the future. An example of this was a speech in the summer of 1979 made by a TVA official on social well-being in the valley. Objections were voiced by some critics who objected to the TVA having "programs for the aged, the handicapped, children and Indians." Assistance has been given by the Authority in providing attic and floor insulation.

Of course the nuclear accident at Three Mile Island in Pennsylvania on March 28, 1979, caused concern among TVA officials, especially those directly in charge of nuclear power. But an initial warning about the flaw in the reactors at Three Mile Island was issued to the company there by Carl Michelson, a nuclear safety expert with the Tennessee Valley Authority, in late 1977. Following the accident in Pennsylvania, it was reported that Chairman Freeman and another board member, Richard Freeman, a former Chicago lawyer and a TVA employee, had issued a directive that no one but themselves in the TVA was authorized to comment on the effects of the number of nuclear reactors on line in the 1980s. Construction of these reactors has been delayed a number of times. As a result of the Three Mile Island accident, additional precautionary measures are being taken by the TVA.

Even so, an engineer with the Lockheed Missile and Space Company in Huntsville, Alabama, told a symposium of the American Association for the Advancement of Science (which dealt with scientific ventures in space) that such possible projects were so enormous that a public corporation along the lines of the TVA might have to be created to handle them. She even offered a name for such an agency: The Space Utilization Authority. A poll of Purdue University engineers in mid-1979 listed the TVA as one of the "Seven Engineering Wonders in the Modern World." Others named were the computer, mass production of the automobile, development of jets, rockets and space travel, nuclear power, and television. The TVA was described as "a rather fabulous technical experiment—an example of what can be done with total planning involving the economy and environment of a region."

After decades of promoting all-electric homes, the TVA in late 1978 asked some customers to try another energy source for heat: wood stoves. At first 120 such stoves were given to residents in six low-income counties in East Tennessee. Later the program was expanded to provide interest-free loans to 1,000 residents in six north Georgia counties. It was found that heating bills dropped 60 to 80 percent. The stoves are not like those of 50 years ago. They have thermostats and controlled combustion chambers which allow a single piece of wood to burn for 10 to 12 hours.

Analysis

The significant value of the Tennessee Valley Authority can be said to be in the eye of the beholder. It is not all good and not all bad, depending upon one's relationship to the huge organization and to the judgment of time. To be overly positive about its merits and faults can only lead to oversimplification and inevitable error.

This writer, having grown up with the TVA, is greatly tempted to be subjective in its favor. But the years of research and close contact with its friends and enemies have led me to present, as far as possible, both positive and negative aspects of the unique organization and then to let the reader be the judge. Few, it is believed, will be neutral.

Born in the dismal days of the Great Depression, it represented (during those lean years) food, clothing, and healthful comfort for countless people of the basically rich but economically deprived Tennessee Valley. There can be no argument concerning its benefits then. One thing is certain in my mind, and probably obvious in the preceeding pages: it could not have happened in a better place. Not only did the TVA lift the economic status and physical well-being of the people of the valley, but, perhaps more importantly, it lifted their spirits as high as the lofty mountains which majestically border the eastern rim.

As to the debate over whether the TVA pays taxes, whether it is a government subsidy or a self-supporting body or whether it sells cheaper power partly paid for by the citizens of the United States to only a portion of the country, this argument will probably go on forever. Indeed, at this writing, it seems so will the TVA. The beneficiaries in seven southern states will cheer, albeit not so much lately with higher prices for their electricity, while the high-paying customers of Consolidated Edison in New York City will vociferously scoff at the idea that a federally operated power company can be functioning on a reasonably fair basis.

Navigation is there, where it was not before. Now shipping can move on the Tennessee River from Knoxville to Paducah uninterruptedly. True, much of the river was navigable before the TVA, but not enough. Freight rates in the South were 40 percent higher than in other parts of the country. Now they are relatively lower, but big shippers have the choice of rail or water. Private industry might have brought this about; but like the bringing of electric lights to remote rural communities, it didn't.

Flood control is so obviously improved from what it was before the Authority appeared that it is only necessary to recall the disastrous inundation of some adjacent Southern states in early 1979 to realize the difference. Years ago this writer was almost a victim of the heavy Tennessee rains, driving through Sweetwater one night with water up to the mid-radiator of his car and miraculously escaping death on the same stretch of city highway where some two hours later a couple in their car were drowned.

It is hard to write excitingly about fertilizer. But one of the most important achievements of the TVA is in this field. From the beginning the Authority has rather quietly moved forward in improving and making available to farmers here and abroad highly productive kinds of soil nutrients along with showing how properly to use them. Recreation along the river is a welcome by-product of the TVA. Some believe it is not vital; all agree it is invigorating and restful.

The TVA has been hit by inflation like everything else, as shown in its higher power rates and increased costs. Its nuclear power plants have come under attack from environmentalists, and its cartel-like structure has been criticized as being an inland empire. Nevertheless, with full consideration of its shortcomings, if this writer were subjected to a yes or no vote about the Tennessee Valley Authority, his vote would have to be "Yes!"

Epilogue

Forty-five years after my initial entry into the realm of the Tennessee Valley Authority, I stood on the landscaped elevation above Norris Dam and looked upon the scene. My memory had not dimmed with the years any more than had my eyes. I hoped that both were clear enough to properly record the past and present.

Spring had come to the valley in wondrous ways. In a leafy, spreading oak tree above my head, a mockingbird trilled out its liquid

The landscaped elevation beside Norris Dam where the author stood, as described in his Epilogue, and warmly recalled his first presence there almost half a century ago.

notes, and from the huge, sweeping dam could be heard the resonant hum of the great electric power transformers, enlivened by the surging waters of the lake above.

Here was a marvelous blending of the handiwork of nature and mankind. It appeared to be a good combination.

To my left, across the undulating foothills and beyond the city of Knoxville, towered the majestic, bluish peaks of the Great Smoky Mountains. Long years ago I had grown up in their soft shadows, stayed awhile near them, and then went away. But I remembered that Thomas Wolfe who lived across these mountains in North Carolina had written, "You Can't Go Home Again." I did not believe this. He, too, had gone to The Big City and also had taught at New York University and then played out his life all too soon. Maybe he had a point.

My ancestors had come over from England and Ireland and had settled in this beauteous, green valley and felt that they belonged to it, and in a visionary way, it to them. They came through wars, a depression, and recovery. They always believed in the future here and hereafter. I could do no less.

Bibliography

Historical Background

"A.E.C. Wants Muscle Shoals Under Water-Power Act." *Electrical World*, 3 May 1924.

"Again the Bugaboo of a Power Trust." *Electrical World*, 10 January 1925.

"Alabama Power's Muscle Shoals Offer Makes Favorable Impression." *Electrical World*, 25 February 1922.

American Farm Bureau Federation, Report of the Muscle Shoals Committee of the American Farm Bureau Federation (Chicago, May 31, 1921), in General Records of the Department of Agriculture Correspondence of the Secretary of Agriculture, Muscle Shoals Nitrate Plant, National Archives.

"American Farm Bureau Weekly News Letter," 1 February 1923. General Records of the Department of Agriculture, Correspondence of the Secretary of Agriculture, Muscle Shoals Nitrate Plant, National Archives.

Baker, Benjamin. "Muscle Shoals Plans and Issues Before Congress." *Annalist,* 9 March 1928.

———. "Political Forces in the Muscle Shoals Struggle." *Annalist* 2 March 1928.

———. "Some Hope for Some Action on Muscle Shoals." *Annalist,* 14 February 1928.

Bauer, John. "Muscle Shoals and the President's Veto." *National Municipal Review,* April 1931.

"Bill Leasing Muscle Shoals to Ford Strongly Backed." *Electrical World,* 22 December 1923.

Blee, C. E. "Development of the Tennessee River Waterway." *American Society of Civil Engineers, Centennial Transactions,* 1953.

Bulletin, League of Women Voters (17 May 1928), in Papers of George W. Norris, Division of Manuscripts, Library of Congress.

Bulletin No. 43, National Popular Government League (14 January 1931), in Papers of George W. Norris, Division of Manuscripts, Library of Congress.

Campbell, James B. "East Tennessee During the Federal Occupation, 1863–1865." Knoxville, Tenn. *The East Tennessee Historical Society's Publications,* 1947.

Chase, Stuart. *Rich Land, Poor Land; a Study of Waste in the Natural Resources of America*. New York: McGraw-Hill, 1936.

"City All Main Street." *Literary Digest*, 8 April 1922.

Clark, Farley G. "Muscle Shoals Relative to Conservation." *Transactions of the American Electrochemical Society*, September 1929.

"Committee for Ford Offer." *Electrical World*, 2 February 1924.

"The Conference Report on Muscle Shoals Should be Defeated." *Manufacturers' Record*, 19 February 1925.

"Congressman Quin Still Favors Muscle Shoals Bill." *Electrical World*, 30 October 1926.

"Consideration of Muscle Shoals Deferred." *Electrical World*, 6 December 1924.

Coyle, D. C. *Conservation: an American Story of Conflict and Accomplishment*. New Brunswick, N.J.: Rutgers University Press, 1957.

Dakin, Edwin. "Henry Ford—Man or Superman?" *Nation*, 26 March 1924.

"The Dance on Muscle Shoals." *Outlook*, 28 January 1925.

Daniel, A. G. "Navigational Development of Muscle Shoals, 1807–1880." *Alabama Review*, October 1961.

Davis, R. O. E. "Muscle Shoals, Nitrogen and Farm Fertilizers." *Annals of the American Academy of Political and Social Science*, January 1928.

"Deadlock in Congress Over Muscle Shoals." *Electrical World*, 8 April 1922.

"Defenders of Water-Power Act Attack Ford Plan." *Electrical World*, 17 February 1923.

"Developing the Tennessee." *Electrical World*, 2 May 1925.

"Editorial Views of the Ford Offer." *Congressional Digest*, II, October 1922.

"Effort to Report Ford Bill Fails." *Electrical World*, 24 May 1924.

"Facing a Dilemma with Very Sharp Horns." *Electrical World*, 12 March 1921.

"Facts about TVA Operations." Knoxville, Tenn: TVA, 1967.

"Facts and Fancies About Muscle Shoals." *Outlook*, 3 February 1926.

"Farm Bureau Federation Decries Muscle Shoals Bill." *Electrical World*, 22 May 1926.

"Farmers' National Council." *Nation*, 15 March 1919.

Finer, Herman. *T.V.A.: Lessons for International Application*. Montreal: International Labour Office, 1944.

Folmsbee, Stanley J. *Sectionalism and Internal Improvements in Tennessee*. Knoxville, Tenn.: East Tennessee Historical Society, 1939.

"Fooling the Farmers Again." *New Republic*, 7 December 1927.

"Ford Mesmerism and Muscle Shoals." *Current Opinions*, May 1924.

"Ford Politics in Muscle Shoals." *Literary Digest*, 27 October 1923.

"Ford Winning Muscle Shoals." *Literary Digest*, 29 March 1924.

"Ford Withdraws Offer for Muscle Shoals." *Electrical World*, 18 October 1924.

"Ford's Muscle Shoals Offer and Public Policy." *Electrical World*, 20 August 1921.

Friedmann, John R. P. *The Spatial Structure of Economic Development in the Tennessee Valley.* Chicago: University of Chicago Press, 1955.

Garrett, Garet. "Over the Dam with TVA." *Saturday Evening Post*, 7 May 1938.

Gilford, Duff. "The Muscle Shoals Lobby." *New Republic*, 16 April 1930.

Govan, G. E., and Livingood, J.W. *Chattanooga Country, 1540–1962, From Tomahawks to TVA.* Chapel Hill: University of North Carolina Press, 1963. Copyright 1963 University of Chattanooga, excerpted by permission.

"Government Moves Slowly on Muscle Shoals Offer." *Electrical World*, 13 August 1921.

Gray, Coolidge. "Norris and Muscle Shoals." *Electrical World*, 1 March 1930.

Greenwood, Ernest. "The Myth of Muscle Shoals." *Independent*, 28 February 1925.

Hamer, Philip. *Tennessee: A History.* New York: American Historical Society, Inc., 1933.

Hard, William. "Mr. Ford Is So Good." *Nation*, 26 March 1924.

Hearings before the Military Affairs Committee, on the TVA Bill, House, 74th Cong., 1st Sess., 1933.

Hill, Lister. "TVA: Democracy in Action." *Progressive*, May 1958.

Holt, Albert C. "Economic and Social Beginnings of Tennessee." *Tennessee Historical Magazine*, January 1922.

Hubbard, P. J. *Origins of the TVA; the Muscle Shoals Controversy, 1920–1932.* Nashville, Tenn.: Vanderbilt University Press, 1961.

———. "Story of Muscle Shoals." *Current History*, May 1958.

King, Judson. *Conservation Fight from Theodore Roosevelt to the Tennessee Valley Authority.* Washington, D. C.: Public Affairs Press, 1959.

———. *The Legislative History of Muscle Shoals*, Vols. 1–5. Knoxville, Tenn., TVA, 1936.

———. *Shall Coolidge and Congress Railroad the Underwood Bill and Deliver Muscle Shoals to the Power Trust?* Bulletin 96, National Popular Government League (20 January 1925), in Papers of

George W. Norris, Division of Manuscripts, Library of Congress.

Ladd, Edwin F. "Why I am for Henry Ford's Offer for Muscle Shoals." *Saturday Evening Post,* 22 and 29 November 1924.

Lane, Alfred P. "Muscle Shoals—Bonanza or White Elephant?" *Scientific American,* May 1925.

Livingood, James W. "The Tennessee Valley in America's History." *The East Tennessee Historical Society's Publications,* No. 21, Knoxville, Tenn., 1949.

McClung, Littel. "Building of the World's Largest Monolith." *Scientific American,* July 1923.

———. "The Seventy-Five Mile City." *Scientific American,* 22 September 1922.

McMurray, K. C. "The Geographic Setting of Muscle Shoals." Bulletin of the *Geographical Society of Philadelphia,* July 1924.

"Merrill on Muscle Shoals." *Electrical World,* 4 July 1925.

Merz, Charles. "Muscle Shoals." *Century Magazine,* September 1924.

Message from the President Requesting Legislation to Create a Tennessee Valley Authority. House Doc. 15, 73rd Cong., 1st Sess., 1933.

Milton, George F., Jr. "The South and Muscle Shoals." *Independent,* 19 January 1924.

Mississippi Valley Association. Report of the Special Committee of the Mississippi Valley Association, 28 May 1921, in General Records of the Department of Agriculture, Correspondence of the Secretary of Agriculture, Muscle Shoals Nitrate Plant, National Archives.

"Mr. Hoover Defies the Senate on Muscle Shoals." *Literary Digest,* 9 August 1930.

"Muscle Shoals." *Outlook and Independent,* 23 April 1930.

Muscle Shoals: A Groundwork of Facts. Washington, D.C.: U.S. Chamber of Commerce, 1930.

"Muscle Shoals: A Scandal in the Making?" *New Republic,* 23 April 1924.

"Muscle Shoals Again." *New Republic,* 10 March 1926.

"Muscle Shoals as a Hot Air Plant." *Current Opinion,* February 1925.

"The Muscle Shoals Bill." *Outlook and Independent,* 4 March 1931.

Muscle Shoals Commission. *Muscle Shoals: A Plan for the Use of the United States Properties on the Tennessee River by Private Industry for "the Manufacture of Fertilizers and Other Useful Products,"* Washington, D.C., 1931.

"Muscle Shoals Commissioners Confer Informally." *Electrical World,* 9 May 1925.

"Muscle Shoals in Crisis." *New Republic,* 30 May 1928.

"Muscle Shoals May Yet Be Leased to Highest Bidder." *Business Week*, 23 April 1930.

"Muscle Shoals Nearing Its Climax." *Literary Digest*, 19 April 1930.

"Muscle Shoals Open for Bids." *Literary Digest*, 27 March 1926.

"Muscle Shoals—Ours." *Nation*, 17 December 1924.

"Muscle Shoals Power Soon a Reality." *Electrical World*, 28 March 1925.

"Muscle Shoals Rededicated to Fertilizer and Power Production." *Electrical World*, 23 January 1932.

"The Muscle Shoals Situation." *Manufacturers' Record*, 2 March 1922.

"The Muscle Shoals Situation as Viewed in Mississippi." *Manufacturers' Record*, 19 February 1925.

"Muscle Shoals to Plague the 1932 Campaign." *Literary Digest*, 14 March 1931.

National Fertilizer Association, "Proceedings of the Third Annual Convention of the National Fertilizer Association." Washington, D.C.: 1927.

"New England and the South's Interest in Muscle Shoals." *Manufacturers' Record*, 23 September 1926.

"New Muscle Shoals Idea Falls Flat." *Electrical World*, 9 April 1927.

Norris, George W. "Shall We give Muscle Shoals to Henry Ford?" *Saturday Evening Post*, 24 May 1924.

———. "Why Henry Ford Wants Muscle Shoals." *Nation*, 26 December 1923.

"Norris' Power Fight." *Nation*, 26 March 1928.

"Officials Not Backing Ford." *Electrical World*, 22 September 1923.

"One Million Primary Horsepower Could be Developed at Muscle Shoals." *Manufacturers' Record*, 3 May 1923.

Owen, Marguerite. *Muscle Shoals and the Public Welfare*. Washington, D.C.: National League of Women Voters, 1929.

Pinchot, Amos. "Hoover and Power." *Nation*, 12 August 1931.

"President Gives a Free Hand to Muscle Shoals Commissioners." *Electrical World*, 11 April 1929.

Pritchett, C. H. "Development of the Tennessee Valley Authority Act." *Tennessee Law Review*, February 1938.

"The Problem of Muscle Shoals." *Current History*, August 1928. Introduction by William M. Jardine, Part 1 by Robert Stewart, and Part 2 by George W. Norris.

"The Rejection of Ford's Muscle Shoals Offer." *Electrical World*, 22 July 1922.

"The Rival Bids for Muscle Shoals." *Literary Digest*, 10 May 1924.

"The Senate Navigating the Shoals." *Outlook*, 21 June 1925.

Correspondence of the Secretary of Agriculture, Muscle Shoals Nitrate Plant, National Archives.

"Senator Harrison Optimistic on Muscle Shoals Bills." *Electrical World*, 14 August 1926.

"Smoke Screen Over Muscle Shoals." *New Republic*, 21 October 1931.

"Snell and Garrett to Confer." *Electrical World*, 26 December 1925.

Southern Appalachian Power Conference. Report of the *Southern Appalachian Power Conference* (15 October 1927), in Records of the Bureau of Plant Industry, Soils, and Agriculture Engineering, Fertilizer Investigations, National Archives.

Southern States Republican League, *Report of the Muscle Shoals Committee of the Southern States Republican League* (21 February 1927), in General Records of the Department of Agriculture,

Spurm, Henry C. "Will the Public Utilities Be a Major Political Issue?" *Public Utilities Fortnightly*, 10 July 1930.

"Stubborn Dr. Morgan of the TVA—Glimpse into his Private Life." *Liberty Magazine*, 28 May 1938.

"Such a Lovely Green Valley," *Time*, 26 April 1963.

"Sweetness and Light vs Power and Light." *Today*, 6 February 1937.

Switzer, John A. "The Muscle Shoals Question." *Manufacturers' Record*, 13 January 1927.

Tennessee Valley Authority. *Report to the Congress on the Unified Development of the Tennessee River System*. Knoxville, Tenn.: TVA, 1936.

————. *Historical Roots of TVA*. (In its Annual Report, 1953.) Washington, D.C.: GPO, 1954.

————.*TVA: the First Twenty Years; a Staff Report*. Edited by Roscoe C. Martin. University, Ala.: University of Alabama Press; Knoxville, Tenn.: University of Tennessee Press, 1956.

————. "Report to the Nation from the Tennessee Valley Authority on Its First Twenty-Five Years." Knoxville, Tenn.: 1958

————. "Short History of the Tennessee Valley Authority, 1933–1963." Knoxville, Tenn.: 1964.

————. "TVA Today, 1967–1968." Knoxville, Tenn.: TVA, March 1967.

Tennessee Valley Authority Act., May 18, 1933, with Amendments. Washington, D.C.: GPO.

"The Tennessee Valley Region; Highlights of Growth and Change." Knoxville, Tenn.: 1968.

"Three Honest to Goodness Bidders Startle Muscle Shoals Board." *Business Week*, 30 September 1931.

"The Troublous Muscle Shoals Veto." *Literary Digest*, 23 June 1928.

TVA—Valley of Light, 1933–1963. Washington, D.C.: GPO, 1964.

TVA-Two Decades of Progress. Washington, D.C.: GPO, 1953.

"The Unsolved Problem of Muscle Shoals." *Review of Reviews*, April 1931. Tennessee Manufacturers' Association. "The Muscle Shoals Situation was Viewed by the Press of America," in General Records of the Department of Agriculture, Correspondence of the Secretary of Agriculture, Muscle Shoals Nitrate Plant, National Archives. Nashville, Tenn.: 1924.

U.S. Corps of Engineers. *Tennessee River and Tributaries-North Carolina, Tennessee, Alabama, and Kentucky*. Washington, D.C.: GPO, 1930. 71st Cong., H. Doc. 328, Part 1.

U.S. Congress. Joint Committee on the Investigation of the Tennessee Valley Authority. *Report 1939*, 76th Cong., S. Doc. 56, Part 3.

Welliver, Judson C. "The Muscle Shoals Power and Industrial Project." *American Review of Reviews*, April 1922.

Wells, Philip. "Our Federal Power Policy." *Survey Graphic*, March 1924.

Wengert, Norman. "Antecedents of TVA: The Legislative History of Muscle Shoals." *Agricultural History*, October 1952.

"What Next at Muscle Shoals?" *Literary Digest*, 8 November 1924.

Whitman, Willson. "Morgan and Morgan and Lilienthal." *Harpers*, September 1938.

"Whole Country Should Back Ford-Edison Scheme for Muscle Shoals Development." *Manufacturers' Record*, 19 January 1922.

"Why Henry Ford Wants the Muscle Shoals Property." *Current Opinion*, February 1922.

Wooton, Paul. "Chances for Muscle Shoals Bill Improve." *Electrical World*, 8 May 1926.

———. "Cyanamid and Farmers' Bids Rejected." *Electrical World*, 9 April 1927.

———. "Muscle Shoals City's Plea for Power." *Electrical World*, 9 July 1927.

———. "Tennessee Senator's Views." *Electrical World*, 12 June 1926.

Wyer, Samuel S. *Fundamentals of Our Fertilizer Problem*. Columbus, Ohio: Fuel-Power-Transportation-Educational Foundation, 1927.

———. *Niagara Falls: Its Power Possibilities and Preservation*, Washington, D.C.: Study of Natural Resources 2820, Smithsonian Institution, 1925.

———. *Power Possibilities at Muscle Shoals*. (Reprint of paper presented at Annual Convention of American Institute of Electrical Engineers, 22–26 June 1925), in Papers of Calvin Coolidge, Division of Manuscripts. National Archives.

General

"A Second Spring Stirs the TVA." *Business Week,* 29 October 1966.

Ackerman, E. A. "Regional Research—Emerging Concepts and Techniques in the Field of Geography." *Economic Geography,* July 1953.

Adamic, Louis. *My America.* New York: 1938.

Barr, Stringfellow. *Citizens of the World.* New York: Doubleday, 1952.

Biddle, Francis. *In Brief Authority.* New York: Doubleday, 1962.

Billings, Henry. *All Down the Valley.* New York: The Viking Press, 1952.

Callahan, North. "Coming of TVA." In *Smoky Mountain Country.* New York: Little, Brown-Duell, Sloan & Pearce, 1952.

Chase, Stuart. *Roads to Agreement.* New York: Harper & Bros., 1951.

Clapp, Gordon R. *TVA; an Approach to the Development of a Region.* Chicago: University of Chicago Press, 1955.

———. "The Tennessee Valley Authority." In *Regionalism in America.* Edited by Merrill Jensen. Madison, Wis.: University of Wisconsin Press, 1951.

Cole, William E., and Price Crowe, Hugh. *Recent Trends in Rural Planning.* New York: Prentice-Hall, 1937.

Curtis, H. A. "TVA: The Tennessee Valley Authority." *World Crops,* February 1950.

Daniels, Jonathan. "Three Men in a Valley." *New Republic,* 17 August, 1938.

Davidson, Donald. "TVA Makes a New River." In *The Tennessee,* Vol. 2. New York: Rinehart & Co., 1948.

Dimock, M. E. "Regional Conservation and the TVA." In *Business and Government,* 4th ed. New York: Holt, Rinehart and Winston, 1961.

Duffus, R. L. *The Valley and Its People.* New York: Alfred A. Knopf, 1946.

———. "TVA's Challenge—After Twenty-Five Years." *New York Times Magazine,* 18 May 1958.

Durisch, L. L., and Macon, H. L. *Upon Its Own Resources.* Tuscaloosa, Ala.: University of Alabama Press, 1951.

Durisch, L. L., and Lowry, R. E. "Scope and Content of Administrative Decision—the TVA Illustration." *Public Administrative Review,* Autumn 1953.

Federal Writers Project. *North Carolina, A Guide to the Old North State.* Chapel Hill: University of North Carolina Press, 1939.

Fly, J. L. "Role of the Federal Government in the Conservation and Utilization of Water Resources." *Pennsylvania Law Review,* January 1938.

Folmsbee, S. J. "A New Era in Tennessee: TVA." In *History of Tennessee*. New York: Lewis Historical Publishing Co., 1960.

Frank, Bernard, and Netboy, Anthony. *Water, Land and People*. New York: Alfred A. Knopf, 1951.

Garrett, Garet. *The Wild Wheel*. New York: Pantheon Books, 1952.

Glover, Katherine. *America Begins Again; the Conquest of Waste in Our Natural Resources*. New York: McGraw-Hill, 1939.

"Government and Water Resources: A Symposium." *American Political Science Review*, September 1950.

Gunther, John. *Story of TVA*. New York: Harper & Brothers, 1951.

———. *Inside U.S.A.* New York: Harper & Bros., 1947.

Hays, Brooks. "Instrument of Freedom." *National Civic Review*, January 1961.

Hofstadter, Richard. "The Patrician as Opportunist." In *The American Political Tradition*. New York: Alfred A. Knopf, 1948.

Hoover, C. B., and Ratchford, B. U. *Economic Resources and Policies of the South*. New York: Macmillan, 1951.

Howard, Waldorf V. *Authority in TVA Land*. Kansas City, Mo. Frank Glenn Publishing Company, 1948.

Hubbert, M. K. *Resources and Man*. San Francisco: Freeman, 1969.

Huxley, J. S. *TVA, Adventure in Planning*. Cheam, Surrey: The Architectural Press, 1943.

———. "The TVA, a Great American Experiment." *The Times*, London, May 21 and 22, 1935.

Joubert, William H. *Southern Freight Rates in Transition*. Gainesville: University of Florida Press, 1949.

Kerr, R. S. *Land, Wood and Water*. New York: Fleet Publishing Co., 1960.

Kerwin, Jerome G. *Federal Water-Power Legislation*. New York: Columbia University Press, 1926.

Krutilla, John V., and Eckstein, Otto. *Multiple Purpose River Development: Studies in Applied Economic Analysis*. Baltimore: Johns Hopkins Press, 1958.

Lewis, T. M. N., and Madeline Kneberg. *Hiwassee Island, and Archaeological Account of Four Tennessee Indian Peoples*. Knoxville, Tenn.: University of Tennessee Press, 1946.

Lilienthal, David E. *Journals of David E. Lilienthal*, Vols. 1–5, *The TVA Years*. New York and London: Harper & Bros., 1964–1969.

———. *TVA, Democracy on the March*. New York: Harper & Row, 1953.

Lilienthal, D. E., and Marquis, R. H. "Conduct of Business Enterprises by the Federal Government." *Harvard Law Review*, February 1941.

————. "Administrative Decentralization of Federal Functions." *Advanced Management*, January–March, 1940.

————. "The TVA and Decentralization." *Survey Graphic*, June 1940.

Loeb, Carl M. Rhoades and Company. *Aluminum: An Analysis of the Industry in the United States*. New York: Loeb, Rhoades, 1950.

McCarthy, C. J. "TVA and the Tennessee Valley." *Town Planning Review*, July 1950.

McCraw, Thomas K. *Morgan vs. Lilienthal: The Feud Within the TVA*. Chicago: Loyola University Press, 1960.

————. *TVA and the Power Fight, 1933–1939*. Philadelphia: Lippincott, 1971.

McKay, Kenneth C. *The Progressive Movement of 1924*. New York: Columbia University Press, 1947.

McKinley, Charles. *Uncle Sam in the Pacific Northwest*. Berkeley: University of California Press, 1952.

McLaughlin, G. E., and Robock, S. H. *Why Industry Moves South*. Washington, D.C.: National Planning Association, 1949.

Manuscripts: Library of Congress. Papers of William E. Borah, Calvin Coolidge, Charles L. McNary, George W. Norris, Gifford Pinchot, and Thomas J. Walsh.

Mason, Lucy Randolph. *To Win These Rights*. New York: Harper & Bros., 1952.

Mayer, Albert. *The Urgent Future*. New York: McGraw-Hill, 1967.

Moore, John R., ed. *The Ecoomic Impact of TVA*. Knoxville, Tenn.: University of Tennessee Press, 1967.

Morgan, Arthur E. The American Bent for Planning." *Survey Graphic*, April 1936.

————. "Autobiography" (incomplete, unpublished).

————. Bench-Marks in the Tennessee Valley." *Survey Graphic*, January and November 1934.

————. *Diary*, 1910 (unpublished).

————. Edward Bellamy, New York: Columbia University Press, 1944.

————. "Engineers' Share in Democracy." *Civil Engineering Magazine*, November 1939.

————. The First Social Revolt in America" (unpublished).

————. *"For a Wilderness Program."* The Living Wilderness, November 1936.

————. "Good Will in a World of Aggression" (unpublished).

————. The Long Road. Washington, D.C.: 1936.

————. *The Making of the TVA*. Yellow Springs, Ohio: 1974.

————. *The Miami Conservancy District*, Private Files, New York: 1951.

————. *My World*. Yellow Springs, Ohio: 1927.

————. *Not by Eastern Windows Only*. Yellow Springs, Ohio: 1936.

————. *Nowhere was Somewhere; How History Makes Utopias and How Utopias Make History*. Chapel Hill: University of North Carolina, 1946.

————. "A Personal View on the Power Issue." *New York Times*, 17 January 1937.

————. *The Small Community*, New York: Harper & Bros., 1942.

————. *"Sociology in the TVA."* American Sociological Review, April 1937.

————. "TVA—How Did it Happen?" *Civil Engineering*, August 1956.

Morgan, Lucy Griscom. *Finding His World*. Yellow Springs, Ohio: 1927.

Munzer, Martha E. *Valley of Vision: The TVA Years*. New York: Alfred A. Knopf, 1969.

Neal, Harry E. *The People's Giant: The Story of TVA*. New York: Julian Messner, 1970. (A children's book.)

Neuberger, Richard L., and Kahn, Stephan B. *Integrity: The Life of George W. Norris*. New York: The Vanguard Press, 1937.

Nicholson, Max. *The Environmental Revolution: a Guide for the New Masters of the World*. New York: McGraw-Hill, 1970.

Norris, George W. *The Fighting Liberal: The Autobiography of George W. Norris*. New York: Macmillan, 1945.

Odum, Howard W., and Moore, Harry E. *American Regionalism*. New York: Henry Holt and Co., 1938.

Owen, Marguerite. *The Tennessee Valley Authority*. New York: Praeger Publishers, 1973.

Parkins, Almon E. "The Tennessee Valley Project: Facts and Fancies." *Journal of the Tennessee Academy of Science*, October 1933.

Pearson, Drew. "Washington Merry-go-Round." *Washington Post*, 20 August 1933; 23 May 1936; and 25 November 1936.

Pinchot, Gifford. *The Power Monopoly: It's Make-Up and Its Menace*. Milford, Pa.: 1928.

Poe, J. C. "The Morgan-Lilienthal Feud," *Nation*, 3 October 1936.

President's Water Resources Policy Commission. *Ten Rivers in America's Future*. Washington, D.C.: 1950.

Pritchett, C. H. *Tennessee Valley Authority; a Study in Public Administration*. Chapel Hill: University of North Carolina Press, 1943.

Ransmeier, J. S. *Tennessee Valley Authority; a Cast Study in the Economics of Multiple Purpose Stream Planning*. Nashville, Tenn.: Vanderbilt University Press, 1942.

Reeves, F. W. "Adult Education as Related to the Tennessee Valley Authority." *School and Society*, 1936.

Richards, William C. *The Last Billionaire: Henry Ford.* New York: Charles Scribner's Sons, 1948.

Sandstrom, Gosta E. *Man the Builder.* Stockholm, Sweden: A. Bonniers, 1950.

Satterfield, M. H. *Soil and Sky; the Development and Use of Tennessee Valley Resources.* Knoxville, Tenn.: University of Tennessee, May 1950.

Schlesinger, A. M. "Power for the People." In *The Age of Roosevelt.* Boston: Houghton Mifflin Company, 1960.

Seay, M. F. "The Educational Program of the Tennessee Valley Authority." *Peabody Reflector and Educational News,* 1936.

Selznick, Philip. *TVA and The Grass Roots.* Berkeley, Calif.: University of California Press, 1949.

Shapiro, Edward. "The Southern Agrarians and the TVA," *American Quarterly,* Winter 1970. (Copyright 1970, Trustees of the U. of Penn.)

Sinclair, Upton B. *The Flivver King: A Story of Ford-America.* Pasadena, Calif.: Upton Sinclair, 1937.

Smith, Frank E. *Land Between the Lakes; Experiment in Recreation.* Lexington: University of Kentucky Press, 1971.

————. *Politics of Conservation.* New York: Pantheon Books, 1966.

Tennessee Valley Public Power Association. "Answers to Questions that are Frequently Asked about TVA." Chattanooga, Tenn.: May 1967 (folder).

Tunis, J. R. *Son of the Valley.* New York: W. Morrow, 1949 (fiction).

TVA Annual Reports, 1934–1979, Tennessee Valley Authority, Knoxville, Tenn.

U.S. General Accounting Office. *Report on the Audit of Tennessee Valley Authority, 1945 to Date.* Washington, D.C.: GPO.

U.S. National Science Foundation. "Scientific Information Activities of Federal Agencies: Tennessee Valley Authority." Washington, D.C.: GPO, 1960.

U.S. President's Water Resources Policy Commission. "The Tennessee River Basin." In the Commission's Report, Vol. 2. Washington, D.C.: GPO, 1950.

Vivian, Charles H. "Remaking the Tennessee Valley." *Compressed Air Magazine,* August 1934.

Vogel, H. D. "Competition and Administered Prices." *Electrical World,* 6 November 1961.

Wagner, A. J. "Emerging South." *Torch,* July 1964.

Webb, W. S., and D. L. DeJarnette. *An Archaeological Survey of Pickwick Basin in the Adjacent Portions of the States of Alabama, Mississippi, and Tennessee.* Washington, D.C.: GPO, 1942.

Whitman, Willson. *God's Valley; People and Power Along the Tennessee River.* New York: The Viking Press, 1939.

Zimmerman, Erich V. *World Resources and Industries,* rev. ed. New York: Harper & Bros., 1950.

Agriculture

Association of American Fertilizer Control Officials and Tennessee Valley Authority. "New Frontiers in Fertilizer Technology and Use." Wilson Dam, Ala.: 1964.

Ball, C. R. *Study of the Work of the Land-Grant Colleges in the Tennessee Valley Area in Cooperation with the Tennessee Valley Authority.* Knoxville, Tenn.: TVA, 1939.

Brittain, Robert. *Let There Be Bread.* New York: Simon and Schuster, 1952.

Bunce, A. C. *Economics of Soil Conservation.* Ames, Iowa: Iowa State College Press, 1942.

Childs, Marquis. *The Farmer Takes a Hand.* New York: Doubleday, 1952.

Douglas, J. R., Jr. "Market of Growth." *Commercial Fertilizer and Plant Food Industry,* March 1964.

Engelstad, O. P., and Terman, G. L. "Importance of Water Solubility in Fertilizers." *Commercial Fertilizer,* December 1966.

England, C. B., and Lesesne, E. H. "Efforts of Single Crop Covers on Runoff." *Journal of Soil and Water Conservation,* January–February 1962.

———. "Evaportranspiration Research in Western North Carolina." *Agricultural Engineering,* September 1962.

Hardin, Charles M. *The Politics of Agriculture.* Glencoe, Ill.: The Free Press, 1952.

Hill, Lister. "Increased Food Production—Phosphate Essential of a Fighting Soil." *Congressional Record,* 29 April 1943.

Jones, R. J., and Rogers, H. T. "New Fertilizers and Fertilizer Practices." *Advances in Agronomy,* Vol. 1. New York: The Academic Press, 1949.

Jones, W. Lewis, ed. *The Changing Status of the Negro in Southern Agriculture.* Tuskegee Institute, Ala.: The Rural Life Council, 1950.

Lee, Chi Yuen. "The Impact on Agriculture." Unpublished Master's Thesis, University of Tennessee, 1949.

Lord, Russell. *Growth: Unit Test Demonstration Farms in Georgia,* Bulletin 506. Athens: The University of Georgia Agricultural Extension Service, June 1944.

Mays, D. A. "Description of an Improved Forage Sample Dryer." *Agronomy Journal,* September–October 1966.

Mays, D. A., and Tinsley, V. L. "A Computer Program for Processing Forage Research Data." *Agronomy Journal,* July–August 1966.

Mississippi State College, Extension Service. *Test Demonstration:*

Farm Improved Programs on 103 Unit Test Demonstration Farms, Extension Bulletin 138. Miss.: State College, July 1947.

National Archives. General Records of the Dept. of Agriculture, Correspondence of the Secretary of Agriculture, Muscle Shoals Nitrate Plant. Records of the Bureau of Plant Industry, Soils, and Agricultural Engineering: Correspondence of the Bureau of Soils, Muscle Shoals; Fertilizer Investigations, Muscle Shoals; Fixed Nitrogen Laboratory Research Reports, Muscle Shoals.

North Carolina State College, Agriculture Extension Service. *Mountain Agriculture Moves Forward: A Report of Agricultural Development and Watershed Protection in the Tennessee Valley Area of North Carolina, 1935–1948*. Raleigh: undated.

————. Agricultural Extension Service. New Prosperity for Hayood County. Raleigh: Oct. 1966. (Misc. Extension Pub. No. 21.)

Papendick, R. I., and Giordano, P. M. "A Technique for Continuous Monitoring of pH in Soil Systems." Soil Science Society of America, *Proceedings*, May–June 1966.

Parris, D. W., and McClendon, S. P. "The Pickens Farm—Demonstration in Solving Farm Adjustment Problems." Auburn, Ala.: Auburn University, no date.

Raushenbush, Winifred. "Farmers Join Hands for a Better Life: The Thing to Do is Get Up a Contest." *Survey Graphic*, May 1948.

Robock, S. H. "Rural Industries and Agricultural Development." *Journal of Farm Economics*, August 1952.

Ruttan, V. W. "Impact of Urban-Industrial Development on Agriculture in the Tennessee Valley and the Southeast." *Journal of Farm Economics*, February 1955.

Tennessee Valley Authority. *An Inventory of Land and Its Use by Major Land Resource Areas in the Tennessee Valley*, by Wesley G. Smith and John M. Soileau. Muscle Shoals, Ala.: April 1966.

————. *Agriculture, Fertilizer and Forestry Activities of the Tennessee Valley Authority*. Knoxville, Tenn.: January 1950.

————. "APP Goes to Hawaii." Muscle Shoals, Ala.: no date, unpublished.

————. "Change and Challenge, Fertilizer Dealers View Their Sales and Services, Their Need for Knowledge and Training." Muscle Shoals, Ala.: 1966, unpublished.

————. *A Comparative Study of the Tennessee Valley with Special Reference to Agriculture* by Wesley G. Smith. Muscle Shoals, Ala.: July 1966.

————. "Census of Agriculture for the 125 Tennessee Valley Watershed Counties." Part 1: State and County Data. Part 2: Percentages and Totals for 14 Sub-areas. Wilson Dam, Ala.: 1963.

————. "Crop Response to Nitric Phosphate Fertilizers," by O. P. Engelstad and G. L. Terman. Muscle Shoals, Ala.: March 1966.

———. "Estimated World Fertilizer Production Capacity as Related to Future Needs." Report of the Agency for International Development. U. S. Dept. of State; prepared by Donald L. McCune, Travis P. Hignett, and John R. Douglas, Jr. Muscle Shoals, Ala.: February, 1966.

———. "Farm Income Estimates and Related Statistics; Tennessee Elk River Counties, 1959–1966." Muscle Shoals, Ala.: September 1966.

———. "Fertilizer Demonstrations for Forage Crops, Small Grains, and Row Crops." Wilson Dam, Ala.: July 1963.

———. *Fertilizer Production and Marketing Conference: the Impact of New Technology.* Muscle Shoals, Ala.: 1967.

———. *Fertilizer Science and the American Farmer.* Knoxville, Tenn.: 1966.

———. *Fertilizer Summary Data . . . by States and Geographic Areas.* Muscle Shoals, Ala.: 1966.

———. *Fertilizer Trends . . . and TVA's Fertilizer Activities.* Muscle Shoals, Ala.: 1967.

———. *Food at the Grass Roots: The Nation's Stake in Soil Minerals.* Knoxville, Tenn.: 1947.

———. *Greenhouse Techniques for Soil-Plant-Fertilizer Research.* Compiled by G. L. Terman, S. E. Allen, and L. B. Clements. Muscle Shoals, Ala.: June 1966.

———. *Morocco: Role of Fertilizer in Agricultural Development, with Special Emphasis on Wheat.* Prepared for the Agency for International Development, by Thurman M. Kelson, Ralph E. McKnight, Jon H. Nevins, and Darrell A. Russel. Muscle Shoals, Ala.: 1967.

———. *Movement of Labor Between Farm and Nonfarm Sectors and Multiple-Jobholding by Farm Operators in the Tennessee Valley* by Wesley G. Smith and Venkareddy Chennareddy. Muscle Shoals, Ala.: March 1967.

———. *New Developments in Fertilizer Technology, 6th Demonstration, Oct. 4–5, 1966.* Muscle Shoals, Ala.: 1966.

———. *Nitrogen Sources for Rice and Flooded Soils,* by O. P. Engelstad. Muscle Shoals, Ala.: February 1967.

———. *The Potential for Soybean Production in the Tennessee Valley,* by Curtis L. Ahrens. Muscle Shoals, Ala.: no date.

———. *Problems and Suggested Programs for Low-Income Farmers with Special Reference to the Tennessee Valley* by Arthur B. Mackie and E. L. Baum. Knoxville, Tenn.: October 1959.

———. *Projected Fertilizer Needs for Korea, 1967–1971,* by Wesley G. Smith and Orvis P. Engelstad. Muscle Shoals, Ala.: 30 June 1965.

———. *Response of Millet to Nitrogen and Irrigation—An Application of Simulation to the Problem of Weather Uncertainty,* by Wesley G. Smith and W. L. Parks. Muscle Shoals, Ala.: August 1967.

———. *Seminar for Latin America Fertilizer Executives, Sept. 18–29, 1967*. Muscle Shoals, Ala.: 1967.

———. Soil, People, and Fertilizer Technology. Washington, D.C.: GPO, 1949.

———. *South Vietnam: an Evaluation of the Fertilizer Industry* by John R. Douglas, Jr., John A. Burnett, Jr., and William N. Sutherland. Muscle Shoals, Ala.: 1967.

———. *Southern Bulk Blending Fertilizer Conference. January 21–23, 1963*. Knoxville, Tenn.: 1963.

———. Tennessee Valley Agriculture; "A Profile Change 1949–1959." Wilson Dam, Ala.: 1964.

———. *Uruguay's Fertilizer Supply and Need; a Preliminary Study*, by Fred G. Heil, Jr. Muscle Shoals, Ala.: 1967.

Wadleigh, Cecil H. "Wastes in Relation to Agriculture and Forestry." USDA, March 1968.

Wengert, Norman. "The Land, TVA, and the Fertilizer Industry." *Land Economics*, February 1949.

———. "Valley of Tomorrow; the TVA and Agriculture." Knoxville, Tenn.: University of Tenn., July 1952.

Williams, G. G. "Crop Response to Fertilizers." *Agricultural Chemicals*, May 1964.

Yeager, J. H., Belcher, O. D., and Walkup, H. G. *Fertilizer Use and Practices by Alabama Farmers*. Auburn, Ala.: Auburn University, January 1960.

Architecture

Augur, T. B. "The Planning of the Town of Norris." *American Architect*, April 1936.

Gutheim, F. A. "Tennessee Valley Authority; a New Phase in Architecture." *Magazine of Art*, September 1940.

Hackett, Brian. "TVA: Creator of Landscape." *Town Planning Institute, Journal*, November 1950.

Hamlin, T. F. "Architecture of the TVA." *Pencil Points*, November 1939.

———, ed. *Forms and Functions of Twentieth-Century Architecture*. New York: Columbia University Press, 1952.

Kyle, J. H. *Building of TVA: An Illustrated History*. Baton Rouge: Louisiana State University Press, 1958.

Mayer, Albert, and Stein, Clarence. "Synthesis and Sublimation: The Role of the Architect." *Architectural Record*, October 1964.

Reid, Kenneth. "Design in TVA Structures." *Pencil Points*, November 1939.

"Tennessee Valley Authority." *Architectural Forum*, August 1939.

Tour, H. B. "TVA—Ten Years of Concrete." *Architectural Concrete,* July 1943.

Towne, C. A. "Portable Housing; TVA Experience Leads to Trailer-Houses." *Pencil Points,* July 1952.

"Trailer House, TVA's New Approach to Mobile Shelter." *Architectural Record,* February 1943.

Wank, R. A. "Architecture in Rural Areas—a Report on TVA Experience." *New Pencil Points,* December 1942.

―――. "Some Recent Work of the Tennessee Valley Authority." *Pencil Points,* July 1941.

Area Development

Barrett, Roy, and Ramsey, Brownie K. *Basic Sanitation Facilities in the Upper Hiwassee Development Association Area.* Knoxville, Tenn.: February 1967. TVA

Baskoff, Alvin. *The Sociology of Urban Regions.* New York: Appleton-Century-Crofts, 1962.

Buchanan, James M. *Cost and Choice.* Chicago: Markham, 1969.

Carter, Edna Ann. "Education Resources and Needs in Hancock County, Tennessee." TVA, September 1965.

Hicks, J. R. *Value and Capital.* Oxford: Clarendon Press, 1961.

Mississippi State University. *Delineation of Trade Areas and Communities in the Yellow Creek Watershed,* by Carlton R. Sollie and Wilfrid C. Bailey. November 1961–1962.

―――. *Survey of Families in the Yellow Creek Watershed,* by Wilfrid C. Bailey and Mary Wilkinson, April 1962.

North Carolina State. *Economic Development of the Upper French Broad Area; Summary of Needs and Opportunities.* Knoxville, Tenn.: TVA, 1964.

Polhemus, James H. *Assistance Programs in Campbell County, Tennessee.* Knoxville, Tenn.: TVA, 1964.

Raulston, J. Leonard, and Livingood, J. W. *Sequatchie: a Story of the Southern Cumberlands.* Knoxville, Tenn. University of Tennessee Press, 1974.

Smith, H. A. "Chestuee Watershed Project." In Society of American Foresters, *Proceedings,* 1956.

Smith, Nicholas A. *A Survey of Legal Problems Among Rural and Indigent Residents of Anderson and Union Counties, Tennessee.* Knoxville, Tenn.: September 1965.

Tennessee, University of. "Ten Years of Progress in Beech River Agriculture." Knoxville, Tenn.: May 1966.

Tennessee Valley Authority. "Bear Creek Watershed; Summary of Resources." Knoxville, Tenn.: October 1962.

———. "Clinch-Powell Valley; Summary of Resources." Knoxville, Tenn.: July 1963.

———. "Elk River Valley; Growth and Development." Knoxville, Tenn.: 1967.

———. "Elk River Watershed; Summary of Resources." Knoxville, Tenn.: August 1962.

———. "Farming Along the Elk." Knoxville, Tenn.: University of Tennessee and Auburn University, 1966.

———. "Lower Hiwassee Valley; Summary of Resources." Knoxville, Tenn.: August 1962.

———. "Lower Hiwassee Valley; Summary of Resources." Knoxville, Tenn.: November 1963.

———. *Nature's Constant Gift; a Report on the Water Resource of the Tennessee Valley.* Knoxville, Tenn.: June 1966.

———. "Northwest Georgia; Walker-Catoosa-Dade Counties; Summary of Resources." Knoxville, Tenn.: June 1967.

———. *Office of Tributary Area Development. Annual Report, 1967.* Knoxville, Tenn.: 1967.

———. "Sequatchie Valley; Summary of Resources." Knoxville, Knoxville, Tenn.: September 1965.

———. "Southwest Virginia; Lee-Scott-Wise Counties." Knoxville, Tenn.: July 1964.

———. "Tributary Area Development Activities; Selected List of Reports and Publications." Knoxville, Tenn.: 1963.

———. "Tributary Area Development in the Tennessee Valley." Knoxville, Tenn.: 1964.

———. *Upper Duck River Development; Columbia Reservoir Area Investments.* Knoxville, Tenn.: August 1967.

———. "Upper Duck River Valley; Summary of Resources." Knoxville, Tenn.: July 1965.

———. "Upper French Broad River Basin; a Cooperative Plan for Economic Growth." Knoxville, Tenn.: September 1967.

———. "Upper Hiwassee Valley; Summary of Resources." Knoxville, Tenn.: May 1965.

———. "Yellow Creek Watershed Area; Summary of Resources." Knoxville, Tenn.: September 1965.

Wells, D. T. *The Tributary Area Development Program.* University, Ala., University of Alabama Press, 1964.

Chemical Engineering

Allbaugh, L. G. "Fertilizer-Munitions and Agriculture." In *TVA: the First Twenty Years; a Staff Report.* Edited by Roscoe C. Martin. University, Ala.: University of Alabama Press, 1956.

Allgood, H. Y.; Lancaster, F. E. Jr.; McCollum, J. A.; and Simpson, J. P. "A High Temperature Superphosphoric Acid Plan." *Industrial and Engineering Chemistry,* June 1967.

Hignett, T. P. Bulk Blending of Fertilisers: Practices and Problems."
The Fertiliser Society, *Proceedings No. 87.* London: 25 March
1965.

———. "Granulation of Fertilizers." *Farm Chemicals,* January 1963;
February 1963; March 1963; April 1963.

Hignett, T. P., and Newman, E. L. "Fluid Fertilizer—Research and
Development." In Liquid Fertilizer Round-Up, *Proceedings.* St.
Louis, July 1967.

Hignett, T. P., and Striplin, M. M., Jr. "Elemental Phosphorus in
Fertilizer Manufacture." *Chemical Engineering Progress,* May
1967.

Johansen, R. W., and Crow, G. L. "Liquid Phosphate Fire Retardant
Concentrates." *Fire Control Notes,* April 1965.

Nelson, L. B. "Advances in Fertilizers." In *Advances in Agronomy.*
New York: Academic Press, 1965.

———. "Fertilizer Forecast." *Agricultural Chemicals,* November
1966.

Parker, F. W., and Nelson, L. B. "More Fertilizers for More Food."
In *National Academy of Sciences.* Prospects of the World Food
Supply—A Symposium. Washington, D.C.: September 1966.

Scott, W. C. "Production of Clear Liquid Fertilizers." In Liquid
Fertilizer Round-Up, *Proceedings.* St. Louis: July 1967.

Scott, W. C.; Wilbanks, J. A.; and Burns, M. R. "Suspension Fertilizers Produced with TVA's 12–40–0." *Fertilizer Solutions,*
March–April, 1967.

Silverberg, Julius. "Storage Properties and Conditioning Requirements
of Various Fertilizers." In *Proceedings* of the Fertilizer Industry
Round Table, 1966. Washington, D.C.: 1967.

Slack, A. V. *Chemistry and Technology* of Fertilizers. New York:
Interscience Publishers, 1966.

———. "History and Growth of Liquid Fertilizers." In Liquid Fertilizer Round-Up, *Proceedings.* St. Louis: July 1967.

Tennessee Valley Authority. *Chemical Engineering Bulletins.* Wilson
Dam, Alabama: 1957–1967.

———. *Chemical Engineering Reports, 1949–1951.* Washington, D.C.:
GPO.

———. *Developments in Technology of Fertilizer Production. 4th
Demonstration.* Wilson Dam, Ala.: 1962.

———. *Fertilizer Science and the American Farmer: the Research and
Education Programs of the Tennessee Valley Authority.* Knoxville, Tenn.: 1966.

———. *General Outline of Chemical Engineering Activities* by H. A.
Curtis. Revised 1949.

———. National Fertilizer Development Center. *Annual Report, 1967.*
Muscle Shoals, Ala.: 1967.

———. *New Developments in Fertilizer Technology, 6th Demonstration.* Muscle Shoals, Ala.: 1966.

————. *Pilot-Plant Demonstrations of the Production of Granular Fertilizers.* Wilson Dam, Ala.: 1959.

————. "Production of Liquid Fertilizers from Liquid Base 11-37-0." Muscle Shoals, Ala.: January 1967.

U.S. Agricultural Research Service and TVA. *Superphosphate: Its History, Chemistry and Manufacture.* Washington, D.C.: GPO, 1964.

Wilbanks, J. A. "Suspension and Slurry Fertilizers." In Liquid Fertilizer Round-Up, *Proceedings.* St. Louis: July 1967.

Young, R. D., and I. W. McCamy. "TVA Development Work and Experience with Pan Granulation of Fertilizers." *Canadian Journal of Chemical Engineering,* February 1967.

Engineering

Annual Reports of the Chief of Engineers, United States Army, Washington, 1876–1955.

"At Nickajack, TVA Controls both Concrete and a River." *Engineering News-Record,* 26 May 1966.

"Biggest Shovel Goes to Work." *Excavating Engineer,* October 1962.

Blee, C. E. "Engineering Features of TVA." American Society of Civil Engineers, *Proceedings, 79.* August 1953.

Bolieu, C. W. "Hydraulics of Circulating Systems." American Society of Civil Engineers, *Proceedings, 85.* February 1959.

Bowden, N. W. "Multiple-Purpose Reservoir Operation." *Civil Engineering,* May and June 1941.

————. "Multiple-Purpose Reservoirs; General Problems of Design and Operation." American Society of Civil Engineers, *Proceedings,* March 1949.

DeMerit, Merrill. "Engineering Gains Mark TVA's Progress." *Public Power,* May 1958.

Design of Tennessee Valley Authority Projects: Civil and Structural Design. Technical Report No. 24, Washington, D.C.: 1952.

Elder, R. A.; Price, J. T.; and Engle, W. W. Navigation Locks: TVA's Multiport Lock Filling and Emptying System." American Society of Civil Engineers, *Proceedings, 90.* February 1964.

Elliott, R. A. "Navigation, Flood Control, Power—TVA Develops Its Rivers." *Civil Engineering,* January 1957.

Elliot, R. A., and LeRoy Engstrom. "Controlling Floods on the Tennessee." *Civil Engineering,* June 1959.

Emmons, W. F., and W. C. Boop. "Civil Engineering Design on TVA Steam Stations." American Society of Civil Engineers, *Proceedings, 88.* September 1962.

Fox, A. J., Jr. "TVA Dambuilders Turn to Steam." *Engineering News-Record*. 25 February 1954.

Fry, A. S. "Effects of Major River Basin Development on Watershed Improvement." *Journal of Soil and Water Conservation*. March 1957.

Gardner, R. M. "TVA Builds 500-Mw Steam Unit, Largest Yet Ordered in U.S.A." *Electrical World*, 18 May 1959.

Kesler, S. J. "Coal Handling at Paradise." *Mining Engineering*, October 1962.

Kesler, Stanley, and J. H. Boehms. "7,200-ton Coal Train Unloads in Twenty Minutes." *Electrical World*, 9 January 1967.

Leonard G. K. "Record Blast Provides 1.8 Million Cubic Yards of Rock for South Holston Dam." *Civil Engineering*, March 1950.

Leonard, G. K., and H. T. Lofft. "TVA Builds a Floating Guard Wall for New Wilson Lock." *Engineering News-Record*. 1 October 1959.

Lewis, Fred J. "An Engineer Looks at the Tennessee Valley Project," *Journal of the Tennessee Academy of Science*. July 1934.

McCain, E. H. "Measurement of Sedimentation in TVA Reservoirs." American Society of Civil Engineers, *Proceedings, 83*. June 1957.

Mattern, D. H. "TVA Installing Largest Pump-Turbine at Hiwassee." *Electrical World*, 5 July 1954.

Moneymaker, B. C. "Earthquakes in Tennessee and Nearby Sections of Neighboring States—1901–1925." *Tennessee Academy of Science Journal*, April 1957.

———. "Earthquakes in Tennessee and Nearby Sections of Neighboring States—1926–1950." *Tennessee Academy of Science Journal*, July 1958.

Monroe, R. A. "Addition to Generating Capacity at Wilson Dam." American Society of Civil Engineers, *Proceedings, 85*, October 1959.

———. "Some Factors in the Economic Generation of Power by the TVA System." American Power Conference. *Proceedings, 1957*. Chicago: Illinois Institute of Technology, 1957.

More Steam Plants for TVA Goals Set by Chief Engineer. *Engineering News-Record*, 24 July 1952.

Ouellette, Edward F. "Character in a Great Engineer." *Character Magazine*, April 1936.

Palo, G. P. "Coal-Handling Design for TVA Steam Plans." American Society of Civil Engineers, *Proceedings, 80*, February 1954.

Palo, G. P., and Weaver, D. B. "TVA's First Nuclear Plant." *Power Engineering*, April 1967.

Parker, T. B. "Allocation of the Tennessee Valley Authority Projects." American Society of Civil Engineers, *Proceedings*, December 1941.

Petersen, H. J. "Shawnee—TVA to AEC." *Power Engineering*, September 1952.

"Progress of the Tennessee Valley Authority." *Engineer*, 3 March 1967.

Snyder, W. M. "Hydrologic Studies by Electronic Computers in TVA." American Society of Civil Engineers, *Proceedings, 86*, February 1960.

Tennessee Valley Authority. *Comparison of Coal-Fired and Nuclear Power Plants for the TVA System.* Chattanooga: June 1966.

———. *Engineering Geology and Mineral Resources of the Tennessee Valley Authority Region*, by E. C. Eckel. Knoxville, Tenn.: June 1934.

———. *Technical Reports:* Concrete Production and Control, Tennessee Valley Authority Projects, 1948. Geology and Foundation Treatment, Tennessee Valley Authority Projects, 1949. Surveying, Mapping and Related Engineering, Tennessee Valley Authority, 1951. Tennessee River Navigation System, 1964. Floods and Flood Control, 1961. Washington, D.C.: GPO.

———. *Influences of Reforestation and Erosion Control Upon the Hydrology of the Pine Tree Branch Watershed 1941 to 1950.* Knoxville, Tenn.: 1955.

———. Tennessee and Cumberland Valley Reservoirs Level Storage Tables and Profile Storage Charts. Knoxville: August 1960.

———. *Water Temperature of Streams and Reservoirs in the Tennessee River Basin.* Knoxville: September 1966.

"Tennessee's High Speed Dam." *Engineering*, 2 December 1966.

"TVA's Giant Generators." *Engineering*, 2 June 1967.

Vogel, Herbert D. "Role of the Civil Engineer in Multipurpose River Development." *Civil Engineering*, July 1956.

Wagner, A. J. "Water Resources Engineering in the Tennessee Valley." *Indian Journal of Power & River Valley Development*, July 1963.

Wiersema, H. A. "Responsibilities of the Engineer Employer." *Civil Engineering*, October 1956.

Woodruff, W. W., et al. *Standard Handbook for Electrical Engineers*, 9th ed. New York: McGraw-Hill, 1957.

Financial Operations

Brown, Richard E. *The GAO, Untapped Source of Congressional Power.* Knoxville: University of Tennessee Press, 1970.

Durisch, L. L., and H. L. Macon. "Payments in Lieu of Taxes by the Tennessee Valley Authority." *Journal of Politics*, August 1941.

Financial Control System of the Tennessee Valley Authority, Rev. ed. Washington, D.C.: American University Press, 1945.

Glaeser, Martin. "Those Joint TVA Costs." *Public Utilities Fortnightly,* 1939.

Jones, Arnold R. "Financing of TVA." In *Law and Contemporary Problems.* Durham, N.C.: Duke University, Autumn 1961.

Kohler, E. L. "Accounting for the TVA." *Accounting Forum,* June 1941.

————. "TVA and Its Power-Accounting Problems." *Accounting Review,* January 1948.

Kull, D. C. *Budget Administration in the Tennessee Valley Authority.* Knoxville, Tenn.: University of Tennessee, 1948.

Neuner, E. J. *Financial and Operating Characteristics of the Municipal and Cooperative Distributors of TVA Power.* Knoxville, Tenn.: University of Tennessee, May 1949.

Parker, T. B. "Allocation of the Tennessee Valley Authority Projects." American Society of Civil Engineers, *Proceedings,* December 1941.

Revenue Bond Financing by TVA. *Hearings* before the Senate Subcommittee of the Committee on Public Works, 86 Cong., 1st Sess. Washington, D.C. GPO 1959.

Selected Financial and Operating Statistics from Annual Reports of Carriers by Water, 1944. Bureau of Transport Economics and Statistics, Washington, D.C.: 1945.

Society for the Advancement of Management. *Financial Control System of the Tennessee Valley Authority,* Rev. ed. Washington, D.C.: American University Press, 1945.

Stekler, Herman. "Critique of TVA Accounting Practices." *Public Utilities Fortnightly,* 27 March 1958.

Tennessee Valley Authority. Budget Staff. *Progress in the Tennessee Valley (1932–1952).* A statement made before the subcommittee to Study Civil Works of the Committee on Public Works, H. 82 Cong., 2nd Sess., Washington, D.C. GPO May 1952.

————. Basic Data on TVA and Its Revenue Bond Financing. Knoxville, Tenn.: 1960.

————. "Investment of the TVA in Wilson, Norris, and Wheeler Projects." H. 75 Cong., Doc. 709, Washington, D.C. GPO 1938.

————. *Municipalities & Cooperatives, Purchasing Power from Tennessee Valley Authority.* Knoxville, Tenn.: 1967.

U.S. Congress. House. Committee on Public Works. TVA Financing. *Hearings,* 85 Cong., 1st Sess., on H.R. 3236 and H.R. 4266. Washington, D.C.: GPO, 1957.

————. TVA *Hearings,* 86th Cong., 1st Sess., on H.R. 3460 and H.R. 3461. 10–11 March 1959. Washington, D.C.: GPO, 1959.

U. S. Congress. Senate. Committee on Public Works. TVA Financing. *Hearings,* 84 Cong., 1st Sess., on S. 2373, a Bill to Amend the

Tennessee Valley Authority Act of 1933. 21, 22, and 27 July, 1955. Washington, D.C.: GPO 1955.

————. Committee on Public Works. Amending the TVA Act. *Hearings*, 85 Cong., 1st Sess., on S. 1855, S. 1869, S. 1986, and S. 2145. Washington, D.C.: GPO, 1957.

————. Committee on Public Works. Revenue Bond Financing by TVA. *Hearings*, 86 Cong., 2nd Sess., on S. 931 and H.R. 3460. 9–10 June 1959. Washington, D.C.: GPO, 1959.

————. Committee on Public Works. Revenue Bond Financing by the TVA. *Hearings*, 89 Cong., 2nd Sess., on H.R. 15225, S. 3419, and S. 2827, to Increase the Borrowing Authority of the TVA. 28 June 1966. Washington,D.C.: GPO, 1966.

U.S. Federal Power Commission. Report on Review of Allocations of Costs of the Multiple-Purpose Water Control System in the Tennessee River Basin, as Determined by the TVA and Approved by the President Under the Provisions of the TVA Act of 1933 as Amended. Washington, D.C.: FPC, 23 March 1949.

Vogel, H. D. "Is TVA's Allocation of Costs Fair?" *Public Utilities Fortnightly*, 9 June 1955.

Wallace, R. L. "Cost and Revenue Associated with Increased Sales of TVA Power." *Southern Economic Journal*, April 1967.

Flood Prevention

Barrows, H. K. *Floods, Their Hydrology and Control*. New York: McGraw-Hill, 1948.

Bowden, N. W. "Multiple-Purpose Reservoirs; General Problems of Design and Operation." American Society of Civil Engineers, *Proceedings*, March 1949.

Cooper, A. J. "Water-Flow Data Keep Hydro Plants Efficient." *Electrical World*, 20 March 1967.

Dunham, Allison. "Flood Control Via the Public Power." *University of Pennsylvania Law Review*, June 1939.

Elliot, R. A. "Navigation, Flood Control Power—TVA Develops Its Rivers," *Civil Engineering*, January 1957.

————. "TVA Water Control System Pays More Dividends in the Great Flood of 1957." *Tennessee Valley Engineer*, June 1957.

Elliott, Reed A., and LeRoy Engstrom. "Controlling Floods on the Tennessee," *Civil Engineering*, June 1959.

Goddard, J. E. "Considerations in Preserving Reservoir Sites." *Proceedings, 91*, American Society of Civil Engineers, January 1965.

————. "Flood Damage Prevention in the Tennessee Valley." *Military Engineer*, March–April 1960.

————. "Flood Plain Management Improves Man's Environment." *Proceedings, 90*, American Society of Civil Engineers, November 1964.

————. "Flood Proofing and Flood Damage Prevention." *Tennessee Town and City*, February 1961.

————. "Floods and How to Avoid Them." *Industrial Development*, July 1958.

Gray, A. J. "Communities and Floods," *National Civic Review*, March 1961.

Hibdon, J. E. "Flood Control Benefits and the Tennessee Valley Authority," *Southern Economic Journal*, July 1958.

Moore, J. A. *Planning for Flood Damage Prevention.* Atlanta: Georgia Institute of Technology, June 1958.

Morse, H. F. *Role of the States in Guiding Land Use in Flood Plains.* Atlanta: Georgia Institute of Technology, 1962.

Rutter, E. J. "Flood-Control Operation of Tennessee Valley Authority Reservoirs." *Proceedings, 76,* American Society of Civil Engineers, May 1950.

Sheaffer, J. R. *Introduction to Flood Proofing; an Outline of Principles and Methods.* Chicago: University of Chicago, April 1967.

Tennessee Valley Authority. Chattanooga Flood Control Problem. 76 Cong., H. Doc. No. 91. Washington, D. C.: GPO 9 January 1939.

————. *Floods and Flood Control.* Knoxville, Tenn.: 1961.

————. *Program for Reducing the National Flood Damage Potential.* Committee on Public Works, Senate 85 Cong., 1st Sess., Washington, D.C.: GPO, 1959.

————. *Report to the Congress on the Unified Development of the Tennessee River System.* Knoxville,: Tenn. 1936.

————. Value of Flood Height Reduction from TVA Reservoirs to the Alluvial Valley of the Lower Mississippi River. 76 Cong., H. Doc. 455. Washington, D.C.: GPO, 1939.

U. S. President's Water Resources Policy Commission. "The Tennessee River Basin." Washington, D.C.: GPO, 1950.

Vogel, H. D. "Reasoning Behind the Tennessee Valley Authority's New Concept of Avoiding Flood." *Waterways Journal,* 18 April 1959.

Weathers, J. W. "Comprehensive Flood Damage Prevention." *Proceedings, 91,* American Society of Civil Engineers, January 1965.

Forestry and Wildlife

Artman, J. O. "Forest Development in the Tennessee Valley." *Unasylva,* October–December 1951.

————. "Tennessee Valley Forests." Norris, Tenn.: Tennessee Division of Forestry Relations, 1950.

Baker, William M. "TVA Approach to Forest Development." Durham, N.C.: Duke University, School of Forestry Lectures, No. 6, June 1946.

Boardman, D. S. "The 300-Board-Footers." *Forest Farmer*, February 1963.

Chase, S. B. "New Tree Crops in the Tennessee Valley." *Southern Lumberman*, 15 December 1947.

Clapp, G. R. "Our Forests and the Future of the Tennessee Valley." *Journal of Forestry*, May 1947.

————. "Valley of Faith and Works." *American Forests*, November 1948.

Collins, Chapin. "Selling Forestry to the Farmer." *American Forests*, January 1948.

Coufal, J. E. "Logging in Municipal Watershed." *Journal of Soil and Water Conservation*, March–April 1965.

Gulick, L. H. *American Forest Policy, A Study of Government Administration and Economic Control*. New York: Duell, Sloan and Pearce, 1951.

Kline, L. V. "Tree Crops for the Tennessee Valley." American Forestry Association, Washington, D.C.: October 1941

Lehman, J. W., and R. A. Vogenberger. "Role of a Regional Agency in Forest Fire Control." *Journal of Forestry*, June 1955.

Schnell, R. L. "Harvesting Costs for Hardwood Pulpwood in the Tennessee Valley." *Pulpwood Production and Sawmill Logging*, February 1964.

————. "Pulpwood Marketing Trends in the Tennessee Valley." *Pulpwood Production and Sawmill Logging*, November 1963.

Seigworth, K. J. "Reforestation in the Tennessee Valley." *Public Administration Review*, Autumn, 1948.

Smith, F. E. "What TVA is Doing to Foster Forestry Development." *Forest Farmer*, July 1964.

Taft, K. A. "TVA at Work—Better Hardwood for the Future." *American Forests*, January 1965.

Tennessee Valley Authority. "Forest Resources and Industries in the Tennessee Valley." Norris, Tenn.: 1967.

————. "A Forest Restored, an Industry Expanded, Twenty Years of Progress on the Hassell and Hughes Lumber Company Forest Management Demonstration." Norris, Tenn.: 1964.

————. "Furniture Industry Expansion in the Tennessee Valley." Norris, Tenn.: 1963.

————. "Hardwood Logging Methods and Costs in the Tennessee Valley." Norris, Tenn.: 1960.

————. "Hardwood Utilization Centers, Their Potential for the Tennessee Valley." Norris, Tenn.: 1964.

————. "Hickory—Wood with a Future." Norris, Tenn.: 1964.

———. *Influence of Woodland and Owner Characteristics on Forest Management.* Norris, Tenn.: 1956.

———. "Inventory Forest Properties; Suggested Standard Procedure and Specifications for Use in the Tennessee Valley." Norris, Tenn.: May 1956.

———. "Managed Forests Create Industrial Opportunity." Norris, Tenn.: 1965.

———. "North Georgia Forest Industry Outlook." Norris, Tenn.: 1966.

———. "Private Forest Management Trends in the Tennessee Valley." Norris, Tenn.: 1961.

———. "Public Building Furniture—Expansion Prospects in the Tennessee Valley." Norris, Tenn.: 1967.

———. "Reclaiming a Strip Mine in Morgan County, Tennessee. In Cooperation with Owners." Norris, Tenn.: 1963.

———. "A Report on 85,700 Forest Plantations in the Tennessee Valley." Norris, Tenn.: 1962.

———. *Reforestation and Erosion Control Influences Upon the Hydrology of the Pine Tree Branch Watershed, 1941 to 1960.* Knoxville, Tenn.: 1962.

———. "Tennessee River Mussel Investigation, a Progress Report." Norris, Tenn.: 1965.

———. "Thank you, Mr. Treeplanter." Norris, Tenn.: 1964.

———. "TVA and Forestry." Norris, Tenn.: 1967.

———. "Why Invest in Forest Land? Some Forest Owners Give Their Answers." Norris, Tenn.: 1962.

Wiesehuegel, E. G. "Forest Research in the Tennessee Valley." *Southern Lumberman,* 15 January 1953.

———. "Forest Tree Improvement Progress in Tennessee." *Southern Lumberman,* 1 June 1956.

———. "Studies Relating to Soil and Water Resources." *Alabama Academy of Science Journal,* December 1953.

Governmental Relationships

Chase, Stuart. "TVA: The New Deal's Best Asset." *Nation,* 10 June 1936.

Clapp, G. R. "Public Administration in an Advancing South." *Public Administration Review,* Summer 1948.

Durisch, L. L. "States and Decentralized Administration of Federal Functions." *Journal of Politics,* February 1950.

Greene, L. S., and G. S. Parthemos. Tennessee Valley Authority. In *American Government, Policies and Functions.* New York: Scribners, 1967.

Hunger, M. F. "U.S. Coast Guard on the Tennessee River." *Tennessee River Journal,* September 1944.

Johnson, H. B. "Federal-State-Local Cooperation: the Tennessee Valley." *State Government,* October 1948.

Leuchtenburg, W. E. "Roosevelt, Norris and the Seven Little TVA's." *Journal of Politics,* 1952.

Lilienthal, David E.: The Partnership of Federal Government and Local Communities in the Tennessee Valley: "A Study of Grass-Roots Democracy in Action." Address to Decatur Chamber of Commerce, 30 July 1942. TVA, Knoxville, Tenn. Mimeo.

Macon, H. L. Payments in Lieu of Taxes by the Tennessee Valley Authority. In National Tax Association, *Proceedings,* 1943.

Merton, Robert K., Ed. *Reader in Bureaucracy.* Glencoe, Ill.: The Free Press, 1951.

Mitrany, D. "The New Deal." *Agenda,* Vol. 1, 1942.

Ray, J. M. "Influence of the Tennessee Valley Authority on Government in the South." *American Political Science Review,* October 1949.

Roberts, Elliott. *One River-Seven States. TVA-State Relations in the Development of the Tennessee River.* Knoxville: University of Tennessee, June 1955.

Satterfield, M. H. "TVA-State-Local Relationships." *American Political Science Review,* October 1946.

Shelton, B. C. "TVA: Partner of the People." *Progressive,* May 1958.

Stephenson, Gordon. "Report on the Tennessee Valley Authority." City Planning Administration, Massachusetts Institute of Technology, Cambridge; 1938. Typescript.

Tennessee Valley Authority. *Manufacturing Structure and Change in the Tennessee Valley Region.* Knoxville: November 1964.

———. *Manufacturing Employment in the Tennessee Valley Region.* Knoxville: October 1961.

———. "The Tennessee Valley Region: Important Features and Recent Trends." Knoxville: November 1956.

"Truth About TVA and Taxes." *Public Power,* June 1957.

Tugwell, R. G. and E. C. Banfield. "Grass-Roots Democracy—Myth or Reality?" *Public Administration Review,* Winter 1950.

Wilbur, Ray L. and Arthur M. Hyde. *The Hoover Policies.* New York: Scribners, 1937.

Willbern, York. *Cities and Riverfront Lands.* University, Ala.: University of Alabama Bureau of Public Administration, 1947.

Health and Safety

Bishop, E. L. "Health and Safety Services of the Tennessee Valley Authority." *Public Personnel Review*, January 1943.

————. "The Coordination of Health Programs of a Regional Agency," Paper presented before the Industrial Hygiene, Engineering, and Public Health Nursing Sections of TVA, 11 November 1942.

Bishop, E. L., and E. Harold Hinman. "Malaria Control Trends on Impounded Waters of the Tennessee Valley." *National Malaria Society Journal*, March 1948.

Childress, W. H. *Experience of TVA in Cooperative Health Work*, unpublished, University of Syracuse.

Christopher, G. S., and N. W. Bowden. "Mosquito Control in Reservoirs by Water Level Management." *Mosquito News*, December 1957.

Churchill, M. A. "Effects of Storage Impoundments on Water Quality." *Transactions*, American Society of Civil Engineers, 1958.

Churchill, M. A., H. L. Elmore, and R. A. Buckingham. "Prediction of Stream Reaeration Rates." *Proceedings 88*, American Society of Civil Engineers, July 1962.

Churchill, M. A., and W. R. Nicholas. "Effects of Impoundments on Water Quality." *Proceedings 93*, American Society of Civil Engineers, December 1967.

Clark, R. N. "Stream Sanitation in the Tennessee Valley." *Proceedings*, American Society of Civil Engineers, November 1949.

Derryberry, O. M. "Health Conservation Activities of TVA." *Public Health Reports*, March 1953.

Derryberry, O. M., and Gartrell, F. E. "Trends in Malaria Control Program of the Tennessee Valley Authority." *American Journal of Tropical Medicine and Hygiene*, May 1952.

Derryberry, O. M.; Kochtitzky, O. W.; and Stone, G. F. "Radiological Health Program for an Experimental Power Reactor." *Health Physics*, 1964.

Garner, J. M., Jr., and Kochtitzky, O. W. "Radioactive Sediments in the Tennessee River System." *Proceedings 82*, American Society of Civil Engineers, August 1956.

Gartrell, Francis E. "Malaria Control in the Tennessee Valley." *Industry and Tropical Health*, October 1951.

Gartrell, F. E., and J. C. Barber. "Pollution Control Interrelationships." *Chemical Engineering Progress*, October 1966.

Kiker, C. C. "Management of Water to Control Anopheline Mosquito Breeding." Fourth International Congress of Tropical Medicine and Malaria, 10–18 May, 1948. Washington, D.C.: GPO, 1948.

Nolting, D. E. "Safety Is Part of TVA Plans." *National Safety News*, May 1958.

Smith, G. E.; Hall, T. F. Jr.; and Stanley, R. A. "Eurasian Watermil-foil in the Tennessee Valley." *Weeds,* April 1967.

Snow, W. E. "Production and Control of Floodwater Mosquitoes Incidental to Water Level Operations of Reservoirs of the Tennes-see Valley Authority." *Proceedings,* Tenth International Con-gress of Entomology, 1956.

Stromquist, W. G. "Stream Pollution Problems of the Tennessee Valley." *Paper Trade Journal,* 25 May 1944.

Tennessee Valley Authority. "Health and Safety, TVA." Knoxville, Tenn.: 1967.

———. "Malaria Control in the Tennessee Valley," Chattanooga, Tenn.: September 1960.

———. "Stream Sanitation in the Tennessee Valley," Chattanooga, Tenn.: December 1952.

Thomas, F. W. "TVA Air Pollution Studies Program." *Air Repair,* August 1954.

Thomas, F. W.; Carpenter, S. B.; and Gartrell, F. E. "Stacks—How High?" *Air Pollution Control Association, Journal,* May 1963.

U.S. Public Health Service. *Malaria Control on Impounded Water,* by the Public Health Service and TVA, Washington, D.C.: GPO, 1947.

Wiley, J. S. and Kochtitzky, O. W. "Composting Developments in the United States." *Compost Science,* Summer 1965.

Industrial Economics

Curtis, H. A. "Electroprocess Plants in the TVA Power Service Area." *Electrochemical Society. Journal,* May 1954.

Friedmann, John R. P. "Industrial Opportunities on the Tennessee River," a study of water-front sites and industrial use of the Tennessee River, Knoxville, Tenn.: TVA, 1954.

Herring, H. L. *Southern Industry and Regional Development.* New York: Oxford University Press, 1941.

Lancaster, John L. *County Income Estimates for the Seven Southeast-ern States.* Charlottesville: University of Virginia, 1952.

Robock, S. H. "Industrialization and Economic Progress in the South-east." *Southern Economic Journal,* April 1954.

———. "The Negro in the Industrial Development of the South." *Phylon,* Third Quarter, 1953.

———. "Regional Markets and Industrial Development," Athens: University of Georgia, June 1950.

———. "Rural Industries and Agricultural Development." *Journal of Farm Economics,* August 1952.

Robock, S. H., and J. M. Peterson. "Fact and Fiction About Southern Labor." *Harvard Business Review,* March–April 1954.

Simon, Sir Ernest. "The Tennessee Valley Authority." Manchester, England; 1943.

Smith, F. E. "Water Route to Economic Progress." *Trinity Valley Progress*, March–April 1964.

Stephenson, C. M. "Local Government Improvement to Aid Industrial Development." *Tennessee Town and City*, January 1963.

Land Acquisition

Conover, H. S. *Grounds Maintenance Handbook*, 2nd ed. New York: F. W. Dodge Corp., 1958.

Graves, O. H. "TVA Land Planning: Landscape Architecture in a Resource Development Agency." *Landscape Architecture*, July 1953.

Hackett, Brian. "TVA" Creator of Landscape." *Journal of The Town Planning Institute*, November 1950.

Knetsch, J. L., and C. J. Parrott. "Estimating the Influence of Large Reservoirs on Land Values." *Appraisal Journal*, October 1964.

McCarthy, C. J. "Land Acquisition Policies and Proceedings in TVA—A Study of the Role of Land Acquisition in a Regional Agency." *Ohio Law Journal*, Winter 1949.

Snyder, John I. *TVA's Land Buying Program*. Knoxville, Tenn.: TVA, February 1946.

White, L. C., and Murray, J. L. "TVA Condemnation Practice Under the Federal Rules." *Tennessee Law Review*, April 1952.

Land Reclamation

Conover, H. S. "Improvement and Maintenance Techniques at TVA Dams." *Landscape Architecture*, January 1949.

Greene, Lee S., *Rescued Earth*. Knoxville, Tenn.: University of Tennessee, Bureau of Public Administration, 1948.

Greene, Lee S., and Williamson, Rene D. eds. *Resources and Policy: Current Issues in Conservation*. Gainesville, Fla.: Kollman, 1951.

"Tapping U.S. Knowhow to Reclaim Wasteland." *Business Week*, 8 November 1952.

Legal Aspects

Arrow Transportation Company, et al. v. U.S. of America and Interstate Commerce Commission, et al. Civil Action No. 961 (Northern District of Alabama, 1959).

Ashwander et al. v. Tennessee Valley Authority. 9 Federal Supplement, 965 (Northern District of Alabama, 1935).

Clapp, G. R. "TVA, A Democratic Method for the Development of a Region's Resources." *Vanderbilt Law Review*, February 1948.

Opinion of the Supreme Court of the United States . . . in the case of George Ashwander et. al., Petitioners, vs. Tennessee Valley Authority, etc. 74 Cong., 2nd Sess., *Document No. 176*, GPO, 1936.

Pritchett, C. Herman. "The Transplantability of TVA." *Iowa Law Review*, January 1947.

Publications, United States Congress, general, *Congressional Directory*, 66 Cong., through 72 Cong. (1918–1933); *Congressional Record*, 66 Cong. through 72 Cong. (1918–1933); and *United States Statutes at Large*, XXXIX (1915–1917), XLI (1919–1921).

Swidler, J. C. "Legal Foundations." In *TVA: the First Twenty Years*, Ed. Roscoe C. Martin. University, Ala.: University of Alabama Press; Knoxville, Tenn.: University of Tennessee Press, 1956.

Swidler, Joseph C., and Robert H. Marquis. "TVA in Court: A Study of TVA's Constitutional Litigation," *Iowa Law Review*, January 1947.

Tennessee Electric Power Companies v. Tennessee Valley Authority. 21 Federal Supplement 845 Eastern District of Tennessee, 1938; "Transcript of Record" Washington, D.C.: Judd and Detweiler, Printers, 1938.

Local Planning

Cole, W. E. "What's Ahead for our Communities?" *Tennessee Planner*, April–June 1960.

Durisch, L. L. "Southern Regional Planning and Development." *Journal of Politics*, February 1964.

Gober, J. L. "Federalism at Work." *National Civic Review*, May 1967.

Gray, A. J. "Planning for Local Flood Damage Prevention." *American Institute of Planners Journal*, Winter 1956.

Lepawsky, Albert. *State Planning and Economic Development in the South*. Washington, D.C.: National Planning Association, 1949.

Menhinisk, H. K., and Durisch, L. L. "Tennessee Valley Authority: Planning in Operation." *Town Planning Review*, July 1953.

Tennessee. State Planning Commission. *Local Planning in Tennessee*, 1956–57. Nashville, Tenn.: 1957.

————. *Reservoir Shore Line Development in Tennessee; a Study of Problems and Opportunities*. Prepared by Walter L. Criley, Nashville, Tenn.: 1958.

Wagner, A. J. "Natural Resources—A Challenge for Planning." *Tennessee Planner*, March 1965.

Weber, Dickson. "Tennessee River Gorge Study—An Evaluation." *Tennessee Planner*, September 1961.

Navigation and Transportation

A History of Navigation on the Tennessee River System, House Doc. 254, 75 Cong., 1st Sess., 1937. Washington, D.C. GPO.

Barker, C. T. "Barge Delivery of Coal to TVA Steam Plants." *Waterways,* January 1953.

————. "Navigation on the Tennessee River." *Engineering News-Record,* Part I, 21 February 1946; Part II, 7 March 1946.

————. "Developments in Tennessee River Navigation." *Waterways,* July and August 1953.

Droze, W. H. *High Dams and Slack Waters.* Baton Rouge: Louisiana: State University Press, 1965.

Evans, P. L. "Cruising the Inland Waterways; The Tennessee River Valley—Paducah to Knoxville." Chicago: *Great Lakes Cruising Club,* 1965.

Inland Waterways: Facts and Figures. Washington, D.C.: American Waterways Operators, 1950.

Joubert, W. H. "Tennessee River—A New Frontier in Navigation." *Transport and Communications Review,* July–September 1951.

Lilienthal, D. E. "Navigation on the Tennessee River: Its Effect Upon the Economic Future of the South," speech before Southern Economic Association, Knoxville, 5 November 1937.

————. "Tennessee River Provides Big Trade Vein." *Tennessee River Journal,* May 1944.

Locher, H. O., Ed. *Waterways of the United States: Rivers, Harbors, Lakes, Canals.* 2nd ed. New York: National Association of River and Harbor Contractors, 1963.

Menhinick, H. K. "Local Riverfront Development." *American City,* November 1950.

Morgan, Charles S. *Problems in the Regulation of Domestic Transportation by Water.* ICC Ex Parte No. 165, Washington, D.C.: 1946.

New Dimensions in Transportation. Washington, D.C.: American Waterways Operators, 1956.

Nichols, R. B. "How a Waterway Improvement Changed Environment." *Proceedings, 89,* American Society of Civil Engineers, November 1963.

Pope, James P. "The Tennessee Waterway Moves On," speech before Chattanooga Kiwanis Club, 30 June 1942.

Shaub, E. L. "Navigation on Tennessee River Enriches Valley." *Tennessee Conservationist,* August 1958.

Smith, F. E. "What River Shipping Means to a Region's Growth," *Waterways Journal,* 1 July 1967.

Taylor, C. T. "Transportation on the Tennessee." *Federal Reserve Bank of Atlanta, Monthly Review,* 28 February 1949.

Taylor, J. P. "Navigation: A Tool in Industrial Development," speech before the Tennessee Valley Public Power Association, Nashville, 17 April 1958.

Tennessee Valley Authority. *History of Navigation on the Tennessee River System; an Interpretation of the Economic Influence of This River System on the Tennessee Valley.* Washington, D.C.: GPO, 1937.

———. *Major Freight Terminals on the Tennessee River Waterway.* Knoxville, Tenn.: 1963.

———. *Navigation and Economic Growth: Tennessee River Experience.* Knoxville, Tenn.: 1966.

———. *Tennessee River Navigation System. History, Development and Operation.* Knoxville, Tenn.: 1964

———. *The Barge Grain Case—Its Significance to the Tennessee Valley and the Southeast.* Knoxville, Tenn.: November, 1951.

Waterborne Commerce of the United States, Parts 2 and 5, Board of Engineers for Rivers and Harbors. Washington, D.C.: 1954–1957.

Waterside Site Plant Locations and Expansions Since 1952. 2nd ed. Washington, D.C.: March 1962.

Wright, D. T. "Paducah to Knoxville on the Tennessee River." *Waterways Journal,* 24 April 1954.

Personnel Administration

Angle, Carl. "How TVA Built Its Data Computing Center." *The Office,* November 1958.

Avery, R. S. *Experiment in Management; Personnel Decentralization in the Tennessee Valley Authority.* Knoxville: University of Tennessee Press, 1954.

Case, H. L. "Cornerstones of Personnel Administration in TVA." *Personnel Administration,* January 1949.

———. *Personnel Policy in a Public Agency: the TVA Experience.* New York: Harper & Bros. 1955.

———. "Wage Negotiations in the Tennessee Valley Authority." *Public Personnel Review,* July 1947.

Chase, Stuart. *Roads to Agreement.* New York: Harper & Bros., 1951.

Clapp, G. R. "Problems of Union Relations in Public Agencies." *American Economic Review,* March 1943.

———. *TVA; an Approach to the Development of a Region.* Chicago, Ill.: University of Chicago Press, 1955.

———. "The Rule of Three, It Puzzles Me." *Public Administration Review,* Spring 1941.

Dodd, Thelma. "Teamwork Approach to Productivity," *Personnel Administration,* January 1952.

Duke, C. A. and H. B. Cummings, Jr. "How TVA Trains Its Engineers," *Electrical World* 22 October 1951.

Fredriksen, C. W., and Helmer Martinson. "Helping Supervisors Train Themselves in Human Relations; a Cast Study," *Personnel,* January 1955.

Given, William B., Jr. "Reaching Out in Management." *Harvard Business Review,* March–April 1952.

Godine, Morton Robert. *Labor Problem in the Public Service; A Study in Political Pluralism.* Cambridge, Mass.: Harvard University Press, 1951.

Gregory, B. F. "Authority vs. Competence." *The Office,* April 1955.

———. "Developing a Filing System." *Records Management Journal,* Autumn 1963.

———. "Growing Pains of a Record Management Program." *American Archivist,* Jan. 1956.

———. "TVA's 25 Years on Records Management." *The Office,* May–June, 1958.

Kampelman, M. M. "TVA Labor Relations: A Laboratory in Democratic Human Relations." *Minnesota Law Review,* April 1946.

King, Judson. *TVA Labor Relations Policy at Work; Successful Cooperation Between Public Power and Organized Labor in the Public Interest,* Rev ed. Washington, D.C.: National Popular Government League, 19 April 1940.

Libby, C. O. "Have You a Modern Office?" *The Office,* July 1951.

———. "Paper Tells Your Story." *Office Management and Equipment,* February and April 1953.

———. "What Is Records Management?" *Office Economist.* March–April 1953.

McGlothlin, W. J. "Apprentice Program of TVA." *Personnel Administration,* April 1946.

———. "Union-Management Administration of Employee Training: The Experience of TVA." *Advanced Management,* April–June 1943.

Massey, J. E. "What are the Prospects and Problems of Management-Employee Cooperation in the Federal Service." *Personnel Administration,* January–February 1963.

———. "Labor-Management Cooperation in TVA." *Public Personnel Review,* July 1965.

Mitchell, J. P. "TVA Apprenticeship Program." *Power,* November 1960.

Patchen, Martin. "Labor-Management Consultation at TVA: Its Impact on Employees." *Administrative Science Quarterly,* September 1965

Pritchett, Charles Herman. *The Tennessee Valley Authority, A Study in Public Administration*. Chapel Hill: University of North Carolina Press, 1943.

Pritchett, C. H. "Lessons of the TVA Power Program." *Public Affairs*, Winter 1946.

Raushenbush, Stephen. *High Power Propaganda*. New York: New Republic, 1928.

——. *The Power Fight*. New York: New Republic, 1932.

——. "Electricity in Dairying." Chattanooga, Tenn.: no date.

——. Electricity Sales Statistics, Monthly Reports. Chattanooga, Tenn.: 1935 to present.

——. *Fire Protection Manual*. Chattanooga: 1963.

Schneider, J. D. "Collective-Bargaining in the Field of Job Classification." *Personnel*, July 1953.

Schultz, E. B. "Selective Retirement and Preretirement Counseling in the TVA." *Industrial and Labor Relations Review*, January 1959.

Tennessee Valley Authority. *Comparison of Coal-Fired and Nuclear Power Plants for the TVA System*. Chattanooga: June 1966.

Tennessee Valley Authority. *Effectiveness of Apprentice Training in TVA*. Knoxville: Tenn.: December 1951.

——. *Records Administration in TVA*. Rev. ed. Chattanooga, Tenn.: October 1964.

Thompson, A. A. "Collective Bargaining in the Public Service—The TVA Experience and Its Implications for Other Government Agencies," *Labor Law Journal*, February 1966.

——. "Employee Participation in Decision Making: the TVA Experience," *Public Personnel Review*, April 1967.

Thompson, A. A., and Irwin Weinstock. "White-Collar Employees and the Unions at TVA," *Personnel Journal*, January 1967.

Van Mol, L. J. "Collective Bargaining in the Public Service: Theory and Practice," Chicago: *Public Personnel Association*, 1967.

——. "Effective Procedures for the Handling of Employee Grievances," Chicago: *Civil Service Assembly*, 1953.

Warner, K. O., Ed. *Development in Public Employee Relations: Legislative, Judicial, Administrative*. Chicago: Public Personnel Association, 1965.

Weinstock, Irwin, and A. A. Thompson. "Administrative Sensitivity to Economic Needs of Employees: Some Distorting Mechanisms," *Academy of Management Journal*, March 1967.

Williamson, M. W. "TVA and the TVA Engineers Association." *Engineers and Scientists of America, News Digest*, February 1954.

Young, C. H., and Martinson, H. M. "TVA's Training Program for Chemical Plant Operations," *Chemical and Engineering News*, 10 February, 1945.

Power

Bauer, John, and Costello, Peter. *Public Ownership of Electric Power: Conditions, Policies and Program.* New York: Harper and Bros., 1949.

Brudenell, R. N. and Gilbreath, J. H. "Economic Complementary Operation of Hydro Storage and Steam Power in the Integrated TVA System." *American Institute of Electrical Engineers, Transactions*, Vol. 78, Part 3A, 1959.

————. "How TVA Coordinates Use of Hydro and Steam Generation," *Electric Light and Power*, June 1962.

Clapp, G. R. "On Whose Side of the Bus Bar?—The Experience of the Tennessee Valley Authority." *American Public Power Association, Proceedings*, 1947.

————. "TVA—A National Asset," *American Public Power Association, Proceedings*, 1951.

Dupree, W. G. and West, J. A. *United States Energy Through the Year 2000.* U.S. Department of the Interior, 1972.

Freeman, R. M. "Regional and River Valley Public Power Development." *Nebraska Law Review*, March 1951.

Glaeser, M. G. *Utilities in American Capitalism.* New York: Macmillan, 1957.

Haffley, S. S. "Load Building in the Tennessee Valley: Why and How," *American Public Power Association, Proceedings*, 1964.

Hill, E. C. "Tennessee Valley Authority . . . Coal Industry's Largest Customer." *Coal-Today and Tomorrow*, January 1965.

Krug, J.A. "Testimony of the TVA Power Program." Joint Committee on the Investigation of the Tennessee Valley Authority. *Hearings*, 75 Cong., GPO, 1939.

Lilienthal, D. E. "The Yardstick in Action," Address to American Historical Association and American Political Science Association, 29 December 1935. Knoxville, Tenn.: TVA, 1936.

McKinley, Charles. *Uncle Sam in the Pacific Northwest.* Berkeley: University of California Press, 1952.

McWhorter, Jr., A. D., and H. S. Gangwer. "Computer Develops Design Data for Distribution System Planning." *Electrical World*, 28 January 1963.

Martin, B.H. "Space Heating Stimulates Electric Consumption." *Electrical World*, 5 December 1960.

Mitchell, J. P. "TVA Apprenticeship Program," *Power*, November 1960.

"More Power for Bomber Production." *Engineering News-Record*, 26 February 1942.

New, W. R. "Electric Heating in the Tennessee Valley—A Pattern for the Future." *Proceedings*, American Power Conference, 1957. Chicago: Illinois Institute of Technology, 1957.

———. "Financial Effect of Heating Load on Utility System." *Proceedings,* American Public Power Association, 1960. Washington, D.C.: 1960.

———. "Three Decades of Electrical Heating." *Public Power,* October 1966.

New, W. R., and Bell, W. A., Jr. "Serving the All-Electric Home." *Electrical World,* 19 March 1956.

Northeast Power Failure, Nov. 9–10, 1965. A report to the President, 10 December 1965, by the Federal Power Commission.

Pinchot, Gifford. *The Power Monopoly: Its Make-Up and Its Menace.* Milford, Pa.: 1928.

Pritchett, C. H. "Lessons of the TVA Power Program." *Public Affairs,* Winter 1946.

"The Proposed Power Pool." *Nation,* 5 December 1936.

Raushenbush, Stephen. *High Power Propaganda.* New York: New Republic, 1928.

———. *The Power Fight.* New York: New Republic, 1932.

Tennessee Valley Authority. *Comparison of Coal-Fired and Nuclear Power Plants for the TVA System.* Chattanooga: June 1966.

———. Electricity Sales Statistics, Monthly Reports. Chattanooga: 1935 to present.

"Fire Protection Manual." Chattanooga: 1963.

———. "TVA Power—1952," Knoxville, Tenn.: 1952

———. "TVA's Influence on Electric Rates." Knoxville, Tenn.: 1965.

Tennessee Valley Public Power Association. "All-Electric Schools . . . in the Tennessee Valley," Special Report on the Growing Use of Electricity in Modern Schools. 3rd ed. Chattanooga: TVA, 1966.

U.S. Atomic Energy Commission. 1971. *Forecast of Growth of Nuclear Power* Washington, D.C.

U.S. Department of the Interior, 1972. "United States Energy: a Summary Review." (The energy outlook to 1985).

Vogel, H. D. "Some Operational Aspects of the TVA's Large Integrated Power System." *Proceedings,* American Power Conference. Chicago: Illinois Institute of Technology, 1956.

Wagner, A. J. "Power Tale of Two Cities." *Public Power,* February 1962.

———. "Public Power: In the American Tradition," *Public Power,* August 1964.

Wessenauer, G. O. "Necessity for a Load Building Program." *Proceedings,* American Public Power Association, 1959.

———. "Story of TVA—Multipurpose Development," *Power Engineering,* February 1963.

———. "What of Your Future?" *Public Power,* March 1964.

Recreation

Cohen, M. L. "L-B-L; An Accessible Wilderness." *Boating,* June 1966.

"Conservation Education Center Is Big Land Between Lakes Attraction." *Tennessee Conservationist,* April 1967.

Eschmeyer, R. W. "Facts of Fish Conservation." *Tennessee Conservationist,* May–June 1947.

————. *Fish and Fishing in TVA Impoundments.* Nashville, Tenn.: Department of Conservation, 1950.

Eschmeyer, R. W.; Manges, D. E.; and Hasbauer, O. F. "Fishing Management Methods—Reservoirs." *Fisherman's Encyclopedia.* Edited by Ira N. Gabrielson. New York: Stackpole and Heck, 1950.

Eschmeyer, R. W., and Tarzwell, C. M. "An Analysis of Fishing in the TVA Impoundments during 1939. *Wildlife Management,* Vol. r (1), 1941.

Evans, P. L. "TVA Lakes . . . A 'Stairway' of Trees, Water and Fish." *Southern Living,* April 1966.

Howes, R. M. "Land Between the Lakes—Vast Recreation Project." *Journal of Soil and Water Conservation,* November–December, 1964.

Kraft, Virginia. "Discovery: the Tennessee Valley." *Sports Illustrated,* 7 July 1958.

Laycock, George. "Land Between the Lakes." *Field & Stream,* March 1965.

Lesure, T. B. "Thriving Vacation Area." *Travel,* September 1952.

Morgan, H. V. "Parks, Recreation and Open Space." *Tennessee Planner,* December 1962.

Morriss, Mack. "New Holiday Motor Tour—Asheville-TVA-Chattanooga." *Holiday,* July 1958.

Nixon, H. Clarence. *The Tennessee Valley, A Recreation Domain.* Nashville, Tenn.: Vanderbilt University Press, June 1945.

Recreation Potentialities of the Tennessee River Lakes. TVA, 1941.

Simpich, Frederick. "Around the 'Great Lakes of the South.' " *National Geographic Magazine,* April 1948.

Tennessee Valley Authority. "Fish and Wildlife in the Tennessee Valley." Norris, Tenn.: 1950.

————. "Fish and Wildlife, Valuable Natural Resources." Norris, Tenn.: 1963–1964.

————. *Outdoor Recreation for a Growing Nation; TVA's Experience with Man-Made Reservoirs.* Knoxville, Tenn.: 1961.

————. *Recreation Development of the Tennessee River System,* 76 Cong., *H. Doc. No. 565,* Washington, D.C.: GPO, 1940.

————. *Scenic Resources of the Tennessee Valley; a Descriptive and Pictorial Inventory.* Washington, D.C.: GPO, 1938.

————. "The Land Between the Lakes; A Demonstration in Recreation Resource Development. Revised Concept Statement." Knoxville, Tenn.: April 1964.

Wagner, A. J. "Water: The Riddle and the Answer." *Trends in Parks and Recreation*, January 1966.

Wolf, Bill. "These Southerners Just Love Yankees." *Saturday Evening Post*, 5 September, 1953.

Social Impact

Brown, Ralph G. "Family Removal in the Tennessee Valley," thesis submitted to the Committee on Graduate Study, University of Tennessee, May, 1951.

Cole, W. E. "Impact of TVA Upon the Southeast." *Social Forces*, May 1950.

————. "Urban Development in the Tennessee Valley." *Social Forces*, 1947.

"A Contemptible Effort to Arouse Hatred in New England to the South." *Manufacturers' Record*, 2 September, 1926.

de Castro, Josue. *The Geography of Hunger*. Boston: Little Brown, 1952.

Dolson, Hildegard. "Meet a TVA Family." *Ladies Home Journal*, June 1948.

Hayes, Wayland J. "Planning Process in Tennessee Valley Communities." In *The Small Community Looks Ahead*. New York: Harcourt, Brace, 1947.

Hymans, Edward. *Soil and Civilization*. London: Thames and Hudson, 1952.

Leonard, F. H., and Dobbins, W. O. "Community Planning in North Alabama." *Public Administration Review*, Summer 1944.

Lewin, Kurt. *Field Theory in Social Sciences*. New York: Harper & Bros., 1951.

Lilienthal, D. E., and Clapp, G. R. "Progress in Regional Planning in the U.S.A." In Eighth International Congress for Scientific Management, *Papers and Proceedings*, 1947.

MacIver, R. M. *Social Causation*. Boston: Ginn and Company, 1942.

Malinowski, B. *The Dynamics of Culture Change*. New Haven: Yale University Press, 1945.

Meier, Richard L. *Science and Economic Development: New Patterns of Living*. Cambridge, Mass., and London: The M.I.T. Press, 1966.

Menhinick, H. K., and Durisch, L. L. "The Tennessee Valley Authority: Planning in Operation." *Town Planning Review*, July 1953.

Nielsen, Ralph Leighton. "Socio-Economic Readjustment of Families in Norris Area." University of Tennessee, August 1940.

Odum, H. W., and Moore, H. E. *American Regionalism*. New York: Henry Holt, 1938.

Smith, Frank E. "Improving the Southern Environment." *New South*, Fall 1970.

"Tennessee Revisited: The Technique of Democratic Planning." *The Times*, London, 25 June 1942.

Tennessee Valley Authority. "Graves Removed in Reservoir Areas." 1946.

———. "Manual for Grave Relocation Activities." Chattanooga, 1948, unpublished.

"The TVA Program—The Regional Approach to General Welfare." *Journal of Educational Sociology*, November 1941.

Vance, R. B. *All These People: The Nation's Human Resources in the South*. Chapel Hill: University of North Carolina Press, 1945.

Yale University, Directive Committee on Regional Planning. *The Case for Regional Planning with Special Reference to New England*. New Haven: Yale University Press, 1947.

Watershed Development

Barton, J. H. "Famous Pine Tree Branch Demonstration Watershed." *Tennessee Conservationist*, May 1958.

Baum, E. L., and Coutu, A. J. "Economic and Hydrologic Developments in the Parker Branch Watershed." *Journal of Soil and Water Conservation*, November 1959.

Bowman, J. S. "Trend Toward Multipurpose Developments." *Civil Engineering*, September 1952.

Cooper, A. J., and Snyder, W. M. "Evaluating Effects of Land-Use Changes on Sediment Load." *Proceedings, 82*, American Society of Civil Engineers, February 1956.

Durisch, L. L., and Lowry, R. E. "State Watershed Policy and Administration in Tennessee." *Public Administration Review*, Winter 1955.

Fry, A. S. "Effects of Major River Basin Development on Watershed Improvement." *Journal of Soil and Water Conservation*, March 1957.

Kilbourne, Richard. "Watershed Improvement in the Tennessee Valley." *Journal of Forestry*, April 1960.

Knetsch, J. L., and Hart, W. J. "Watershed as an Entity for Development Planning." *Journal of Farm Economics*, November 1961.

Missouri Basin Survey Commission. *Missouri: Land and Water*. Washington, D.C.: GPO, 1953.

Ratchford, B. U. "Government Action or Private Enterprise in River Valley Development: An Economist's View." *American Economic Review*, May 1951.

Riggs, F. E. *Economics of Watershed Planning*. Ames, Iowa: Iowa State University Press, 1961.

Scott, Ronald F. "Cardview Plans and Builds." The *Tennessee Planner*, February 1948

Seigworth, K. J. "Some Watershed Activities and Results." *Proceedings*, Society of American Foresters, 1960.

Tennessee Valley Authority. "Nature's Constant Gift." A report on the Water Resource of the Tennessee Valley, Knoxville, Tenn. 1966.

Tolley, G. S., and F. E. Riggs, eds. *Economics of Watershed Planning Sponsored by the Southeast Land Tenure Research Committee, the Farm Foundation, and the Tennessee Valley Authority*. Ames, Iowa: State University Press, 1961.

U.S. Senate, Joint Committees. *Report of the President's Water Resources Policy Commission*. Washington, D.C.: 1950. GPO.

Index

413